3rd Workshop on Cross-Cultural Considerations in NLP (C3NLP 2025)

Albuquerque, New Mexico, USA
4 May 2025

ISBN: 979-8-3313-1912-0

Printed from e-media with permission by:

Curran Associates, Inc.
57 Morehouse Lane
Red Hook, NY 12571

Some format issues inherent in the e-media version may also appear in this print version.

Association for Computational Linguistics
209 N. Eighth Street
Stroudsburg, Pennsylvania 18360

Phone: 1-570-476-8006
Fax: 1-570-476-0860

acl@aclweb.org

Additional copies of this publication are available from:

Curran Associates, Inc.
57 Morehouse Lane
Red Hook, NY 12571 USA
Phone: 845-758-0400
Fax: 845-758-2633
Email: curran@proceedings.com
Web: www.proceedings.com

C3NLP 2025

The 3rd Workshop on Cross-Cultural Considerations in NLP (C3NLP 2025)

Proceedings of the Workshop

May 4, 2025

The C3NLP organizers gratefully acknowledge the support from the following sponsors.

Gold

Apple Google

Order copies of this and other ACL proceedings from:

Association for Computational Linguistics (ACL)
317 Sidney Baker St. S
Suite 400 - 134
Kerrville, TX 78028
USA
Tel: +1-855-225-1962
acl@aclweb.org

Introduction

Natural Language Processing has seen impressive gains in recent years. This research includes the demonstration by NLP models to have turned into useful technologies with improved capabilities, measured in terms of how well they match human behavior captured in web-scale language data or through annotations. However, human behavior is inherently shaped by the cultural contexts humans are embedded in, the values and beliefs they hold, and the social practices they follow, part of which will be reflected in the data used to train NLP models, and the behavior these NLP models exhibit. Not accounting for this factor could cause incongruencies and misalignments between the cultural contexts that underpin the NLP model development process and the multi-cultural ecosystems they are expected to operate in. These misalignments may result in various harms, including barriers to those from under-represented cultures, violating cultural norms and values, and erasure of cultural knowledge.

While recent work in the field has started to acknowledge this issue, it is important to build a long-term research agenda for the NLP community around (1) deeper understanding of how global cultures and NLP technologies intersect, in a way that goes beyond multi-lingual and cross-lingual research, (2) how to detect, measure, and attempt to mitigate potential biases and harms in NLP technology in ways that reflect local cultures and values, and (3) how to build more cross-culturally competent NLP systems. This agenda requires looking beyond the NLP community, bringing in multi-disciplinary expertise to shape the inquiries in this important area.

We propose this workshop as a way to bring together the growing number of NLP researchers interested in this topic, along with a community of scholars with multi-disciplinary expertise spanning linguistics, social sciences, and cultural anthropology. Our aim is to build this important inquiry within NLP on a solid basis of cultural theories from social sciences. To this end, the workshop program will focus on the following themes: Inclusivity and Representation of cultures in NLP, Cultural harms of NLP technologies, and Culture Sensitive lens on Social Biases and Harms in NLP.

In the interest of having a broad conversation, inclusive of different disciplinary norms, we invited submissions of different kinds. Authors were able to choose between: (1) archival papers which will be published in the C3NLP proceedings as well as presented during the workshop, and (2) non-archival papers which are not published in the proceedings but are given a presentation slot during the workshop. Archival papers may be long (up to 9 pages) or short (up to 5 pages), and went through mutually anonymous peer review by our program committee members or were already reviewed through ACL Rolling Review (ARR). Non-archival papers include extended abstracts which were also subjected to mutually anonymous peer review by our program committee, or papers that were already reviewed through ARR or accepted for publication at another peer-reviewed venue.

We received 24 direct submissions and 4 submissions through ARR, accepting 15 direct submissions (4 short and 10 long, including 11 archival and 4 non-archival) and 2 ARR submissions (1 short and 1 long, all non-archival). Additionally, we received 7 already accepted submissions. All accepted submissions include an oral presentation (virtual or in-person) and a poster session (in-person only). Oral presentations are 3 minutes for long papers and 2 minutes for short papers. In addition, our program includes presentations of selected papers on this topic accepted by other venues, a panel discussion of selected accepted authors, a panel discussion with world-leading researchers in cross cultural NLP, and an interdisciplinary panel discussion.

Welcome to the 3rd Workshop on Cross-Cultural Considerations in NLP! We extend our heartfelt gratitude to our program committee for their thorough and insightful reviews, as well as to our authors for contributing outstanding and innovative research to this workshop. We eagerly anticipate a day of engaging discussions and the fostering of future collaborations.

– Vinodkumar Prabhakaran, Sunipa Dev, Luciana Benotti, Daniel Hershcovich, Yong Cao, Li Zhou, Laura Cabello, Ife Adebara

Organizing Committee

Vinodkumar Prabhakaran, Google Research
Sunipa Dev, Google Research
Luciana Benotti, Universidad Nacional de Córdoba
Daniel Hershcovich, University of Copenhagen
Yong Cao, University of Tübingen
Li Zhou, The Chinese University of Hong Kong, Shenzhen
Laura Cabello, University of Copenhagen
Ife Adebara, The University of British Columbia

Program Committee

Nikola Ljubešić, Jožef Stefan Institute
Michael Bloodgood, The College of New Jersey
Aida Mostafazadeh Davani, Research, Google
Kevin Robinson, Google
Bin Wang, I2R, A*STAR
Shravan Nayak, Université de Montréal
Steven R Wilson, University of Michigan - Flint
Mehar Bhatia, Mila - Quebec Artificial Intelligence Institute
Charvi Rastogi, Google
Agrima Seth, University of Michigan - Ann Arbor
Kiki Ferawati, Universitas Sebelas Maret
Sunny Rai, School of Engineering and Applied Science, University of Pennsylvania
Aubrie Amstutz, Apple
Sidney Wong, University of Canterbury
A. Seza Doğruöz, Ghent University
Partha Talukdar, Google Research and Indian Institute of Science, Bangalore
Preetam Prabhu Srikar Dammu, University of Washington
Taelin Karidi
Guijin Son
Razan Baltaji
Alice Oh, Korea Advanced Institute of Science and Technology
Kristen Johnson, Michigan State University
Luis Chiruzzo, Facultad de Ingeniería - Universidad de la República - Uruguay
Dan Simonson, BlackBoiler, Inc.
Laura Alonso Alemany, Universidad Nacional de Córdoba
Shangrui Nie
Rifki Afina Putri, Universitas Gadjah Mada
Junho Myung, Korea Advanced Institute of Science and Technology
Valerio Basile, University of Turin
Dipankar Srirag, University of New South Wales
Nisansa De Silva, University of Moratuwa
Siddhesh Milind Pawar, Copenhagen University
Dan Goldwasser, Purdue University and Purdue University
Yuu Jinnai, CyberAgent, Inc.
Nayeon Lee, Korea Advanced Institute of Science and Technology
Akhila Yerukola
Shreya Havaldar, University of Pennsylvania
Sunipa Dev, Google

Keynote Talk

Ekaterina Shutova
University of Amsterdam

Bio: Ekaterina Shutova is an Associate Professor at the ILLC, University of Amsterdam and a Visiting Associate Professor at Stanford University. At the ILLC, she leads the Amsterdam Natural Language Understanding Lab and the Natural Language Processing & Digital Humanities research unit. She received her PhD from the University of Cambridge, and then worked as a research scientist at the University of California, Berkeley. Ekaterina's current research focuses on multilingual and multicultural NLP, generalisability and robustness of NLP models and LLM alignment. Her prominent service roles include Program Chair of ACL 2025, Senior Action Editor of ACL Rolling Review, Action Editor of Computational Linguistics and Demonstrations chair at EMNLP 2022. She is also an ELLIS scholar.

Keynote Talk

Elisabeth Maier
Universidad Nacional Autónoma de México

Bio: Elisabeth A. Mager Hois holds a Bachelor's degree in Pedagogy (University of Munich, 1971), a Bachelor's degree in Social Anthropology (ENAH, 2004), a Master's degree in Mexico-United States Studies (UNAM, 2001), and a PhD in Anthropology (UNAM, 2008). She is a national researcher at the SNI (National Institute of National Research) and a Professor-Researcher of German at the FES Acatlán-UNAM. She won the CISAN Award (2009) and the Honorable Mention of the Aguirre Beltrán Chair by CIESAS of the Gulf and the University of Veracruz (2010). She has published several books: Struggle and Resistance of the Kickapoo Tribe, Kickapoo, Casinos and Power: The Kickapoo Lucky Eagle Casino Case, and Relationship between Dialectics and Social Consciousness in the Poetry of Bertolt Brecht, among others. She has written several articles and book chapters on group cohesion, assimilation, cultural assimilation, resistance and ethnic consciousness, migration, ideology and power, and polysynthetic languages, among others.

Keynote Talk

Isabelle Augenstein
University of Copenhagen

Bio: Isabelle Augenstein is a Professor at the University of Copenhagen, Department of Computer Science, where she heads the Copenhagen Natural Language Understanding research group as well as the Natural Language Processing section. Her main research interests are fair and accountable NLP, including challenges such as explainability, factuality and bias detection. Prior to starting a faculty position, she was a postdoctoral researcher at University College London, and before that a PhD student at the University of Sheffield. In October 2022, Isabelle Augenstein became Denmark's youngest ever female full professor. She currently holds a prestigious ERC Starting Grant on 'Explainable and Robust Automatic Fact Checking', as well as the Danish equivalent of that, a DFF Sapere Aude Research Leader fellowship on 'Learning to Explain Attitudes on Social Media'. She is a member of the Royal Danish Academy of Sciences and Letters, and co-leads the Danish Pioneer Centre for AI.

Keynote Talk

Monojit Choudhury
MBZUAI

Bio: Monojit Choudhury is a professor of Natural Language Processing at Mohommed Bin Zayed University of Artificial Intelligence (MBZUAI), Abu Dhabi. Prior to this, he was a principal scientist at Microsoft Research India and Microsoft Turing. Prof Choudhury's research interests lie in the intersection of NLP, Social and Cultural aspects of Technology use, and Ethics. In particular, he has been working on multilingual and multicultural aspects of large language models (LLMs), their use in low resource languages and making LLMs more inclusive and safer. Prof Choudhury takes a keen interest in popularizing linguistics and AI through puzzle solving; he is the general chair of Indian national linguistics Olympiad, the founding co-chair of Asia-Pacific linguistics Olympiad, and a founding board-member of International AI Olympiad. He holds a BTech and PhD degree in Computer Science and Engineering from IIT Kharagpur.

Table of Contents

LLM Alignment for the Arabs: A Homogenous Culture or Diverse Ones?

Amr Keleg
Institute for Language, Cognition and Computation
School of Informatics, University of Edinburgh
a.keleg@sms.ed.ac.uk

Abstract

Large language models (LLMs) have the potential of being useful tools that can automate tasks and assist humans. However, these models are more fluent in English and more aligned with Western cultures, norms, and values. Arabic-specific LLMs are being developed to better capture the nuances of the Arabic language, as well as the views of the Arabs. Yet, Arabs are sometimes assumed to share the same culture. In this position paper, I discuss the limitations of this assumption and provide preliminary thoughts for how to build systems that can better represent the cultural diversity within the Arab world. The invalidity of the cultural homogeneity assumption might seem obvious, yet, it is widely-adopted in developing multilingual and Arabic-specific LLMs. I hope that this paper will encourage the NLP community to be considerate of the cultural diversity within various communities speaking the same language.

1 Introduction

Even in the global world we live in, people residing in different parts of the world nourish different ideas, have different interests, and face different challenges. These differences can be too extreme to the extent that people could be considered to be living in totally distinct worlds (Sapir, 1929, p. 209 as cited in Bird, 2024, p. 3). For instance, Kirk et al. (2024) found that US participants questioned Large Language Models (LLMs) about abortion more than non-US ones. People from different regions can also have different perceptions of the same topic, as exemplified by English speakers from the US, UK, Singapore, Kenya, and South Africa disagreeing on what counts as Hate Speech (Lee et al., 2024). All these differences could be attributed to the cultural diversity among various communities across the world.

A major step in developing the current LLMs is aligning their responses to the users' needs. With the popularized one-model-fits-all paradigm, it is challenging to build models that can produce personalized responses that appeal to people of different demographics (Kirk et al., 2024). Current models tend to generate responses that better match the expectations of Western users (Cao et al., 2023; Naous et al., 2024; Wang et al., 2024; AlKhamissi et al., 2024; Ryan et al., 2024; Mihalcea et al., 2024). Moreover, the views of Arabs—one group of many underrepresented non-Western communities—tend to be ignored,[1] sometimes unconsciously and other times with deliberate intent, putting people of these communities at a higher risk of discrimination (Alimardani and Elswah, 2021; Shahid and Vashistha, 2023; Magdy et al., 2025).

Arabic is privileged by having (a) a community of Arab NLP experts (Habash and Vogel, 2014; Habash et al., 2015, 2017; El-Hajj et al., 2019; Zitouni et al., 2020; Habash et al., 2021; Bouamor et al., 2022; Sawaf et al., 2023; Habash et al., 2024; Al-Khalifa et al., 2020, 2022, 2024; El-Haj et al., 2019; Ezzini et al., 2025), and (b) interest backed by funding from some Arab countries to build Arabic-focused models that serve its speakers. Jais (Sengupta et al., 2023), AceGPT (Huang et al., 2024), Allam (Bari et al., 2024), and Fanar (Fanar Team et al., 2025) are Arabic-centric LLMs developed in 2023 and 2024. While earlier models like Jais focused on better modeling the linguistic features of Arabic, AceGPT, ALLaM, and Fanar are marketed as models that better align to the *Arabic/Arab Culture*.

It is well-known that local varieties of Dialectal Arabic (DA) exist in different Arabic-speaking regions, in addition to a standardized variety (MSA)

[1]Despite the attempt of curating model alignment data from different multi-cultural demographics, the PRISM Alignment dataset (Kirk et al., 2024) had only 51 participants (out of 1,500) who reported that they reside in the Middle East, out of which 47 reside in Israel, 2 in Turkey, and 1 in each of Sudan and Kuwait. Moreover, only 14 participants self-reported themselves as *Middle Eastern/ Arab*.

Proceedings of the 3rd Workshop on Cross-Cultural Considerations in NLP (C3NLP 2025), pages 1–9
May 4, 2025

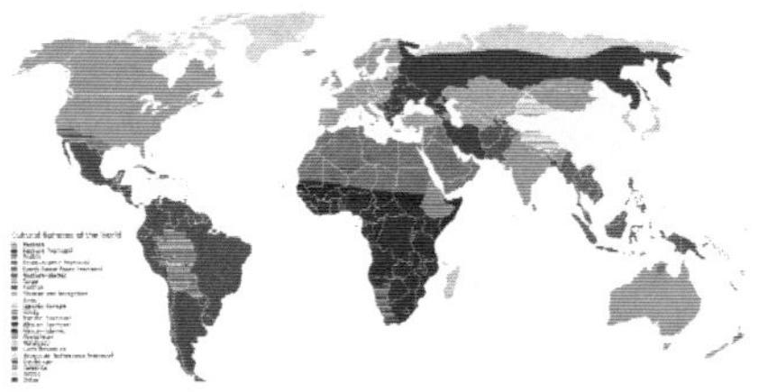

(a) Culture Areas: Zones of high cultural overlap due to shared geography and long-term contact (Source: VividMaps)

Figure 1: A visualization of the areas with substantial cultural similarities as in (Bird, 2024, p. 3). Arabic speakers (green color) are grouped into a single region.

that is generally perceived as a shared variety across the Arabic-speaking communities. (Habash, 2010). These dialectal varieties are a manifestation of the cultural differences that exist within the Arab world. However, the notion of a single *Arabic Culture* only focuses on the shared values and norms among the Arabs, marginalizing any regional differences between them. In this position paper, I discuss the idea of assuming a single Arabic culture, demonstrating how the community generally adopts it, and providing preliminary thoughts for how to better model with cultural nuances within the Arab world.

2 Arabs - a Single or Multiple Cultures?

Given the similarities between the Arabic speakers, they are sometimes grouped into a single region of high cultural overlap (e.g., Figure 1). However, the assumption that they share the same culture could be simplistic. Conceptually, there are multiple ways to define who an Arab is. A broader definition is that *anyone having Arabic as their native language is an Arab*. Accordingly, there are more than 420 million Arabs distributed across the Arab region (Bergman and Diab, 2022), a large proportion of which reside in North Africa and the Arabian peninsula. I discuss two contrasting extreme views of the Arabic culture:[2]

View #1 - One Culture Arab nationalism is an ideology that started to gain traction in the 20th century, with the goal of unifying the Arab countries under a single goal, fostering economic cooperation between them. Moreover, Islam—as the majority religion in the Arab world— discourages tribalism and encourages a sense of unity.[3]

View #2 - Multiple Unrelated Cultures A contrasting ideology fosters the notion of local national identities, focusing on what makes these identities different from other Arab nations. Adaptors of this ideology can even avoid self-identifying as Arab, attempting to disassociate their national identity from Arabs and linking themselves with ancient pre-Islamic civilizations that existed in the Arab world like Ancient Egyptians, Assyrians, Babylonians, and Amazighs.

It is worth mentioning that the distinction between *Arabic Culture* and *Arab Culture* in English—the former linking the culture to the Arabic language, while the latter links it to Arabs—does not exist in Arabic, as both are termed الثقافة العربية. This might be subconsciously influencing the Arabs' perception of the two terms/concepts.

3 How is the Arabic Culture Currently Represented?

On surveying more than 90 papers related to cultural representation in LLMs, Adilazuarda et al. (2024) found that none of the papers explicitly mention how they operationalize the concept of a culture. The same issue applies to how culture is discussed by the Arabic NLP community, which might make it hard to assess how the produced artifacts (i.e., models and datasets) are culturally representative.[4] Hence, I taxonomize the datasets into three different categories according to their intended use as follows:

Classical Task-specific Datasets The community widely acknowledges the presence of different varieties of DA, with many datasets having samples from multiple dialects to model this linguistic variation (Mubarak et al., 2017; Alsarsour

[2]These contrasting views are manifested in the Wikipedia articles for عرب (Arab), in which the MSA and the Moroccan Arabic versions are more representative of the first view, while the Egyptian Arabic version link the Arabs to the Gulf and Levantine countries while excluding Egypt and the other North African countries. **Note:** The links to عرب (Arab) article in MSA, Moroccan and Egyptian Arabic respectively: `ar.wikipedia.org/wiki/%D8%B9%D8%B1%D8%A8`, `ary.wikipedia.org/wiki/%D9%84%D8%B9%D8%B1%D8%A8`, `arz.wikipedia.org/wiki/%D8%B9%D8%B1%D8%A8`

[3]Christianity is another religion that is adopted by a significant minority of Arabs (e.g., in Lebanon and Egypt). Moreover, Arab Jews used to be a vital part of Arab societies until the 20th century (Atta, 2023), and are still a minority in some countries like Morocco.

[4]Notably, AlKhamissi et al. (2024) provide a comprehensive discussion of what a culture is.

	English Translation	Arabic
Instruction	Suggest men's clothing for a family gathering	أقترح ملابس رجالية تناسب اجتماع عائلي
Choice (A)	Casual pants and a T-shirt	بنطلون كاجوال وتيشيرت
Choice (B)	Shorts and a polo shirt	شورت وتيشيرت بولو
Choice (C)	Formal shirt and pants	قميص وبنطلون رسمي
Choice (D)	Jellabiya and ghutra	جلابية وغترة
Answer	Choice (D)	

Instruction	I ate Kabsa using	اكلت الكبسة باستخدام
Choice (A)	a fork	الشوكة
Choice (B)	a spoon	الملعقة
Choice (C)	my hand	يدي
Choice (D)	a knife	السكين
Answer	Choice (C)	

Table 1: Two cherry-picked examples of edited instructions with multiple choices from *CIDAR-MCQ-100*. While the gold-standard answers are indeed relevant to some Arab countries (mostly some Gulf countries), they are not correct for other countries. **Note:** I provide the English translations for clarity.

et al., 2018; Ousidhoum et al., 2019; Chowdhury et al., 2020; Abu Farha and Magdy, 2020; Alturayeif et al., 2022). Given that dialects are signs of cultural diversity (Falck et al., 2012 as cited in Singh et al., 2024), this implies that such diversity might be modeled in the datasets. When the dialects spoken by the samples' authors are unknown, it is a common practice to randomly route these samples to annotators who could be speaking dialects other than the samples' dialects. *This assumes that Arabic is a monolith language, and disregards the cultural differences between its speakers.*[5]

Two independent papers found that Arabic-speaking annotators are harsher in labeling hate speech (Bergman and Diab, 2022), and less capable of identifying sarcasm (Abu Farha and Magdy, 2022), on annotating samples written in dialects that the annotators do not speak. On analyzing 15 publicly available datasets covering 5 different tasks, and having samples from multiple dialects that were randomly routed to annotators, Keleg et al. (2024) found that the interannotator agreement scores decreased as the level of dialectness of the samples increased. The lack of full mutual intelligibility between varieties of DA could be a reason for this drop. *However, cultural nuances form another plausible cause.* Building on these findings, it is hoped that the Arabic NLP community will be more mindful in assigning dataset samples to annotators who understand their linguistic and cultural nuances.

Less Subjective Culture Understanding Benchmarks Country-level sample curation was used to allow for capturing the cultural diversity in the Arab world. Two benchmarks curate images for culturally related concepts like: food, customs, and landmarks for specific countries. *CVQA* (Romero et al., 2024) has about 300 images related to Egypt, that were manually curated and are accompanied by QA pairs. Conversely, *Henna* (Alwajih et al., 2024) has 10 images from each of 11 Arab countries, accompanied by automatically generated image captions.

Similarly, *ArabicMMLU* (Koto et al., 2024) consists of multiple-choice questions (MCQs) in MSA covering different subjects, that were sourced from the school exams of 8 different Arab countries.[6] *AraDICE-Culture* (Mousi et al., 2025) has 180 MCQs from 6 different Arab countries (30 each) that were manually curated. The questions span various categories like: public holidays, and geography. *DLAMA (Arab-West)* (Keleg and Magdy, 2023) has Wikidata factual triplets from 20 predicates, equally balanced between Arab countries

[5] On analyzing the errors of a hate-speech detection model, Keleg et al. (2020) found two Egyptian Arabic quotes from films that were used sarcastically, yet labeled as hate speech. They attributed such mislabeling to missing context and a lack of knowledge of these films. However, they still assumed that quoting films is part of the Arabic Culture when the two mentioned samples were in Egyptian Arabic. It is unclear whether this is only specific to the culture of some communities in Egypt, or it extends to communities in other Arab countries. Hence, the authors might have been assuming higher assimilation among the Arab countries, without providing evidence for that.

[6] *ArabicMMLU*'s authors acknowledge the data is not equally representative of the different countries.

and a comparable set of Western countries. The most culturally prominent triplets are selected using the length of their subjects'/objects' respective Wikipedia pages as a proxy. *Cultural ArabicMTEB* (Bhatia et al., 2024) contains 1,000 queries automatically synthesized using Command-R+ from Wikipedia articles related to multiple categories such as: history, local movies, and food items for 20 different Arab countries. Lastly, *BLEnD* (Myung et al., 2024) has 1,000 MCQs about everyday knowledge of the cultures existing in Algeria.

Values Alignment Datasets Surprisingly, all Arabic-specific LLMs but ALLaM and Fanar perform alignment only using Supervised Fine-Tuning (SFT), with datasets that are either machine-translated or repurposed from task-specific datasets.

CIDAR (Alyafeai et al., 2024) is the first open Arabic instruction-tuning dataset composed of manually localized instruction/output pairs, edited by speakers of different varieties of Arabic.[7] While the authors focused on localizing person names and country names in the dataset to Arabic ones, which makes most of them culturally representative, few outputs are still biased by the annotator's views/country of origin, as exemplified in Table 1.

This issue is much more prominent in the *Arabic Cultural Value Alignment (ACVA)* benchmark (Huang et al., 2024), which is introduced to evaluate the alignment of different LLMs to *the Arabic Culture* (Huang et al., 2024; Bari et al., 2024). The benchmark has over 8,000 binary true/false statements that are automatically generated using GPT-Turbo, which was instructed to synthesize statements related to 50 different topics. Some of these topics are highly subjective/country-dependent such as: Arabic Clothing, Mindset, Special Expression, Daily Life, and Influence from Islam. Figure 2 lists two examples of non-inclusive statements, *which are a result of assuming a single homogenous Arabic culture.*

4 Recommendations

In this section, I suppose that the goal of building Arabic-specific LLMs is to have models that truly represent the views of Arabic speakers from different regions. Following the discussion and the examples in §3, it is clear that assuming a single

An example statement for *Communications*:
في الثقافة العربية، يمكن للرجال والنساء الجلوس معًا في الكافيهات.
In the Arabic culture, men and women can sit together in cafes.

Verdict: False (خطأ).

An example statement for *Influnce From Islam*:
العرب يعتبرون الإسلام جزءًا لا يتجزأ من هويتهم الثقافية.
Arabs consider Islam an integral part of their cultural identity.

Verdict: True (صح).

Figure 2: Two statements from the ACVA benchmark showcasing misrepresentation of the cultural nuances within the Arab world. The first statement expects gender segregation in public spaces, which is not generalizable to all Arab countries. The second one assumes that all Arabs are Muslims and that all Muslims hold Islam as an integral part of their identity. Adding a quantifier like "معظم العرب (Most Arabs)" would make the statement more precise and less controversial.

Arabic culture is not inclusive of the cultural diversity within the Arab world. Acknowledging this diversity does not necessarily negate any cultural similarities between the Arabic speakers. In contrast, it provides a more inclusive view of them.

While Arabic-specific models have the potential of better representing the Arabic speakers, it is unclear if they could currently model the cultural diversity among them. Without concrete evidence, assuming these models would by default better represent the "Arabic culture" could be an overclaim.

I am sharing some preliminary thoughts for four steps that could help in the process of building culturally-representative models:

Step #1 - Improving the Diversity of the Research Teams A first step is to ensure that the research teams responsible for building the models are representative of the different regions of the Arab World. Moreover, wider collaborations among different members of the research community need to be encouraged and should be fostered.

Step #2 - Understanding the Topics of Interest of the Speakers across the Arab World Many AI systems are developed without a clear vision of what they solve and how they would serve the needs of their users (Mihalcea et al., 2024). Given that people from different regions engage differently with LLMs (Kirk et al., 2024), we should start identifying the topics of interest of Arabic speakers from different regions, especially that their views were excluded in building the PRISM dataset (Kirk

[7] *CIDAR*'s creators acknowledge that the responses could be biased by the views of the different dataset contributors.

et al., 2024) on which the aforementioned finding is based. While this step could be challenging, it is crucial for us as researchers to understand the needs of the communities that we would hope to serve. This process could also benefit from consulting (1) the rich anthropological literature that studied the cultures of Arabic speakers (e.g., Deeb and Winegar, 2012), and (2) the recommendations from the Human-Computer Interaction (HCI) field for designing surveys and tools to understand the Arabic speakers' needs.

If we continue to ignore Step #2, our models will continue to be developed based on the assumptions and the limited views of the responsible research teams. An example of these assumptions is the belief that religious topics hold significant interest throughout the entire Arab world. Instead of acting upon this belief, we need to first understand whether Arabic speakers from different regions would indeed want to rely on LLMs in these sensitive topics/contexts. Doing so would allow for identifying the contexts in which the LLMs should engage in religious topics, if any, which in turn could help in controlling the dangers of shipping public-facing models that engage in religious discussions (Keleg and Magdy, 2022; Alyafeai et al., 2024).

Step #3 - Identifying the Languages/Varieties that Arabic Speakers Use on Engaging with Technologies On adapting the ArabicMMLU dataset to Moroccan Arabic (also known as Moroccan Darija), Shang et al. (2024) discarded the samples that they deemed as "too technical" and "beyond the user's needs" for an LLM that generates responses in Darija. This again indicates that researchers have some preconceived assumptions on the users' needs and the language varieties they would generally use to engage with the different technological systems.

In order to determine the language or variety that Arabic speakers would use when interacting with technology, we can first draw insights from the lessons of Blaschke et al.'s (2024) study, which analyzed the German users' preferences for having their local varieties supported as inputs or outputs of different language technologies such as virtual assistants and machine-translation systems.

However, the new study needs to also acknowledge that a non-negligible portion of the Arabic speakers in some regions are bilingual. Hence, English and French can be more preferred in different regions over using Standard Arabic or the regional local variety of Arabic to interact with technology in specific contexts. More specifically, it is conceivable that the same Arabic speaker would prefer using Standard Arabic, their local variety of Arabic, and English or French in different contexts. Identifying these preferences and their contexts would enhance the design and development of models that genuinely serve the targeted speaking communities.

Step #4 - Collecting More Inclusive Alignment Data There is a clear need for collecting alignment and preference data to improve the Arabic-specific LLMs. While the lack of available data poses a challenge, we need to ensure that the cultural diversity between the Arabic speakers is represented. Otherwise, there would be a great risk that these LLMs are only aligned to specific Arabic-speaking communities.

5 Conclusion

Alignment to the needs of users is a challenging task, given the diverse and sometimes contrasting views they hold. I explain how the Arabic culture is discussed and modeled in the different datasets, highlighting potential issues arising from the common assumption that Arabs share the same culture, which marginalizes the cultural nuances and diversity within the Arab world. Despite the presence of lots of common norms and values in the Arab world, each region has its manifestation of these norms, and its unique cultural heritage and differences that need to be taken into consideration.

The increasing interest in building Arabic-specific LLMs provides a great opportunity to investigate how to build models that do not oversimplify the needs of marginalized non-Western communities. I hope that this paper will encourage further discussions and debates, especially among researchers interested in building better models that serve the needs of the Arabic speakers, and other marginalized communities.

Limitations

I hope that a better understanding of the needs of the Arabs from diverse regions across the Arab World would allow for designing and building models that are more suited to their needs. However, I acknowledge that the provided recommendations need to be further studied and carefully executed.

Acnowledgments

I am grateful to Merham Keleg for attentively listening to the preliminary arguments that led to this paper. I also thank SMASH for their feedback on an earlier version of the paper. Special thanks to Walid Magdy, Björn Ross, Maria Walters, and Xue Li for their valuable comments and suggestions. Lastly, I really appreciate the anonymous reviewers' insightful feedback.

This work was supported by the UKRI Centre for Doctoral Training in Natural Language Processing, funded by the UKRI (grant EP/S022481/1) and the University of Edinburgh, School of Informatics.

References

Ibrahim Abu Farha and Walid Magdy. 2020. From Arabic sentiment analysis to sarcasm detection: The ArSarcasm dataset. In *Proceedings of the 4th Workshop on Open-Source Arabic Corpora and Processing Tools, with a Shared Task on Offensive Language Detection*, pages 32–39, Marseille, France. European Language Resource Association.

Ibrahim Abu Farha and Walid Magdy. 2022. The effect of Arabic dialect familiarity on data annotation. In *Proceedings of the Seventh Arabic Natural Language Processing Workshop (WANLP)*, pages 399–408, Abu Dhabi, United Arab Emirates (Hybrid). Association for Computational Linguistics.

Muhammad Farid Adilazuarda, Sagnik Mukherjee, Pradhyumna Lavania, Siddhant Shivdutt Singh, Alham Fikri Aji, Jacki O'Neill, Ashutosh Modi, and Monojit Choudhury. 2024. Towards measuring and modeling "culture" in LLMs: A survey. In *Proceedings of the 2024 Conference on Empirical Methods in Natural Language Processing*, pages 15763–15784, Miami, Florida, USA. Association for Computational Linguistics.

Hend Al-Khalifa, Kareem Darwish, Hamdy Mubarak, Mona Ali, and Tamer Elsayed, editors. 2024. *Proceedings of the 6th Workshop on Open-Source Arabic Corpora and Processing Tools (OSACT) with Shared Tasks on Arabic LLMs Hallucination and Dialect to MSA Machine Translation @ LREC-COLING 2024*. ELRA and ICCL, Torino, Italia.

Hend Al-Khalifa, Tamer Elsayed, Hamdy Mubarak, Abdulmohsen Al-Thubaity, Walid Magdy, and Kareem Darwish, editors. 2022. *Proceedings of the 5th Workshop on Open-Source Arabic Corpora and Processing Tools with Shared Tasks on Qur'an QA and Fine-Grained Hate Speech Detection*. European Language Resources Association, Marseille, France.

Hend Al-Khalifa, Walid Magdy, Kareem Darwish, Tamer Elsayed, and Hamdy Mubarak, editors. 2020. *Proceedings of the 4th Workshop on Open-Source Arabic Corpora and Processing Tools, with a Shared Task on Offensive Language Detection*. European Language Resource Association, Marseille, France.

Mahsa Alimardani and Mona Elswah. 2021. Digital orientalism: #SaveSheikhJarrah and Arabic content moderation. *SSRN Scholarly Paper*.

Badr AlKhamissi, Muhammad ElNokrashy, Mai Alkhamissi, and Mona Diab. 2024. Investigating cultural alignment of large language models. In *Proceedings of the 62nd Annual Meeting of the Association for Computational Linguistics (Volume 1: Long Papers)*, pages 12404–12422, Bangkok, Thailand. Association for Computational Linguistics.

Israa Alsarsour, Esraa Mohamed, Reem Suwaileh, and Tamer Elsayed. 2018. DART: A large dataset of dialectal Arabic tweets. In *Proceedings of the Eleventh International Conference on Language Resources and Evaluation (LREC 2018)*, Miyazaki, Japan. European Language Resources Association (ELRA).

Nora Saleh Alturayeif, Hamzah Abdullah Luqman, and Moataz Aly Kamaleldin Ahmed. 2022. Mawqif: A multi-label Arabic dataset for target-specific stance detection. In *Proceedings of the Seventh Arabic Natural Language Processing Workshop (WANLP)*, pages 174–184, Abu Dhabi, United Arab Emirates (Hybrid). Association for Computational Linguistics.

Fakhraddin Alwajih, El Moatez Billah Nagoudi, Gagan Bhatia, Abdelrahman Mohamed, and Muhammad Abdul-Mageed. 2024. Peacock: A family of Arabic multimodal large language models and benchmarks. In *Proceedings of the 62nd Annual Meeting of the Association for Computational Linguistics (Volume 1: Long Papers)*, pages 12753–12776, Bangkok, Thailand. Association for Computational Linguistics.

Zaid Alyafeai, Khalid Almubarak, Ahmed Ashraf, Deema Alnuhait, Saied Alshahrani, Gubran Abdulrahman, Gamil Ahmed, Qais Gawah, Zead Saleh, Mustafa Ghaleb, Yousef Ali, and Maged Al-shaibani. 2024. CIDAR: Culturally relevant instruction dataset for Arabic. In *Findings of the Association for Computational Linguistics: ACL 2024*, pages 12878–12901, Bangkok, Thailand. Association for Computational Linguistics.

Zubaydah Mohamed Atta. 2023. اليهود في العالم العربي *Jews in the Arab World*. Elain Publishing House.

M Saiful Bari, Yazeed Alnumay, Norah A. Alzahrani, Nouf M. Alotaibi, Hisham A. Alyahya, Sultan Al-Rashed, Faisal A. Mirza, Shaykhah Z. Alsubaie, Hassan A. Alahmed, Ghadah Alabduljabbar, Raghad Alkhathran, Yousef Almushayqih, Raneem Alnajim, Salman Alsubaihi, Maryam Al Mansour, Majed Alrubaian, Ali Alammari, Zaki Alawami, Abdulmohsen Al-Thubaity, Ahmed Abdelali, Jeril Kuriakose, Abdalghani Abujabal, Nora Al-Twairesh, Areeb Alowisheq, and Haidar Khan. 2024. ALLaM: Large language models for Arabic and English. *Preprint*, arXiv:2407.15390.

A. Bergman and Mona Diab. 2022. Towards responsible natural language annotation for the varieties of Arabic. In *Findings of the Association for Computational Linguistics: ACL 2022*, pages 364–371, Dublin, Ireland. Association for Computational Linguistics.

Gagan Bhatia, El Moatez Billah Nagoudi, Abdellah El Mekki, Fakhraddin Alwajih, and Muhammad Abdul-Mageed. 2024. Swan and ArabicMTEB: Dialect-aware, Arabic-centric, cross-lingual, and cross-cultural embedding models and benchmarks. *Preprint*, arXiv:2411.01192.

Steven Bird. 2024. Must NLP be extractive? In *Proceedings of the 62nd Annual Meeting of the Association for Computational Linguistics (Volume 1: Long Papers)*, pages 14915–14929, Bangkok, Thailand. Association for Computational Linguistics.

Verena Blaschke, Christoph Purschke, Hinrich Schuetze, and Barbara Plank. 2024. What do dialect speakers want? a survey of attitudes towards language technology for German dialects. In *Proceedings of the 62nd Annual Meeting of the Association for Computational Linguistics (Volume 2: Short Papers)*, pages 823–841, Bangkok, Thailand. Association for Computational Linguistics.

Houda Bouamor, Hend Al-Khalifa, Kareem Darwish, Owen Rambow, Fethi Bougares, Ahmed Abdelali, Nadi Tomeh, Salam Khalifa, and Wajdi Zaghouani, editors. 2022. *Proceedings of the Seventh Arabic Natural Language Processing Workshop (WANLP)*. Association for Computational Linguistics, Abu Dhabi, United Arab Emirates (Hybrid).

Yong Cao, Li Zhou, Seolhwa Lee, Laura Cabello, Min Chen, and Daniel Hershcovich. 2023. Assessing cross-cultural alignment between ChatGPT and human societies: An empirical study. In *Proceedings of the First Workshop on Cross-Cultural Considerations in NLP (C3NLP)*, pages 53–67, Dubrovnik, Croatia. Association for Computational Linguistics.

Shammur Absar Chowdhury, Hamdy Mubarak, Ahmed Abdelali, Soon-gyo Jung, Bernard J. Jansen, and Joni Salminen. 2020. A multi-platform Arabic news comment dataset for offensive language detection. In *Proceedings of the Twelfth Language Resources and Evaluation Conference*, pages 6203–6212, Marseille, France. European Language Resources Association.

Lara Deeb and Jessica Winegar. 2012. Anthropologies of Arab-majority societies. *Annual Review of Anthropology*, 41(Volume 41, 2012):537–558.

Mahmoud El-Haj, Paul Rayson, Eric Atwell, and Lama Alsudias, editors. 2019. *Proceedings of the 3rd Workshop on Arabic Corpus Linguistics*. Association for Computational Linguistics, Cardiff, United Kingdom.

Wassim El-Hajj, Lamia Hadrich Belguith, Fethi Bougares, Walid Magdy, Imed Zitouni, Nadi Tomeh, Mahmoud El-Haj, and Wajdi Zaghouani, editors. 2019. *Proceedings of the Fourth Arabic Natural Language Processing Workshop*. Association for Computational Linguistics, Florence, Italy.

Saad Ezzini, Hamza Alami, Ismail Berrada, Abdessamad Benlahbib, Abdelkader El Mahdaouy, Salima Lamsiyah, Hatim Derrouz, Amal Haddad Haddad, Mustafa Jarrar, Mo El-Haj, Ruslan Mitkov, and Paul Rayson, editors. 2025. *Proceedings of the 4th Workshop on Arabic Corpus Linguistics (WACL-4)*. Association for Computational Linguistics, Abu Dhabi, UAE.

Oliver Falck, Stephan Heblich, Alfred Lameli, and Jens Südekum. 2012. Dialects, cultural identity, and economic exchange. *Journal of Urban Economics*, 72(2):225–239.

Fanar Team, Ummar Abbas, Mohammad Shahmeer Ahmad, Firoj Alam, Enes Altinisik, Ehsannedin Asgari, Yazan Boshmaf, Sabri Boughorbel, Sanjay Chawla, Shammur Chowdhury, Fahim Dalvi, Kareem Darwish, Nadir Durrani, Mohamed Elfeky, Ahmed Elmagarmid, Mohamed Eltabakh, Masoomali Fatehkia, Anastasios Fragkopoulos, Maram Hasanain, Majd Hawasly, Mus'ab Husaini, Soon-Gyo Jung, Ji Kim Lucas, Walid Magdy, Safa Messaoud, Abubakr Mohamed, Tasnim Mohiuddin, Basel Mousi, Hamdy Mubarak, Ahmad Musleh, Zan Naeem, Mourad Ouzzani, Dorde Popovic, Amin Sadeghi, Husrev Taha Sencar, Mohammed Shinoy, Omar Sinan, Yifan Zhang, Ahmed Ali, Yassine El Kheir, Xiaosong Ma, and Chaoyi Ruan. 2025. Fanar: An Arabic-centric multimodal generative AI platform. *Preprint*, arXiv:2501.13944.

Nizar Habash, Houda Bouamor, Ramy Eskander, Nadi Tomeh, Ibrahim Abu Farha, Ahmed Abdelali, Samia Touileb, Injy Hamed, Yaser Onaizan, Bashar Alhafni, Wissam Antoun, Salam Khalifa, Hatem Haddad, Imed Zitouni, Badr AlKhamissi, Rawan Almatham, and Khalil Mrini, editors. 2024. *Proceedings of The Second Arabic Natural Language Processing Conference*. Association for Computational Linguistics, Bangkok, Thailand.

Nizar Habash, Houda Bouamor, Hazem Hajj, Walid Magdy, Wajdi Zaghouani, Fethi Bougares, Nadi Tomeh, Ibrahim Abu Farha, and Samia Touileb, editors. 2021. *Proceedings of the Sixth Arabic Natural Language Processing Workshop*. Association for Computational Linguistics, Kyiv, Ukraine (Virtual).

Nizar Habash, Mona Diab, Kareem Darwish, Wassim El-Hajj, Hend Al-Khalifa, Houda Bouamor, Nadi Tomeh, Mahmoud El-Haj, and Wajdi Zaghouani, editors. 2017. *Proceedings of the Third Arabic Natural Language Processing Workshop*. Association for Computational Linguistics, Valencia, Spain.

Nizar Habash and Stephan Vogel, editors. 2014. *Proceedings of the EMNLP 2014 Workshop on Arabic Natural Language Processing (ANLP)*. Association for Computational Linguistics, Doha, Qatar.

Nizar Habash, Stephan Vogel, and Kareem Darwish, editors. 2015. *Proceedings of the Second Workshop on Arabic Natural Language Processing*. Association for Computational Linguistics, Beijing, China.

Nizar Y Habash. 2010. *Introduction to Arabic natural language processing*. Morgan & Claypool Publishers.

Huang Huang, Fei Yu, Jianqing Zhu, Xuening Sun, Hao Cheng, Song Dingjie, Zhihong Chen, Mosen Alharthi, Bang An, Juncai He, Ziche Liu, Junying Chen, Jianquan Li, Benyou Wang, Lian Zhang, Ruoyu Sun, Xiang Wan, Haizhou Li, and Jinchao Xu. 2024. AceGPT, localizing large language models in Arabic. In *Proceedings of the 2024 Conference of the North American Chapter of the Association for Computational Linguistics: Human Language Technologies (Volume 1: Long Papers)*, pages 8139–8163, Mexico City, Mexico. Association for Computational Linguistics.

Amr Keleg, Samhaa R. El-Beltagy, and Mahmoud Khalil. 2020. ASU_OPTO at OSACT4 - offensive language detection for Arabic text. In *Proceedings of the 4th Workshop on Open-Source Arabic Corpora and Processing Tools, with a Shared Task on Offensive Language Detection*, pages 66–70, Marseille, France. European Language Resource Association.

Amr Keleg and Walid Magdy. 2022. SMASH at qur'an QA 2022: Creating better faithful data splits for low-resourced question answering scenarios. In *Proceedinsg of the 5th Workshop on Open-Source Arabic Corpora and Processing Tools with Shared Tasks on Qur'an QA and Fine-Grained Hate Speech Detection*, pages 136–145, Marseille, France. European Language Resources Association.

Amr Keleg and Walid Magdy. 2023. DLAMA: A framework for curating culturally diverse facts for probing the knowledge of pretrained language models. In *Findings of the Association for Computational Linguistics: ACL 2023*, pages 6245–6266, Toronto, Canada. Association for Computational Linguistics.

Amr Keleg, Walid Magdy, and Sharon Goldwater. 2024. Estimating the level of dialectness predicts interannotator agreement in multi-dialect Arabic datasets. In *Proceedings of the 62nd Annual Meeting of the Association for Computational Linguistics (Volume 2: Short Papers)*, pages 766–777, Bangkok, Thailand. Association for Computational Linguistics.

Hannah Rose Kirk, Alexander Whitefield, Paul Rottger, Andrew M. Bean, Katerina Margatina, Rafael Mosquera-Gomez, Juan Ciro, Max Bartolo, Adina Williams, He He, Bertie Vidgen, and Scott Hale. 2024. The PRISM alignment dataset: What participatory, representative and individualised human feedback reveals about the subjective and multicultural alignment of large language models. In *Advances in Neural Information Processing Systems*, volume 37, pages 105236–105344. Curran Associates, Inc.

Fajri Koto, Haonan Li, Sara Shatnawi, Jad Doughman, Abdelrahman Sadallah, Aisha Alraeesi, Khalid Almubarak, Zaid Alyafeai, Neha Sengupta, Shady Shehata, Nizar Habash, Preslav Nakov, and Timothy Baldwin. 2024. ArabicMMLU: Assessing massive multitask language understanding in Arabic. In *Findings of the Association for Computational Linguistics: ACL 2024*, pages 5622–5640, Bangkok, Thailand. Association for Computational Linguistics.

Nayeon Lee, Chani Jung, Junho Myung, Jiho Jin, Jose Camacho-Collados, Juho Kim, and Alice Oh. 2024. Exploring cross-cultural differences in English hate speech annotations: From dataset construction to analysis. In *Proceedings of the 2024 Conference of the North American Chapter of the Association for Computational Linguistics: Human Language Technologies (Volume 1: Long Papers)*, pages 4205–4224, Mexico City, Mexico. Association for Computational Linguistics.

Walid Magdy, Hamdy Mubarak, and Joni Salminen. 2025. Who should set the standards? Analysing censored Arabic content on Facebook during the Palestine-Israel conflict. In *Proceedings of the 2025 CHI Conference on Human Factors in Computing Systems*, CHI '25, New York, NY, USA. Association for Computing Machinery.

Rada Mihalcea, Oana Ignat, Longju Bai, Angana Borah, Luis Chiruzzo, Zhijing Jin, Claude Kwizera, Joan Nwatu, Soujanya Poria, and Thamar Solorio. 2024. Why AI is WEIRD and should not be this way: Towards AI for everyone, with everyone, by everyone. *Preprint*, arXiv:2410.16315.

Basel Mousi, Nadir Durrani, Fatema Ahmad, Md. Arid Hasan, Maram Hasanain, Tameem Kabbani, Fahim Dalvi, Shammur Absar Chowdhury, and Firoj Alam. 2025. AraDiCE: Benchmarks for dialectal and cultural capabilities in LLMs. In *Proceedings of the 31st International Conference on Computational Linguistics*, pages 4186–4218, Abu Dhabi, UAE. Association for Computational Linguistics.

Hamdy Mubarak, Kareem Darwish, and Walid Magdy. 2017. Abusive language detection on Arabic social media. In *Proceedings of the First Workshop on Abusive Language Online*, pages 52–56, Vancouver, BC, Canada. Association for Computational Linguistics.

Junho Myung, Nayeon Lee, Yi Zhou, Jiho Jin, Rifki Putri, Dimosthenis Antypas, Hsuvas Borkakoty, Eunsu Kim, Carla Perez-Almendros, Abinew Ali Ayele, Victor Gutierrez Basulto, Yazmin Ibanez-Garcia, Hwaran Lee, Shamsuddeen H Muhammad, Kiwoong Park, Anar Rzayev, Nina White, Seid Muhie Yimam, Mohammad Taher Pilehvar, Nedjma Ousidhoum, Jose Camacho-Collados, and Alice Oh. 2024. BLEnD: A benchmark for llms on everyday knowledge in diverse cultures and languages. In *Advances in Neural Information Processing Systems*, volume 37, pages 78104–78146. Curran Associates, Inc.

Tarek Naous, Michael J Ryan, Alan Ritter, and Wei Xu. 2024. Having beer after prayer? measuring cultural bias in large language models. In *Proceedings of the 62nd Annual Meeting of the Association for Computational Linguistics (Volume 1: Long Papers)*, pages 16366–16393, Bangkok, Thailand. Association for Computational Linguistics.

Nedjma Ousidhoum, Zizheng Lin, Hongming Zhang, Yangqiu Song, and Dit-Yan Yeung. 2019. Multilingual and multi-aspect hate speech analysis. In *Proceedings of the 2019 Conference on Empirical Methods in Natural Language Processing and the 9th International Joint Conference on Natural Language Processing (EMNLP-IJCNLP)*, pages 4675–4684, Hong Kong, China. Association for Computational Linguistics.

David Romero, Chenyang Lyu, Haryo Wibowo, Santiago Góngora, Aishik Mandal, Sukannya Purkayastha, Jesus-German Ortiz-Barajas, Emilio Cueva, Jinheon Baek, Soyeong Jeong, Injy Hamed, Yong Zheng-Xin, Zheng Wei Lim, Paula Silva, Jocelyn Dunstan, Mélanie Jouitteau, David LE MEUR, Joan Nwatu, Ganzorig Batnasan, Munkh-Erdene Otgonbold, Munkhjargal Gochoo, Guido Ivetta, Luciana Benotti, Laura Alonso Alemany, Hernán Maina, Jiahui Geng, Tiago Timponi Torrent, Frederico Belcavello, Marcelo Viridiano, Jan Christian Blaise Cruz, Dan John Velasco, Oana Ignat, Zara Burzo, Chenxi Whitehouse, Artem Abzaliev, Teresa Clifford, Gráinne Caulfield, Teresa Lynn, Christian Salamea-Palacios, Vladimir Araujo, Yova Kementchedjhieva, Mihail Mihaylov, Israel Azime, Henok Ademtew, Bontu Balcha, Naome A. Etori, David Adelani, Rada Mihalcea, Atnafu Lambebo Tonja, Maria Cabrera, Gisela Vallejo, Holy Lovenia, Ruochen Zhang, Marcos Estecha-Garitagoitia, Mario Rodríguez-Cantelar, Toqeer Ehsan, Rendi Chevi, Muhammad Adilazuarda, Ryandito Diandaru, Samuel Cahyawijaya, Fajri Koto, Tatsuki Kuribayashi, Haiyue Song, Aditya Khandavally, Thanmay Jayakumar, Raj Dabre, Mohamed Imam, Kumaranage Nagasinghe, Alina Dragonetti, Luis Fernando D'Haro, Niyomugisha Olivier, Jay Gala, Pranjal Chitale, Fauzan Farooqui, Thamar Solorio, and Alham Aji. 2024. CVQA: Culturally-diverse multilingual visual question answering benchmark. In *Advances in Neural Information Processing Systems*, volume 37, pages 11479–11505. Curran Associates, Inc.

Michael J Ryan, William Held, and Diyi Yang. 2024. Unintended impacts of LLM alignment on global representation. In *Proceedings of the 62nd Annual Meeting of the Association for Computational Linguistics (Volume 1: Long Papers)*, pages 16121–16140, Bangkok, Thailand. Association for Computational Linguistics.

E. Sapir. 1929. The status of linguistics as a science. *Language*, 5(4):207–214.

Hassan Sawaf, Samhaa El-Beltagy, Wajdi Zaghouani, Walid Magdy, Ahmed Abdelali, Nadi Tomeh, Ibrahim Abu Farha, Nizar Habash, Salam Khalifa, Amr Keleg, Hatem Haddad, Imed Zitouni, Khalil Mrini, and Rawan Almatham, editors. 2023. *Proceedings of ArabicNLP 2023*. Association for Computational Linguistics, Singapore (Hybrid).

Neha Sengupta, Sunil Kumar Sahu, Bokang Jia, Satheesh Katipomu, Haonan Li, Fajri Koto, William Marshall, Gurpreet Gosal, Cynthia Liu, Zhiming Chen, Osama Mohammed Afzal, Samta Kamboj, Onkar Pandit, Rahul Pal, Lalit Pradhan, Zain Muhammad Mujahid, Massa Baali, Xudong Han, Sondos Mahmoud Bsharat, Alham Fikri Aji, Zhiqiang Shen, Zhengzhong Liu, Natalia Vassilieva, Joel Hestness, Andy Hock, Andrew Feldman, Jonathan Lee, Andrew Jackson, Hector Xuguang Ren, Preslav Nakov, Timothy Baldwin, and Eric Xing. 2023. Jais and Jais-chat: Arabic-centric foundation and instruction-tuned open generative large language models. *Preprint*, arXiv:2308.16149.

Farhana Shahid and Aditya Vashistha. 2023. Decolonizing content moderation: Does uniform global community standard resemble utopian equality or western power hegemony? In *Proceedings of the 2023 CHI Conference on Human Factors in Computing Systems*, CHI '23, New York, NY, USA. Association for Computing Machinery.

Guokan Shang, Hadi Abdine, Yousef Khoubrane, Amr Mohamed, Yassine Abbahaddou, Sofiane Ennadir, Imane Momayiz, Xuguang Ren, Eric Moulines, Preslav Nakov, Michalis Vazirgiannis, and Eric Xing. 2024. Atlas-Chat: Adapting large language models for low-resource Moroccan Arabic dialect. *Preprint*, arXiv:2409.17912.

Shivalika Singh, Angelika Romanou, Clémentine Fourrier, David I. Adelani, Jian Gang Ngui, Daniel Vila-Suero, Peerat Limkonchotiwat, Kelly Marchisio, Wei Qi Leong, Yosephine Susanto, Raymond Ng, Shayne Longpre, Wei-Yin Ko, Madeline Smith, Antoine Bosselut, Alice Oh, Andre F. T. Martins, Leshem Choshen, Daphne Ippolito, Enzo Ferrante, Marzieh Fadaee, Beyza Ermis, and Sara Hooker. 2024. Global MMLU: Understanding and addressing cultural and linguistic biases in multilingual evaluation. *Preprint*, arXiv:2412.03304.

Wenxuan Wang, Wenxiang Jiao, Jingyuan Huang, Ruyi Dai, Jen-tse Huang, Zhaopeng Tu, and Michael Lyu. 2024. Not all countries celebrate thanksgiving: On the cultural dominance in large language models. In *Proceedings of the 62nd Annual Meeting of the Association for Computational Linguistics (Volume 1: Long Papers)*, pages 6349–6384, Bangkok, Thailand. Association for Computational Linguistics.

Imed Zitouni, Muhammad Abdul-Mageed, Houda Bouamor, Fethi Bougares, Mahmoud El-Haj, Nadi Tomeh, and Wajdi Zaghouani, editors. 2020. *Proceedings of the Fifth Arabic Natural Language Processing Workshop*. Association for Computational Linguistics, Barcelona, Spain (Online).

Multi-Step Reasoning in Korean and the Emergent Mirage

Guijin Son[1,2,3] **Hyunwoo Ko**[1] **Dasol Choi**[2]

OneLineAI[1] Yonsei University[2] MODULABS[3]
spthsrbwls123@yonsei.ac.kr

Abstract

We introduce HRMCR (HAE-RAE Multi-Step Commonsense Reasoning), a benchmark designed to evaluate large language models' ability to perform multi-step reasoning in culturally specific contexts, focusing on Korean. The questions are automatically generated via templates and algorithms, requiring LLMs to integrate Korean cultural knowledge into sequential reasoning steps. Consistent with prior observations on emergent abilities, our experiments reveal that models trained on fewer than $2 \cdot 10^{25}$ training FLOPs struggle to solve any questions, showing near-zero performance. Beyond this threshold, performance improves sharply. State-of-the-art models (e.g., O1) still score under 50%, underscoring the difficulty of our tasks. Notably, stepwise analysis suggests the observed emergent behavior may stem from compounding errors across multiple steps rather than reflecting a genuinely new capability. We publicly release the benchmark and commit to regularly updating the dataset to prevent contamination.

1 Introduction

Large language models (LLMs) have shown notable success in solving complex reasoning tasks across STEM (Rein et al., 2023) and mathematics (Cobbe et al., 2021), facilitated by methods such as chain-of-thought prompting (Wei et al., 2022b) and inference-time scaling (Brown et al., 2024). However, it is unclear how beneficial these high-level problem-solving abilities—particularly for Olympiad-level math problems—are in real-world, everyday scenarios. Moreover, most existing reasoning benchmarks emphasize universal knowledge (Hendrycks et al., 2021; Fang et al., 2024) that remains constant across different cultures and languages. While these benchmarks (Ko et al., 2025) effectively measure a model's general reasoning capabilities, they are less suited for evaluating the

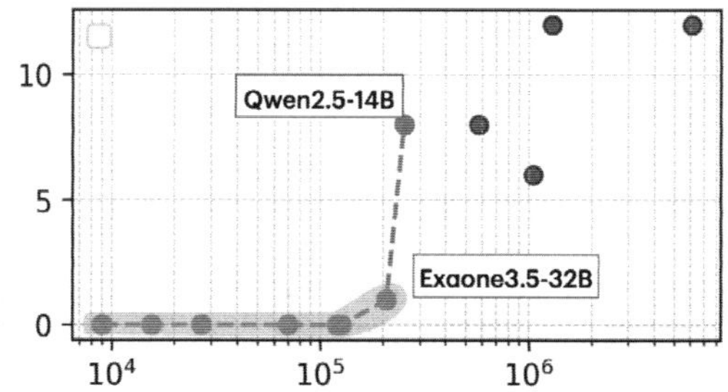

Figure 1: The X-axis represents the training compute scale in ExaFLOPs (10^{18} floating-point operations), calculated as $6 \times$ #parameters $\times$ #tokens following Kaplan et al. (2020). The Y-axis indicates the performance of the models on HRMCR.

model's proficiency in language-specific or culturally grounded reasoning.

To address this gap, we introduce HRMCR (HAE-RAE Multi-Step Commonsense Reasoning), a systematically generated benchmark that requires LLMs to integrate Korean cultural knowledge into multi-step reasoning. Our generation algorithm, which uses randomly selected seeds, generates questions and step-by-step solutions. Each of the two subsets in our benchmark comprises 50 questions. We make the *question–answer set* publicly available but withhold the algorithm itself to prevent contamination and overfitting. Instead, we commit to regularly updating the benchmark[1].

As illustrated in Figure 1, models with fewer than $2 \cdot 10^{25}$ training FLOPs struggle to solve any questions on the benchmark. Once training surpasses this threshold, however, scores increase sharply—a phenomenon often described as an emergent ability. Despite this improvement, even state-of-the-art (SOTA) LLMs (e.g., O1, GPT-4o, Claude-3.5-Sonnet) fall below 50% accuracy, underscoring the benchmark's difficulty. Notably, a stepwise performance analysis indicates that this apparent "emergence" may stem from cumulative

[1]Link has been removed for anonymous submission. It will be publicly available.

Proceedings of the 3rd Workshop on Cross-Cultural Considerations in NLP (C3NLP 2025), pages 10–21
May 4, 2025 ©2025 Association for Computational Linguistics

errors across multiple reasoning steps, rather than a genuinely new capability.

2 Related Works

Korean Benchmarks Most publicly available Korean benchmarks primarily focus on knowledge (Son et al., 2024b; Kim et al., 2024; Son et al., 2023) or safety (Lee et al., 2023a,b), leaving a gap in assessing more advanced reasoning skills. Consequently, the evaluation of Korean LLMs often relies on English benchmarks (Research et al., 2024b,a; Yoo et al., 2024), to evaluate the reasoning capability of LLMs. This highlights the need for Korean-specific reasoning benchmarks that demand both linguistic and cultural competencies.

Multi-Step Reasoning As LLMs continue to enhance their reasoning abilities through improved pre-training (Yang et al., 2024; Lu et al., 2024) and post-training (Wu et al., 2024), many existing benchmarks no longer pose meaningful challenges or offer practical utility. Frontier LLMs (OpenAI, 2024) can now achieve near-expert performance on specialized tasks (Rein et al., 2023; Gao et al., 2024), prompting the creation of even more demanding problem sets (Glazer et al., 2024). However, those tasks often require domain-specific expertise—particularly in STEM—making them less representative of the broader range of reasoning tasks encountered in daily life.

One way to create challenging yet broadly accessible questions is to design multi-step problems that do not require deep expert knowledge. Such tasks can be generated by concatenating simpler subproblems (Hosseini et al., 2024; Son et al., 2024a) or by using template-based algorithms (Sprague et al., 2023), with the latter offering greater diversity. Building on prior work, we develop a fully algorithm-based benchmark that systematically generates multi-step reasoning problems demanding Korean commonsense knowledge. Additionally, we provide an automatic explanation generator, enabling more effective error analysis and evaluation for each step of the reasoning process.

3 HRMCR

In this section, we introduce the HRMCR (HAE-RAE Multi-Step Commonsense Reasoning) benchmark, describing its two subsets (Section 3.1) and key design choices (Section 3.2).

3.1 Subsets

HRMCR comprises two subsets: **Date** and **Zodiac**, each created to require multiple steps of reasoning. We release 50 questions per subset.

Date The Date subset contains concise, two-sentence questions involving Korean holidays and traditional date expressions. To solve these, the model must recall Korean cultural knowledge, perform basic arithmetic, and convert between solar and lunar calendars. Each question requires a five-step solution.

Zodiac The Zodiac subset features longer questions, typically spanning 10–12 lines. These tasks require handling a range of Korean cultural elements—such as the country's unique age system[1], conversational age expressions, and honorifics. The model must then extract logical inferences from the given premises and perform arithmetic to determine the zodiac sign. Each solution requires seven steps of reasoning at maximum.

3.2 Design Choice

Each subset is generated by a dedicated algorithm comprising roughly 500 lines of code, and each algorithm includes a built-in solution generator that derives a gold-standard solution step-by-step. This built-in solver is a unique feature of our benchmark, as it facilitates comprehensive error analysis at each reasoning stage.

Benchmark contamination has become a pressing issue (Xu et al., 2024; Zhang et al., 2024), and one common approach to address it is using private test sets (Chollet, 2019). However, private benchmarks have drawbacks: over the long term, repeated attempts can lead to overfitting, with models effectively using the test scores as a training signal (Park et al., 2024). Additionally, keeping questions private hinders error analysis and limits opportunities for diagnosing and improving model performance. To balance these concerns, we publicly release our test set but keep the exact generation code confidential. If contamination arises, we can easily regenerate a new question–answer set by varying random seeds. By withholding the generation algorithm, we ensure that every newly released set remains unseen, making the benchmark more robust over time.

Algorithm 1 illustrates the pseudo-code used to create the Date questions, and the algorithm for the

[1]Korea calculates age differently from Western countries.

Question	Solution
On 개천절 (Korean Foundation Day) in 1993, I heard someone say, "그제 (the day before yesterday) was my birthday." What is the lunar calendar date three days after that birthday?	[STEP 0] Year is 1993. [STEP 1] The 개천절 is 10.3 [STEP 2] Expression='그제' (offset=-2), so birthday is 1993.10.1 [STEP 3] Adding 3 days to 1993.10.1 → 1993.10.4 (solar) [STEP 4] Converting to lunar: 1993.10.4 → 1993.8.19

Question	Solution
I was born on December 10, 2000. Today is my 25th birthday, so I decided to have a birthday party. I met two people, A and B: A always to someone older than them. B always speaks informally to someone younger than them. B and I have a 3-year age difference. A is three years ahead of me in university, is a 빠른 년생 (early-born), and entered university after retaking the college entrance exam 삼수 (three times). A asked B, "어떻게 오셨어요?" B replied, "저 차 타고 왔어요" What is B's zodiac sign (띠)?	[STEP 0] Birth year = 2000, N-th birthday = 25 -> My age = 25 [STEP 1] A's relation: 3년 선배, birth condition: 빠른 년생이고, education: 삼수를 한 뒤 [STEP 2] Calculating A's age: University: 3년 선배 → +3 years (Age: 28) Birth condition: 빠른 년생 → -1 year (Age: 27) Education: 삼수 → +2 years (Age: 29) [STEP 3] Determining relationships: B's age <= A's age (B used formal speech) [STEP 4] Age analysis: Case: me < A & B <= A Given: my_age = 25, A's age = 29 From earlier: B has 3 year age gap, so B could be either age: [22, 28] [Step 5] Since the current year is 2024, birth year of b is [2003, 1997] [Step 6] The zodiac animal can be calculated by dividing the birth year by 12 and acquiring its remaining, accordingly: ['양', '소']

Figure 2: Example of generated questions in the HRMCR benchmark. The figure showcases generated questions (left) alongside their automatically generated solutions (right). The top panel represents the "date" subset, while the bottom corresponds to the "zodiac" subset. Questions are translated into Korean to enhance accessibility.

Algorithm 1 Question Generator for Date Subset

Require: Database of cultural events with calendar types and dates

function GENERATEQUESTION
- *// Step 1: Select base components*
- year, event ← Random(valid_year_range), RandomSelect(cultural_events)
- cal_type ← event.calendar_type
- *// Step 2: Select expressions*
- date_expr, target_cal ← RandomSelect(date_expressions), RandomSelect(calendar_types)
- *// Step 3: Generate question*
- question ← Template(year, event.name, date_expr, target_cal)
- **return** question

end function

Zodiac subset is provided in Appendix A. Figure 2 and 5 show examples of generated questions and their gold solutions.

4 Experimental Setup

In this section, we describe how responses were generated (Section 4.1) and evaluated (Section 4.2).

4.1 Response Generation

We evaluate a total of 20 LLMs, including proprietary models such as GPT-4o, GPT-4o-Mini (Hurst et al., 2024), O1, O1-Mini (Jaech et al., 2024), and Claude-3.5-Sonnet (Anthropic, 2024), as well as open models like Qwen2.5 (Yang et al., 2024), Llama3 (Dubey et al., 2024), Exaone3.5 (Research et al., 2024a), and DeepSeek3 (DeepSeek-AI et al., 2024). All models are evaluated in a greedy setting. For models up to 32B parameters, we run inference on a local GPU server; larger models are accessed via the OpenRouter API.[1] For additional details on the evaluated models, see Appendix A.

4.2 Response Evaluation

For evaluation, we use GPT-4o as an LLM-as-a-Judge (Zheng et al., 2023). The judge takes the question, the model-generated response, and the gold step-by-step solution. As shown in Figure 4 (Appendix A), the judge first provides a brief comparison with the gold solution and then determines whether the model's response is correct. If it is incorrect, the judge identifies the specific step at which the error occurred. All evaluations use greedy decoding.

[1] https://openrouter.ai/

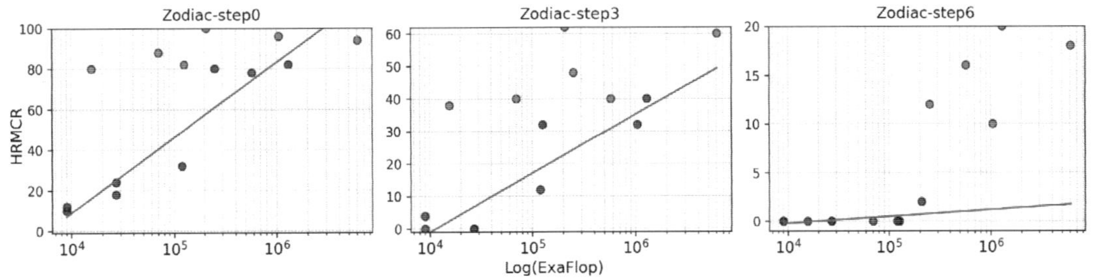

Figure 3: Breakdown of performance results for selected steps in the Zodiac subset. The green line represents the regression line, the blue points are instances used for fitting the regression, and the red points represent the test set. Only at the last step, the regression fails. For the entire results, see Appendix B.

5 Evaluation Results

Models	Date	Zodiac	Av.
o1	**34**	**56**	**45**
GPT-4o	28	32	30
DeepSeek-V3	32	14	23
Claude-3.5-Sonnet	**34**	8	21
Qwen2.5-72B	4	20	12
Llama3.1-405B	6	18	12
EXAONE3.5-32B	0	2	1

Table 1: Evaluation results on HRMCR. We only display the performance of top-performing models per model family. The best-performing model is highlighted in **bold**.

Table 1 presents the evaluation results, from which we derive three key observations. First, the HRMCR benchmark is highly challenging: leading models such as GPT-4o, DeepSeek-V3, and Claude-3.5-Sonnet all score under 30%. This is particularly noteworthy given that the benchmark is built on fixed, deterministic rules rather than specialized domain knowledge. Second, OpenAI's latest reasoning-oriented LLM, O1, achieves an average score of 45, substantially outperforming earlier models. This suggests that inference-time scaling can generalize effectively to previously unseen domains. Finally, EXAONE3.5-32B, despite its size, shows near-zero performance on the benchmark. This indicates that solving HRMCR requires not just model scale but also advanced training strategies and sufficient computational resources.

6 The Emergent Mirage

Emergent at First Sight Emergent capability refers to abilities absent in smaller models but present in larger ones, making them unpredictable based solely on the performance of smaller models (Wei et al., 2022a). In Figure 1, we plot the performance of 19 models, with log compute on the X-axis and average performance on HRMCR on the Y-axis. Models exhibit near-zero performance until reaching $2 \cdot 10^{25}$ training FLOPs, followed by a sudden upsurge between Exaone3.5-32B and Qwen2.5-14B. This indicates that performance is driven primarily by training compute rather than model size: Qwen2.5-14B outperforms EXAONE3.5-32B by training on three times more tokens.

Alternative Interpretation Wei et al. (2022a) suggests that the sudden "emergence" of abilities may be attributed to multi-step reasoning. To investigate this hypothesis in our benchmark, we analyze the performance at each intermediate step. In Figure 3, we plot step-wise accuracy and test for emergent behavior using linear regression. We train a regression model on smaller models (excluding the top five performers) to predict performance at each step. Surprisingly, while this regression accurately predicts the performance of larger models at all intermediate steps, it fails only at the final step. This pattern holds for both Date and Zodiac subsets, despite their final steps involving different types of operations. Given that the final step in the Zodiac subset involves basic arithmetic (simple division), which is not typically considered an emergent capability, we propose an alternative interpretation: rather than true emergence, this pattern may result from error accumulation across steps. We hypothesize that further decomposing tasks into smaller steps would reveal purely linear performance trends, challenging the notion of emergence in this context.

7 Conclusion

We introduced HRMCR, a Korean multi-step reasoning benchmark that combines cultural knowledge with systematic generation. Our analysis revealed that seemingly emergent capabilities in LLMs may be artifacts of accumulated errors, prompting a reconsideration of how we evaluate model capabilities.

Acknowledgments

This research was supported by Brian Impact Foundation, a non-profit organization dedicated to the advancement of science and technology for all.

References

AI Anthropic. 2024. Claude 3.5 sonnet model card addendum. *Claude-3.5 Model Card*, 3.

Bradley Brown, Jordan Juravsky, Ryan Ehrlich, Ronald Clark, Quoc V Le, Christopher Ré, and Azalia Mirhoseini. 2024. Large language monkeys: Scaling inference compute with repeated sampling. *arXiv preprint arXiv:2407.21787*.

François Chollet. 2019. On the measure of intelligence. *arXiv preprint arXiv:1911.01547*.

Karl Cobbe, Vineet Kosaraju, Mohammad Bavarian, Mark Chen, Heewoo Jun, Lukasz Kaiser, Matthias Plappert, Jerry Tworek, Jacob Hilton, Reiichiro Nakano, et al. 2021. Training verifiers to solve math word problems. *arXiv preprint arXiv:2110.14168*.

DeepSeek-AI, Aixin Liu, Bei Feng, Bing Xue, Bingxuan Wang, Bochao Wu, Chengda Lu, Chenggang Zhao, Chengqi Deng, Chenyu Zhang, Chong Ruan, Damai Dai, Daya Guo, Dejian Yang, Deli Chen, Dongjie Ji, Erhang Li, Fangyun Lin, Fucong Dai, Fuli Luo, Guangbo Hao, Guanting Chen, Guowei Li, H. Zhang, Han Bao, Hanwei Xu, Haocheng Wang, Haowei Zhang, Honghui Ding, Huajian Xin, Huazuo Gao, Hui Li, Hui Qu, J. L. Cai, Jian Liang, Jianzhong Guo, Jiaqi Ni, Jiashi Li, Jiawei Wang, Jin Chen, Jingchang Chen, Jingyang Yuan, Junjie Qiu, Junlong Li, Junxiao Song, Kai Dong, Kai Hu, Kaige Gao, Kang Guan, Kexin Huang, Kuai Yu, Lean Wang, Lecong Zhang, Lei Xu, Leyi Xia, Liang Zhao, Litong Wang, Liyue Zhang, Meng Li, Miaojun Wang, Mingchuan Zhang, Minghua Zhang, Minghui Tang, Mingming Li, Ning Tian, Panpan Huang, Peiyi Wang, Peng Zhang, Qiancheng Wang, Qihao Zhu, Qinyu Chen, Qiushi Du, R. J. Chen, R. L. Jin, Ruiqi Ge, Ruisong Zhang, Ruizhe Pan, Runji Wang, Runxin Xu, Ruoyu Zhang, Ruyi Chen, S. S. Li, Shanghao Lu, Shangyan Zhou, Shanhuang Chen, Shaoqing Wu, Shengfeng Ye, Shengfeng Ye, Shirong Ma, Shiyu Wang, Shuang Zhou, Shuiping Yu, Shunfeng Zhou, Shuting Pan, T. Wang, Tao Yun, Tian Pei, Tianyu Sun, W. L. Xiao, Wangding Zeng, Wanjia Zhao, Wei An, Wen Liu, Wenfeng Liang, Wenjun Gao, Wenqin Yu, Wentao Zhang, X. Q. Li, Xiangyue Jin, Xianzu Wang, Xiao Bi, Xiaodong Liu, Xiaohan Wang, Xiaojin Shen, Xiaokang Chen, Xiaokang Zhang, Xiaosha Chen, Xiaotao Nie, Xiaowen Sun, Xiaoxiang Wang, Xin Cheng, Xin Liu, Xin Xie, Xingchao Liu, Xingkai Yu, Xinnan Song, Xinxia Shan, Xinyi Zhou, Xinyu Yang, Xinyuan Li, Xuecheng Su, Xuheng Lin, Y. K. Li, Y. Q. Wang, Y. X. Wei, Y. X. Zhu, Yang Zhang, Yanhong Xu, Yanhong Xu, Yanping Huang, Yao Li, Yao Zhao, Yaofeng Sun, Yaohui Li, Yaohui Wang, Yi Yu, Yi Zheng, Yichao Zhang, Yifan Shi, Yiliang Xiong, Ying He, Ying Tang, Yishi Piao, Yisong Wang, Yixuan Tan, Yiyang Ma, Yiyuan Liu, Yongqiang Guo, Yu Wu, Yuan Ou, Yuchen Zhu, Yuduan Wang, Yue Gong, Yuheng Zou, Yujia He, Yukun Zha, Yunfan Xiong, Yunxian Ma, Yuting Yan, Yuxiang Luo, Yuxiang You, Yuxuan Liu, Yuyang Zhou, Z. F. Wu, Z. Z. Ren, Zehui Ren, Zhangli Sha, Zhe Fu, Zhean Xu, Zhen Huang, Zhen Zhang, Zhenda Xie, Zhengyan Zhang, Zhewen Hao, Zhibin Gou, Zhicheng Ma, Zhigang Yan, Zhihong Shao, Zhipeng Xu, Zhiyu Wu, Zhongyu Zhang, Zhuoshu Li, Zihui Gu, Zijia Zhu, Zijun Liu, Zilin Li, Ziwei Xie, Ziyang Song, Ziyi Gao, and Zizheng Pan. 2024. Deepseek-v3 technical report. *Preprint*, arXiv:2412.19437.

Abhimanyu Dubey, Abhinav Jauhri, Abhinav Pandey, Abhishek Kadian, Ahmad Al-Dahle, Aiesha Letman, Akhil Mathur, Alan Schelten, Amy Yang, Angela Fan, et al. 2024. The llama 3 herd of models. *arXiv preprint arXiv:2407.21783*.

Meng Fang, Xiangpeng Wan, Fei Lu, Fei Xing, and Kai Zou. 2024. Mathodyssey: Benchmarking mathematical problem-solving skills in large language models using odyssey math data. *arXiv preprint arXiv:2406.18321*.

Bofei Gao, Feifan Song, Zhe Yang, Zefan Cai, Yibo Miao, Qingxiu Dong, Lei Li, Chenghao Ma, Liang Chen, Runxin Xu, et al. 2024. Omni-math: A universal olympiad level mathematic benchmark for large language models. *arXiv preprint arXiv:2410.07985*.

Elliot Glazer, Ege Erdil, Tamay Besiroglu, Diego Chicharro, Evan Chen, Alex Gunning, Caroline Falkman Olsson, Jean-Stanislas Denain, Anson Ho, Emily de Oliveira Santos, et al. 2024. Frontiermath: A benchmark for evaluating advanced mathematical reasoning in ai. *arXiv preprint arXiv:2411.04872*.

Dan Hendrycks, Collin Burns, Saurav Kadavath, Akul Arora, Steven Basart, Eric Tang, Dawn Song, and Jacob Steinhardt. 2021. Measuring mathematical problem solving with the math dataset. *arXiv preprint arXiv:2103.03874*.

Arian Hosseini, Alessandro Sordoni, Daniel Toyama, Aaron Courville, and Rishabh Agarwal. 2024. Not all llm reasoners are created equal. *arXiv preprint arXiv:2410.01748*.

Aaron Hurst, Adam Lerer, Adam P Goucher, Adam Perelman, Aditya Ramesh, Aidan Clark, AJ Ostrow, Akila Welihinda, Alan Hayes, Alec Radford, et al. 2024. Gpt-4o system card. *arXiv preprint arXiv:2410.21276*.

Aaron Jaech, Adam Kalai, Adam Lerer, Adam Richardson, Ahmed El-Kishky, Aiden Low, Alec Helyar,

Aleksander Madry, Alex Beutel, Alex Carney, et al. 2024. Openai o1 system card. *arXiv preprint arXiv:2412.16720.*

Jared Kaplan, Sam McCandlish, Tom Henighan, Tom B Brown, Benjamin Chess, Rewon Child, Scott Gray, Alec Radford, Jeffrey Wu, and Dario Amodei. 2020. Scaling laws for neural language models. *arXiv preprint arXiv:2001.08361.*

Eunsu Kim, Juyoung Suk, Philhoon Oh, Haneul Yoo, James Thorne, and Alice Oh. 2024. Click: A benchmark dataset of cultural and linguistic intelligence in korean. *arXiv preprint arXiv:2403.06412.*

Hyunwoo Ko, Guijin Son, and Dasol Choi. 2025. Understand, solve and translate: Bridging the multilingual mathematical reasoning gap. *arXiv preprint arXiv:2501.02448.*

Hwaran Lee, Seokhee Hong, Joonsuk Park, Takyoung Kim, Meeyoung Cha, Yejin Choi, Byoung Pil Kim, Gunhee Kim, Eun-Ju Lee, Yong Lim, et al. 2023a. Square: A large-scale dataset of sensitive questions and acceptable responses created through human-machine collaboration. *arXiv preprint arXiv:2305.17696.*

Hwaran Lee, Seokhee Hong, Joonsuk Park, Takyoung Kim, Gunhee Kim, and Jung-Woo Ha. 2023b. Kosbi: A dataset for mitigating social bias risks towards safer large language model application. *arXiv preprint arXiv:2305.17701.*

Zimu Lu, Aojun Zhou, Ke Wang, Houxing Ren, Weikang Shi, Junting Pan, Mingjie Zhan, and Hongsheng Li. 2024. Mathcoder2: Better math reasoning from continued pretraining on model-translated mathematical code. *arXiv preprint arXiv:2410.08196.*

OpenAI. 2024. Learning to reason with llms.

Chanjun Park, Hyeonwoo Kim, Dahyun Kim, Seonghwan Cho, Sanghoon Kim, Sukyung Lee, Yungi Kim, and Hwalsuk Lee. 2024. Open ko-llm leaderboard: Evaluating large language models in korean with ko-h5 benchmark. *arXiv preprint arXiv:2405.20574.*

David Rein, Betty Li Hou, Asa Cooper Stickland, Jackson Petty, Richard Yuanzhe Pang, Julien Dirani, Julian Michael, and Samuel R Bowman. 2023. Gpqa: A graduate-level google-proof q&a benchmark. *arXiv preprint arXiv:2311.12022.*

LG Research, Soyoung An, Kyunghoon Bae, Eunbi Choi, Kibong Choi, Stanley Jungkyu Choi, Seokhee Hong, Junwon Hwang, Hyojin Jeon, Gerrard Jeongwon Jo, et al. 2024a. Exaone 3.5: Series of large language models for real-world use cases. *arXiv preprint arXiv:2412.04862.*

LG Research, Soyoung An, Kyunghoon Bae, Eunbi Choi, Stanley Jungkyu Choi, Yemuk Choi, Seokhee Hong, Yeonjung Hong, Junwon Hwang, Hyojin Jeon, et al. 2024b. Exaone 3.0 7.8 b instruction tuned language model. *arXiv preprint arXiv:2408.03541.*

Guijin Son, Sangwon Baek, Sangdae Nam, Ilgyun Jeong, and Seungone Kim. 2024a. Multi-task inference: Can large language models follow multiple instructions at once? *arXiv preprint arXiv:2402.11597.*

Guijin Son, Hanwool Lee, Sungdong Kim, Seungone Kim, Niklas Muennighoff, Taekyoon Choi, Cheonbok Park, Kang Min Yoo, and Stella Biderman. 2024b. Kmmlu: Measuring massive multitask language understanding in korean. *arXiv preprint arXiv:2402.11548.*

Guijin Son, Hanwool Lee, Suwan Kim, Huiseo Kim, Jaecheol Lee, Je Won Yeom, Jihyu Jung, Jung Woo Kim, and Songseong Kim. 2023. Hae-rae bench: Evaluation of korean knowledge in language models. *arXiv preprint arXiv:2309.02706.*

Zayne Sprague, Xi Ye, Kaj Bostrom, Swarat Chaudhuri, and Greg Durrett. 2023. Musr: Testing the limits of chain-of-thought with multistep soft reasoning. *arXiv preprint arXiv:2310.16049.*

Jason Wei, Yi Tay, Rishi Bommasani, Colin Raffel, Barret Zoph, Sebastian Borgeaud, Dani Yogatama, Maarten Bosma, Denny Zhou, Donald Metzler, et al. 2022a. Emergent abilities of large language models. *arXiv preprint arXiv:2206.07682.*

Jason Wei, Xuezhi Wang, Dale Schuurmans, Maarten Bosma, Fei Xia, Ed Chi, Quoc V Le, Denny Zhou, et al. 2022b. Chain-of-thought prompting elicits reasoning in large language models. *Advances in neural information processing systems*, 35:24824–24837.

Yangzhen Wu, Zhiqing Sun, Shanda Li, Sean Welleck, and Yiming Yang. 2024. Inference scaling laws: An empirical analysis of compute-optimal inference for problem-solving with language models. *arXiv preprint arXiv:2408.00724.*

Cheng Xu, Shuhao Guan, Derek Greene, M Kechadi, et al. 2024. Benchmark data contamination of large language models: A survey. *arXiv preprint arXiv:2406.04244.*

An Yang, Baosong Yang, Beichen Zhang, Binyuan Hui, Bo Zheng, Bowen Yu, Chengyuan Li, Dayiheng Liu, Fei Huang, Haoran Wei, et al. 2024. Qwen2. 5 technical report. *arXiv preprint arXiv:2412.15115.*

Kang Min Yoo, Jaegeun Han, Sookyo In, Heewon Jeon, Jisu Jeong, Jaewook Kang, Hyunwook Kim, Kyung-Min Kim, Munhyong Kim, Sungju Kim, et al. 2024. Hyperclova x technical report. *arXiv preprint arXiv:2404.01954.*

Hugh Zhang, Jeff Da, Dean Lee, Vaughn Robinson, Catherine Wu, Will Song, Tiffany Zhao, Pranav Raja, Dylan Slack, Qin Lyu, et al. 2024. A careful examination of large language model performance on grade school arithmetic. *arXiv preprint arXiv:2405.00332.*

Lianmin Zheng, Wei-Lin Chiang, Ying Sheng, Siyuan Zhuang, Zhanghao Wu, Yonghao Zhuang, Zi Lin,

Zhuohan Li, Dacheng Li, Eric Xing, et al. 2023. Judging llm-as-a-judge with mt-bench and chatbot arena. *Advances in Neural Information Processing Systems*, 36:46595–46623.

A Evaluated Models

Llama-3 (Dubey et al., 2024). The Llama-3 series, spanning from Llama-3 to Llama-3.3, comprises large language models ranging from 1 to 405 billion parameters developed by Meta. While these multilingual models are pretrained on datasets comprising 9 to 15 trillion tokens across multiple languages, they do not officially support Korean. The suite also provides instruction-tuned models.

Qwen2.5 (Yang et al., 2024). Qwen2.5 is a suite of multilingual language models ranging from 0.5 to 72 billion parameters developed by Alibaba. Each model within the series is pretrained on a dataset of 18 trillion multilingual tokens, including Korean. Furthermore, the Qwen2.5 series officially support Korean and includes instruction-tuned variants for instruction-following.

DeepSeek-V3 (DeepSeek-AI et al., 2024). DeepSeek-V3 is a Mixture-of-Experts (MoE) language model with 671 billion parameters, utilizing 37 billion active parameters per token. It is trained on a dataset of 14.8 trillion multilingual tokens, making it robust across diverse languages and contexts. Additionally, they introduce the instruction-tuned version of the model.

EXAONE-3.5 (Research et al., 2024a). EXAONE 3.5 is a suite of multilingual language models with sizes of 2.4B, 7.8B, and 32B parameters developed by LG AI Research. These models are pretrained on datasets comprising up to 9 trillion tokens, evenly balanced between Korean and English, to ensure strong bilingual capabilities. Only the instruction-tuned versions of the models were made publicly available.

GPT-4o & o1 (Hurst et al., 2024; Jaech et al., 2024). GPT-4o, an advanced version of GPT-4, accepts multimodal inputs–including text, audio, image, and video–and demonstrate significant improvements on text in non-English languages. The o1 is a model designed to perform high-quality reasoning on complex tasks that require extensive thought processes, leveraging inference-time scaling through more elaborate reasoning steps and reflection. Both models are developed by OpenAI, and the latest versions of each were utilized in the experiments.

Claude-3.5 (Anthropic, 2024). Claude-3.5 series is the next generation of the Claude

Algorithm 2 Question Generator for Zodiac Subset

Require: Database of relationships, speech levels, and age modifiers
Ensure: Question about age relationships and zodiac sign

```
function GENERATEQUESTION
    // Step 1: Generate base timeline
    birth_year, current_year ← Random(valid_range), Random(valid_range)
    my_age ← CalculateKoreanAge(birth_year, current_year)
    // Step 2: Generate person A's profile
    relationship ← RandomSelect(university_relationships)
    modifiers ← RandomSelect(age_modifiers)
    a_age ← CalculateAge(my_age, relationship, modifiers)
    // Step 3: Generate conversation
    speech_level_a, speech_level_b ← RandomSelect(speech_levels), RandomSelect(speech_levels)
    age_relationship ← DetermineRelationship(speech_level_a, speech_level_b)
    // Step 4: Generate question text
    question ← Template(my_age, relationship, modifiers, conversation)
      return question
end function
```

3 series with significant improvements in commonsense and STEM reasoning benchmarks developed by Anthropic. We utilize the `claude-3.5-sonnet-20241022` for the experiments.

B Details in Evaluation

In this section, we provide samples of the prompts used for evaluation, responses generated by GPT-4o as LLM-as-a-Judge, and additional evaluation results.

B.1 Evaluation Prompt

We use GPT-4o as an LLM-as-a-Judge for evaluation; in Figure 4, we provide the prompt used for evaluation. The evaluation is done in greedy decoding settings.

B.2 Sample Responses

In Figure 5, we provide sample responses by models, and judgements generated by GPT-4o.

B.3 Additional Results

In this section, we present additional results. For the performance of all 20 models broken down by steps, see Table 2 and 3. In Figures 7 and 6, we provide continue from Section 6 and provide regression results for all steps of both subsets. Our findings remain consistent with the additional results.

System Prompt:
Please act as an impartial judge and evaluate the quality of the response provided by an AI assistant to the provided question. You will be given a question, a gold step-by-step answer, and a response from an AI assistant. Review the response by the AI assistant. Compare it with the gold step-by-step answer.

Begin your evaluation by providing a comparison with the gold answer. Be as objective as possible. After providing your explanation, return whether the model has reached the correct answer, and if not specify which step it has first failed at. For example:

if correct -> correct: [[true]] step: [[-1]]
if wrong -> correct: [[false]] step: [[3]]

User Prompt:
Question :
{question}

Gold Answer :
{gold}

Model Response :
{response}

Figure 4: Prompt used for judging responses.

Models	**Step 0**	**Step 1**	**Step 2**	**Step 3**	**Final**
Exaone3.5-2.4B	94	38	20	6	0
Exaone3.5-7.8B	86	56	42	14	0
Exaone3.5-32B	100	74	52	16	0
Qwen2.5-0.5B	56	30	14	6	0
Qwen2.5-1.5B	42	12	4	0	0
Qwen2.5-7B	100	72	40	22	0
Qwen2.5-14B	100	82	50	30	4
Qwen2.5-32B	100	76	54	28	0
Qwen2.5-72B	100	74	50	30	4
Llama3.2-1B	48	26	14	2	0
Llama3.2-3B	84	48	30	6	0
Llama3.1-8B	100	70	38	8	0
Llama-3.3-70B	100	78	48	14	2
Llama3.1-405B	100	72	48	24	6
DeepSeek3	100	70	54	40	32
Claude-3.5-Sonnet	100	70	60	48	34
GPT-4o-mini	100	68	44	32	10
GPT-4o	100	76	54	40	28
o1-mini	100	76	46	32	0
o1	100	76	64	60	34

Table 2: Performance of all models on the Date subset, broken down per step.

Question:
On 새해 첫날 (New Year's Day) in 1999, I heard someone say, "이튿날" (the day after tomorrow) was my birthday. What is the lunar calendar date 57 days after that birthday?

Gold Solution:
STEP 0: Year is 1999.
STEP 1: The 새해 첫날 is 1.1
STEP 2: Expression='이튿날' (offset=+1), so birthday is 1999.1.2
STEP 3: Adding 57 days to 1999.1.2 → 1999.2.28 (solar)
STEP 4: Converting to lunar: 1999.2.28 → 1999.1.13

Response by O1:
1999년 음력 설날(새해 첫날)은 **1월 1일**로, 그 다음 날인 **1월 2일**이 생일입니다. 이 생일로부터 57일 후의 음력 날짜를 계산해 보겠습니다.

1. **1월 2일부터 1월 말까지:**
- 1월은 30일로 구성되어 있으므로, 1월 2일부터 1월 30일까지는 총 **29일**입니다.

2. **2월:**
- 1999년 음력 2월은 **29일**입니다.
- 57일에서 1월에 사용된 29일을 제외하면, **28일**이 남습니다.
- 따라서 2월 1일부터 2월 28일까지가 됩니다.

결론적으로, **1월 2일**로부터 57일 후의 음력 날짜는 **2월 28일**입니다.

답: 음력 2월 28일

LLM-as-a-Judge:
The AI assistant's response does not align with the gold step-by-step answer. Here's a comparison:

1. **Year Identification:**
- Both the gold answer and the AI response correctly identify the year as 1999.

2. **New Year's Day Identification:**
- The gold answer identifies the solar New Year's Day as January 1st, 1999, and the birthday as January 2nd, 1999.
- The AI response incorrectly assumes the lunar New Year's Day as January 1st, 1999, and the birthday as January 2nd, 1999, without clarifying the calendar system.

3. **Calculation of 57 Days After Birthday:**
- The gold answer correctly calculates 57 days after January 2nd, 1999, in the solar calendar, resulting in February 28th, 1999.
- The AI response incorrectly calculates the days using the lunar calendar, leading to a different conclusion.

4. **Conversion to Lunar Date:**
- The gold answer converts February 28th, 1999, from the solar calendar to the lunar calendar, resulting in the lunar date of January 13th, 1999.
- The AI response does not perform this conversion and instead provides a lunar date of February 28th, which is incorrect.

The AI assistant fails to correctly interpret the calendar system and does not perform the necessary conversion from the solar to the lunar calendar. The first failure occurs at step 3, where the AI incorrectly calculates the 57 days using the lunar calendar instead of the solar calendar.

Correct: [[false]] Step: [[3]]

Figure 5: A full example including a sample question, gold solution, model response (by o1) and judgment (by GPT-4o).

Models	Step 0	Step 1	Step 2	Step 3	Step 4	Step 5	Final
Exaone3.5-2.4B	80	76	54	38	34	4	0
Exaone3.5-7.8B	88	84	52	40	34	8	0
Exaone3.5-32B	100	98	66	62	40	22	2
Qwen2.5-0.5B	10	4	0	0	0	0	0
Qwen2.5-1.5B	24	16	2	0	0	0	0
Qwen2.5-7B	82	68	36	32	26	10	0
Qwen2.5-14B	80	80	58	48	42	28	12
Qwen2.5-32B	78	78	46	40	38	28	16
Qwen2.5-72B	82	80	40	40	32	28	20
Llama3.2-1B	12	12	12	4	0	0	0
Llama3.2-3B	18	8	0	0	0	0	0
Llama3.1-8B	32	22	14	12	4	2	0
Llama-3.3-70B	96	92	52	32	30	20	10
Llama3.1-405B	94	90	72	60	54	32	18
DeepSeek3	94	94	70	60	48	20	14
Claude-3.5-Sonnet	32	30	26	14	8	8	8
GPT-4o-mini	96	90	72	64	52	22	20
GPT-4o	88	84	54	50	42	32	32
o1-mini	92	90	70	64	48	44	44
o1	98	98	72	68	58	56	56

Table 3: Performance of all models on the Zodiac subset, broken down per step.

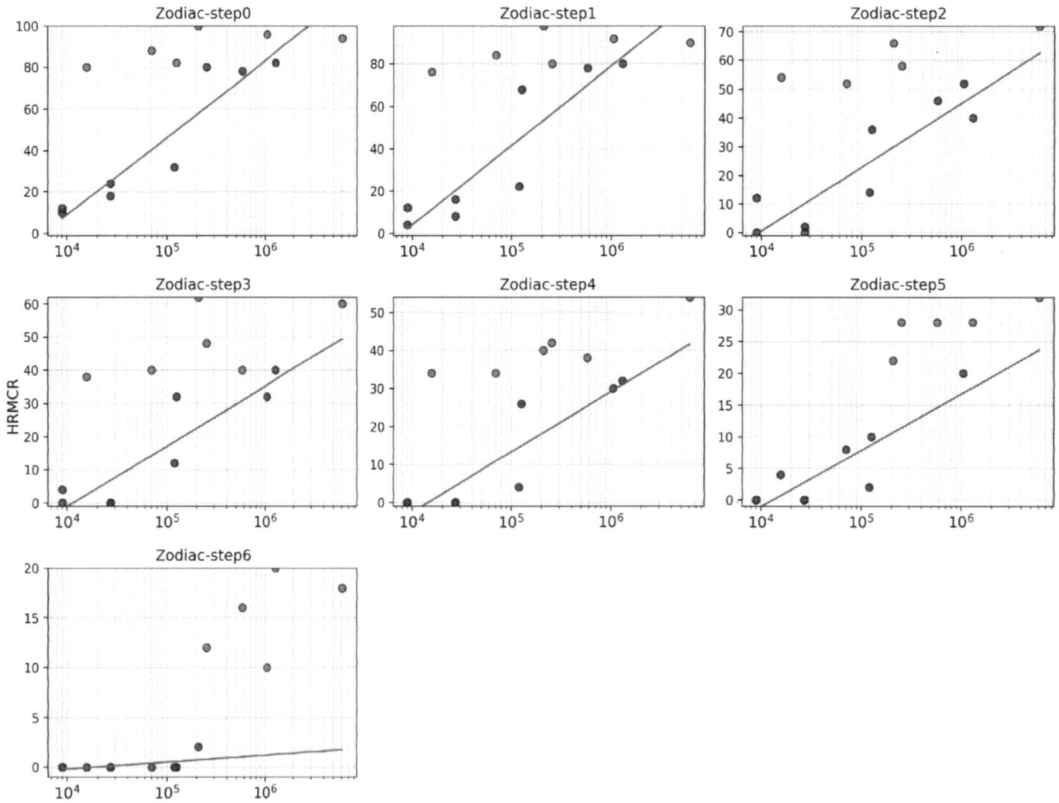

Figure 6: Breakdown of performance results for all steps in the Zodiac subset. The green line represents the regression line, the blue points are instances used for fitting the linear regression, and the red points represent the test set. Only at the final step the regression fails.

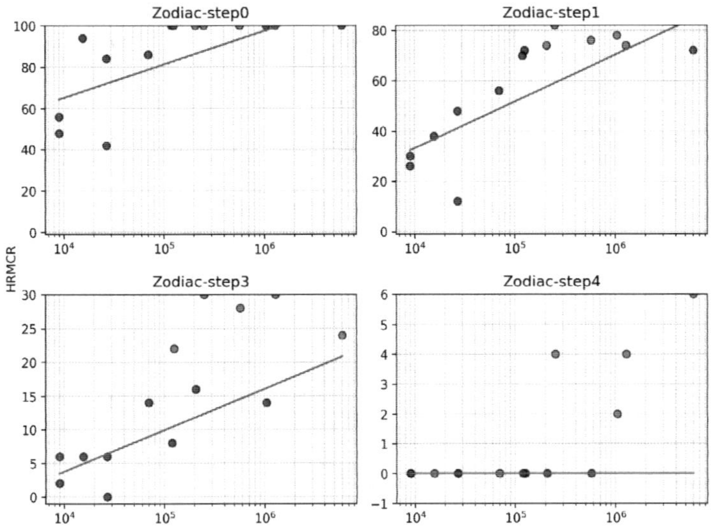

Figure 7: Breakdown of performance results for all steps in the Date subset. The green line represents the regression line, the blue points are instances used for fitting the linear regression, and the red points represent the test set. Only at the final step the regression fails.

Fair Summarization: Bridging Quality and Diversity in Extractive Summaries

Sina Bagheri Nezhad, Sayan Bandyapadhyay, Ameeta Agrawal
Department of Computer Science
Portland State University, USA
{sina5,sayanb,ameeta@pdx.edu}

Abstract

Fairness in multi-document summarization of user-generated content remains a critical challenge in natural language processing (NLP). Existing summarization methods often fail to ensure equitable representation across different social groups, leading to biased outputs. In this paper, we introduce two novel methods for fair extractive summarization: `FairExtract`, a clustering-based approach, and `FairGPT`, which leverages GPT-3.5-turbo with fairness constraints. We evaluate these methods using `Divsumm` summarization dataset of White-aligned, Hispanic, and African-American dialect tweets and compare them against relevant baselines. The results obtained using a comprehensive set of summarization quality metrics such as SUPERT, BLANC, SummaQA, BARTScore, and UniEval, as well as a fairness metric F, demonstrate that `FairExtract` and `FairGPT` achieve superior fairness while maintaining competitive summarization quality. Additionally, we introduce composite metrics (e.g., SUPERT+F, BLANC+F) that integrate quality and fairness into a single evaluation framework, offering a more nuanced understanding of the trade-offs between these objectives. Our code is available online.[1]

1 Introduction

Multi-document summarization, which condenses multiple documents into a concise summary, is a fundamental task in natural language processing (NLP). Summarization methods are typically either *extractive*, selecting the most important sentences, or *abstractive*, where the content is rephrased.

Early research focused on summarizing formal text sources such as news articles. However, with the rise of social media, attention has shifted to summarizing user-generated content, which is diverse in style and language (Dash et al., 2019; Jung et al., 2019; Keswani and Celis, 2021; Olabisi et al., 2022). Social media platforms bring together users from varied backgrounds, introducing linguistic diversity through informal language, slang, and emojis. This diversity raises the challenge of ensuring fairness in summarization for a balanced representation of various social groups. In social media, where public opinion is shaped, fair summaries are essential to include different perspectives and avoid underrepresentation of one or more social groups as without proper representation, certain voices might be excluded or misrepresented. Therefore, ensuring that all groups—across race, gender, and linguistic diversity—are fairly represented is critical for generating balanced summaries that reflect the diversity of public opinion (Dash et al., 2018). In particular, the dialectal variations among White-aligned, Hispanic, and African-American groups not only reflect different linguistic styles but also embody distinct cultural expressions that influence how users communicate.

Despite advancements, bias remains a concern in automated summarization (Dash et al., 2019; Jung et al., 2019; Keswani and Celis, 2021; Olabisi et al., 2022) as most existing summarization methods focus on quality but fall short in optimizing fairness. Improving fairness can sometimes lower quality (Jung et al., 2019). This gap leads to the key question: if a summarization method is optimized for fairness, how does it affect the overall summary quality?

In this paper, we address two research questions:

1. How does achieving perfectly fair summaries affect overall quality?

2. How well do current methods perform when considering both fairness and quality?

To illustrate the performance of fairness-aware summarization models, we compare summaries generated by ChatGPT-EXT (Zhang et al., 2023)

[1] `https://github.com/PortNLP/FairEXTSummarizer`

Proceedings of the 3rd Workshop on Cross-Cultural Considerations in NLP (C3NLP 2025), pages 22–34
May 4, 2025

ChatGPT-EXT (Zhang et al., 2023)	FairGPT (Ours)
If you see on the news something about the Chicago Kitchen Clown Bandits then it will be referring me my friend Eten and I. Turns out not all White Castles are the same. Why do you push me away Chicago?! I mean I'm from Chicago. I'll cheer for the Bears, but I'm a bigger 49ers fan. Is this new wave of Chicago Rap gonna be like the Hyphy movement? Don't talk shot about Chicago, or those big shoulders will plow right into your little Boston ass. Nothing makes me happier than seeing the Bulls win #ChicagoBasketball #Bullieve.	Don't talk shot about Chicago, or those big shoulders will plow right into your little Boston ass. Nothing makes me happier than seeing the Bulls win #ChicagoBasketball #Bullieve. Truuu we tryna find sum to do too.. I dnt wanna b n Chicago if ain't nobody here. Turns out not all White Castles are the same. Why do you push me away Chicago?! I mean I'm from Chicago. I'll cheer for the Bears, but I'm a bigger 49ers fan. Is this new wave of Chicago Rap gonna be like the Hyphy movement?

Table 1: Comparison of summaries generated by ChatGPT-EXT and FairGPT. Tweets from different groups are highlighted: Group 1 (e.g., White-aligned) and Group 2 (e.g., African-American).

and our proposed FairGPT model on a sample instance from Divsumm dataset (Olabisi et al., 2022). As shown in Table 1, FairGPT ensures equal representation of tweets from different groups, while ChatGPT-EXT shows a slight imbalance.

We make the following contributions:

- We propose FairExtract, a fair clustering-based extractive summarization method that achieves perfect fairness while preserving competitive summarization quality, as demonstrated through evaluations against baseline models using standard and composite quality-fairness metrics.
- We develop FairGPT, a large language model-based extractive summarization method that enforces fairness through equal representation and accurate content extraction using the longest common subsequence, producing fair summaries without sacrificing competitive summarization quality.
- We introduce composite metrics combining normalized quality scores with fairness, providing a comprehensive analysis of the quality-fairness trade-off in summarization models.

2 Related Work

The field of NLP has increasingly focused on addressing bias and fairness, with research focused along two key dimensions: intrinsic bias, stemming from text representations, and extrinsic bias, reflecting performance disparities across demographic groups (Han et al., 2023).

Early work on fairness in summarization (Shandilya et al., 2018; Dash et al., 2019) revealed that summaries often fail to represent source data fairly, even when source texts from different groups have similar quality. This led to the development of fairness-aware algorithms across various stages of summarization, including pre-processing, in-processing, and post-processing techniques. For example, Keswani and Celis (2021) proposed a post-processing method to mitigate dialect-based biases. Olabisi et al. (2022) introduced the DivSumm dataset, focusing on dialect diversity in summarization and evaluating algorithms on fairness.

Recent work has explored bias related to the position of input data. Olabisi and Agrawal (2024) studied position bias in multi-document summarization, showing that the order of input texts affects fairness. Similarly, Huang et al. (2023) analyzed clustering-based summarization models, which may introduce political or opinion bias, emphasizing the need for fair representation.

Recent work highlights that large language models often reflect dominant Western cultural norms, resulting in cultural bias (Tao et al., 2024). Liu et al. (2024) provided a taxonomy for culturally aware NLP that emphasizes the role of values, norms, and linguistic diversity. Moreover, Hershcovich et al. (2022) discussed cross-cultural challenges in NLP and advocate for strategies that integrate cultural insights into model development.

Fair clustering, another key technique, has also seen significant research. Chierichetti et al. (2017) introduced the concept of fairlets—small, balanced clusters that ensure fair representation across protected groups. Building on this, Chen et al. (2019) proposed proportional centroid clustering to eliminate biases in cluster-based models.

Further advancements include scalable techniques for fair clustering, such as the fair k-median clustering method (Backurs et al., 2019), and approaches that generalize fairness constraints across multiple protected groups (Bera et al., 2019). Esmaeili et al. (2020) extended this work to probabilistic fair clustering, offering solutions for uncertain group memberships.

In the domain of clustering methodologies, Micha and Shah (2020) explored fairness in centroid clustering, while Li et al. (2020) proposed Deep Fair Clustering (DFC), which leverages deep learning to filter sensitive attributes, improving both fairness and performance. This underscores the growing importance of combining fairness with robust clustering methods in NLP tasks.

3 Task Formulation

In this work, we address the challenge of diversity-preserving multi-document extractive summarization. Given a collection of documents $\mathcal{D} = \{d_1, d_2, \ldots, d_n\}$ from two diverse social groups, G_1 and G_2, the goal is to produce an extractive summary $\mathcal{S} = \{s_1, s_2, \ldots, s_k\} \subset \mathcal{D}$ of length $k << n$, ensuring balanced representation from both groups.

In this context, each document is a tweet from a specific dialect group, which serves as an indicator of its social group. Traditionally, various metrics like ROUGE (Lin, 2004) and BERTScore (Zhang et al., 2019) have been used to evaluate summary quality. However, our primary focus is on balancing both quality and fairness, particularly in terms of representing different social groups equitably. To measure fairness, we use the *Representation Gap (RG)* metric, as proposed by Olabisi et al. (2022). This metric captures how well the summary reflects the proportions of the original groups. A lower RG score indicates better balance and thus a fairer summary.

For a summary $\mathcal{S}$ of length k, let $N_1(\mathcal{S})$ and $N_2(\mathcal{S})$ represent the number of documents from groups G_1 and G_2, respectively. The Representation Gap is defined as:

$$\text{RG}(\mathcal{S}) = \frac{\max\{N_1(\mathcal{S}), N_2(\mathcal{S})\} - \min\{N_1(\mathcal{S}), N_2(\mathcal{S})\}}{k}. \quad (1)$$

For example, if $k = 6$, with 4 documents from G_1 and 2 from G_2, the RG is 0.333. When both groups are equally represented, the RG is 0, indicating a *perfectly fair* summary.

At this point, we recognize two key challenges: (1) While quality metrics improve with larger values, fairness improves with smaller Representation Gap (RG) values. (2) Quality and fairness metrics differ greatly in scale, making direct comparison difficult.

To address these issues, we introduce a new fairness metric, F, defined as:

$$F(\mathcal{S}) = 1 - \text{RG}(\mathcal{S}) \quad (2)$$

This transformation ensures that larger F values indicate better fairness, aligning it with the behavior of quality metrics. Furthermore, we apply min-max normalization to rescale all metrics to the range $[0, 1]$, ensuring comparability across different scales. The normalization formula is given by:

$$\frac{\text{value} - \min}{\max - \min} \quad (3)$$

where $\min$ and $\max$ are the minimum and maximum observed values for the respective metric.

Finally, we introduce composite metrics, such as **SUPERT+F**, **BLANC+F**, **SummaQA+F**, **BARTScore+F**, and **UniEval+F**, which are the averages of the normalized quality metrics (e.g., SUPERT (Gao et al., 2020), BLANC (Vasilyev et al., 2020), SummaQA (Scialom et al., 2019), BARTScore (Yuan et al., 2021), and UniEval (Zhong et al., 2022)) and the fairness score F, providing a balanced assessment of both quality and fairness.

4 Fair Extractive Summarizers

In this work, we introduce two novel methods for fair extractive summarization: FairExtract and FairGPT. FairExtract utilizes clustering techniques with fairlet decomposition to ensure diversity in summaries while maintaining high-quality representation across different groups. FairGPT, on the other hand, leverages large language models (LLMs) such as GPT-3.5, incorporating fairness constraints and the longest common subsequence (LCS) method to match and fairly select content from different groups. Both methods prioritize fairness and ensure equitable representation in the generated summaries.

4.1 FairExtract: A Clustering-based Fair Extractive Summarization Method

The task of clustering is central to the FairExtract process, which aims to generate diversity-preserving summaries. The method combines document embeddings, fairlet decomposition, and clustering techniques to ensure both fairness and quality. Below, we describe the steps involved in detail:

1. **Embedding Documents:** We begin by embedding each document (tweet) into a high-dimensional space (e.g., using a pretrained model such as BERT (Devlin et al., 2019)), capturing its semantic content in Euclidean space. This embedding enables us to compute meaningful distances between documents, which is crucial for clustering.

2. **Fairlet Decomposition:** To ensure fairness in the summarization process, we decompose the dataset into fairlets. A fairlet is the smallest set of documents that maintains proportional balance between two groups, G_1 and G_2 (Backurs et al., 2019). Assume the desired ratio of documents from G_1 to G_2 is $g_1 : g_2$, where g_1 and g_2 are coprime (i.e., $\gcd(g_1, g_2) = 1$). Then, a fairlet is defined as the smallest group of documents that exactly preserves this ratio, containing exactly g_1 documents from G_1 and g_2 documents from G_2. This ensures that the composition of the fairlet reflects the required ratio between the two groups, maintaining fairness at the smallest possible scale. The decomposition aims to minimize the sum of Euclidean distances between documents within the same fairlet.

3. **Finding the Fairlet Center:** Once the dataset is divided into fairlets, we compute the center of each fairlet. The center is the document within the fairlet that minimizes the sum of distances to all other documents in the same fairlet. This document acts as the representative of the fairlet, summarizing the content while maintaining group balance.

4. **k-Median Clustering on Fairlet Centers:** After identifying the centers of all fairlets, we apply the k-median clustering algorithm to these centers. In the k-median problem, we are given a set of points P in a d-dimensional space, and we aim to partition them into k clusters $\Pi = \{P_1, \ldots, P_k\}$ that minimize the following cost:

$$\min_{C \subset P : |C| = k} \sum_{c_i \in C | 1 \leq i \leq k} \sum_{p \in P_i} ||p - c_i||. \quad (4)$$

   The number of clusters k is selected such that $k \times (g_1 + g_2)$ equals the desired number of documents in the summary. This step ensures that the clusters formed are representative of both social groups.

5. **Summary Construction:** From each k-median cluster, we select the center fairlet and include all documents within that fairlet in the final summary. By selecting one fairlet from each cluster, we maintain both quality and fairness, as the summary reflects the balanced representation of both groups. The resulting extractive summary ensures that the most salient information is captured while maintaining equitable representation of the social groups.

For a formal representation of the process, see Appendix A.1.

4.2 FairGPT: An LLM-based Fair Extractive Summarization Method

FairGPT leverages an LLM generate fair extractive summaries by selecting an equal number of sentences from different social groups. It applies fairness checks and uses the longest common subsequence (LCS) to match generated summaries with the original tweets. Below are the detailed steps:

1. **Input Preparation:** The dataset is split into two groups (e.g., White-aligned and Hispanic dialects), and a document with sentences for each group is created as input for the summarization process.

2. **Summarization using an LLM:** We use an LLM (GPT-3.5-turbo) to generate a summary of length L, selecting $L/2$ sentences from each group to ensure balanced representation. The specific prompt used for this task is available in the Prompt 1.

3. **Matching using Longest Common Subsequence (LCS):** As GPT sometimes extracts partial sentences, we apply LCS to match the generated summary with the closest original tweets. The full tweets corresponding to the longest common subsequences are added to the final summary.

4. **Output Check:** After generating the summary, we verify two key aspects. First, at least 50% of the content in each GPT-generated sentence must match the corresponding original tweet using the LCS. Second, we ensure that the summary is perfectly fair, with equal representation from each group.

FairGPT Prompt

```
system:  "You are an extractive fair summarizer that follows the output pattern. A fair summarizer
          should select the same number of sentences from each group of people."

user:    "Please extract sentences as the summary. The summary should contain {L} sentences
          which means select {L/2} number of sentences from each group of people to represent
          the idea of all groups in a fair manner.
          Document:{document}"
```

Prompt 1: Prompt used in FairGPT. The variable L refers to the total number of sentences to be extracted.

Algorithm 1 FairGPT Algorithm

Input:

- Document set $\mathcal{D}$ divided into groups G_1 and G_2
- Desired summary length L with $L/2$ sentences from each group

Output: Fair extractive summary $\mathcal{S}$

Step 1: Input Preparation
Create documents for G_1 and G_2, clearly labeling each sentence based on its group.

Step 2: Summarization using LLM
Instruct LLM (GPT-3.5-turbo) using Prompt 1 to select $L/2$ sentences from each group, ensuring fair representation.

Step 3: Matching using Longest Common Subsequence (LCS)
Use LCS to match the GPT-generated sentences with the original dataset to identify the closest matching tweets and include the full sentences in the summary.

Step 4: Ensuring 50% Similarity
Ensure that at least 50% of the content in each generated sentence matches the corresponding original tweet using LCS.

Step 5: Fairness Check
Verify that the summary contains an equal number of sentences from G_1 and G_2. If fairness or similarity conditions are not met, go to Step 2.

Step 6: Final Output
Save the final summary $\mathcal{S}$ once both fairness and quality thresholds are satisfied.

Return: The final summary $\mathcal{S}$.

This output check is crucial because large language models, such as GPT-3.5-turbo, sometimes generate unexpected outputs that do not align with the input instructions. To ensure the generated summaries meet both fairness and content similarity criteria, we repeat the process if either condition is not satisfied. In our tests of generating 75 summaries, the repetition process never exceeded 10 iterations, and the average number of repetitions across all tests was 1.6, indicating the efficiency and reliability of the output check mechanism.

5. **Final Output:** Once the summary satisfies both fairness and similarity requirements, it is saved as the final output.

For a formal representation of the process, see Algorithm 1.

5 Experimental Setup

Next, we describe the dataset, baseline methods, and evaluation metrics that are used to comprehensively assess the quality and fairness of the generated summaries.

5.1 Dataset

The dataset used in this study is *DivSumm* (Olabisi et al., 2022), consisting of tweets from three dialect groups—White-aligned, Hispanic, and African-American—across 25 topics, with 30 tweets per group per topic, totaling 2,250 tweets.

Our model works with two groups at a time, so we explore three pairings: White-Hispanic, Hispanic-African American, and White-African American. Each pairing maintains proportional representation from both groups to ensure an equitable balance in the summarization process. Table 2 presents a sample of the dataset used in this study, containing tweets from different social groups about Chicago.

Group	Tweet
White-aligned	Turns out not all White Castles are the same. Why do you push me away Chicago?!
African American	"I mean I'm from Chicago. I'll cheer for the Bears, but I'm a bigger 49ers fan."
White-aligned	Nothing makes me happier than seeing the Bulls win _____ #ChicagoBasketball #Bullieve
White-aligned	If you see on the news something about the Chicago Kitchen Clown Bandits, then it will be referring to me, my friend Eten, and I.
African American	Truuu we tryna find sum to do too.. I dnt wanna b n Chicago if ain't nobody here.
White-aligned	Oh yeah.. I'm good. Hangin' up here in Chicago today. :)
Hispanic	You girls have a safe flight.! See you in Chicago (:
...	**... (Dataset continues with more examples)**

Table 2: Sample of tweets from different social groups in the dataset. The full dataset contains many more examples.

For our experiments, we formed 60 tweets per group pair (30 from each group) and generated a 6-tweet summary per pair, covering all 25 topics. This yielded 75 distinct summaries per model, allowing us to evaluate both fairness and quality comprehensively.

5.2 Baseline Methods

Here, we provide a detailed description of the baseline methods used in our comparative analysis:

Naive: In the Naive baseline method, L tweets are randomly chosen from the input without any specific criteria. This approach represents a straightforward, non-strategic selection process and serves as a basic reference point for evaluating other methods.

NaiveFair: The NaiveFair baseline method involves randomly selecting $L/2$ tweets from each social group. This method ensures equal representation from each group, providing a basic notion of fairness without any sophisticated processing.

For the Naive and NaiveFair methods, which involve randomness in selecting summaries, we conducted the experiment five times for each summary, resulting in 375 different summaries for each of these methods.

TextRank: TextRank is an unsupervised graph-based ranking method used for extractive summarization (Mihalcea and Tarau, 2004). This standard `vanilla` baseline approach uses a single aggregated set of randomized documents from all groups as input for summarization, without any pre-processing.

BERT-Ext: BERT-Ext is an extractive summarization model that utilizes pre-trained embeddings from BERT and k-means clustering to select sentences closest to the centroid as summaries (Miller, 2019). Similar to the TextRank baseline, we implemented BERT-Ext `vanilla` method.

Cluster-Heuristic (Cluster-H): This method first partitions the input documents into group-based subsets before generating separate group summaries of length . These group-level summaries are shuffled, combined and then used to generate a final, unified summary (Dash et al., 2019; Olabisi et al., 2022). As summarization models, we use TextRank and BERT-Ext.

Cluster-Automatic (Cluster-A): In this attribute-agnostic approach, documents are clustered automatically into m subsets, and corresponding summaries of length are generated. The summaries are concatenated and used to generate a final summary (Olabisi et al., 2022). As summarization models, we experiment with TextRank and BERT-Ext.

ChatGPT-EXT: This approach uses GPT-3.5 for extractive summarization by employing in-context learning and chain-of-thought reasoning to identify key sentences. It focuses on extracting salient content from documents to generate coherent summaries while maintaining the structure of the original text (Zhang et al., 2023).

5.3 Evaluation Metrics

Below, we list the several reference-free metrics which do not rely on human-written reference text used for evaluation in this study.

- **SUPERT:** SUPERT (Gao et al., 2020) evaluates the quality of a summary by measuring its semantic similarity with a pseudo reference summary. It employs contextualized embeddings and soft token alignment techniques, providing an in-depth analysis of the semantic fidelity of generated summaries.

- **BLANC:** BLANC (Vasilyev et al., 2020) is a reference-less metric that measures the improvement in a pretrained language model's performance during language understanding tasks when given access to a summary.

- **SummaQA:** SummaQA (Scialom et al., 2019) employs a question-answering model based on BERT to answer cloze-style questions using the system-generated summaries, providing insights into the summarization's factual accuracy and coherence.

- **BARTScore:** BARTScore (Yuan et al., 2021) is a parameter- and data-efficient metric that supports the evaluation of generated text from multiple perspectives, including informativeness and coherence.

- **UniEval:** UniEval (Zhong et al., 2022) is a unified multi-dimensional evaluator that reframes natural language generation evaluation as a Boolean Question Answering (QA) task, guiding the model with different questions to evaluate from multiple dimensions. It is reference-free in three dimensions (coherence, consistency, fluency), but not relevance. For our evaluation, we focused on the reference-free dimensions of UniEval and reported the overall average performance.

- **Fairness (F):** To align fairness with the quality metrics, we define $F = 1 - \text{RG}$, where larger values represent better fairness. The Representation Gap (RG) metric (Olabisi et al., 2022) assesses the fairness of summaries by measuring the balance in the representation of different groups. We define *perfect fairness* as $F = 1$, meaning the summary includes an equal number of documents from each social group. This metric only captures numerical balance and does not address other dimensions such as content diversity or semantic nuances, which we leave for future work.

- **Composite Metrics (Metric+F):** For each quality metric (e.g., SUPERT, BLANC, SummaQA, BARTScore, and UniEval), we introduce a composite metric that combines the normalized quality score with the fairness score F. These composite metrics, such as **SUPERT+F**, **BLANC+F**, **SummaQA+F**, **BARTScore+F**, and **UniEval+F**, are computed by taking the average of the normalized quality metric and the fairness score F. A higher value of these composite metrics reflects a better balance between the summary's quality (as measured by the respective metric) and fairness.

6 Results and Discussion

In this section, we present the results of our evaluation, comparing the performance of various summarization models on both quality and fairness metrics.

6.1 Results of Quality and Fairness

The models were assessed using SUPERT, BLANC, SummaQA, BARTScore, UniEval, and the fairness metric F. Table 3 presents the results.

Naive and NaiveFair Baselines: The `Naive` baseline, which randomly selects sentences without any fairness consideration, performs relatively poorly across most quality metrics, particularly on SummaQA and BARTScore, where it scores significantly lower. However, it achieves a reasonable fairness score ($F = 0.732$), despite its lack of sophisticated fairness mechanisms. The `NaiveFair` model, which ensures equal representation from both groups, shows a slight improvement in fairness, achieving the maximum F value of 1. However, this fairness comes at a slight cost to quality, as it falls behind on some metrics like UniEval.

TextRank Models: The `TextRank Vanilla` method shows a balanced performance in terms of quality, with the highest SummaQA score (0.081), but suffers in BLANC and BARTScore. Variations of TextRank, such as `Cluster-A` and `Cluster-H`, show slight improvements in specific metrics like SUPERT and BLANC, but they still struggle in ensuring fairness, with scores in the range of $F = 0.693$ to $F = 0.727$.

BERT-Ext Models: The `BERT-EXT` models generally outperform the TextRank methods in quality metrics. `BERT-EXT Vanilla` achieves higher SUPERT and BARTScore scores compared to TextRank, with `BERT-EXT Cluster-A` further improving on these metrics, particularly in SUPERT (0.553) and BLANC (0.138). However, the fairness scores for these models remain moderate, with F values ranging from 0.680 to 0.728, indicating room for improvement in terms of group representation balance.

ChatGPT-Ext: The `ChatGPT-Ext` method stands out as the top performer in terms of quality, achieving the highest scores in SUPERT

Model	SUPERT	BLANC	SummaQA	BARTScore	UniEval	F
Naive	0.525	0.135	0.063	-1.788	0.391	0.732
NaiveFair	0.526	0.137	0.065	-1.776	0.386	**1.000**
TextRank Vanilla	0.527	0.108	**0.081**	-1.852	0.401	0.727
TextRank Cluster-A	0.530	0.107	0.075	-1.827	0.383	0.693
TextRank Cluster-H	0.530	0.107	0.077	-1.922	0.387	0.709
BERT-EXT Vanilla	0.544	0.137	0.070	-1.427	0.396	0.680
BERT-EXT Cluster-A	0.553	0.138	0.071	-1.535	0.399	0.728
BERT-EXT Cluster-H	0.554	0.133	0.070	-1.486	0.365	0.689
ChatGPT-EXT	**0.668**	**0.140**	0.065	**-0.642**	**0.434**	0.698
FairExtract (Ours)	0.530	**0.140**	0.066	-1.801	0.411	**1.000**
FairGPT (Ours)	0.644	0.139	0.075	-0.821	0.418	**1.000**

Table 3: Evaluation results for various summarization methods. The best values for each metric are shown in bold.

(0.668), BLANC (0.140), BARTScore (-0.642), and UniEval (0.434). This demonstrates its effectiveness in producing semantically rich and coherent summaries. However, its fairness score of $F = 0.698$ indicates that while it excels in quality, there is still room for improvement in terms of group representation.

FairExtract and FairGPT (Ours): Our proposed models, FairExtract and FairGPT, were designed with fairness as a core objective. Both models achieve perfect fairness, with $F = 1$, while still maintaining competitive quality. FairExtract performs comparably to TextRank in terms of quality metrics, excelling in BLANC (0.140) and achieving respectable scores in SUPERT and UniEval. FairGPT, leveraging the power of GPT-3.5, shows a strong balance between quality and fairness, with particularly high SUPERT (0.644) and BARTScore (-0.821) scores. These results suggest that our models successfully balance the trade-off between quality and fairness, making them robust options for fairness-aware summarization tasks.

Overall, ChatGPT-Ext achieves the highest quality metrics, while FairExtract and FairGPT lead in fairness without compromising quality; notably, FairGPT emerges as the best model, striking an optimal balance between quality and diversity, underscoring the success of our proposed methods in achieving fair and high-quality summarizations.

6.2 Results Aggregating Quality and Fairness

The composite evaluation metrics are presented in Table 4. These metrics aggregate both quality and fairness, both receiving equal weight (50%) in the overall score. Our results show that FairExtract, the proposed clustering-based summarization method, consistently outperforms other clustering-based models across most composite metrics, including SUPERT+F, BLANC+F, SummaQA+F, and UniEval+F. Although NaiveFair scores slightly higher on BARTScore+F, the difference is minimal, at just 0.003 (or 0.35% in percentage terms), indicating that FairExtract achieves near-optimal performance in balancing quality and fairness.

Similarly, among the large language model (LLM)-based methods, FairGPT stands out as the best performer, achieving the highest composite scores across almost all metrics, including SUPERT+F, BLANC+F, SummaQA+F, BARTScore+F, and UniEval+F. This demonstrates that FairGPT effectively balances quality and fairness, setting a new benchmark in fair summarization using LLMs.

To assess the impact of varying the weight on fairness, we explored a composite metric formula: $(1 - \alpha) \times \text{Quality} + \alpha \times F$, where α controls the fairness weight. When $\alpha = 0.5$, fairness and quality are equally weighted, as in the results presented in Table 4. We further experimented with reducing the fairness weight to find the minimum value of α at which FairExtract still outperforms other clustering-based methods.

Table 5 in Appendix A.2 shows the results for $\alpha = 0.16$ (i.e., a 16% fairness incentive). Even with this reduced fairness weight, FairExtract continues to outperform all clustering-based methods across most metrics. Similarly, FairGPT remains the best-performing LLM-based method, maintaining dominance even with the lower fairness incentive.

In summary, our experimental results clearly demonstrate that FairExtract and FairGPT, the two fair summarization models proposed in this

Clustering-based Methods					
Model	SUPERT+F	BLANC+F	SumQA+F	BARTSc+F	UniEval+F
Naive	0.585	0.609	0.468	0.713	0.601
NaiveFair	0.720	0.749	0.606	**0.848**	0.732
TextRank Vanilla	0.585	0.531	0.494	0.703	0.605
TextRank Cluster-A	0.571	0.513	0.467	0.689	0.577
TextRank Cluster-H	0.579	0.521	0.478	0.687	0.588
BERT-EXT Vanilla	0.582	0.590	0.453	0.725	0.578
BERT-EXT Cluster-A	0.616	0.615	0.479	0.737	0.604
BERT-EXT Cluster-H	0.598	0.583	0.457	0.723	0.564
FairExtract (Ours)	**0.724**	**0.758**	**0.607**	0.845	**0.747**
LLM-based Methods					
ChatGPT-EXT	0.737	0.607	0.454	0.817	0.611
FairGPT (Ours)	**0.837**	**0.760**	**0.615**	**0.945**	**0.751**

Table 4: Evaluation results using composite metrics for clustering-based and LLM-based summarization methods with equal weighting of quality and fairness ($\alpha = 0.5$). The best values for each metric are highlighted in bold.

paper, achieve a robust balance between quality and fairness across multiple metrics. FairExtract consistently surpasses other clustering-based models when fairness is weighted equally with quality, while FairGPT sets new benchmarks among LLM-based methods, showing superior performance in both quality and fairness. Even when the fairness incentive is reduced to 16%, FairExtract continues to perform better than most competing models, underscoring the strength of our approach in ensuring diverse representation without compromising summary quality. These findings highlight the importance of incorporating fairness into summarization tasks and demonstrate the effectiveness of our proposed methods in achieving this balance.

7 Conclusion

In this paper, we introduced two novel methods, FairExtract and FairGPT, to address the critical challenge of fairness in multi-document extractive summarization. Both methods were designed to ensure equitable representation of social groups while maintaining competitive summarization quality. Our extensive experiments demonstrated that both FairExtract and FairGPT achieve perfect fairness without significantly compromising on standard quality metrics.

We also introduced new composite metrics (e.g., SUPERT+F, BLANC+F) that combine quality and fairness scores, offering a more nuanced evaluation of the trade-offs between these two dimensions. The results showed that our methods strike a strong balance between quality and fairness, with FairExtract performing exceptionally well in clustering-based approaches and FairGPT setting new benchmarks among LLM-based methods.

These findings highlight the importance and feasibility of integrating fairness into summarization tasks, where diverse representation is crucial. Future work can build on these models by extending them to abstractive summarization, exploring additional fairness constraints, and applying them to larger, more diverse datasets. Our work serves as a significant step toward building fair and inclusive summarization systems for real-world applications.

8 Limitations

While FairExtract and FairGPT show advances in ensuring fairness in multi-document summarization, several limitations remain.

First, our methods focus on extractive summarization, which, while preserving input fidelity, may not capture the semantic richness of abstractive methods (Lebanoff et al., 2019). Extending our approach to abstractive models presents additional challenges, particularly in balancing fairness with coherence and fluency.

Second, the dataset consists of social media content, which may limit generalization to other domains like news or scientific articles. The informal nature of social media language introduces variability that might not translate to more formal text types.

Third, our work focuses on monolingual inputs, specifically in English. Future research could extend these methods to multilingual inputs, where additional factors such as language diversity and cross-lingual transfer (Bagheri Nezhad and Agrawal, 2024; Bagheri Nezhad et al., 2025), would need to be addressed to ensure fairness across languages.

Additionally, while we employ standard quality and fairness metrics, they do not fully capture subjective factors such as readability or user trust. Human evaluation could provide deeper insights into the practical implications of fairness and quality. Also, our evaluation primarily relies on quantitative metrics, we acknowledge that a deeper qualitative error analysis—examining specific examples and error cases—would further illuminate the limitations of fairness-aware summarization, and we consider this an important direction for future investigation.

Finally, the computational complexity of fair clustering and large language models may limit scalability in real-time or resource-constrained environments

9 Acknowledgments

We would like to thank Aravind Inbasekaran for his valuable assistance throughout this project. We also appreciate the constructive feedback provided by the anonymous reviewers. This research has been supported by the National Science Foundation under Grants AF 2311397 and CRII:RI 2246174.

References

Arturs Backurs, Piotr Indyk, Krzysztof Onak, Baruch Schieber, Ali Vakilian, and Tal Wagner. 2019. Scalable fair clustering. In *International Conference on Machine Learning*, pages 405–413. PMLR.

Sina Bagheri Nezhad and Ameeta Agrawal. 2024. What drives performance in multilingual language models? In *Proceedings of the Eleventh Workshop on NLP for Similar Languages, Varieties, and Dialects (VarDial 2024)*, pages 16–27, Mexico City, Mexico. Association for Computational Linguistics.

Sina Bagheri Nezhad, Ameeta Agrawal, and Rhitabrat Pokharel. 2025. Beyond data quantity: Key factors driving performance in multilingual language models. In *Proceedings of the First Workshop on Language Models for Low-Resource Languages*, pages 225–239, Abu Dhabi, United Arab Emirates. Association for Computational Linguistics.

Suman Bera, Deeparnab Chakrabarty, Nicolas Flores, and Maryam Negahbani. 2019. Fair algorithms for clustering. In *Advances in Neural Information Processing Systems*, volume 32. Curran Associates, Inc.

Xingyu Chen, Brandon Fain, Liang Lyu, and Kamesh Munagala. 2019. Proportionally fair clustering. In *Proceedings of the 36th International Conference on Machine Learning*, volume 97 of *Proceedings of Machine Learning Research*, pages 1032–1041. PMLR.

Flavio Chierichetti, Ravi Kumar, Silvio Lattanzi, and Sergei Vassilvitskii. 2017. Fair clustering through fairlets. In *Advances in Neural Information Processing Systems*, volume 30. Curran Associates, Inc.

Abhisek Dash, Anurag Shandilya, Arindam Biswas, Kripabandhu Ghosh, Saptarshi Ghosh, and Abhijnan Chakraborty. 2018. Summarizing user-generated textual content: Motivation and methods for fairness in algorithmic summaries. *Proceedings of the ACM on Human-Computer Interaction*, 3:1 – 28.

Abhisek Dash, Anurag Shandilya, Arindam Biswas, Kripabandhu Ghosh, Saptarshi Ghosh, and Abhijnan Chakraborty. 2019. Summarizing user-generated textual content: Motivation and methods for fairness in algorithmic summaries. *Proceedings of the ACM on Human-Computer Interaction*, 3(CSCW):1–28.

Jacob Devlin, Ming-Wei Chang, Kenton Lee, and Kristina Toutanova. 2019. BERT: Pre-training of deep bidirectional transformers for language understanding. In *Proceedings of the 2019 Conference of the North American Chapter of the Association for Computational Linguistics: Human Language Technologies, Volume 1 (Long and Short Papers)*, pages 4171–4186, Minneapolis, Minnesota. Association for Computational Linguistics.

Seyed Esmaeili, Brian Brubach, Leonidas Tsepenekas, and John Dickerson. 2020. Probabilistic fair clustering. In *Advances in Neural Information Processing Systems*, volume 33, pages 12743–12755. Curran Associates, Inc.

Yang Gao, Wei Zhao, and Steffen Eger. 2020. SUPERT: Towards new frontiers in unsupervised evaluation metrics for multi-document summarization. In *Proceedings of the 58th Annual Meeting of the Association for Computational Linguistics*, pages 1347–1354, Online. Association for Computational Linguistics.

Xudong Han, Timothy Baldwin, and Trevor Cohn. 2023. Fair enough: Standardizing evaluation and model selection for fairness research in NLP. In *Proceedings of the 17th Conference of the European Chapter of the Association for Computational Linguistics*, pages 297–312, Dubrovnik, Croatia. Association for Computational Linguistics.

Daniel Hershcovich, Stella Frank, Heather Lent, Miryam de Lhoneux, Mostafa Abdou, Stephanie Brandl, Emanuele Bugliarello, Laura Cabello Piqueras, Ilias Chalkidis, Ruixiang Cui, Constanza Fierro, Katerina Margatina, Phillip Rust, and Anders Søgaard. 2022. Challenges and strategies in cross-cultural NLP. In *Proceedings of the 60th Annual Meeting of the Association for Computational Linguistics (Volume 1: Long Papers)*, pages 6997–7013, Dublin, Ireland. Association for Computational Linguistics.

Nannan Huang, Lin Tian, Haytham Fayek, and Xiuzhen Zhang. 2023. Examining bias in opinion summarisation through the perspective of opinion diversity. In *Proceedings of the 13th Workshop on Computational Approaches to Subjectivity, Sentiment, & Social Media Analysis*, pages 149–161, Toronto, Canada. Association for Computational Linguistics.

Taehee Jung, Dongyeop Kang, Lucas Mentch, and Eduard Hovy. 2019. Earlier isn't always better: Subaspect analysis on corpus and system biases in summarization. In *Proceedings of the 2019 Conference on Empirical Methods in Natural Language Processing and the 9th International Joint Conference on Natural Language Processing (EMNLP-IJCNLP)*, pages 3324–3335, Hong Kong, China. Association for Computational Linguistics.

Vijay Keswani and L. Elisa Celis. 2021. Dialect diversity in text summarization on twitter. In *Proceedings of the Web Conference 2021*, WWW '21, page 3802–3814, New York, NY, USA. Association for Computing Machinery.

Logan Lebanoff, Kaiqiang Song, Franck Dernoncourt, Doo Soon Kim, Seokhwan Kim, Walter Chang, and Fei Liu. 2019. Scoring sentence singletons and pairs for abstractive summarization. In *Proceedings of the 57th Annual Meeting of the Association for Computational Linguistics*, pages 2175–2189, Florence, Italy. Association for Computational Linguistics.

Peizhao Li, Han Zhao, and Hongfu Liu. 2020. Deep fair clustering for visual learning. In *Proceedings of the IEEE/CVF Conference on Computer Vision and Pattern Recognition (CVPR)*.

Chin-Yew Lin. 2004. ROUGE: A package for automatic evaluation of summaries. In *Text Summarization Branches Out*, pages 74–81, Barcelona, Spain. Association for Computational Linguistics.

Chen Cecilia Liu, Iryna Gurevych, and Anna Korhonen. 2024. Culturally aware and adapted nlp: A taxonomy and a survey of the state of the art. *Preprint*, arXiv:2406.03930.

Evi Micha and Nisarg Shah. 2020. Proportionally Fair Clustering Revisited. In *47th International Colloquium on Automata, Languages, and Programming (ICALP 2020)*, volume 168 of *Leibniz International Proceedings in Informatics (LIPIcs)*, pages 85:1–85:16, Dagstuhl, Germany. Schloss Dagstuhl–Leibniz-Zentrum für Informatik.

Rada Mihalcea and Paul Tarau. 2004. TextRank: Bringing order into text. In *Proceedings of the 2004 Conference on Empirical Methods in Natural Language Processing*, pages 404–411, Barcelona, Spain. Association for Computational Linguistics.

Derek Miller. 2019. Leveraging bert for extractive text summarization on lectures. *arXiv preprint arXiv:1906.04165*.

Olubusayo Olabisi and Ameeta Agrawal. 2024. Understanding position bias effects on fairness in social multi-document summarization. In *Proceedings of the Eleventh Workshop on NLP for Similar Languages, Varieties, and Dialects (VarDial 2024)*, pages 117–129, Mexico City, Mexico. Association for Computational Linguistics.

Olubusayo Olabisi, Aaron Hudson, Antonie Jetter, and Ameeta Agrawal. 2022. Analyzing the dialect diversity in multi-document summaries. In *Proceedings of the 29th International Conference on Computational Linguistics*, pages 6208–6221, Gyeongju, Republic of Korea. International Committee on Computational Linguistics.

Thomas Scialom, Sylvain Lamprier, Benjamin Piwowarski, and Jacopo Staiano. 2019. Answers unite! unsupervised metrics for reinforced summarization models. In *Proceedings of the 2019 Conference on Empirical Methods in Natural Language Processing and the 9th International Joint Conference on Natural Language Processing (EMNLP-IJCNLP)*, pages 3246–3256, Hong Kong, China. Association for Computational Linguistics.

Anurag Shandilya, Kripabandhu Ghosh, and Saptarshi Ghosh. 2018. Fairness of extractive text summarization. In *Companion Proceedings of the The Web Conference 2018*, WWW '18, page 97–98, Republic and Canton of Geneva, CHE. International World Wide Web Conferences Steering Committee.

Yan Tao, Olga Viberg, Ryan S Baker, and René F Kizilcec. 2024. Cultural bias and cultural alignment of large language models. *PNAS Nexus*, 3(9):pgae346.

Oleg Vasilyev, Vedant Dharnidharka, and John Bohannon. 2020. Fill in the BLANC: Human-free quality estimation of document summaries. In *Proceedings of the First Workshop on Evaluation and Comparison of NLP Systems*, pages 11–20, Online. Association for Computational Linguistics.

Weizhe Yuan, Graham Neubig, and Pengfei Liu. 2021. Bartscore: Evaluating generated text as text generation. *Advances in Neural Information Processing Systems*, 34:27263–27277.

Haopeng Zhang, Xiao Liu, and Jiawei Zhang. 2023. Extractive summarization via ChatGPT for faithful summary generation. In *Findings of the Association for Computational Linguistics: EMNLP 2023*, pages 3270–3278, Singapore. Association for Computational Linguistics.

Tianyi Zhang, Varsha Kishore, Felix Wu, Kilian Q Weinberger, and Yoav Artzi. 2019. Bertscore: Evaluating text generation with bert. *arXiv preprint arXiv:1904.09675*.

Ming Zhong, Yang Liu, Da Yin, Yuning Mao, Yizhu Jiao, Pengfei Liu, Chenguang Zhu, Heng Ji, and

Jiawei Han. 2022. Towards a unified multi-dimensional evaluator for text generation. In *Proceedings of the 2022 Conference on Empirical Methods in Natural Language Processing*, pages 2023–2038, Abu Dhabi, United Arab Emirates. Association for Computational Linguistics.

A Appendix / supplemental material

A.1 Fair Extract Formal Algorithmic Processes

In this section, we provide a detailed breakdown of the formal procedures used in our proposed method, `FairExtract`. These algorithm ensure fairness and quality in extractive summarization, addressing the core objectives of balanced representation and high-quality content extraction from diverse groups.

The `FairExtract` algorithm utilizes clustering techniques combined with fairlet decomposition to ensure that summaries reflect an equitable representation of the input groups. This process involves embedding documents using BERT, dividing the dataset into fairlets, and applying k-median clustering to construct a diversity-preserving summary.

The formal descriptions of the algorithm are presented in Algorithm 2.

A.2 Impact of Varying Fairness Weight on Composite Metrics

In this section, we present the results of an experiment where we varied the weight assigned to fairness in the composite metric formula. Specifically, we explored the performance of `FairExtract` and `FairGPT` under different fairness weights to assess their robustness in balancing quality and fairness. Table 5 summarizes the results for the setting where the fairness weight α is reduced to 0.16, representing a 16% incentive toward fairness and an 84% incentive toward quality.

Algorithm 2 FairExtract Algorithm

Input:

- Document set $\mathcal{D}$ of size N
- Groups G_1 and G_2
- Proportions g_1 (for G_1) and g_2 (for G_2) where $\gcd(g_1, g_2) = 1$
- Desired summary length L, where $L \ll N$

Output:

- Diversity-preserving extractive summary $\mathcal{S}$

Step 1: Embedding Documents
Embed each document $d_i \in \mathcal{D}$ into a vector in $\mathbb{R}^{768}$ using BERT.

Step 2: Fairlet Decomposition
Decompose $\mathcal{D}$ into fairlets, each containing g_1 documents from G_1 and g_2 from G_2, minimizing the sum of Euclidean distances.

Step 3: Finding Fairlet Centers
For each fairlet, select the document that minimizes the sum of distances to other documents.

Step 4: k-Median Clustering on Fairlet Centers
Calculate $k = \frac{L}{g_1+g_2}$ and perform k-median clustering on the fairlet centers.

Step 5: Summary Construction
From each cluster, select the fairlet corresponding to the cluster center and add all documents from that fairlet to the final summary $\mathcal{S}$.

Return: The final summary $\mathcal{S}$

Clustering-based Methods					
Model	SUPERT+F	BLANC+F	SumQA+F	BARTSc+F	UniEval+F
Naive	0.485	0.525	0.288	0.699	0.343
NaiveFair	0.530	0.578	0.337	0.744	0.373
TextRank Vanilla	0.488	0.397	0.335	0.687	0.323
TextRank Cluster-A	0.488	0.390	0.313	0.686	0.283
TextRank Cluster-H	0.491	0.394	0.321	0.672	0.285
BERT-EXT Vanilla	0.515	0.529	0.298	**0.756**	0.338
BERT-EXT Cluster-A	**0.539**	0.538	0.309	0.744	0.355
BERT-EXT Cluster-H	0.536	0.511	0.299	0.746	0.315
FairExtract (Ours)	0.537	**0.593**	**0.339**	0.740	**0.396**
LLM-based Methods					
ChatGPT-EXT	**0.764**	0.545	0.288	0.899	0.396
FairGPT (Ours)	0.726	**0.597**	**0.354**	**0.907**	**0.446**

Table 5: Evaluation results using composite metrics for clustering-based and LLM-based summarization methods with reduced fairness weighting ($\alpha = 0.16$). The best values for each metric are highlighted in bold.

INSPAIRED: Cross-cultural Inspiration Detection and Analysis in Real and LLM-generated Social Media Data

Oana Ignat[1*] **Gayathri Ganesh Lakshmy**[2*] **Rada Mihalcea**[3]
[1]Santa Clara University - Santa Clara, USA
[2]Carnegie Mellon University - Pittsburgh, USA
[3]University of Michigan - Ann Arbor, USA
oignat@scu.edu *gganeshl@andrew.cmu.edu* *mihalcea@umich.edu*

Abstract

Inspiration is linked to various positive outcomes, such as increased creativity, productivity, and happiness. Although inspiration has great potential, there has been limited effort toward identifying content that is *inspiring*, as opposed to just engaging or positive. Additionally, most research has concentrated on Western data, with little attention paid to other cultures. This work is the first to study cross-cultural inspiration through machine learning methods. We aim to identify and analyze real and AI-generated cross-cultural inspiring posts. To this end, we compile and make publicly available the INSPAIRED dataset, which consists of 2,000 real inspiring posts, 2,000 real non-inspiring posts, and 2,000 generated inspiring posts evenly distributed across India and the UK. The real posts are sourced from Reddit, while the generated posts are created using the GPT-4 model. Using this dataset, we conduct extensive computational linguistic analyses to (1) compare inspiring content across cultures, (2) compare AI-generated inspiring posts to real inspiring posts, and (3) determine if detection models can accurately distinguish between inspiring content across cultures and data sources.

1 Introduction

Inspiration has been a part of our world for millennia, starting with ancient Greece, where Muses were responsible for delivering divine knowledge by whispering in a poet's ear (Leavitt and Leavitt, 1997), all the way to today's creativity domain, where it is still common for artists and scientists to attribute their best ideas to a higher power, independent of their own control.

According to Thrash and Elliot (2003, 2004), inspiration is a general construct that consists of three core characteristics: *evocation*, *transcendence*, and *approach motivation*. Evocation refers to the process of being triggered by a stimulus, either from within (such as a creative idea that comes from the subconscious) or from outside (such as a person, object, music, or nature). Transcendence allows one to perceive something beyond their usual concerns (Milyavskaya et al., 2012). Finally, an inspired person is motivated to express, transmit, or *act* on their inspiration (Elliot and Thrash, 2002).

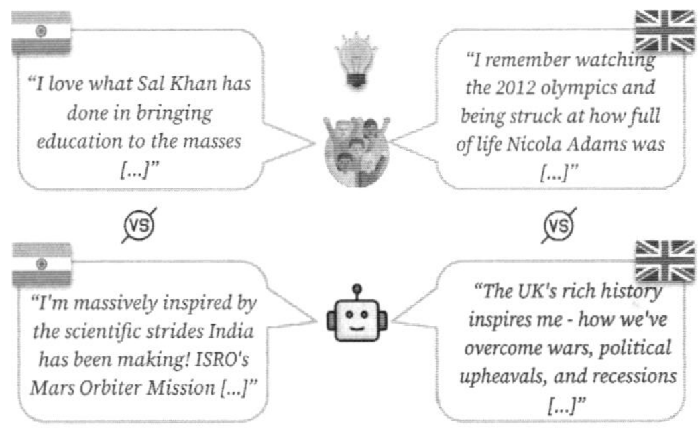

Figure 1: We compare AI-generated and human-written inspiring Reddit content across India and the UK. Although it is challenging for a person to distinguish between them, we find significant linguistic cross-cultural differences between generated and real inspiring posts.

Inspiration is an area of study with promising cross-disciplinary applications in creative fields (e.g., advertisement, storytelling), education, therapy, mentorship, coaching, or social media. For instance, social network recommendation systems can mitigate potential harms by showing more positive and inspiring content to users (Ignat et al., 2021). Access to inspiring content can have a positive impact on people's lives by offering them a fresh perspective and motivating them to take action, particularly during periods of uncertainty and concern (Oleynick et al., 2014). Moreover, inspiration facilitates progress towards goals (Milyavskaya et al., 2012) and increases overall well-being (Thrash et al., 2010).

Despite the compelling motivation, little re-

*Oana Ignat and Gayathri Ganesh Lakshmy contributed equally to the manuscript

Proceedings of the 3rd Workshop on Cross-Cultural Considerations in NLP (C3NLP 2025), pages 35–49
May 4, 2025 ©2025 Association for Computational Linguistics

search has been done on the automatic identification of content that is *inspiring*, as opposed to simply positive (Ignat et al., 2021), and no studies have been conducted on how inspiration varies across different cultures, and whether it can be automatically generated. At the same time, the impressive generative ability of LLMs can create new opportunities for automatically generating inspiring content.

In this work, we aim to address these research gaps by focusing on three main research questions. First, *RQ1: How do inspiring posts compare across cultures?* Second, *RQ2: How do AI-generated inspiring posts compare to real inspiring posts across cultures?* Finally, *RQ3: Can detection models effectively differentiate inspiring posts across diverse cultures and data sources?*

We summarize our contributions as follows. First, we share **a novel dataset comprised of cross-cultural real and generated inspiring and non-inspiring posts**, for a total of 2,000 real inspiring posts, 2,000 non-inspiring posts, and 2,000 LLM-generated posts, balanced across India and the UK. Second, we make use of the dataset to conduct **extensive computational linguistic analyses to compare inspiring content across cultures and data sources**, i.e., India vs. the UK and AI-generated vs. human-written. Finally, **we explore the effectiveness of machine learning models for detecting inspiration** across diverse data sources and cultures.

2 Related Work

Automatic Inspiration Detection. There have been a limited number of research studies conducted on inspiration, with the majority of them being carried out by the psychology and sociology communities. These studies, such as the ones by Thrash and Elliot (2003, 2004) and Elliot and Thrash (2002), have established the fundamental characteristics of inspiration. Additionally, they have developed a scale to measure the frequency with which people experience inspiration in their daily lives. These studies found that individuals who are inspired tend to be more open to new experiences and show greater absorption in their tasks. They are also more intrinsically motivated, have a strong drive to master their work, and are less competitive.

The work most similar to ours is from Ignat et al. (2021), who are the first to study inspiration through machine learning methods. To facilitate research in this domain, they release a weakly labeled dataset consisting of inspiring and non-inspiring posts collected from Reddit and annotate these posts with their effect on the reader and the emotions they transmit. They also provide a RoBERTa (Liu et al., 2019) classifier fine-tuned on human labels to provide a strong baseline for determining whether a post is inspiring. Finally, they perform extensive data analyses to gain insights into which topics inspire readers and how they influence them. Our work builds on Ignat et al. (2021) by extending it to other cultures, India and the UK, and by collecting AI-generated inspiring posts in order to compare them to human-written posts.

Human vs. LLM-generated cross-cultural text. With the rapid development of LLMs, these models demonstrate remarkable proficiency in generating human-like text across multiple languages and styles (Wu et al., 2023; Tang et al., 2023).

In particular, LLMs excel at creative writing, such as story generation (Yuan et al., 2022), advertising slogan creation (Murakami et al., 2023), and news composition (Yanagi et al., 2020). Tools like Yuan et al. (2022) can help users in their creative pursuits. By generating inspiring content, our work provides a more indirect approach, with the same final goal of helping the user express, transmit, and act on their insight.

More similar to our work, LLMs have also started to be applied to motivate people (Cox et al., 2023). For example, Karinshak et al. (2023) used GPT-3 to generate messages to persuade people to receive the Covid-19 vaccine. To the best of our knowledge, we are the first to generate inspiring content using LLMs. Our work is also part of the emerging work on modeling cultural factors in LLMs (Huang and Yang, 2023; Fung et al., 2022; Ramezani and Xu, 2023). Inspiration varies across cultures. Therefore, we test the cultural knowledge of LLMs about inspiration in India and the UK, and compare it to inspiring Reddit posts from users in these countries.

Computational Linguistics for Social Media Analysis. The advent of computational linguistics techniques has enabled researchers to analyze vast amounts of social media data for various purposes, including sentiment analysis, topic modeling, and linguistic variation across cultures (Pennebaker et al., 2007; Pang et al., 2008; Imran et al.,

2020). These works have facilitated the extraction of meaningful insights from diverse linguistic contexts, paving the way for studies on cross-cultural communication in online environments.

Social media is a key source of inspiring content for younger audiences (Raney et al., 2018). Features such as hope and appreciation of beauty and excellence trigger self-transcendent emotions in videos tagged with "inspiration" on YouTube (Dale et al., 2017), as well as in #inspiring and #meaningful Tumblr memes and Facebook posts (Rieger and Klimmt, 2019; Dale et al., 2020). Similarly, we collect Reddit posts from subreddits related to inspiration across UK and Indian cultures and analyze them using computational linguistic tools such as Pennebaker et al. (2007).

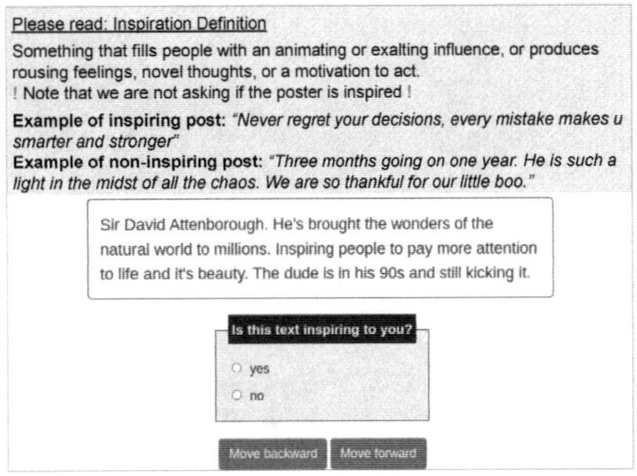

Figure 2: We use the Potato (Pei et al., 2022) annotation platform and provide workers with guidelines to annotate whether a given text is inspiring.

3 The INSPAIRED Dataset

To answer our research questions, we compile a novel dataset, which we refer to as INSPAIRED - AI-generated Inspiring Reddit Content. Our dataset contains inspiring and non-inspiring posts from India and the UK, from two different sources: (1) crawled from Reddit and (2) generated by an LLM.

3.1 Real Inspiring Content

We collect 2,000 weakly labeled inspiring posts and 2,000 weakly labeled non-inspiring posts, balanced across India and the UK. We describe our data collection and annotation process below.

Data Collection. We scrape around 5,300 posts from Reddit, a popular online platform, specifically focusing on culturally inspiring content. Following the data collection process from Ignat et al. (2021), we conduct searches within culture-related or discussion-related flairs of the subreddits using keywords, such as "inspiration" and "motivation", to identify the relevant data in the form of both posts and comments.

More specifically, for Indian data, we primarily target the regions of *Kerala, Karnataka, Maharashtra*, and *Tamil Nadu*. Besides the general "r/india", we also explore subreddits at the *state* level, such as "r/Kerala", "r/Karnataka", "r/Maharashtra", and "r/TamilNadu", which serve as hubs for focused discussions on regional culture, traditions, and social issues. Finally, we also examine subreddits from specific *cities*, including capital cities like *Chennai* and *Bangalore*, to capture more local perspectives and experiences. For the UK data, we follow a similar strategy to collect Reddit posts, targeting both *state* level subreddits, such as "r/UnitedKingdom", as well as *regional* subreddits representing areas and capital cities, such as "r/London".

We group the collected posts into two main categories: inspiring posts from India and inspiring posts from the UK. Initially, we attempted to create a more fine-grained split at the region or city level, but we faced difficulties in finding annotators from those specific regions. However, we encourage future research to explore this direction and investigate how inspiration varies within a country or within a region, along with exploring other demographic information such as language, age, gender, or income.

Data Filtering. The collected posts are further filtered with an inspiration classifier model. We use the XLM-RoBERTa base (Conneau et al., 2019) from `HuggingFace`.[1] The model is a multilingual version of RoBERTa (Liu et al., 2019), and is pre-trained on 2.5TB of filtered CommonCrawl (Wenzek et al., 2020)[2]. We fine-tune the model for five epochs using the dataset described below, with a learning rate of $2e-5$ and a batch size of 8. More implementation details can be found in the Appendix A.1.

For fine-tuning, we use the data from Ignat et al. (2021). The data contains around 12,000 annotated "general", i.e., no target culture, balanced Reddit inspiring and non-inspiring posts. More details about the fine-tuning data can be found in Ignat et al. (2021). Next, we evaluate the quality of the

[1] `https://huggingface.co/FacebookAI/xlm-roberta-base`

[2] We choose a multilingual model, as the Indian data contains code-mix data.

	# NON-INSPIRING ✗		# INSPIRING	
	Annotated	Weakly-Labeled	Annotated	Weakly-Labeled
	100	900	100	900
	100	900	100	900

Table 1: Final number of inspiring ( ) and non-inspiring (✗) posts across India and the UK.

fine-tuned model predictions by annotating a subset of the posts and comparing them with the model predictions.

Data Annotation. The posts are annotated by crowd-sourced workers from India and the UK. For each country, we select a sample of 200/ 1,000 posts equally sampled from inspiring and non-inspiring predicted posts, to be labeled by three annotators from that country.

We use Potato (Pei et al., 2022) to create the user interface and store the data. Following the guidelines from Ignat et al. (2021), the user interface contains a definition of inspiration and examples of inspiring and non-inspiring posts, as seen in Figure 2. To find and hire UK annotators, we connect Potato to Prolific.[3] We select annotators who have the following qualifications: an approval rate >98%, living in the UK, and a right to vote (as a proxy for age). The annotators independently label 200 posts each, categorizing the posts based on their subjective judgment of whether they found the content inspiring or not. We conduct a similar annotation process with three reliable Indian annotators to label the data from India. To ensure consistency amongst the annotators, they are provided with the same interface as used for the UK annotators and shown in Figure 2.

Finally, we compute the agreement score between the annotators using the Fleiss Kappa measure (Fleiss and Cohen, 1973). We obtain a score of 0.24 for UK data and 0.29 for Indian data, indicating a fair agreement, expected for a subjective task as inspiration detection.

Given that each post is annotated by three annotators, following Ignat et al. (2021), we mark a post as inspiring if at least one annotator labeled it as inspiring.

We find that the predictions made by the fine-tuned model are quite similar to human annotations. For Indian data, the accuracy rate is 72.9%, and the F1 score is 75.5%. Similarly, for UK data, the accuracy rate is 73.5%, and the F1 score is 80.1%. Therefore, we decide to not annotate more data and instead use the model predictions. Additionally, we further fine-tune the model on the annotated data and use it to collect more weakly labeled data. This approach aims to leverage the insights gained from the initial fine-tuning process and apply them to the user-annotated subset, thereby refining the model to better capture the nuances present in this specific dataset. We use the fine-tuned model predictions and the annotated subset as our final labeled data.

Quality Assurance. We remove posts that are classified as toxic or hate speech using two fine-tuned XLM-RoBERTa classifiers from `HuggingFace`.[4,5] We also remove profanity from posts using a profanity classifier.[6] We acknowledge that automatic detection of profanity, toxicity, and hate speech are active research areas that have yet to be solved (Dale et al., 2021; Vidgen et al., 2021). Finally, for each country, we manually inspect 100 random posts to ensure syntactic and semantic correctness and find the remaining toxic or hate speech posts. We find that around 99% of the posts are of good quality.

Data Statistics. The final data statistics are shown in Table 1.

3.2 LLM-Generated Inspiring Content

We generate 2,000 inspiring posts with GPT-4,[7] balanced across India and the UK. Our study can be conducted with any LLM. However, we chose GPT-4 because it is one of the largest LLMs available and has been shown to effectively emulate human texts. (Achiam et al., 2023)

3.2.1 Prompt Design and Robustness

GPT-4 takes as input a list of *message* objects, and returns an inspiring Reddit post. We use *messages*, which are more interactive and dynamic compared to the classical prompt style. Specifically, we use messages with three different roles: *system*, *user* or *assistant*.[8]

[3] www.prolific.com

[4] https://huggingface.co/textdetox/xlmr-large-toxicity-classifier

[5] https://huggingface.co/facebook/roberta-hate-speech-dynabench-r4-target

[6] https://github.com/snguyenthanh/better_profanity

[7] https://platform.openai.com/docs/guides/text-generation/chat-completions-api

[8] https://help.openai.com/en/articles/7042661-chatgpt-api-transition-guide

The prompt is first formatted with a *system* role, which sets the behavior of the model. This is followed by a conversation between the *user* and *assistant*, in a **few-shot prompting** fashion. Prior work found that LLMs function better with few-shot prompts (i.e., instructions alongside example output) rather than using zero-shot prompts (with no examples). (Brown et al., 2020)

System Prompt. We find that we can obtain high-quality responses with additional context in our prompts. Therefore, we instruct the model to be a Reddit user from either the UK or India. To ensure that the generated data is diverse and reliable, we collect five versions of *system* prompts with different phrasing, with one example shown below.

> *Imagine you're a person from {location} and use Reddit regularly.*

User-Assistant Prompts. We design two rounds of conversations between a *user* and an *assistant*, where the *user* asks for a Reddit post or comment, and the *assistant* responds to the request. We use **few-shot prompting** by providing the *assistant* in the first round of conversation with an inspiring post, which is randomly extracted from the real posts annotated as inspiring by the majority of annotators. Finally, the answer to the second *user* is automatically generated by the *assistant* and used to collect the GPT-4 generated inspiring post. A *user* message is shown below.

> *Write a Reddit post or comment of maximum 100 tokens about what inspires you.*

Quality Assurance. To ensure the quality of our generated data, we conduct sanity checks to review approximately 200 inspiring posts balanced across the UK and India. The posts are checked for cultural knowledge, factuality, semantic and syntax errors, and style. Based on the feedback, we find that the posts are semantically and syntactically accurate, possess cultural knowledge, and are often more complex than real posts.

4 Cross-Cultural Inspiration Analysis across Real and LLM-generated posts

In line with previous work (Jakesch et al., 2023), we also find during manual inspection that it is challenging to differentiate between LLM-generated texts and those written by humans (see Table 2). Therefore, we perform computational linguistic analyses to compare real and LLM-generated text across cultures. This section addresses our first two research questions: *RQ1: How do inspiring posts compare across cultures?* and *RQ2: How do AI-generated inspiring posts compare to real inspiring posts across cultures?*

4.1 Stylistic and Structural Features

We assess the linguistic style and structure of real and LLM-generated inspiring posts across India and the UK in terms of (1) analytic writing, (2) descriptiveness, and (3) readability.

Analytic Writing index measures the complexity and sophistication of the writing, which can be an indicator of advanced thinking. The formula for analytic writing is $[articles + prepositions - pronouns - auxiliaryverbs - adverb - conjunctions - negations]$ from LIWC scores (Jordan et al., 2019; Pennebaker et al., 2014) More information about LIWC can be found in Section 4.2. We display the scores in Table 3. The low complexity scores of Reddit posts are primarily negative due to their high usage of pronouns and lack of articles. We find that *LLM-generated inspiring posts from the UK and India are more complex than real posts*, which aligns with our initial observations from data quality checks. At the same time, there is *no significant difference in text complexity between real inspiring posts from India and those from the UK.*

Descriptiveness can be measured by the frequency of adjectives used in language patterns. Texts with high rates of adjectives tend to be more elaborate and narrative-like compared to texts with low rates of adjectives. (Chung and Pennebaker, 2008) In Table 3, we find that *LLM-generated inspiring posts from the UK and India are more descriptive than real posts.* Additionally, *real inspiring posts from India are more descriptive than those from the UK.*

Readability considers not only word count, but also word complexity. For instance, longer words are more complex than shorter ones. We use the Flesch Reading Ease metric (Flesch, 1948), which counts the number of words per sentence and syllables per word. In Table 3, we find that *LLM-generated inspiring posts from the UK and India are less readable than real posts.* Additionally, *real inspiring posts from India are less readable than those from the UK.* Furthermore, when measuring post length, *LLM-generated UK posts are*

	Real Post 👥	GPT4-generated Post 💻
🇮🇳	💡 *The youngest freedom fighter martyr of the country, the brave boy who refused to take the British cops across the river and was shot to death. His name was Baji Rout and he was 12 at the time of his death.* ✗ *What is a common meal there? I've always thought Indian palates to be quite spicy and rich.*	💡 *Dr. APJ Abdul Kalam - His humble beginnings, insatiable thirst for knowledge, and absolute dedication to his country have been my greatest inspiration. It pushed me to work harder, dream big, and contribute to society.* ✗ N/A
🇬🇧	💡 *Dr. Helen Sharman. I'm very pleased to come from a country whose first astronaut isn't a man by default. Equality shouldn't be about women catching up, it should be about women being first 50% of the time.* ✗ *Mate all he does is play football and misses pens. Not that special*	💡 *Absolutely love Sir David Attenborough's documentaries. His passion and commitment to preserving the environment is truly inspiring in these challenging times.* ✗ N/A

Table 2: Random samples of inspiring (💡) and non-inspiring (✗) posts from India and UK.

	🇮🇳		🇬🇧	
	💡👥	💡💻	💡👥	💡💻
Analytic	-16.7 $\pm$ 18.0	-6.9 $\pm$ 10.0	-17.1 $\pm$ 19.9	-7.0 $\pm$ 11.4
Descriptive	8.2 $\pm$ 7.8	8.9 $\pm$ 3.6	6.6 $\pm$ 5.9	9.1 $\pm$ 3.9
Readable	36.3 $\pm$ 63.1	12.1 $\pm$ 20.6	53.2 $\pm$ 52.2	29.6 $\pm$ 18.0
Word Count	61.1 $\pm$ 59.8	66.9 $\pm$ 20.3	43.9 $\pm$ 49.3	49.9 $\pm$ 16.8

Table 3: To what degree is the LLM-generated text (💻) stylistically and structurally different from the real text (👥)? We compute the mean and standard deviation for the inspiring posts, across cultures. The differences are statistically significant, based on the Student t-test (Student, 1908), p-value < 0.05.

longer than real posts and *UK posts are shorter than Indian posts.*

4.2 Semantic and Psycholinguistic Features

We assess the semantic and psycholinguistic differences between LLM-generated and real inspiring posts across India and the UK, using topic modeling and LIWC psycholinguistic markers.

Data Pre-processing. We use `spaCy` library[9] to pre-process the data: tokenize each post, lowercase tokens, remove stop words, remove numbers, symbols, emojis, links, and lemmatize tokens.

Topic Modeling. We use Scattertext (Kessler, 2017), a tool used to create interactive visualizations of linguistic patterns. After initial pre-processing, we structure the text data for a better representation of information. Next, we use the n-gram representation of the text data to conduct topic extraction through sentence-level clustering. We utilize methods like Non-negative Matrix Factorization (NMF) to decompose the TF-IDF matrix to identify the latent thematic structures within the corpus (Ramos et al., 2003).

Results. We analyze the n-gram and topic distributions by various dimensions: inspiring vs. non-inspiring, Indian vs. UK, and real vs. generated. We display the topic distribution across real and generated UK inspiring posts in Figure 3. Further topic and n-gram distributions are displayed in Appendix A.2.

💡 vs. ✗: Comparing inspiring to non-inspiring real posts, we find that, in the Indian data (Fig. 5, 7), the topic of *people* is frequently discussed in an inspiring context. Moreover, the most commonly occurring theme in non-inspiring posts is *bot*, encompassing textual content regarding Reddit rules and moderators.

In the UK data (Fig. 6, 8), the topic of *life* is amongst the most commonly occurring themes in inspiring posts, with discussions surrounding *career*, *luck*, and *pension*. On the other hand, the non-inspiring posts contain themes like *dark*, including conversations about *rain* and *winter*.

👥 vs. 💻: The LLM-generated Indian data (Fig. 10, 11) often places a significant emphasis on the topic of *inspiring*, within which common words include *dedication* and *motivational*. There is also a significant number of posts surrounding *isro (Indian Space Research Organisation)*, featuring terms such as *space*, *mars*, and *mission*. In contrast, the real data from India contains mentions of *housing*, *summer*, and *living*, grouped under the category *live*. The topic of *movie* is also popular, containing words such as *hype*, *stardom*, and *socialize*, hinting at the culture surrounding the film industry.

In the LLM-generated UK data (Fig. 3, top left), the topic *nhs* is emphasized, where common words include *pandemic*, *heroes*, and *staff*. Additionally,

[9]`https://spacy.io/models`

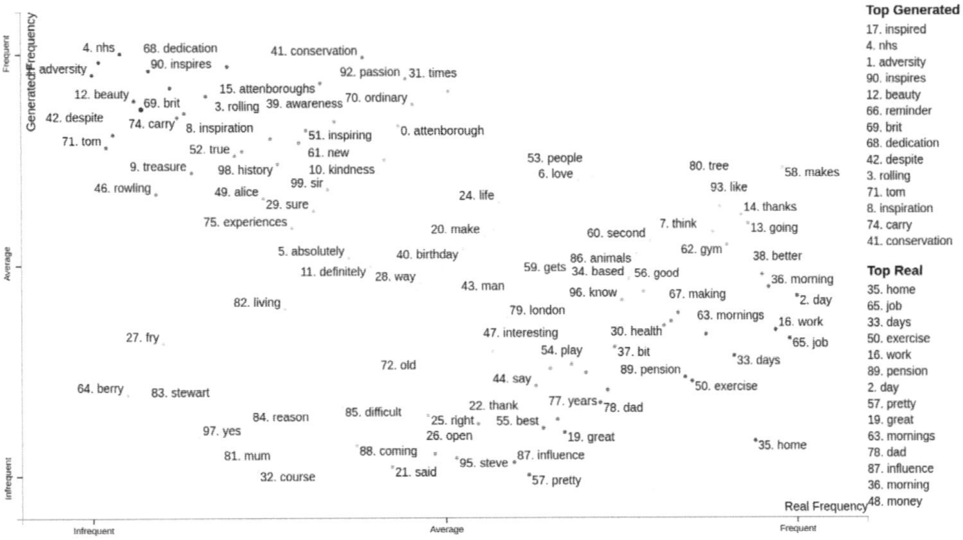

Figure 3: Visualization of **topics** used in the real and generated (👥 vs. 💻) inspiring posts from the **UK**. Points are colored red or blue based on the association of their corresponding terms with UK Real inspiring posts or UK LLM-Generated inspiring posts. The most associated topics are listed under **Top Generated** and **Top Real** headings. Interactive version: `https://github.com/MichiganNLP/cross_inspiration`.

discussions often revolve around *adversity*, with mentions of *resilience*, *determination*, and *spirit*. In contrast, in the real data from the UK (Fig. 3, bottom right), discussions related to *job* dominate, with mentions of *salary*, *savings*, and *time*. Moreover, there is also a significant focus on *exercise*, featuring words like *discipline*, and *motivate*.

LIWC Psycholinguistic Markers. We use Linguistic Inquiry and Word Count (LIWC), a gold-standard text analysis tool (Pennebaker et al., 2007, 2015), to obtain the words related to human cognitive processes from each post. Specifically, we use the LIWC2015 dictionary, which contains 6,400 words and word stems, each related to a cognitive category. As an example, the word "mother" is assigned the following cognitive categories: *female, family, social*.

Results. We display the top 24 categories and their LIWC scores, with the most significant differences across dimensions in Table 4. Across all data, we find that *male* words are more frequent than *female*, the most common pronoun is *I*, the most frequent tense is *present*, and the most common emotion is *positive*.

💡 vs. ✗: Comparing inspiring to non-inspiring real posts, we find that, in the Indian data, inspiring posts are more likely to be related to *socializing, insight, feelings, perception, affection*, and contain *more positive emotions*. Additionally, Indian inspiring posts tend to have *more comparisons* and use more words related to *achievement, health, reward*, and *work*.

UK real inspiring posts contain more words related to *affection, comparisons, feelings, achievement, health, home, leisure, money, reward*, and *work* than non-inspiring posts. Furthermore, compared to Indian inspiring posts, UK inspiring posts have fewer words related to *family, socializing, affection, perception, religion, less positive emotions* and more words related to *achievement, health, home, leisure, money, rewards*, and *work*.

👥 vs. 💻: Comparing real to LLM-generated inspiring posts, we find that real Indian posts tend to include more words related to *family, social interactions, comparisons, feelings, perceptions* as well as *home, leisure* and *rewards*. Conversely, real Indian posts contain fewer words related to *affection, insight, achievement, health*, and *religion*.

UK real inspiring posts contain more words related to *comparisons, feelings, health, home, leisure, money, rewards* and *work* than LLM-generated UK posts. Conversely, real UK posts contain fewer words related to *socializing, affection, insight, perception, achievement* and *religion* than LLM-generated UK posts. Furthermore, compared to LLM-generated Indian posts, LLM-generated UK posts have fewer words related to *socializing, achievement, leisure, money, religion, work* and more words related to *affection, perception* and *more positive emotions*.

LIWC	India 👥	India ✗👥	India 💻	UK 👥	UK ✗👥	UK 💻
			Social Processes			
FAMILY	0.4	0.4	0.2	0.2	0.1	0.2
FRIEND	0.3	0.4	0.2	0.2	0.4	0.2
FEMALE	0.4	0.3	0.2	0.4	0.4	0.2
MALE	1.1	1.0	0.9	0.9	1.3	1.7
SOCIAL	9.3	7.7	8.6	7.4	8.1	8.1
			Affective Processes			
AFFECT	6.1	4.3	8.4	5.4	4.8	9.4
NEGEMO	1.4	1.3	1.0	1.3	1.6	0.9
POSEMO	4.5	3.0	7.3	4.1	3.1	8.3
			Cognitive Processes			
COMPARE	3.0	2.4	1.8	3.0	2.7	1.8
INSIGHT	2.3	2.0	4.8	2.2	2.1	4.9
			Perceptual Processes			
FEEL	0.6	0.4	0.4	0.7	0.3	0.4
PERCEPT	2.4	2.0	2.1	2.1	2.1	2.4
			Personal Concerns			
ACHIEV	1.9	1.0	3.5	2.4	1.6	2.6
HEALTH	0.7	0.4	0.9	1.0	0.8	0.8
HOME	0.3	0.2	0.1	0.7	0.4	0.2
LEISURE	1.5	1.4	1.2	1.7	1.4	0.9
MONEY	0.7	0.8	0.6	1.2	0.8	0.4
RELIG	0.4	0.5	1.1	0.1	0.1	0.6
REWARD	2.0	1.1	1.0	2.2	1.6	1.1
WORK	3.0	1.9	3.0	3.9	2.7	1.9

Table 4: Comparing LIWC scores across cultures (India and the UK) in inspiring vs. non-inspiring (💡 vs. ✗) and real vs. LLM-generated posts (👥 vs. 💻). We present the top 24 categories with the most significant differences across these dimensions.

5 Cross-Cultural Inspiration Detection across Real and LLM-generated Posts

To answer our last research question – *RQ3: Can detection models effectively differentiate inspiring posts across diverse cultures and data sources?* – we fine-tune a multi-label classification model to identify if a post is inspiring, represents India or the UK, and whether it is real or LLM-generated.

Implementation Details. We use the XLM-RoBERTa base model (Conneau et al., 2019), pre-trained on 2.5TB of filtered CommonCrawl (Wenzek et al., 2020). We fine-tune the model on our dataset for five epochs with a learning rate of $2e-5$ and a batch size of 8, while monitoring the validation performance and selecting the best model checkpoint based on the F1 metric.

Model Training Setup. We experiment with two setups to split the data into training, validation, and test sets: a *default* train-val-test split of 64-16-20% and a *few-shot* split of 8-2-90%.

Results. Since the dataset is evenly distributed across classes, a random baseline results in a 50% accuracy score.

The XLM-RoBERTa model with *few-shot* setup achieves an accuracy of 75.0% and F1 score of

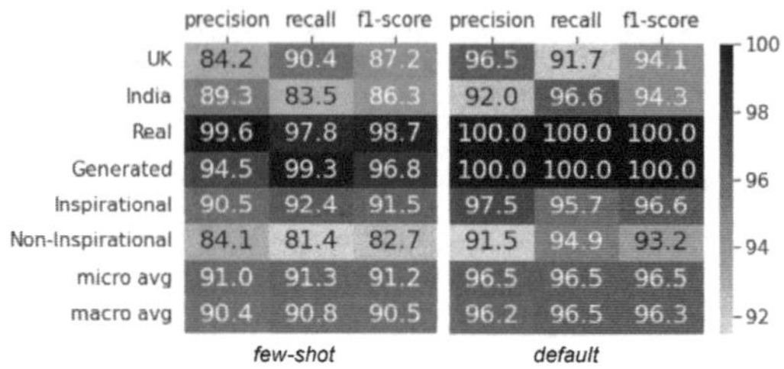

Figure 4: Multi-label classification test results with the *few-shot* and *default* setups with the XLM-RoBERTa base (Conneau et al., 2019) model.

91.1% across all labels, while the *default* setup achieves an accuracy of 89.1% and F1 score of 96.3%. Figure 4 displays the disaggregated results for each label. We find that even with very few training data (600 posts), in the *few-shot* setup, the XLM-RoBERTa model learns to accurately distinguish inspiring content across cultures (India, UK) and data sources (real and generated). Furthermore, we do not find significant differences in performance across cultures and data sources. Finally, the model can accurately distinguish between real and generated inspiring posts in both *few-shot* and *default* training setups.

6 Conclusion

In this paper, we introduced the task of cross-cultural inspiration detection and generation in social media data. To facilitate research in this domain, we released INSPAIRED, a dataset of 2,000 real inspiring posts, 2,000 real non-inspiring posts, and 2,000 LLM-generated inspiring posts, evenly distributed across India and the UK. We performed extensive linguistic data analyses to gain insight into what topics inspire each culture and compare AI-generated inspiring posts to real inspiring posts across various linguistic dimensions. Despite the difficulty humans have in distinguishing between real posts and those generated by LLMs, we found that these posts have noticeable differences in style, structure, and semantics and that, even with little data, fine-tuned models accurately distinguish inspiring content across cultures and data sources.

We hope our work will enable the exploration of various applications to improve creativity and motivation, including storytelling, advertising, and social media, as well as therapy and coaching. Our dataset can be used to test, fine-tune, and analyze other models, and it is publicly available at `https://github.com/MichiganNLP/cross_inspiration`.

Limitations

1. A more fine-grained data split

Our posts are divided into two main categories - inspiring posts from India and inspiring posts from the UK. Initially, we tried to create a more detailed classification at the region or city level, but we faced difficulties in finding annotators from those specific regions. However, we encourage future research to explore this direction and investigate how inspiration varies within a country or region, as well as explore other demographic information, such as language, age, gender, or income.

Study case for India. The extensive discussions on Indian subreddits, like r/AskIndia and r/India, offer straightforward access to text-based motivational narratives. Additionally, region-based subReddits, like r/Chennai and r/Mumbai, provide diverse insights into localized experiences and discussions. The nature of posts on this topic is mostly anecdotal. Reddit users contribute by sharing personal experiences that have inspired them.

2. Limited number of cross-cultural inspiring posts

It is crucial to recognize that inspiration is not always explicitly articulated through words like "inspiring" or "motivation", especially within cultures that aren't as open about talking about such topics. In many instances, it manifests more subtly, embedded within narratives, imagery, or cultural expressions. This implicit nature of inspiration adds another layer of complexity to the data collection process.

The language barrier also introduces an additional barrier, as it requires linguistic fluency and cultural understanding to interpret and analyze inspiring content effectively. Posts in languages other than English may contain nuances and cultural references that are not easily translatable. Moreover, it becomes more challenging to collect inspiring content when data collection is restricted to certain countries. That is why we collected fewer posts compared to Ignat et al.'s "general" inspiring posts.

3. Relevance of LLM-based data to current times

In our reliance on LLM-based data, it's imperative to recognize the temporal limitations inherent in its training corpus. While these models offer remarkable capabilities in understanding and generating text, they might not fully capture the current cultural and societal context in their outputs. This limitation can be primarily attributed to the fact that these models are trained on data only up to a specific cutoff date, i.e., GPT-4 only learned from data dated up to September 2021.

References

Josh Achiam, Steven Adler, Sandhini Agarwal, Lama Ahmad, Ilge Akkaya, Florencia Leoni Aleman, Diogo Almeida, Janko Altenschmidt, Sam Altman, Shyamal Anadkat, et al. 2023. Gpt-4 technical report. *arXiv preprint arXiv:2303.08774*.

Tom Brown, Benjamin Mann, Nick Ryder, Melanie Subbiah, Jared D Kaplan, Prafulla Dhariwal, Arvind Neelakantan, Pranav Shyam, Girish Sastry, Amanda Askell, et al. 2020. Language models are few-shot learners. *Advances in neural information processing systems*, 33:1877–1901.

Cindy K Chung and James W Pennebaker. 2008. Revealing dimensions of thinking in open-ended self-descriptions: An automated meaning extraction method for natural language. *Journal of research in personality*, 42(1):96–132.

Alexis Conneau, Kartikay Khandelwal, Naman Goyal, Vishrav Chaudhary, Guillaume Wenzek, Francisco Guzmán, Edouard Grave, Myle Ott, Luke Zettlemoyer, and Veselin Stoyanov. 2019. Unsupervised cross-lingual representation learning at scale. *CoRR*, abs/1911.02116.

Samuel Rhys Cox, Ashraf Abdul, and Wei Tsang Ooi. 2023. Prompting a large language model to generate diverse motivational messages: A comparison with human-written messages. In *Proceedings of the 11th International Conference on Human-Agent Interaction*, pages 378–380.

David Dale, Anton Voronov, Daryna Dementieva, Varvara Logacheva, Olga Kozlova, Nikita Semenov, and Alexander Panchenko. 2021. Text detoxification using large pre-trained neural models. In *Proceedings of the 2021 Conference on Empirical Methods in Natural Language Processing*, pages 7979–7996, Online and Punta Cana, Dominican Republic. Association for Computational Linguistics.

Katherine R Dale, Arthur A Raney, Sophie H Janicke, Meghan S Sanders, and Mary Beth Oliver. 2017. Youtube for good: A content analysis and examination of elicitors of self-transcendent media. *Journal of Communication*, 67(6):897–919.

Katherine R Dale, Arthur A Raney, Qihao Ji, Sophie H Janicke-Bowles, Joshua Baldwin, Jerrica T Rowlett, Cen Wang, and Mary Beth Oliver. 2020. Self-transcendent emotions and social media: Exploring the content and consumers of inspirational facebook posts. *New Media & Society*, 22(3):507–527.

Andrew J Elliot and Todd M Thrash. 2002. Approach-avoidance motivation in personality: approach and avoidance temperaments and goals. *Journal of personality and social psychology*, 82(5):804.

Joseph L Fleiss and Jacob Cohen. 1973. The equivalence of weighted kappa and the intraclass correlation coefficient as measures of reliability. *Educational and psychological measurement*, 33(3):613–619.

Rudolph Flesch. 1948. A new readability yardstick. *Journal of applied psychology*, 32(3):221.

Yi R Fung, Tuhin Chakraborty, Hao Guo, Owen Rambow, Smaranda Muresan, and Heng Ji. 2022. Normsage: Multi-lingual multi-cultural norm discovery from conversations on-the-fly. *arXiv preprint arXiv:2210.08604*.

Jing Huang and Diyi Yang. 2023. Culturally aware natural language inference. In *Findings of the Association for Computational Linguistics: EMNLP 2023*, pages 7591–7609.

Oana Ignat, Y-Lan Boureau, Jane A. Yu, and Alon Y. Halevy. 2021. Detecting inspiring content on social media. *2021 9th International Conference on Affective Computing and Intelligent Interaction (ACII)*, pages 1–8.

Ali Shariq Imran, Sher Muhammad Daudpota, Zenun Kastrati, and Rakhi Batra. 2020. Cross-cultural polarity and emotion detection using sentiment analysis and deep learning on covid-19 related tweets. *Ieee Access*, 8:181074–181090.

Maurice Jakesch, Jeffrey T Hancock, and Mor Naaman. 2023. Human heuristics for ai-generated language are flawed. *Proceedings of the National Academy of Sciences*, 120(11):e2208839120.

Kayla N Jordan, Joanna Sterling, James W Pennebaker, and Ryan L Boyd. 2019. Examining long-term trends in politics and culture through language of political leaders and cultural institutions. *Proceedings of the National Academy of Sciences*, 116(9):3476–3481.

Elise Karinshak, Sunny Xun Liu, Joon Sung Park, and Jeffrey T Hancock. 2023. Working with ai to persuade: Examining a large language model's ability to generate pro-vaccination messages. *Proceedings of the ACM on Human-Computer Interaction*, 7(CSCW1):1–29.

Jason Kessler. 2017. Scattertext: a browser-based tool for visualizing how corpora differ. In *Proceedings of ACL 2017, System Demonstrations*, pages 85–90, Vancouver, Canada. Association for Computational Linguistics.

J.H. Leavitt and P.J. Leavitt. 1997. *Poetry and Prophecy: The Anthropology of Inspiration*. Studies in Literature and Science. University of Michigan Press.

Yinhan Liu, Myle Ott, Naman Goyal, Jingfei Du, Mandar Joshi, Danqi Chen, Omer Levy, Mike Lewis, Luke Zettlemoyer, and Veselin Stoyanov. 2019. Roberta: A robustly optimized bert pretraining approach. *ArXiv*, abs/1907.11692.

Marina Milyavskaya, Iana Ianakieva, Emily Foxen-Craft, Agnes Colantuoni, and Richard Koestner. 2012. Inspired to get there: The effects of trait and goal inspiration on goal progress.

Soichiro Murakami, Sho Hoshino, and Peinan Zhang. 2023. Natural language generation for advertising: A survey. *Preprint*, arXiv:2306.12719.

Victoria C. Oleynick, Todd M. Thrash, Michael C. LeFew, Emil G. Moldovan, and Paul D. Kieffaber. 2014. The scientific study of inspiration in the creative process: challenges and opportunities. *Frontiers in Human Neuroscience*, 8.

Bo Pang, Lillian Lee, et al. 2008. Opinion mining and sentiment analysis. *Foundations and Trends® in information retrieval*, 2(1–2):1–135.

Jiaxin Pei, Aparna Ananthasubramaniam, Xingyao Wang, Naitian Zhou, Apostolos Dedeloudis, Jackson Sargent, and David Jurgens. 2022. Potato: The portable text annotation tool. In *Proceedings of the 2022 Conference on Empirical Methods in Natural Language Processing: System Demonstrations*.

James W. Pennebaker, Roger John Booth, and Martha E. Francis. 2007. Linguistic inquiry and word count (LIWC2007).

James W. Pennebaker, Ryan L. Boyd, Kayla Jordan, and Kate G. Blackburn. 2015. The development and psychometric properties of LIWC2015.

James W Pennebaker, Cindy K Chung, Joey Frazee, Gary M Lavergne, and David I Beaver. 2014. When small words foretell academic success: The case of college admissions essays. *PloS one*, 9(12):e115844.

Aida Ramezani and Yang Xu. 2023. Knowledge of cultural moral norms in large language models. *arXiv preprint arXiv:2306.01857*.

Juan Ramos et al. 2003. Using tf-idf to determine word relevance in document queries. In *Proceedings of the first instructional conference on machine learning*, volume 242, pages 29–48. Citeseer.

Arthur A Raney, Sophie H Janicke, Mary Beth Oliver, Katherine R Dale, Robert P Jones, and Daniel Cox. 2018. Profiling the audience for self-transcendent media: A national survey. *Mass Communication and Society*, 21(3):296–319.

Diana Rieger and Christoph Klimmt. 2019. The daily dose of digital inspiration: A multi-method exploration of meaningful communication in social media. *New Media & Society*, 21(1):97–118.

Student. 1908. The probable error of a mean. *Biometrika*, pages 1–25.

Ruixiang Tang, Yu-Neng Chuang, and Xia Hu. 2023. The science of detecting llm-generated texts. *arXiv preprint arXiv:2303.07205*.

Todd M. Thrash and Andrew J Elliot. 2003. Inspiration as a psychological construct. *Journal of personality and social psychology*, 84 4:871–89.

Todd M. Thrash and Andrew J Elliot. 2004. Inspiration: core characteristics, component processes, antecedents, and function. *Journal of personality and social psychology*, 87 6:957–73.

Todd M. Thrash, Laura A. Maruskin, Scott E. Cassidy, James W. Fryer, and Richard M. Ryan. 2010. Mediating between the muse and the masses: inspiration and the actualization of creative ideas. *Journal of personality and social psychology*, 98 3:469–87.

Bertie Vidgen, Tristan Thrush, Zeerak Waseem, and Douwe Kiela. 2021. Learning from the worst: Dynamically generated datasets to improve online hate detection. In *ACL*.

Guillaume Wenzek, Marie-Anne Lachaux, Alexis Conneau, Vishrav Chaudhary, Francisco Guzmán, Armand Joulin, and Edouard Grave. 2020. CCNet: Extracting high quality monolingual datasets from web crawl data. In *Proceedings of the Twelfth Language Resources and Evaluation Conference*, pages 4003–4012, Marseille, France. European Language Resources Association.

Junchao Wu, Shu Yang, Runzhe Zhan, Yulin Yuan, Derek F. Wong, and Lidia S. Chao. 2023. A survey on llm-generated text detection: Necessity, methods, and future directions. *ArXiv*, abs/2310.14724.

Yuta Yanagi, Ryohei Orihara, Yuichi Sei, Yasuyuki Tahara, and Akihiko Ohsuga. 2020. Fake news detection with generated comments for news articles. In *2020 IEEE 24th International Conference on Intelligent Engineering Systems (INES)*, pages 85–90. IEEE.

Ann Yuan, Andy Coenen, Emily Reif, and Daphne Ippolito. 2022. Wordcraft: story writing with large language models. In *27th International Conference on Intelligent User Interfaces*, pages 841–852.

A Appendix

A.1 Fine-tuning Process

XLM-RoBERTa Model. Implementation Details. We experiment with three different fine-tuned classification models for the purpose of weakly labeling the presence of inspiration in the dataset. The first attempt involved fine-tuning the model on the general inspiration dataset introduced in (Ignat et al., 2021). In each of the experiments, the data is split into three subsets: training, validation, and test sets, using an 80:10:10 ratio. The fine-tuning process involved training the model for 5 epochs with a learning rate of $2e - 5$ and a batch size of 8. We monitored the model performance on a separate validation set and selected the best model checkpoint based on accuracy metric.

In the second experiment, we focused on a subset of the dataset used in annotation, consisting of 200 posts. These posts were labeled as inspiring if at least one user considered them to be so. We fine-tuned the base XLM-RoBERTa model using this subset, maintaining the same training configurations as in the initial experiment. In the last experiment, we leveraged the user-annotated posts to further refine the model trained on the general inspiration dataset from the first experiment. This approach aimed to leverage the insights gained from the initial fine-tuning process and apply them to the user-annotated subset, thereby refining the model to better capture the nuances present in this specific dataset.

A.2 Topic Analysis

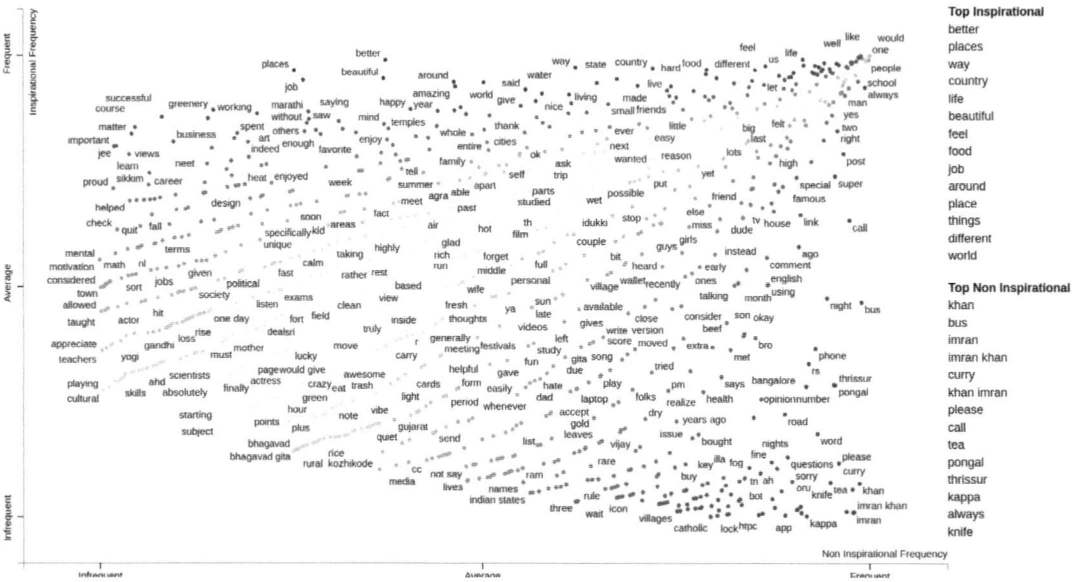

Figure 5: Scattertext visualization of **unigrams** used in the real inspiring and non-inspiring (vs. ✗) Reddit posts from **India**. Points are colored in red or blue based on the association of their corresponding terms with Indian Non-inspiring posts or Indian inspiring posts. The most associated terms are listed under "Top inspiring" and "Top Non-inspiring" headings.

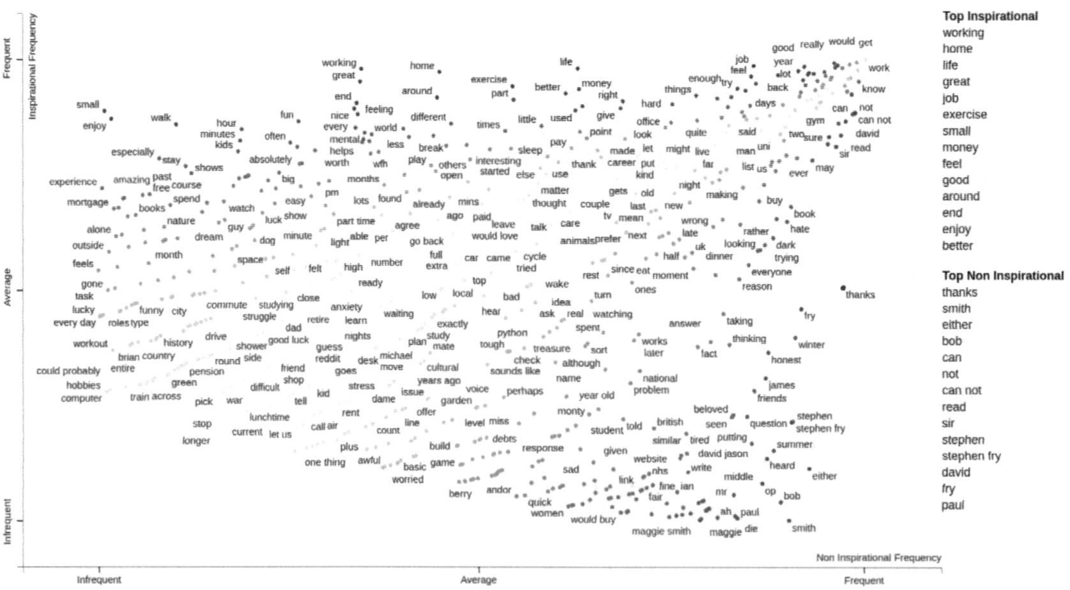

Figure 6: Scattertext visualization of **unigrams** used in the real inspiring and non-inspiring (vs. ✗) Reddit posts from the **UK**. Points are colored in red or blue based on the association of their corresponding terms with UK Non-inspiring posts or UK inspiring posts. The most associated terms are listed under "Top inspiring" and "Top Non-inspiring" headings.

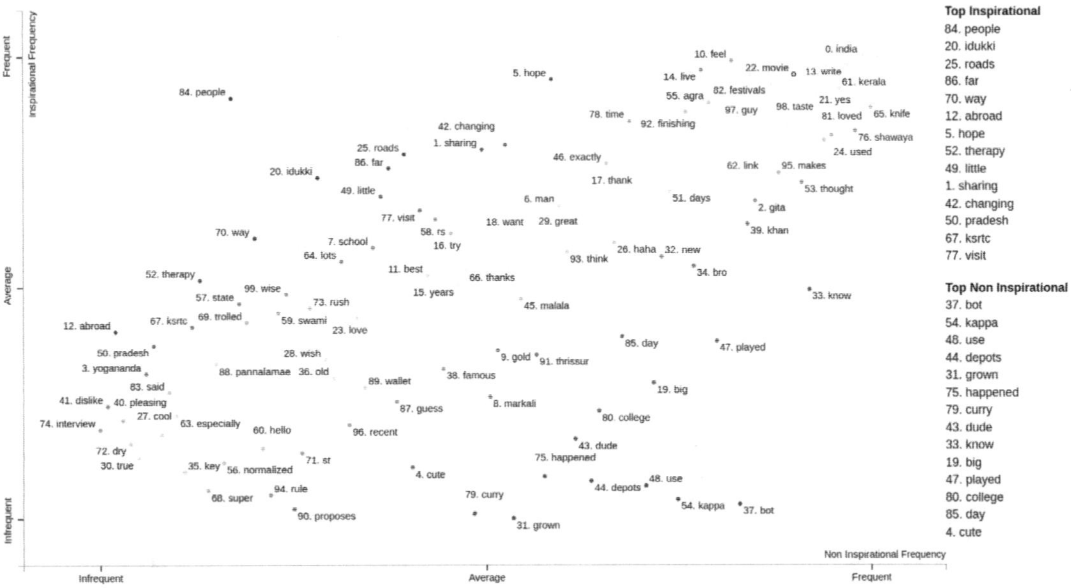

Figure 7: Scattertext visualization of **topics** used in the real inspiring and non-inspiring (✓ vs. ✗) Reddit posts from **India**. Points are colored in red or blue based on the association of their corresponding terms with India Non-inspiring posts or India inspiring posts. The most associated topics are listed under “Top inspiring” and “Top Non-inspiring” headings.

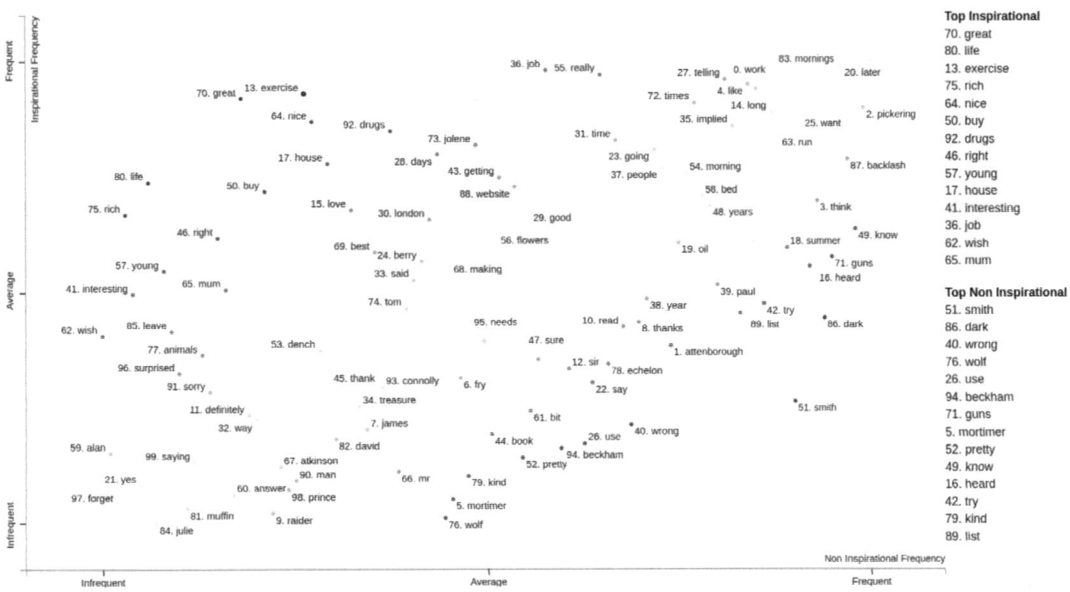

Figure 8: Scattertext visualization of **topics** used in the real inspiring and non-inspiring (✓ vs. ✗) Reddit posts from the **UK**. Points are colored red or blue based on the association of their corresponding terms with UK Non-inspiring posts or UK inspiring posts. The most associated topics are listed under “Top inspiring” and “Top Non-inspiring” headings.

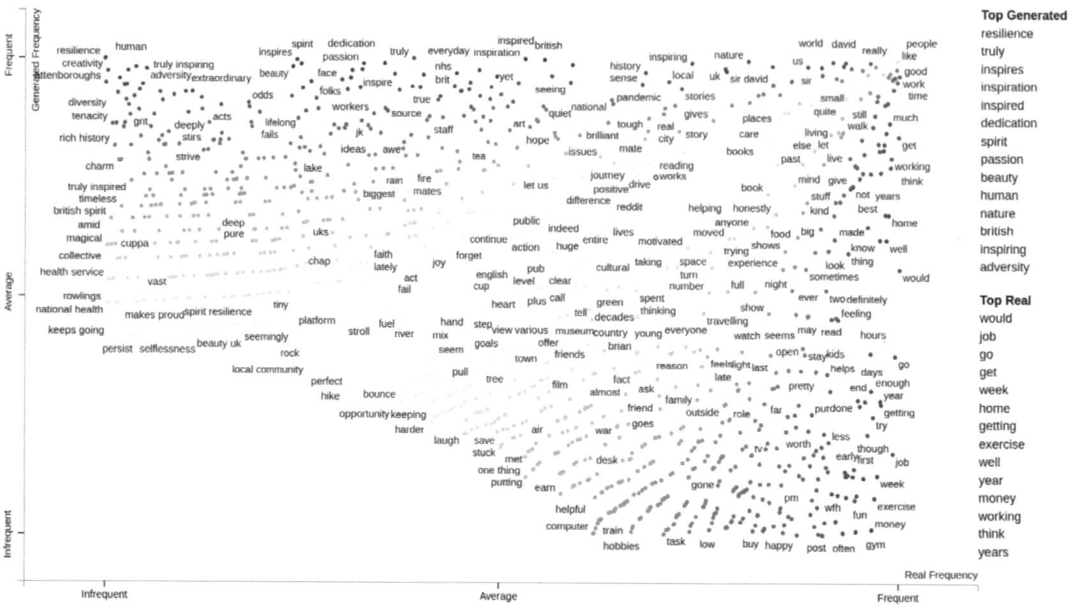

Figure 9: Scattertext visualization of **unigrams** used in the real and generated (👥 vs. 💻) inspiring posts from the **UK**. Points are colored red or blue based on the association of their corresponding terms with the UK Real inspiring posts or the UK LLM-Generated inspiring posts. The most associated topics are listed under **Top Generated** and **Top Real** headings.

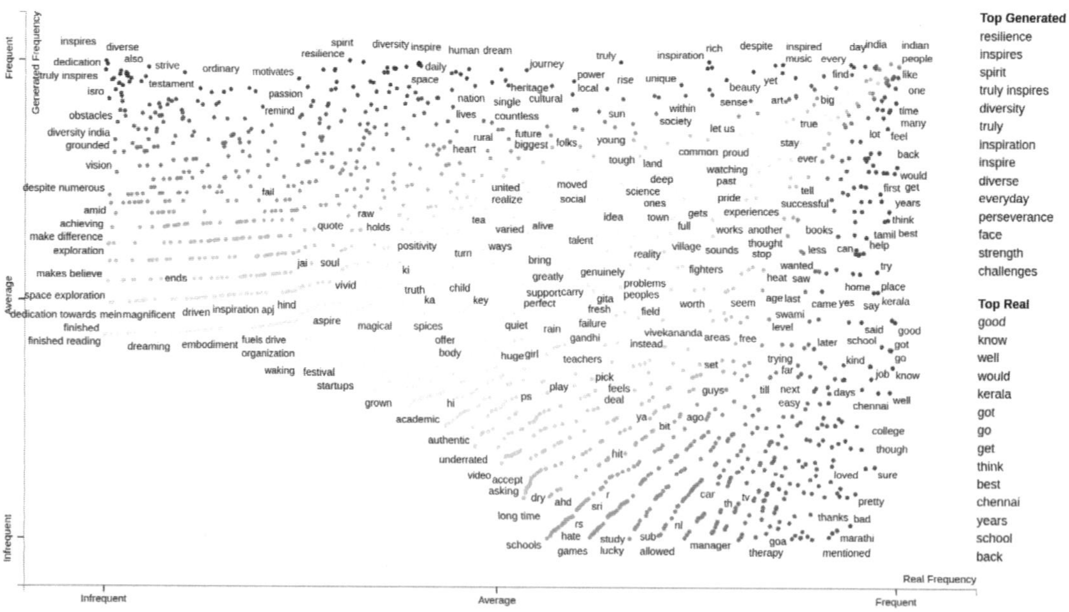

Figure 10: Scattertext visualization of **unigrams** used in the real and generated (👥 vs. 💻) inspiring posts from **India**. Points are colored red or blue based on the association of their corresponding terms with India Real inspiring posts or India LLM-Generated inspiring posts. The most associated topics are listed under **Top Generated** and **Top Real** headings.

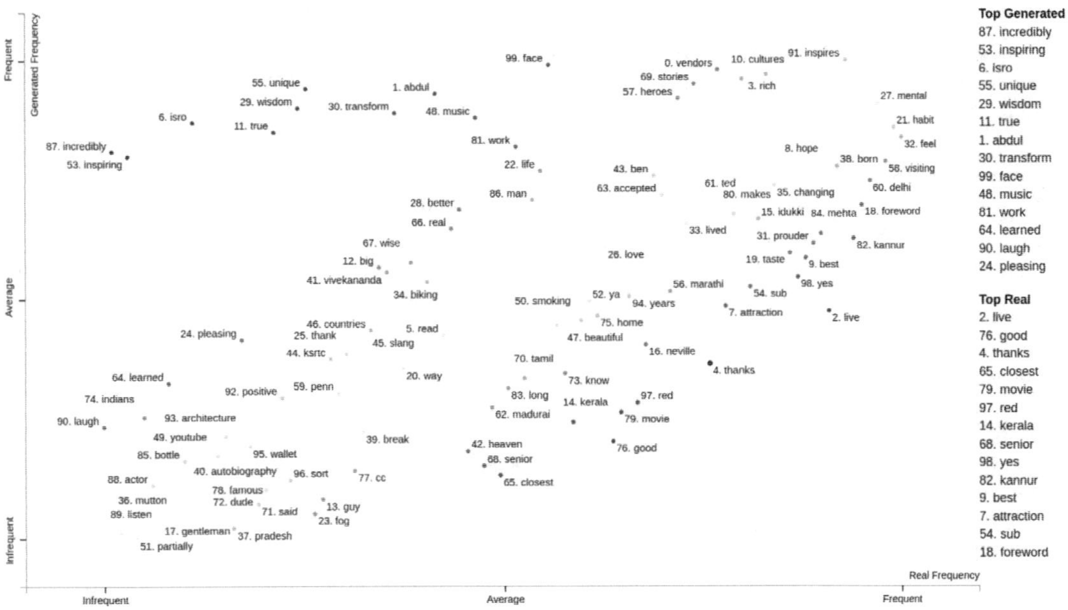

Figure 11: Scattertext visualization of **topics** used in the real and generated (vs.) inspiring posts from **India**. Points are colored red or blue based on the association of their corresponding terms with India Real inspiring posts or India LLM-Generated inspiring posts. The most associated topics are listed under **Top Generated** and **Top Real** headings.

DaKultur: Evaluating the Cultural Awareness of Language Models for Danish with Native Speakers

Max Müller-Eberstein **Mike Zhang**
Elisa Bassignana **Peter Brunsgaard Trolle** **Rob van der Goot**
IT University of Copenhagen, Denmark Aalborg University, Denmark
Pioneer Center for Artificial Intelligence, Denmark
mamy@itu.dk jjz@cs.aau.dk

Abstract

Large Language Models (LLMs) have seen widespread societal adoption. However, while they are able to interact with users in languages beyond English, they have been shown to lack cultural awareness, providing anglocentric or inappropriate responses for underrepresented language communities. To investigate this gap and disentangle linguistic versus cultural proficiency, we conduct the first cultural evaluation study for the mid-resource language of Danish, in which native speakers prompt different models to solve tasks requiring cultural awareness. Our analysis of the resulting 1,038 interactions from 63 demographically diverse participants highlights open challenges to cultural adaptation: Particularly, how currently employed automatically translated data are insufficient to train or measure cultural adaptation, and how training on native-speaker data can more than double response acceptance rates. We release our study data as DaKultur—the first native Danish cultural awareness dataset. [1]

1 Introduction

Culture encompasses shared beliefs, norms, and worldviews (Tylor, 1871; Braff and Nelson, 2020), and tightly interweaves with language (Kramsch, 1998, 2014). These bidirectional influences affect how LLMs perform on culturally-sensitive tasks (Hovy and Yang, 2021). Contemporary LLMs are predominantly trained on English data, yet their global usage has outpaced their cultural coverage (Shi et al., 2023; Huang et al., 2023). Recent findings suggest that many models fail to adequately represent non-anglophone cultures (Hershcovich et al., 2022; Zhang et al., 2023; Liu et al., 2024), resulting in culturally misaligned outputs that undermine user trust (Hovy and Yang, 2021; Litschko et al., 2023; Ge et al., 2024).

Addressing cultural misalignment requires assessing linguistic forms, common ground, aboutness, and values (Hershcovich et al., 2022). Prior efforts to improve alignment across these dimensions include the diversification of training data, as well as involving native speakers in evaluations (Tay et al., 2020; Huang and Yang, 2023; Cao et al., 2023; Naous et al., 2024; Wang et al., 2024). However, it remains unclear which LLM adaptation strategies (i.e., data selection, training methodology) lead to the highest linguistic and cultural alignment–especially for smaller languages.

This work investigates these questions by focusing on Danish, a mid-resource language that shares typological features with English, yet differs culturally to a non-trivial degree. By performing controlled experiments with respect to linguistic and cultural adaptation, we further aim to identify guidelines for culturally adapting LLMs to languages with similar characteristics and resource constraints. Our contributions are:

- DaKultur: The first native Danish dataset for the cultural evaluation of LLMs.
- A corresponding study, showing that native Danish data is critical to improving human acceptance rates (14%→42%), and accurate automatic cultural evaluation.
- An analysis of the effects of demographic factors (region, age, gender) on model alignment across different cultural topics.

2 DaKultur

2.1 Study and Data Collection Setup

To obtain a holistic perspective on Danish culture, we construct DaKultur based on a cultural evaluation study with native speakers in the loop. For

These authors contributed equally.

[1] Dataset and code at https://mxij.me/x/dakultur. This study was approved by the ethics committee of the IT University of Copenhagen on 24th June 2024.

Proceedings of the 3rd Workshop on Cross-Cultural Considerations in NLP (C3NLP 2025), pages 50–58
May 4, 2025

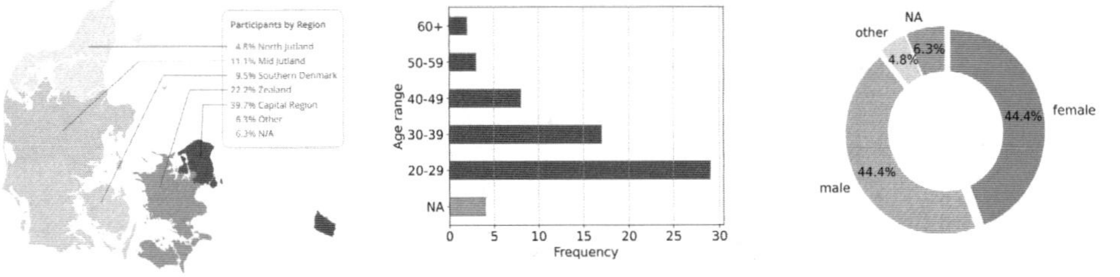

(a) Participants by Region. (b) Participants by Age Range. (c) Participants by Gender Identity.

Figure 1: **Demographic Statistics for Our 63 Study Participants**, who were asked to optionally provide the region, where one grew up (Fig. 1a), age range in decades (Fig. 1b), and gender identity (Fig. 1c). 94% of respondents opted to provide this information.

this purpose, we build an open online interface (Fig. 3a), through which we task participants to compose prompts which require an understanding of Danish culture (Fig. 3c). We then use three different language models (Section 3.1) to generate answers[2], which participants rate with an accept or reject, plus optional comments (Fig. 3d).

While the study is anonymous, we ask for optional demographic information (Fig. 3b), in order to assess the intra-cultural diversity of the respondents. We aim to collect only the minimal set of demographic features most likely to affect cultural responses, while not discouraging casual participation. Namely, we ask for the *region* where one grew up, (the five regions of Denmark, plus *other* for, e.g., people having grown up abroad), *age range* in decades, and *gender identity* (female, male, other).

After data collection, we manually validated the responses for relevance and correctness, and added topic annotations with a distinct set of five Danish speakers (Section 2.3). The resulting validated study data, in the form of DAKULTUR, not only serves to evaluate the cultural capabilities of the examined LLMs, but also constitutes—to the best of our knowledge—the first native Danish instruction dataset, with culturally-specific instructions, and human preference annotations.

2.2 Study Statistics

Our study was conducted over a period of two months, and was mainly advertised across higher educational institutions in Denmark. It attracted 1,038 input-response pairs with human quality judgments, from 63 participants (after validation).

Demographics. 94% of study respondents opted to provide demographic information, for which we find coverage of all regions (Fig. 1a) and gender identities (Fig. 1c), as well as most age ranges except for <20 and >70 (Fig. 1b). We observe a slight skew towards participants who report having grown up in or around the Capital Region, that is 7% above the expected population share, while participants from Mid/Northern Jutland and Southern Denmark are underrepresented by 4–12%.

Quality. Generally, participants provided high-quality input, with 94.49% of prompts passing our post-study validation (Section 2.3). They further cover a diverse range of cultural concepts, as shown in the spread of topics in Fig. 2. Prompts are more frequently phrased as questions than as instructions (e.g., "how does a hot-dog stand look?" versus "describe how a hot-dog stand looks like"). Furthermore, the majority of inputs query the models' cultural knowledge directly instead of via its situational awareness of societal norms (e.g., by prompting models to resolve dilemmatic situations). As prompts in the latter format are much more time-intensive to create, this is likely to be expected. Participants further steered clear of politically and morally-charged topics, despite their anonymity. The resulting collection of cultural prompts therefore contains cultural concepts, that appear to enjoy a more uniform consensus.

2.3 Post-study Validation

Post-study, we validate and analyze the resulting data in another round of annotation with a distinct set of five Danish speakers. The study data is split across annotators, and each annotator is tasked to verify whether an input is dependent on a Danish cultural context (i.e., valid for this study), as well as which broader main topic it belongs to. For annotating topics, we employ an open coding strategy (Strauss, 1987), which resulted in the following 12 topics (+ other):

[2]Answer order was shuffled after each trial.

MODEL	LANGUAGE						CULTURE		
	LA	NER	SA	AS	CSR	QA	PE	CT	**DK**
LLAMA2-7B$_{base}$	33.4	23.7	61.5	65.5	29.8	63.5	38.6	57.7	—
+ INST$_{da}$	36.1	28.5	62.9	66.4	29.0	64.4	49.1	58.5	13.9
LLAMA2-7B$_{chat}$	47.4	24.6	66.2	66.3	**32.2**	61.3	46.7	55.2	—
+ INST$_{da}$	43.4	29.7	65.9	65.8	31.0	62.5	57.3	55.6	15.0
SNAKMODEL	**52.9**	**29.8**	**66.7**	**66.6**	29.5	**64.7**	**71.1**	**71.9**	**42.4**

Table 1: **Results on the ScandEval Benchmark (Test) and DAKULTUR (DK).** Higher scores are better, with exact metrics depending on the sub-task (Section 3.1). We differentiate between linguistic tasks (under LANGUAGE), and cultural tasks (under CULTURE). Additionally, we include scores for the English LLAMA2-7B$_{base}$ and LLAMA2-7B$_{chat}$ (Touvron et al., 2023). The best score per sub-task is highlighted in **bold**.

- **arts**: media and their place in society (e.g., "name five popular Danish TV programs").
- **education**: regarding the education system (e.g., "which university is best to learn about AI in Denmark?").
- **food**: regarding dishes and culinary traditions (e.g., "can I serve herring on french bread?").
- **geography**: regions, cities, and climate (e.g., "where can you go on vacation in the south?").
- **language**: proficiency in appropriate responses and proverbs (e.g., "what does it mean to be a pineapple in its own juice?").
- **lifestyle**: everyday activities that are not as strict as norms (e.g., "what should I prepare when going to a Danish beach?").
- **norms**: implicit rules that are followed in Danish society (e.g., "explain the effect of 'the law of Jante' on Danish mentality").
- **politics**: knowledge of the political system, figures, and parties (e.g., "how do I become a member of the regional parliament?").
- **traditions**: customs and events, observed across multiple generations (e.g., "what do you do with a 25-year-old who's single?").
- **transport**: knowledge and customs regarding transportation systems (e.g., "can you turn left on a bicycle at a traffic light?").
- **trivia**: factual knowledge about people, places, historical events, sports etc., which are not part of the other topics (e.g., "in what year was the reunification of Southern Jutland?").
- **work**: procedures and behaviors, that are appropriate for a professional context (e.g., "how do I ask my manager for a raise?").

3 Cultural Evaluation

We next investigate the results of our cultural evaluation study, and compare the metrics from DAKULTUR with those of automatic benchmarks.

3.1 Experimental Setup

Models. In our study, we use three LLMs based on LLAMA2-7B$_{base}$ (Touvron et al., 2023), adapted to Danish using distinctive training strategies: Danish language modeling training (LMT$_{da}$), and instruction tuning on translated data (INST$_{da}$). The corresponding models are LLAMA2-7B$_{base}$+INST$_{da}$, LLAMA2-7B$_{chat}$+INST$_{da}$, and SNAKMODEL (Zhang et al., 2024; LLAMA2-7B$_{base}$+LMT$_{da}$+INST$_{da}$).

Automatic Evaluation. To compare the human judgments in DAKULTUR with existing automatic metrics, we employ the Danish part of ScandEval (Nielsen, 2023), across its sub-tasks on linguistic acceptability (LA from ScaLA[3]) ; named entity recognition (NER from DANSK; Hvingelby et al., 2020) ; sentiment analysis (SA from AngryTweets; Pauli et al., 2021) ; abstractive summarization (AS from Nordjylland-News; Kinch, 2023) ; commonsense reasoning (CSR from HellaSwag; Zellers et al., 2019) ; and question answering (QA from ScandiQA[4]). ScandEval further includes two culturally-oriented tasks: Danske Talemåder (PE; Nielsen, 2023), which prompts for meanings behind Danish proverbs, and a collection of Danish Citizenship Tests (CT; Nielsen, 2024).

[3]Based on Danish data from the Universal Dependencies dataset from (Kromann and Lynge, 2004).

[4]Note that ScandiQA is a translation of the English MKQA dataset Longpre et al., 2021, and does not strictly focus on Scandinavian knowledge.

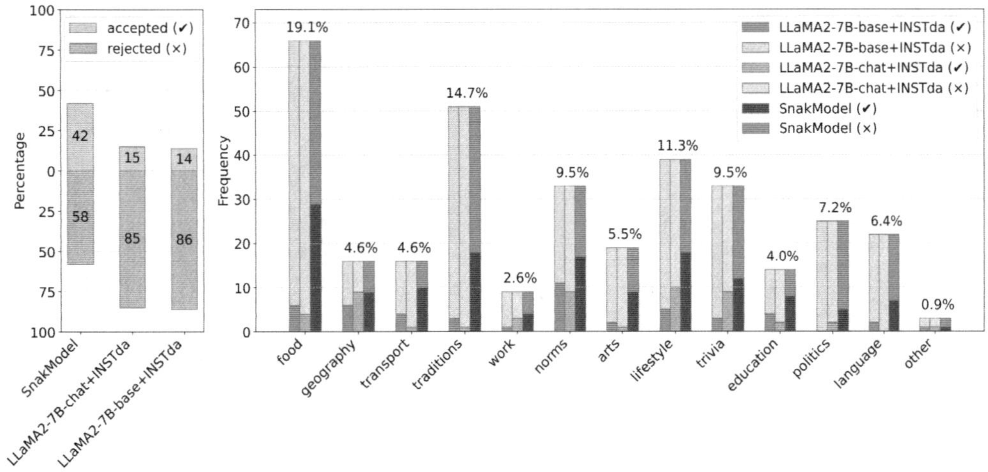

Figure 2: **Acceptance/Rejection Rates** across SNAKMODEL, LLAMA2-7B$_{chat}$+INST$_{da}$ and LLAMA2-7B$_{base}$+INST$_{da}$ as judged by participants in DAKULTUR. Left: overall results; Right: results by topic.

3.2 Results

Automatic Metrics. Results on ScandEval (Table 1) show that training on native Danish data (i.e., SNAKMODEL) leads to the greatest performance gains across the board. While the unadapted English models perform comparably on some tasks, it is important to note that ScandEval employs constrained generation. When prompted without constraint, both LLAMA2-7B$_{base}$ and LLAMA2-7B$_{chat}$ generate English responses. Instruction tuning using translated data is already sufficient to enforce Danish responses (even when prompted in English), which is why we employ the +INST$_{da}$ variants in our human study. Nonetheless, we observe that translated data is insufficient to induce much cultural knowledge into the model, as only SNAKMODEL improves on the cultural tasks of PE and CT to a substantial degree.

DAKULTUR Results. In terms of acceptance rates, SNAKMODEL obtains a rate more than twice as high compared to the other models (Fig. 2). Nonetheless, with a maximum acceptance rate of 42%, none of the models appears to provide particularly well-adapted responses—highlighting the gap between cultural versus linguistic adaptation. Qualitatively, we observe that answers are almost never rejected due to linguistic errors, but rather due to incorrect or incomplete factual content.

Our post-study analysis reveals that the cultural topics of *food* and *traditions* are most popular, and that SNAKMODEL achieves acceptance rates over ten times as high for these topics. While training on native data improves performance across all topics, gains are larger for implicit cultural knowledge (e.g., *lifestyle*, *norms*) than for facts (e.g., *trivia*, *geography*, *politics*). In Appendix C, we further show how topics and acceptance rates vary by demographics. Female-identity participants tend toward *food*, *lifestyle*, *education*, and *norms*, while male-identity participants focus more on *politics*, *trivia*, and *geography*. Additionally, younger participants and those from the capital region report slightly higher acceptance rates.

4 Conclusion

In this work, we introduced DAKULTUR—the first native Danish cultural evaluation dataset. By constructing it via a native-speaker-driven evaluation study, and applying a thorough post-study validation, we are able to share 1,038 high-quality input-response pairs for future Danish NLP research. Our cultural evaluation using DAKULTUR highlights that language modeling training using native data is already sufficient to more than double human-judged cultural awareness—especially for popular cultural topics. Simultaneously, the maximum acceptance rate of 42% highlights that more research is needed to fully align anglocentric LLMs to smaller language communities, such as Danish. In terms of evaluation methodologies, the fact that human judgments align more with the smaller, yet culturally-relevant and non-translated sub-tasks of the automatic ScandEval benchmark (PE, CT, as well as LA) is encouraging, since small amounts of high-quality data may already be sufficient to accurately estimate an LLM's cultural awareness.

Limitations

While we strive for broad coverage of the Danish cultural landscape, culture itself has a high degree of inherent subjectivity and variability. As such, future work using DAKULTUR should be cognizant of the context in which its data was obtained. Our cultural evaluation study was advertised primarily at higher educational institutions. Although we are aware of word-to-mouth advertisement stretching to demographic groups beyond this initial cluster (as evidenced by the range of represented age groups), the study likely does not capture the full breadth of the Danish cultural landscape. By gathering demographics for intra-cultural differences with regard to topics and user acceptance rates, we nonetheless aim to enable analyses with respect to how much cultural consensus might vary with respect to different topics. We believe this is crucial information for practitioners designing downstream systems, as contemporary models seem to, for instance, align slightly better with male-identity participants under 30 from the capital region.

On the technical side, we hope that future work will be able to validate our findings across more base models and languages. Our choice of Danish and LLAMA2-7B-based models was primarily driven by data and compute resource availability. Similarly, while DAKULTUR can theoretically be used for small-scale instruction tuning or model alignment, its size is far from contemporary, automatically generated datasets. For cultural evaluation purposes, we nonetheless believe that it offers a representative out-of-the-box solution for developers of future Danish LMs.

Acknowledgments

We thank the NLPnorth group at ITU and the AAU-NLP group at AAU for feedback on earlier version of this draft. Elisa Bassignana is supported by a research grant (VIL59826) from VILLUM FONDEN. Mike Zhang is supported by a research grant (VIL57392) from VILLUM FONDEN.

References

Lara Braff and Katie Nelson. 2020. Introduction to anthropology. In *Perspectives: An Open Invitation to Cultural Anthropology*, pages 3–28. Society for Anthropology in Community Colleges.

Yong Cao, Li Zhou, Seolhwa Lee, Laura Cabello, Min Chen, and Daniel Hershcovich. 2023. Assessing cross-cultural alignment between ChatGPT and human societies: An empirical study. In *Proceedings of the First Workshop on Cross-Cultural Considerations in NLP (C3NLP)*, pages 53–67, Dubrovnik, Croatia. Association for Computational Linguistics.

Xiao Ge, Chunchen Xu, Daigo Misaki, Hazel Rose Markus, and Jeanne L Tsai. 2024. How culture shapes what people want from ai. In *Proceedings of the CHI Conference on Human Factors in Computing Systems*, CHI '24, New York, NY, USA. Association for Computing Machinery.

Daniel Hershcovich, Stella Frank, Heather Lent, Miryam de Lhoneux, Mostafa Abdou, Stephanie Brandl, Emanuele Bugliarello, Laura Cabello Piqueras, Ilias Chalkidis, Ruixiang Cui, Constanza Fierro, Katerina Margatina, Phillip Rust, and Anders Søgaard. 2022. Challenges and strategies in cross-cultural NLP. In *Proceedings of the 60th Annual Meeting of the Association for Computational Linguistics (Volume 1: Long Papers)*, pages 6997–7013, Dublin, Ireland. Association for Computational Linguistics.

Dirk Hovy and Diyi Yang. 2021. The importance of modeling social factors of language: Theory and practice. In *Proceedings of the 2021 Conference of the North American Chapter of the Association for Computational Linguistics: Human Language Technologies*, pages 588–602, Online. Association for Computational Linguistics.

Haoyang Huang, Tianyi Tang, Dongdong Zhang, Xin Zhao, Ting Song, Yan Xia, and Furu Wei. 2023. Not all languages are created equal in LLMs: Improving multilingual capability by cross-lingual-thought prompting. In *Findings of the Association for Computational Linguistics: EMNLP 2023*, pages 12365–12394, Singapore. Association for Computational Linguistics.

Jing Huang and Diyi Yang. 2023. Culturally aware natural language inference. In *Findings of the Association for Computational Linguistics: EMNLP 2023*, pages 7591–7609, Singapore. Association for Computational Linguistics.

Rasmus Hvingelby, Amalie Brogaard Pauli, Maria Barrett, Christina Rosted, Lasse Malm Lidegaard, and Anders Søgaard. 2020. DaNE: A named entity resource for Danish. In *Proceedings of the Twelfth Language Resources and Evaluation Conference*, pages 4597–4604, Marseille, France. European Language Resources Association.

Oliver Kinch. 2023. Nordjylland news summarization.

Claire Kramsch. 1998. *Language and culture*. Oxford introductions to language study. Oxford University Press, Oxford.

Claire Kramsch. 2014. Language and culture. *AILA Review*, 27(1):30–55.

Matthias Trautner Kromann and Stine Kern Lynge. 2004. The danish dependency treebank v. 1.0.

Robert Litschko, Max Müller-Eberstein, Rob van der Goot, Leon Weber-Genzel, and Barbara Plank. 2023. Establishing trustworthiness: Rethinking tasks and model evaluation. In *Proceedings of the 2023 Conference on Empirical Methods in Natural Language Processing*, pages 193–203, Singapore. Association for Computational Linguistics.

Chen Liu, Fajri Koto, Timothy Baldwin, and Iryna Gurevych. 2024. Are multilingual LLMs culturally-diverse reasoners? an investigation into multicultural proverbs and sayings. In *Proceedings of the 2024 Conference of the North American Chapter of the Association for Computational Linguistics: Human Language Technologies (Volume 1: Long Papers)*, pages 2016–2039, Mexico City, Mexico. Association for Computational Linguistics.

Fangyu Liu, Emanuele Bugliarello, Edoardo Maria Ponti, Siva Reddy, Nigel Collier, and Desmond Elliott. 2021. Visually grounded reasoning across languages and cultures. In *Proceedings of the 2021 Conference on Empirical Methods in Natural Language Processing*, pages 10467–10485, Online and Punta Cana, Dominican Republic. Association for Computational Linguistics.

Shayne Longpre, Yi Lu, and Joachim Daiber. 2021. Mkqa: A linguistically diverse benchmark for multilingual open domain question answering. *Transactions of the Association for Computational Linguistics*, 9:1389–1406.

Tarek Naous, Michael J. Ryan, Alan Ritter, and Wei Xu. 2024. Having beer after prayer? measuring cultural bias in large language models. *Computing Research Repository*, arxiv:2305.14456. Version 4.

Dan Nielsen. 2023. ScandEval: A benchmark for Scandinavian natural language processing. In *Proceedings of the 24th Nordic Conference on Computational Linguistics (NoDaLiDa)*, pages 185–201, Tórshavn, Faroe Islands. University of Tartu Library.

Dan Saattrup Nielsen. 2024. Danish citizen test.

Amalie Brogaard Pauli, Maria Barrett, Ophélie Lacroix, and Rasmus Hvingelby. 2021. DaNLP: An open-source toolkit for Danish natural language processing. In *Proceedings of the 23rd Nordic Conference on Computational Linguistics (NoDaLiDa)*, pages 460–466, Reykjavik, Iceland (Online). Linköping University Electronic Press, Sweden.

Freda Shi, Mirac Suzgun, Markus Freitag, Xuezhi Wang, Suraj Srivats, Soroush Vosoughi, Hyung Won Chung, Yi Tay, Sebastian Ruder, Denny Zhou, Dipanjan Das, and Jason Wei. 2023. Language models are multilingual chain-of-thought reasoners. In *The Eleventh International Conference on Learning Representations*.

Anselm L Strauss. 1987. *Qualitative analysis for social scientists*. Cambridge university press.

Yi Tay, Donovan Ong, Jie Fu, Alvin Chan, Nancy Chen, Anh Tuan Luu, and Chris Pal. 2020. Would you rather? a new benchmark for learning machine alignment with cultural values and social preferences. In *Proceedings of the 58th Annual Meeting of the Association for Computational Linguistics*, pages 5369–5373, Online. Association for Computational Linguistics.

Hugo Touvron, Louis Martin, Kevin Stone, Peter Albert, Amjad Almahairi, Yasmine Babaei, Nikolay Bashlykov, Soumya Batra, Prajjwal Bhargava, Shruti Bhosale, et al. 2023. Llama 2: Open foundation and fine-tuned chat models. *arXiv preprint arXiv:2307.09288*.

Edward Burnett Tylor. 1871. *Primitive culture: researches into the development of mythology, philosophy, religion, art, and custom*, volume 2. J. Murray.

Wenxuan Wang, Wenxiang Jiao, Jingyuan Huang, Ruyi Dai, Jen-tse Huang, Zhaopeng Tu, and Michael Lyu. 2024. Not all countries celebrate thanksgiving: On the cultural dominance in large language models. In *Proceedings of the 62nd Annual Meeting of the Association for Computational Linguistics (Volume 1: Long Papers)*, pages 6349–6384, Bangkok, Thailand. Association for Computational Linguistics.

Rowan Zellers, Ari Holtzman, Yonatan Bisk, Ali Farhadi, and Yejin Choi. 2019. HellaSwag: Can a machine really finish your sentence? In *Proceedings of the 57th Annual Meeting of the Association for Computational Linguistics*, pages 4791–4800, Florence, Italy. Association for Computational Linguistics.

Mike Zhang, Max Müller-Eberstein, Elisa Bassignana, and Rob van der Goot. 2024. Snakmodel: Lessons learned from training an open danish large language model. *Preprint*, arXiv:2412.12956.

Xiang Zhang, Senyu Li, Bradley Hauer, Ning Shi, and Grzegorz Kondrak. 2023. Don't trust ChatGPT when your question is not in English: A study of multilingual abilities and types of LLMs. In *Proceedings of the 2023 Conference on Empirical Methods in Natural Language Processing*, pages 7915–7927, Singapore. Association for Computational Linguistics.

Appendix

A Study Interface

We build a web-based evaluation interface (study flow shown in Fig. 3), which allows study participants to prompt the three LLMs simultaneously[5] with tasks and questions, that require cultural awareness (Fig. 3c), and to rate (accept/reject) and comment on the models' responses (Fig. 3d). The study guidelines (Figs. 3a and 3c) broadly lay out which dimensions of cultural awareness the study aims to investigate—i.e., common ground, aboutness, objectives and values, in addition to linguistic form and style (Hershcovich et al., 2022), which is implicit, given the study's monolingual nature. Following prior work on culturally diverse dataset creation (Liu et al., 2021), we opted for an elicitation setup in order to avoid biasing responses towards a limited set of cultural concepts and topics.

While the study is conducted anonymously, we ask for optional demographic information (Fig. 3b), in order to assess the intra-cultural diversity of the respondents. For this purpose, we aimed to collect only the minimal set of demographic features, that we deemed most likely to affect cultural responses, while not discouraging casual participation. Namely, we ask for the region, where one grew up, (the five regions of Denmark, plus *other* for, e.g., people having grown up abroad), age range in decades, and gender identity (female, male, other).

In test trials, we noticed that, while participants intuitively prompted for a wide variety of culturally-relevant topics, they typically did so in a multi-turn conversational manner, which our single-turn, instruction-tuned models often fail to answer. For instance, the prompt "Hello! Could you tell me about [...]?", frequently produces the response, "Yes, I can.", with no further relevant content. To encourage single-turn instruction-style inputs, we iterated over multiple guideline formulations, of which we found, "Ask one question or give one task about Danish culture [...] to the three virtual assistants below", to produce the most compatible results (see full translations in Appendix B).

[5]Note that the order in which responses are displayed is randomized with each prompt.

B Translations

B.1 Landing Page with Guidelines

Thanks for your interest in our research project!

Purpose We examine cultural skills/competencies with artificial intelligence and would like you to assess our three virtual assistants' knowledge of Danish culture. This includes, for example, norms, art and laws in Danish society, as well as Danes' knowledge, beliefs, customs and habits.

Task On the following pages, you should ask the virtual assistants to perform tasks and assess their answers one-by-one. You can ask them questions or ask them for descriptions, e.g., "tell me how to change the back tire of my bike".

Data policy As this is a research project, input, feedback and optional demographic data are stored in a dataset. All data is collected anonymously.

If you agree to the above terms, continue by clicking Accept below.

B.2 Demographic Information

Your anonymous session ID is:
`SESSION_ID`

Save it in a safe place since it is required if you would like to get your answers removed from our dataset.

Demographics Enter your demographic information below (one or more can be omitted). This helps us to ensure that we get a more diverse data set.

Region (where you grew up)
do not wish to disclose
Age
do not wish to disclose
Gender Identity
do not wish to disclose

Click *Start* to get started!

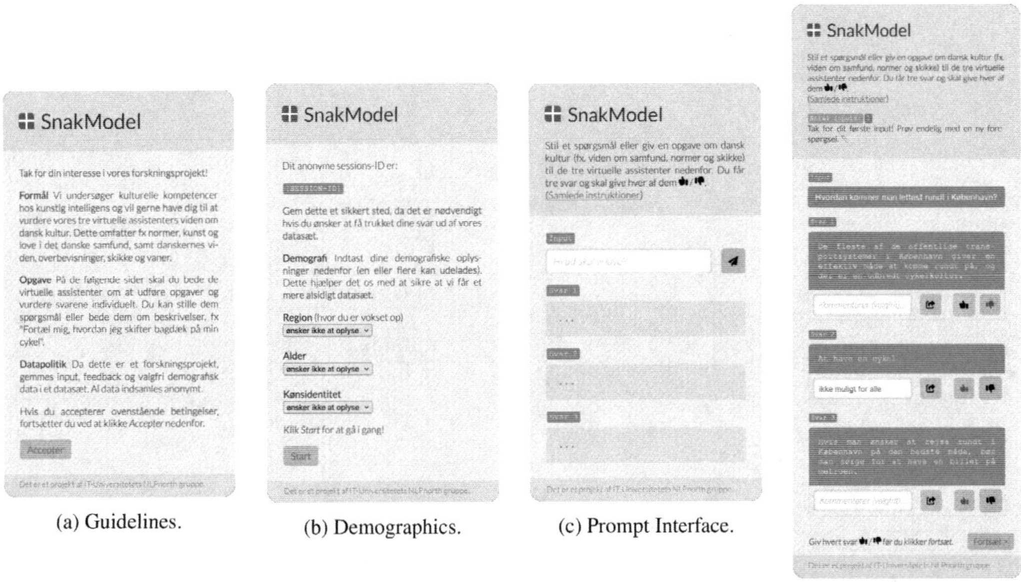

(a) Guidelines. (b) Demographics. (c) Prompt Interface. (d) Evaluation Interface.

Figure 3: **Study Interface for Human Cultural Evaluation**. Participants are guided through the guidelines (Fig. 3a), optional demographic registration (Fig. 3b), before being asked to prompt the three LLMs simultaneously (Fig. 3c), and to evaluate the model responses (Fig. 3d). Translations of the guidelines, interface, and examples can be found in Appendix B.

B.3 Prompt Interface

Ask one question or give one task about Danish culture (e.g., knowledge of society, norms and customs) to the three virtual assistants below. You will receive three answers, which you can each rate with a thumbs-up/down.

Input
What shall we do?

Answer 1
Answer 2
Answer 3

B.4 Response Evaluation Interface

Thanks for your first input! Go ahead, and try another request!

Input
What's the easiest way to get around in Copenhagen?

Answer 1
`Most of the public transport systems in Copenhagen provide an effective way to get around, and there is a widespread cycling-culture.`

Answer 2
`To have a bike`
Comment: not possible for everyone

Answer 3
`If you want to travel around Copenhagen, you should make sure to have a ticket for the subway.`

Give each answer a thumbs-up/down before clicking *Continue*.

C Topics and Acceptance Rates per Demographic

For each demographic dimension, we merge the available categories into two groups, in order to have a large enough amount of information to compare. This leads to splits along male/female, $< 30/\geq 30$, capital region/other regions. The distribution as well as acceptance rates are shown in Fig. 4 for gender, Fig. 5 for age, and Fig. 6 for region.

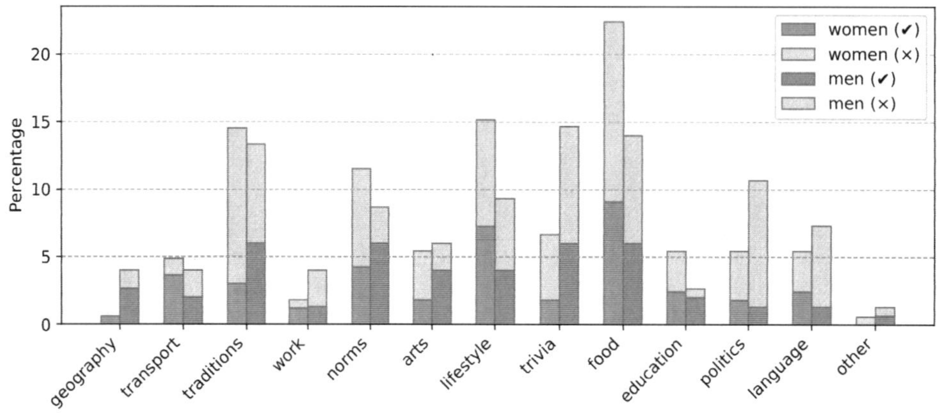

Figure 4: **Acceptance/Rejection Rates and Distribution across Topics** for the female/male gender identity demographic groups.

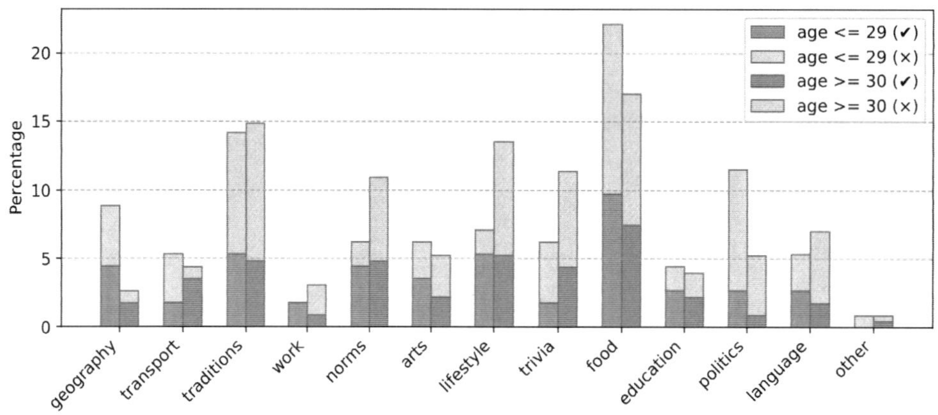

Figure 5: **Acceptance/Rejection Rates and Distribution across Topics** for the age ranges >= 29 and <= 30.

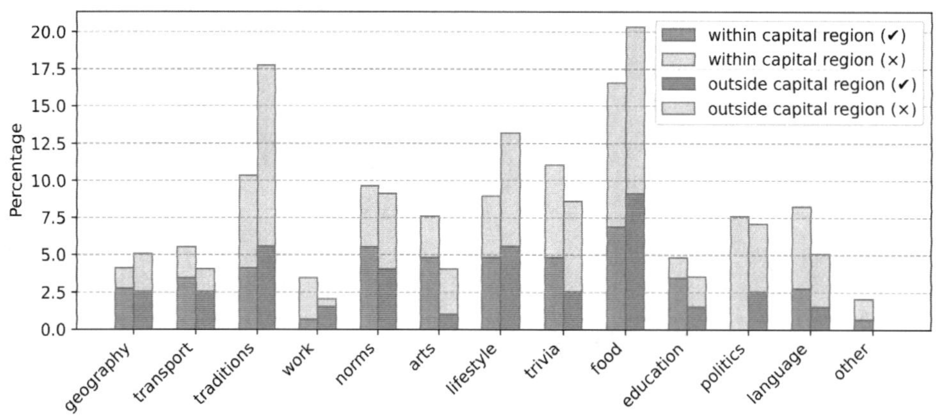

Figure 6: **Acceptance/Rejection Rates and Distribution across Topics** for participants from the capital versus other regions.

Korean Stereotype Content Model: Translating Stereotypes Across Cultures

Michelle YoungJin Kim, Kristen Marie Johnson
Michigan State University, East Lansing, MI, USA
{kimmic16, kristenj}@msu.edu

Abstract

To address bias in language models, researchers are leveraging established social psychology research on stereotyping. This interdisciplinary approach uses frameworks like the Stereotype Content Model (SCM) to understand how stereotypes about social groups are formed and perpetuated. The SCM posits that stereotypes can be defined based on two dimensions: warmth (intent to harm) and competence (ability to harm). This framework has been applied in NLP for various tasks, including stereotype identification, bias mitigation, and hate speech detection. While the SCM has been extensively studied in English language models and Western cultural contexts, its applicability as a cross-cultural measure of stereotypes remains an open research question. This paper explores the cross-cultural validity of the SCM by developing a Korean Stereotype Content Model (KoSCM). We create a Korean warmth-competence lexicon through machine translation of existing English lexicons, validated by an expert translator, and utilize this lexicon to develop a labeled training dataset of Korean sentences. This work presents the first extension of SCM lexicons to a non-English language (Korean), aiming to broaden understanding of stereotypes and cultural dynamics.

1 Introduction

With the growing emphasis on Responsible and Fair AI, researchers are increasingly addressing the challenge of bias in language models. As this area of study within natural language processing (NLP) is still in its formative stages, scholars are drawing upon the insights of social psychology, a field that has extensively examined bias and stereotypes for many years. By employing the concept of stereotyping, researchers aim to elucidate the underlying mechanisms by which individuals form stereotypes about social groups. A prominent framework in this investigation is the Stereotype Content Model (SCM), which offers critical insights into understanding and addressing stereotypes.

The SCM (Fiske et al., 2002) identifies two key dimensions of stereotypes: warmth and competence. When individuals encounter members of an out-group, SCM suggests they instinctively ask two questions: Do these individuals intend to harm me? And are they capable of causing me harm? The first inquiry assesses warmth (characteristics such as friendliness, good-naturedness, sincerity, and warmth), while the second evaluates competence (traits including capability, skillfulness, confidence, and effectiveness). SCM has been utilized in NLP to develop a computational model for identifying stereotypes (Fraser et al., 2021; Herold et al., 2022; Nicolas and Caliskan, 2024; Schuster et al., 2024; Fraser et al., 2024; Mina et al., 2024), to reduce stereotypical bias in language models (Omrani et al., 2023; Ungless et al., 2022; Gaci et al., 2023), and to enhance hate speech detection (Jin et al., 2024).

There has been substantial research into the application of the SCM in language models, particularly regarding English texts and the stereotypes present in English-speaking cultures. However, the computational analysis of stereotypes in other languages and cultures is underexplored. This raises an important research question: Can the computational approach to the SCM be considered a pancultural measure of stereotypes across diverse societies?

In this paper, we explore the potential of the SCM as a pancultural tool by developing a Korean Stereotype Content Model (KoSCM). We begin by curating a Korean dictionary containing warmth-competence seed words. We translate existing English warmth-competence lexicons into Korean using a machine translation model, subsequently validating this translation with an expert translator. The translated lexicons are then utilized to create the training dataset for the KoSCM.

Proceedings of the 3rd Workshop on Cross-Cultural Considerations in NLP (C3NLP 2025), pages 59–70
May 4, 2025

This dataset consists of sentences containing the warmth-competence seed words and two labels: warmth and competence directions.

We evaluate KoSCM by applying the model to do a stereotype analysis on social groups. We perform a stereotype analysis on social groups of age, gender, and religion in Korean texts. We observe whether the computational analysis aligns with and validates the social psychology study (Fiske et al., 2002; Cuddy et al., 2009). Further, we investigate the potential of SCM as a computational method for different languages and cultures. Based on the social psychology theory, we test the three hypotheses of the SCM: (1) the two dimensions hypothesis, (2) the ambivalent stereotypes hypothesis, and (3) the social structural correlates hypothesis. To the best of our knowledge, this is the first attempt to expand the SCM lexicons to a different language. Through this study, we aim to provide valuable insights that expand our understanding of stereotypes and cultural dynamics.

Our contributions are as follows:

- We develop a stereotype analysis model in Korean by curating warmth-competence seed words in Korean and generating training data to map texts to warmth-competence dimensions.
- We propose a social psychology-grounded framework for expanding the Stereotype Content Model to other languages and cultures.

2 Background and Related Work

In this section, we explore the concept of stereotyping. We begin by examining the definitions and research surrounding stereotypes in social psychology (§2.1). Subsequently, we discuss how NLP researchers have utilized findings from social psychology to detect and evaluate stereotypes within data and models (§2.2).

2.1 Stereotyping in Social Psychology

Stereotyping is a cognitive process in which specific attributes are overly generalized to entire social groups. It is a ubiquitous phenomenon that contributes to the perpetuation of social inequalities. When specific qualities are attributed to entire groups, it reinforces existing power dynamics and legitimizes discriminatory practices.

The perpetuation of stereotypes leads to profound consequences, such as the marginalization of certain groups, increased social inequalities, and significant psychological effects on individuals (Timmer, 2011). Marginalization happens when stereotypes justify the exclusion of specific groups from social, economic, and political opportunities. The increase in social inequalities is further fueled by the distribution of resources in ways that uphold existing power dynamics. Additionally, the internalization of stereotypes can severely affect individuals psychologically, undermining their mental well-being and self-image.

Social stereotypes are complex and multifaceted constructs that influence social perception and interaction. Traditional approaches to understanding stereotypes have relied on simplistic categorizations, such as positive or negative. However, the Stereotype Content Model (SCM) (Fiske et al., 2002; Fiske, 2018) offers a more nuanced framework for understanding social stereotypes. The SCM posits that social perception is guided by two fundamental dimensions: warmth and competence. Warmth refers to the perceived intentions and friendliness of a group, while competence refers to the perceived abilities and effectiveness of a group. These dimensions are orthogonal, allowing for the possibility of positive stereotypes along one dimension and negative stereotypes along the other.

A natural follow-up question for researchers is whether these stereotype studies can be generalized across cultures. Given that stereotypes arise from fundamental human phenomena—namely, the need to distinguish between "friends" and "foes" and the ubiquity of hierarchical status differences and resource competition—it is reasonable to assume that these principles are universally applicable.

To investigate this hypothesis, Cuddy et al. (2009) conducted a cross-cultural study spanning seven European (individualist) and three East Asian (collectivist) nations. The findings suggest that the SCM framework is effective across various cultures, reliably indicating group stereotypes based on structural connections with other groups. Using the SCM, the researchers observed parallels in the basic structures of intergroup relations. Building on this study, we expand the computational social study of SCM from English to Korean, leveraging a computational approach to validate the findings of the social psychology study.

2.2 Stereotype Content Model in NLP

The increasing prevalence of NLP models in various applications has raised concerns about the perpetuation of stereotypical biases in AI systems. Social psychological theories present valuable frameworks for understanding and addressing these biases. Consequently, recent studies have applied established social psychological theories to analyze biases in NLP models. In particular, research has concentrated on stereotype dimensions identified by these theories, notably the SCM.

The SCM has been extensively employed in various NLP applications to identify and mitigate stereotypical biases. For instance, researchers have utilized the SCM to detect stereotype subspaces in word embeddings (Fraser et al., 2021) and debias models by removing stereotype dimensions from the embedding space (Ungless et al., 2022; Omrani et al., 2023). Moreover, the SCM has been applied to assess benchmark datasets for bias (Fraser et al., 2021), examine how NLP models relate SCM dimensions to marginalized groups (Herold et al., 2022; Mina et al., 2024), and develop metrics to investigate biases across demographic and intersectional groups (Cao et al., 2022). Recent studies have further refined the SCM by exploring the construct differentiability of direction and representativeness for warmth and competence dimensions (Nicolas and Caliskan, 2024) and fine-graining stereotype dimensions into six psychologically-motivated categories to study occupation-related stereotypes (Fraser et al., 2024).

In recent years, researchers in NLP have expanded the study of bias and fairness to include non-English languages such as Arabic, Bengali, Chinese, Dutch, French, German, Hindi, Japanese, Korean, Spanish, and Telugu (Zhou et al., 2019; Chávez Mulsa and Spanakis, 2020; Kurpicz-Briki, 2020; Lauscher et al., 2020; Liang et al., 2020; Moon et al., 2020; Pujari et al., 2020; Takeshita et al., 2020; Zhao et al., 2020; Malik et al., 2021; Jeong et al., 2022), mirroring developments in social psychology. Bhutani et al. (2024) have expanded the number of languages by releasing a multilingual stereotype dataset that includes 20 languages across 23 regions. Acknowledging that biases are influenced by societal constructs, socio-cultural structures, and historical contexts, researchers are also seeking to adopt a more holistic approach to NLP fairness by taking the geo-cultural context into consideration (Sambasivan et al., 2021; Bhatt et al., 2022). The SeeGULL dataset (Bhutani et al., 2024) includes Korean but differs from our work in that it consists of pairs of associations between an identity term and an attribute generated by a language model. In contrast, our dataset and method are based on stereotyping theory from social psychology, utilizing seed words to identify stereotypes. This approach allows for broader applicability to various identity terms and social groups.

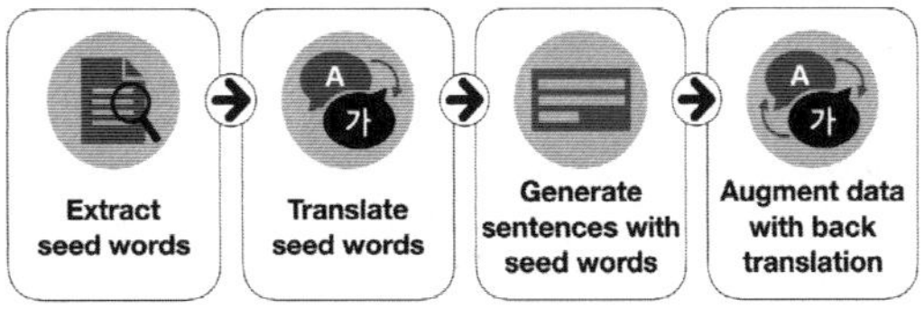

Figure 1: **Stereotype Translation Framework.** This figure illustrates the four steps for generating the data for KoSCM.

3 Translating Stereotype

This section presents a framework for expanding the SCM to a different language. As shown in Figure 1, we adopt the four steps to translate English SCM to Korean and create the dataset for KoSCM [1].

Step 1. Extract seed words The first step is to extract seed words for the stereotype content dictionary (Nicolas et al., 2019). The stereotype content dictionary is a collection of theory-driven seed words used to measure sociability, morality/trustworthiness, ability, assertiveness/dominance, status, political beliefs, and religious beliefs in relation to social groups. The list contains 341 words with their respective theoretical direction—either high or low—on their relevant dimension.

From the list, we select seed words that reflect warmth and competence dimensions. Specifically, words representing sociability and morality measures are classified as warmth seed words, and those related to ability and agency are categorized as competence seed words. There are a total of 157 seed words associated with the warmth dimension and 128 for the competence dimension. Each seed word is labeled with a direction within its respective dimension. For example, the word "warm" is a high-direction seed word in the warmth dimension, whereas "cold" represents a low-direction

[1] The dataset is available in github.com/MSU-NLP-CSS/KoSCM.

Dim	Dir	#	Example
W	high	75	친절한$_{\text{friendly}}$, 호감이 가는$_{\text{likable}}$
	low	82	불친절한$_{\text{unfriendly}}$, 냉담한$_{\text{cold}}$
C	high	68	유능한$_{\text{competent}}$, 영리한$_{\text{clever}}$
	low	60	무능한$_{\text{incompetent}}$, 멍청한$_{\text{stupid}}$

Table 1: **Statistics of Korean Seed Words.** The table shows statistics of translated seed words for KoSCM. The first column denotes dimensions: warmth and competence. The second column indicates a direction in each dimension. The next column lists the number of data points, while the final column provides examples of seed words in Korean.

seed word within the same dimension. Similarly, the word "competent" is an example of a high-direction seed word in the competence dimension, while "incompetent" is classified as having low direction in that dimension.

Step 2. Translate seed words Next, the extracted seed words are translated into Korean. The first step of translation is to adopt a machine translation model. We choose Naver Papago [2], one of the most popular Korean-English AI translators in Korea, to translate English seed words to Korean. Afterward, we validate the translation with an expert translator. The translator is asked to validate the translation by answering the following questions: (1) Is the translation grammatically correct (e.g., a noun is translated as a noun)? (2) Is a word translated into a distinct word (i.e., no recurrence in the translated list)? Through validation, we verify 285 Korean seed words labeled with stereotype dimension and direction in their corresponding dimension. See Table 1 for statistics and examples of seed words.

Step 3. Generate sentences with seed words With the translated stereotype seed words, we generate sentences based on a template. Similar to May et al. (2019), sentences are generated by inserting individual seed words from the list of Korean stereotype words into simple templates such as "그 사람은 <seed word> 사람이다" (That person is a[n] <seed word> person). The templates are selected according to the part-of-speech (POS) tagging of the seed words. Further, The template words are chosen carefully to prevent the generated sentences from referencing specific social groups. For example, the pronouns "he" and "she" indicate a person's gender. We intentionally refrain from using these pronouns as subjects because we aim to create a dataset centered on understanding the dimensions of warmth and competence. For more details, see Appendix A.

[2]https://papago.naver.com/

Step 4. Augment data with back-translation To tackle the limitation of available Korean seed words and address challenges associated with low-resource scenarios, we utilize data augmentation. Sentences generated in Step 3 are augmented using back-translation (Sennrich et al., 2016; Domhan and Hieber, 2017; Belinkov and Bisk, 2018). Back-translation generates paraphrases by leveraging translation models. Initially, a text is translated into another language (forward translation) and then translated back into the original language. This process creates paraphrased sentences, introducing greater variety by allowing for diverse choices in terminology and sentence structure. While the content remains intact, stylistic features that reflect the author's specific traits may be adjusted or omitted during translation.

For our dataset, we first translate the Korean sentences from Step 3 into English and then translate them back into Korean. We use the No Language Left Behind model (Team et al., 2022), a multilingual model that supports translation for 202 languages, for the back-translation step. This model is selected for two key reasons. Firstly, it was designed to assist with low-resource language translations. Secondly, it supports both Korean and English languages. As a result of the back-translation, we obtain a dataset containing 3,420 sentences.

4 Korean Stereotype Content Model

In this section, we detail how the KoSCM dataset, collected through the four steps of the stereotype translation framework, is utilized to build the SCM model. By fine-tuning a model with the dataset, we build KoSCM, which predicts the warmth and competence scores of given Korean sentences.

4.1 Method

We suggest a systematic method to develop a SCM model specific to the language model employed. We introduce two SCM classifier frameworks: the first is designed for embedding models like BERT (Devlin et al., 2019), which excel in processing context-rich information, while the second framework targets large language models (LLMs), leveraging their expansive capabilities in understanding and generating human-like text.

POS	Template	English Translation
NOUN	[SUBJECT]은/는 <seed word>이/가 있다.	[SUBJECT] has <seed word>.
ADJECTIVE	[SUBJECT]은/는 <seed word> 사람이다.	[SUBJECT] is a[n] <seed word> person.

Table 2: **Templates for Sentence Generation.** The table shows two different sentence templates based on the POS tagging of a seed word. English versions of Korean templates are provided for reference.

The first framework utilizes an embedding model as its base, adding two classifiers on top. Each classifier predicts the directions of a given text in the warmth and competence dimensions, respectively. Namely, the two classifiers perform multi-class classification, identifying one of three potential directions: high, low, or none. Formally, we use two classifiers, f_w and f_c, to predict warmth and competence directions, respectively. These prediction tasks are formulated as multi-class classification problems with cross-entropy losses, $\mathcal{L}_w$ and $\mathcal{L}_c$; $\mathcal{L}_w = -\sum_{t \in D} W(t) \cdot \log(f_w(t))$ and $\mathcal{L}_c = -\sum_{t \in D} C(t) \cdot \log(f_c(t))$, where t is a text in the dataset D, and $W(t)$ and $C(t)$ are warmth and competence directions of the text t. The final loss of the model is the sum of the prediction losses: $\mathcal{L} = \alpha\mathcal{L}_w + \beta\mathcal{L}_c$. where α and β are hyperparameters.

As for the second framework, we implement in-context learning with LLMs such as Llama. (Touvron et al., 2023). A small number of samples selected from the KoSCM dataset is provided to an LLM in the prompt. We select four samples for our experiment. In-context learning performance is sensitive to factors such as the selection and order of demonstration examples (Dong et al., 2024). To address this, we test the model using two approaches: first, by utilizing carefully selected samples based on a distance metric, and second, by randomly selecting samples from the KoSCM dataset to eliminate selection bias. The prompt utilized for the experiment is displayed in Table 3.

4.2 Experimental Setup

We evaluate the proposed methods on the following models:

- Multilingual BERT (mBERT): A masked language model pre-trained on 104 languages with 110M parameters. We use `BERT-Base, Multilingual Cased`, which is recommended for languages with non-Latin alphabets.
- Multilingual Sentence Transformer (mST): A modification of the Sentence Transformer (Reimers and Gurevych, 2019) aimed at adapting it for a new language using multilingual knowledge distillation. The pre-trained model `paraphrase-multilingual-MiniLM-L12-v2` is used for the experiment.
- Korean Llama (kLlama): Llama 3.2 fine-tuned with Korean texts using instruction tuning. The model `Bllossom/llama-3.2-Korean-Bllossom-3B` (Choi et al., 2024) uploaded to the HuggingFace models is utilized.
  - $\text{kLlama}_{\text{random}}$: kLlama evaluated using randomly selected samples. In all few-shot learning experiments with kLlama, we utilize four samples.

All models are implemented with PyTorch (Paszke et al., 2019) and Huggingface's Transformers (Wolf et al., 2020). For training, we use the Adam optimizer (Kingma and Ba, 2015) and set the learning rate from $\{1e-05, 2e-05\}$, an epoch as 10, a dropout rate of 0.3, and hyperparameters α and β as 1 . All experiments are conducted on a Nvidia Quatro RTX 5000, 16 GB memory GPU in a machine with Intel(R) Xeon(R) Silver 4214 CPU @ 2.20GHz.

4.3 Evaluation

Using our proposed method, we evaluate how effectively models trained on the KoSCM dataset predict stereotypes. To assess the effectiveness of these models, we measure the accuracy of warmth and competence prediction on the test data. The results are presented in Table 4, which illustrates both the average and standard deviation of the prediction accuracies.

In our analysis, we observe a significant gap between the first and second frameworks. The first framework, which utilizes an embedding model, demonstrates competitive performance with high prediction accuracies for both warmth and competence. Notably, mBERT is the best-performing

Prompt
{"role": "system", "content": "당신은 편견 판별 서비스를 제공합니다. 주어진 글의 온기와 능력 점수를 -1, 0, 1 중에 하나로 매깁니다. You provide a stereotype detection service. Score the warmth and competence of a given sentence in one of the three scores: -1, 0, or 1."},
{"role": "user", "content":<sentence>},   {"role": "assistant", "content": "온기 <warmth>, 능력 <competence>"} } × num. samples

Table 3: **Prompt for Few-Shot Learning.** The table above shows the prompt used for few-shot learning with LLMs. After the system prompt, a sentence is provided as the user prompt, and the assistant predicts warmth and competence directions. The format of the last two prompts can be duplicated based on the chosen number of samples.

Model	Warmth	Competence
mBERT	0.9230 (0.006)	0.9376 (0.005)
mST	0.9172 (0.010)	0.9240 (0.006)
kLlama	0.5376 (0.012)	0.5889 (0.002)
$\text{kLlama}_{\text{random}}$	0.5002 (0.003)	0.5031 (0.005)

Table 4: **Evaluation of KoSCM.** The evaluated performance of the three selected models is displayed. The average accuracy of warmth and competence predictions is presented. The standard deviation is indicated within the parentheses.

model, achieving accuracies of 0.9230 for warmth and 0.9376 for competence prediction. In contrast, the second framework designed for LLMs exhibits much lower performance, with accuracy scores of around 0.5 across all cases. The performance is particularly poor when using prompts with randomly chosen samples for each prediction. Although carefully curating the samples does enhance the performance slightly, the accuracies still remain modest at 0.5376 and 0.5889 for warmth and competence prediction, respectively. We surmise that the performance may have been affected by the limited data distribution of kLlama, as research shows that the diversity of pretraining corpora significantly impacts in-context learning performance (Shin et al., 2022; Raventós et al., 2023).

To evaluate the generalization capacity of the KoSCM, we conduct additional tests to determine whether the computational analysis aligns with and supports the results obtained from the SCM survey conducted in South Korea (Cuddy et al., 2009). We leverage the best-performing model, mBERT, from the evaluation to measure the stereotype directions of various social groups. For this analysis, we utilize the Korean Offensive Language Dataset (KOLD) dataset (Jeong et al., 2022). The dataset consists of comments collected from news articles and videos, with labels indicating group information among the 21 target group labels tailored to Korean culture. We use this group information for analysis. From the existing group labels, we select 19 groups that intersect with the 23 social groups in the survey.

We assess the warmth and competence directions of texts that comment on a target group and calculate the average warmth and competence directions. Then, the groups are clustered using hierarchical cluster analysis, following the method of Cuddy et al. (2009). The results are illustrated in the SCM dimension in Figure 2. In general, we observe a significant overlap between our results and the survey findings. For instance, social groups such as "women," "blue-collar," and "Protestants" fall into the low-competence/high-warmth cluster, while groups like the "poor" and "unemployed" are categorized as low-competence/low-warmth. However, there are also outliers. For example, the group "public functionaries" is positioned in the high-competence/high-warmth cluster in our figure, but it falls within the low-competence/low-warmth cluster in the survey plot. This discrepancy may come from the lack of data since outliers like "public functionaries" have insufficient data, with only nine text samples contributing to their classification.

5 SCM as a Pancultural Tool

In this section, we explore the applicability of the proposed computational method of the SCM for analyzing stereotypes across various languages and cultures. Based on the survey in Cuddy et al. (2009), we examine three key hypotheses of SCM: (1) the two dimensions hypothesis, (2) the ambivalent stereotypes hypothesis, and (3) the social structural correlates hypothesis.

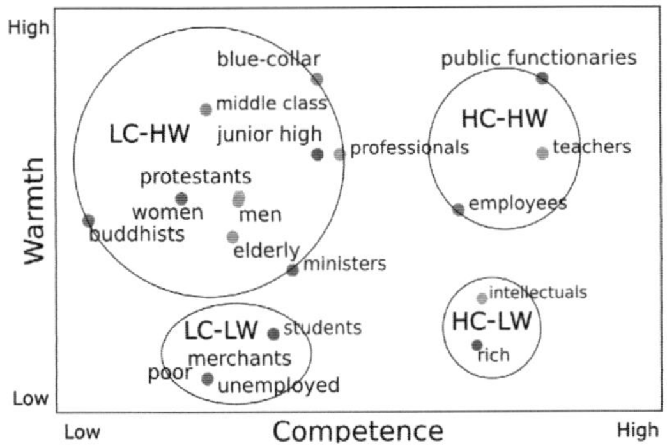

Figure 2: **Stereotypes of Groups Projected to the SCM dimension.** Social groups are mapped onto the SCM dimension according to their predicted warmth and competence by KoSCM.

Two Dimensions Hypothesis The first hypothesis posits that (1) within each sample, groups will be positioned along the dimensions of warmth and competence and that (2) based on their warmth and competence scores, groups will form multiple clusters, including some at both the high and low ends of each dimension. As shown in Figure 2, our results support this hypothesis, as groups are mapped along the warmth and competence dimensions. The figure reveals a structure that aligns with the SCM survey. Notably, we identify four distinct clusters that reflect both high and low scores on each dimension. Consistent with the survey findings, the largest cluster is the low-competence/high-warmth group, which encloses the majority of the sampled groups. Yet we observe that the high-competence/high-warmth cluster in the survey has a lower average warmth score compared to our findings. As discussed in Section 4, this dissimilarity may be attributed to outliers, such as the "public functionaries" category, which suffered from insufficient data.

Ambivalent Stereotypes Hypothesis This hypothesis proposes that (1) within any given sample, there will be significant variations in perceptions of warmth and competence across different social groups and that (2) it predicts that cluster analyses will reveal at least one high-competence/low-warmth cluster and one low-competence/high-warmth cluster. This indicates that numerous groups are characterized as being adept in one area—either warmth or competence—while being perceived as lacking in the other.

Figure 2 shows four distinct clusters at each end, which supports the hypothesis that the four clusters of stereotype content, defined within the warmth-competence space, have universal characteristics. We observe that the groups "women" and "elderly" fall within the low-competence/high-warmth group. This supports the theory that groups seen as gentle but useless—often associated with a "pitying" prejudice—frequently include traditional women and older people. These groups are often viewed as having strong communal traits but lacking agentic qualities, representing a significant stereotype identified in the existing literature. (Jackman, 1994; Glick and Fiske, 2001b,a). In contrast, another significant stereotyped group includes those seen as skilled yet dishonest. Our analysis emphasizes individuals labeled as "intellectuals" and "rich" in this group. It shows that "envious" prejudice frequently targets those considered alarmingly skilled yet untrustworthy (Glick and Fiske, 2001b,a; Fiske et al., 2002; Glick, 2002). This dynamic highlights the complex relationship between admiration and disdain influencing societal perceptions.

Social Structural Correlates Hypothesis The social structural correlates hypothesis suggests that (1) within each sample, perceived status is expected to positively correlate with competence and that (2) perceived competition is anticipated to negatively correlate with warmth. In the survey, participants are asked to evaluate the perceived status and competition of various social groups. As we cannot access the information of commentators in the KOLD dataset, we focus on validating the first part of the hypothesis by examining the relationship between perceived status and competence ratings.

In our analysis, we utilize average wage statistics as a measure of perceived status, recognizing that socioeconomic status is a complex, multidimensional construct influenced by various factors, with income being a key component (Havranek et al., 2015). Individuals with lower incomes often face a lack of economic resources, which leads to social disadvantages such as limited access to quality education, poor working conditions, housing insecurity, and living in unsafe neighborhoods. These factors collectively contribute to a lower perceived status within society. Thus, we use income information as a symbolic indicator of perceived status, emphasizing its significant effect on individuals' overall social standing.

The Korean Ministry of Employment and Labor publishes the Current Status of Wage Distribution

	status-competence corr.
koSCM	0.71
South Korea	0.64
Universal Average	0.79

Table 5: **The correlation between perceived status and competence.** The table displays the correlation coefficient between perceived status and competence

by Business Characteristics every year [3]. We reference the 2024 report to extract the average income across different social groups. This report offers average wage data categorized by labor industry, gender, and years of experience. Due to the ambiguity in categorizing jobs within non-occupational social groups like "intellectuals" and "rich," we exclude these groups from this analysis. The report includes gender data for all jobs, so the average income for each gender is computed to represent the perceived status of the groups "women" and "men."

Next, we calculate the correlation coefficient between the average wage and competence for the social groups. The correlation coefficient is computed as $\mathrm{cov}(\text{wage}, \text{competence})/(\sigma_{\text{wage}} \cdot \sigma_{\text{competence}})$. As shown in Table 5, the calculated correlation value is 0.71, a positive correlation that supports the hypothesis. In the survey, South Korea has a correlation of 0.64, and the average of all 13 surveys shows a correlation of 0.79.

6 Conclusion

In this paper, we propose the Korean Stereotype Content Model (KoSCM), a theory-grounded stereotype model that adapts the existing SCM for the Korean language and culture. We develop a Korean warmth-competence lexicon by translating existing English lexicons and curating a Korean dictionary of seed words. This translated lexicon is used to train the KoSCM, a classification model for predicting directions in warmth and competence dimensions. Then, we utilize KoSCM to analyze stereotypes of age, gender, and religious groups in Korean texts, comparing the results to the social psychology survey. To test whether the computational approach of SCM can be applied cross-culturally, we examine three core hypotheses of the SCM: the two-dimensional structure of stereotypes, the presence of ambivalent stereotypes, and the relationship between stereotypes and social structure.

This study marks the first attempt to adapt the SCM to the Korean language, aiming to enhance the understanding of stereotypes across languages. In the future, we plan to expand our research by incorporating additional languages and utilizing the warmth-competence framework to develop an algorithm that can guide and transform stereotypes present in sentences.

Limitations

We recognize several limitations that may impact the validity of our findings. Despite our efforts to minimize authorial bias, there remains a possibility for such bias to influence both the experimental design and analysis. For example, the process of clustering social groups is inherently affected by the selection of hyperparameters, which can significantly alter the resulting clusters. Additionally, our decisions in curating prompts for sampling from the dataset and crafting the prompt texts introduce further elements of bias. Hence, these decisions may result in selection bias, which could ultimately impact the conclusions drawn from our study.

Furthermore, our data and experiments are limited by scale constraints. Unlike the abundance of resources available for English models and datasets, there is a significant lack of open-source Korean datasets and models, which has limited our efforts. This insufficient data may suggest that the models utilized in this research are not performing at the same level as their English counterparts. For instance, while conducting back-translation in the data curation process, we observed significant noise in the generated data, which might indicate the difficulties posed by limited resources.

Ethical Considerations

We curate and publish the KoSCM dataset, which is used for training and evaluating KoSCM. This dataset is based on a specific social psychology theory known as the SCM, meaning our research investigates stereotypes within this particular framework. As a result, our dataset and analysis do not encompass the complete range of perspectives on stereotypes. Therefore, we advise researchers utilizing the KoSCM dataset and the proposed translation framework to be mindful of these limitations and encourage them to explore additional methodologies to gain a more comprehensive understanding of stereotypes.

[3]Ministry of Employment and Labor website

We strongly recommend against using this research for harmful purposes, including the promotion and dissemination of stereotypical biases.

References

Yonatan Belinkov and Yonatan Bisk. 2018. Synthetic and natural noise both break neural machine translation. In *International Conference on Learning Representations*.

Shaily Bhatt, Sunipa Dev, Partha Talukdar, Shachi Dave, and Vinodkumar Prabhakaran. 2022. Re-contextualizing fairness in NLP: The case of India. In *Proceedings of the 2nd Conference of the Asia-Pacific Chapter of the Association for Computational Linguistics and the 12th International Joint Conference on Natural Language Processing (Volume 1: Long Papers)*, pages 727–740, Online only. Association for Computational Linguistics.

Mukul Bhutani, Kevin Robinson, Vinodkumar Prabhakaran, Shachi Dave, and Sunipa Dev. 2024. SeeGULL multilingual: a dataset of geo-culturally situated stereotypes. In *Proceedings of the 62nd Annual Meeting of the Association for Computational Linguistics (Volume 2: Short Papers)*, pages 842–854, Bangkok, Thailand. Association for Computational Linguistics.

Yang Trista Cao, Anna Sotnikova, Hal Daumé III, Rachel Rudinger, and Linda Zou. 2022. Theory-grounded measurement of U.S. social stereotypes in English language models. In *Proceedings of the 2022 Conference of the North American Chapter of the Association for Computational Linguistics: Human Language Technologies*, pages 1276–1295, Seattle, United States. Association for Computational Linguistics.

Rodrigo Alejandro Chávez Mulsa and Gerasimos Spanakis. 2020. Evaluating bias in Dutch word embeddings. In *Proceedings of the Second Workshop on Gender Bias in Natural Language Processing*, pages 56–71, Barcelona, Spain (Online). Association for Computational Linguistics.

ChangSu Choi, Yongbin Jeong, Seoyoon Park, Inho Won, HyeonSeok Lim, SangMin Kim, Yejee Kang, Chanhyuk Yoon, Jaewan Park, Yiseul Lee, HyeJin Lee, Younggyun Hahm, Hansaem Kim, and KyungTae Lim. 2024. Optimizing language augmentation for multilingual large language models: A case study on Korean. In *Proceedings of the 2024 Joint International Conference on Computational Linguistics, Language Resources and Evaluation (LREC-COLING 2024)*, pages 12514–12526, Torino, Italia. ELRA and ICCL.

Amy J. C. Cuddy, Susan T. Fiske, Virginia S. Y. Kwan, Peter Glick, Stéphanie Demoulin, Jacques-Philippe Leyens, Michael Harris Bond, Jean-Claude Croizet, Naomi Ellemers, Ed Sleebos, Tin Tin Htun, Hyun-Jeong Kim, Greg Maio, Judi Perry, Kristina Petkova, Valery Todorov, Rosa Rodríguez-Bailón, Elena Morales, Miguel Moya, Marisol Palacios, Vanessa Smith, Rolando Perez, Jorge Vala, and Rene Ziegler. 2009. Stereotype content model across cultures: Towards universal similarities and some differences. *British Journal of Social Psychology*, 48(1):1–33.

Jacob Devlin, Ming-Wei Chang, Kenton Lee, and Kristina Toutanova. 2019. BERT: Pre-training of deep bidirectional transformers for language understanding. In *Proceedings of the 2019 Conference of the North American Chapter of the Association for Computational Linguistics: Human Language Technologies, Volume 1 (Long and Short Papers)*, pages 4171–4186, Minneapolis, Minnesota. Association for Computational Linguistics.

Tobias Domhan and Felix Hieber. 2017. Using target-side monolingual data for neural machine translation through multi-task learning. In *Proceedings of the 2017 Conference on Empirical Methods in Natural Language Processing*, pages 1500–1505, Copenhagen, Denmark. Association for Computational Linguistics.

Qingxiu Dong, Lei Li, Damai Dai, Ce Zheng, Jingyuan Ma, Rui Li, Heming Xia, Jingjing Xu, Zhiyong Wu, Baobao Chang, Xu Sun, Lei Li, and Zhifang Sui. 2024. A survey on in-context learning. In *Proceedings of the 2024 Conference on Empirical Methods in Natural Language Processing*, pages 1107–1128, Miami, Florida, USA. Association for Computational Linguistics.

S. T. Fiske, A. J. C. Cuddy, P. Glick, and J. Xu. 2002. A model of (often mixed) stereotype content: competence and warmth respectively follow from perceived status and competition. *Journal of Personality and Social Psychology*, 82:878–902.

Susan T. Fiske. 2018. Stereotype content: Warmth and competence endure. *Current Directions in Psychological Science*, 27(2):67–73. PMID: 29755213.

Kathleen Fraser, Svetlana Kiritchenko, and Isar Nejadgholi. 2024. How does stereotype content differ across data sources? In *Proceedings of the 13th Joint Conference on Lexical and Computational Semantics (*SEM 2024)*, pages 18–34, Mexico City, Mexico. Association for Computational Linguistics.

Kathleen C. Fraser, Isar Nejadgholi, and Svetlana Kiritchenko. 2021. Understanding and countering stereotypes: A computational approach to the stereotype content model. In *Proceedings of the 59th Annual Meeting of the Association for Computational Linguistics and the 11th International Joint Conference on Natural Language Processing (Volume 1: Long Papers)*, pages 600–616, Online. Association for Computational Linguistics.

Yacine Gaci, Boualem Benatallah, Fabio Casati, and Khalid Benabdeslem. 2023. Societal versus encoded stereotypes in text encoders. In *2023 IEEE 35th International Conference on Tools with Artificial Intelligence (ICTAI)*, pages 46–53.

Peter Glick. 2002. Sacrificial lambs dressed in wolves' clothing: Envious prejudice, ideology, and the scapegoating of jews.

Peter Glick and Susan T Fiske. 2001a. An ambivalent alliance: Hostile and benevolent sexism as complementary justifications for gender inequality. *American psychologist*, 56(2):109.

Peter Glick and Susan T. Fiske. 2001b. Ambivalent sexism. volume 33 of *Advances in Experimental Social Psychology*, pages 115–188. Academic Press.

Edward P. Havranek, Mahasin S. Mujahid, Donald A. Barr, Irene V. Blair, Meryl S. Cohen, Salvador Cruz-Flores, George Davey-Smith, Cheryl R. Dennison-Himmelfarb, Michael S. Lauer, Debra W. Lockwood, Milagros Rosal, and Clyde W. Yancy. 2015. Social determinants of risk and outcomes for cardiovascular disease. *Circulation*, 132(9):873–898.

Brienna Herold, James Waller, and Raja Kushalnagar. 2022. Applying the stereotype content model to assess disability bias in popular pre-trained NLP models underlying AI-based assistive technologies. In *Ninth Workshop on Speech and Language Processing for Assistive Technologies (SLPAT-2022)*, pages 58–65, Dublin, Ireland. Association for Computational Linguistics.

Mary R Jackman. 1994. *The velvet glove: Paternalism and conflict in gender, class, and race relations*. Univ of California Press.

Younghoon Jeong, Juhyun Oh, Jongwon Lee, Jaimeen Ahn, Jihyung Moon, Sungjoon Park, and Alice Oh. 2022. KOLD: Korean offensive language dataset. In *Proceedings of the 2022 Conference on Empirical Methods in Natural Language Processing*, pages 10818–10833, Abu Dhabi, United Arab Emirates. Association for Computational Linguistics.

Yiping Jin, Leo Wanner, and Aneesh Moideen Koya. 2024. Disentangling hate across target identities. *Preprint*, arXiv:2410.10332.

Diederik P. Kingma and Jimmy Ba. 2015. Adam: A method for stochastic optimization. In *3rd International Conference on Learning Representations, ICLR 2015, San Diego, CA, USA, May 7-9, 2015, Conference Track Proceedings*.

Mascha Kurpicz-Briki. 2020. Cultural differences in bias? origin and gender bias in pre-trained german and french word embeddings. *Arbor-ciencia Pensamiento Y Cultura*.

Anne Lauscher, Rafik Takieddin, Simone Paolo Ponzetto, and Goran Glavaš. 2020. AraWEAT: Multidimensional analysis of biases in Arabic word embeddings. In *Proceedings of the Fifth Arabic Natural Language Processing Workshop*, pages 192–199, Barcelona, Spain (Online). Association for Computational Linguistics.

Sheng Liang, Philipp Dufter, and Hinrich Schütze. 2020. Monolingual and multilingual reduction of gender bias in contextualized representations. In *Proceedings of the 28th International Conference on Computational Linguistics*, pages 5082–5093, Barcelona, Spain (Online). International Committee on Computational Linguistics.

Vijit Malik, Sunipa Dev, Akihiro Nishi, Nanyun Peng, and Kai-Wei Chang. 2021. Socially aware bias measurements for hindi language representations. *CoRR*, abs/2110.07871.

Chandler May, Alex Wang, Shikha Bordia, Samuel R. Bowman, and Rachel Rudinger. 2019. On measuring social biases in sentence encoders. In *Proceedings of the 2019 Conference of the North American Chapter of the Association for Computational Linguistics: Human Language Technologies, Volume 1 (Long and Short Papers)*, pages 622–628, Minneapolis, Minnesota. Association for Computational Linguistics.

Mario Mina, Júlia Falcão, and Aitor Gonzalez-Agirre. 2024. Exploring the relationship between intrinsic stigma in masked language models and training data using the stereotype content model. In *Proceedings of the Fifth Workshop on Resources and ProcessIng of linguistic, para-linguistic and extra-linguistic Data from people with various forms of cognitive/psychiatric/developmental impairments @LREC-COLING 2024*, pages 54–67, Torino, Italia. ELRA and ICCL.

Jihyung Moon, Won Ik Cho, and Junbum Lee. 2020. BEEP! Korean corpus of online news comments for toxic speech detection. In *Proceedings of the Eighth International Workshop on Natural Language Processing for Social Media*, pages 25–31, Online. Association for Computational Linguistics.

Gandalf Nicolas, Xuechunzi Bai, and Susan Fiske. 2019. Automated dictionary creation for analyzing text: An illustration from stereotype content.

Gandalf Nicolas and Aylin Caliskan. 2024. Directionality and representativeness are differentiable components of stereotypes in large language models. *PNAS Nexus*, 3(11):pgae493.

Ali Omrani, Alireza Salkhordeh Ziabari, Charles Yu, Preni Golazizian, Brendan Kennedy, Mohammad Atari, Heng Ji, and Morteza Dehghani. 2023. Social-group-agnostic bias mitigation via the stereotype content model. In *Proceedings of the 61st Annual Meeting of the Association for Computational Linguistics (Volume 1: Long Papers)*, pages 4123–4139, Toronto, Canada. Association for Computational Linguistics.

Adam Paszke, Sam Gross, Francisco Massa, Adam Lerer, James Bradbury, Gregory Chanan, Trevor Killeen, Zeming Lin, Natalia Gimelshein, Luca Antiga, Alban Desmaison, Andreas Köpf, Edward Z. Yang, Zach DeVito, Martin Raison, Alykhan Tejani, Sasank Chilamkurthy, Benoit Steiner, Lu Fang, Junjie

Bai, and Soumith Chintala. 2019. Pytorch: An imperative style, high-performance deep learning library. *CoRR*, abs/1912.01703.

Arun K. Pujari, Ansh Mittal, Anshuman Padhi, Anshul Jain, Mukesh Jadon, and Vikas Kumar. 2020. Debiasing gender biased hindi words with word-embedding. In *Proceedings of the 2019 2nd International Conference on Algorithms, Computing and Artificial Intelligence*, ACAI '19, page 450–456, New York, NY, USA. Association for Computing Machinery.

Allan Raventós, Mansheej Paul, Feng Chen, and Surya Ganguli. 2023. Pretraining task diversity and the emergence of non-bayesian in-context learning for regression. In *Advances in Neural Information Processing Systems*, volume 36, pages 14228–14246. Curran Associates, Inc.

Nils Reimers and Iryna Gurevych. 2019. Sentence-BERT: Sentence embeddings using Siamese BERT-networks. In *Proceedings of the 2019 Conference on Empirical Methods in Natural Language Processing and the 9th International Joint Conference on Natural Language Processing (EMNLP-IJCNLP)*, pages 3982–3992, Hong Kong, China. Association for Computational Linguistics.

Nithya Sambasivan, Erin Arnesen, Ben Hutchinson, Tulsee Doshi, and Vinodkumar Prabhakaran. 2021. Re-imagining algorithmic fairness in india and beyond. In *Proceedings of the 2021 ACM Conference on Fairness, Accountability, and Transparency*, FAccT '21, page 315–328, New York, NY, USA. Association for Computing Machinery.

Carolin M. Schuster, Maria-Alexandra Dinisor, Shashwat Ghatiwala, and Georg Groh. 2024. Profiling bias in llms: Stereotype dimensions in contextual word embeddings. *Preprint*, arXiv:2411.16527.

Rico Sennrich, Barry Haddow, and Alexandra Birch. 2016. Improving neural machine translation models with monolingual data. In *Proceedings of the 54th Annual Meeting of the Association for Computational Linguistics (Volume 1: Long Papers)*, pages 86–96, Berlin, Germany. Association for Computational Linguistics.

Seongjin Shin, Sang-Woo Lee, Hwijeen Ahn, Sungdong Kim, HyoungSeok Kim, Boseop Kim, Kyunghyun Cho, Gichang Lee, Woomyoung Park, Jung-Woo Ha, and Nako Sung. 2022. On the effect of pretraining corpora on in-context learning by a large-scale language model. In *Proceedings of the 2022 Conference of the North American Chapter of the Association for Computational Linguistics: Human Language Technologies*, pages 5168–5186, Seattle, United States. Association for Computational Linguistics.

Masashi Takeshita, Yuki Katsumata, Rafal Rzepka, and Kenji Araki. 2020. Can existing methods debias languages other than English? first attempt to analyze and mitigate Japanese word embeddings. In *Proceedings of the Second Workshop on Gender Bias in Natural Language Processing*, pages 44–55, Barcelona, Spain (Online). Association for Computational Linguistics.

NLLB Team, Marta R. Costa-jussà, James Cross, Onur Çelebi, Maha Elbayad, Kenneth Heafield, Kevin Heffernan, Elahe Kalbassi, Janice Lam, Daniel Licht, Jean Maillard, Anna Sun, Skyler Wang, Guillaume Wenzek, Al Youngblood, Bapi Akula, Loic Barrault, Gabriel Mejia Gonzalez, Prangthip Hansanti, John Hoffman, Semarley Jarrett, Kaushik Ram Sadagopan, Dirk Rowe, Shannon Spruit, Chau Tran, Pierre Andrews, Necip Fazil Ayan, Shruti Bhosale, Sergey Edunov, Angela Fan, Cynthia Gao, Vedanuj Goswami, Francisco Guzmán, Philipp Koehn, Alexandre Mourachko, Christophe Ropers, Safiyyah Saleem, Holger Schwenk, and Jeff Wang. 2022. No language left behind: Scaling human-centered machine translation. *Preprint*, arXiv:2207.04672.

Alexandra Timmer. 2011. Toward an Anti-Stereotyping Approach for the European Court of Human Rights. *Human Rights Law Review*, 11(4):707–738.

Hugo Touvron, Thibaut Lavril, Gautier Izacard, Xavier Martinet, Marie-Anne Lachaux, Timothée Lacroix, Baptiste Rozière, Naman Goyal, Eric Hambro, Faisal Azhar, Aurelien Rodriguez, Armand Joulin, Edouard Grave, and Guillaume Lample. 2023. Llama: Open and efficient foundation language models. *Preprint*, arXiv:2302.13971.

Eddie Ungless, Amy Rafferty, Hrichika Nag, and Björn Ross. 2022. A robust bias mitigation procedure based on the stereotype content model. In *Proceedings of the Fifth Workshop on Natural Language Processing and Computational Social Science (NLP+CSS)*, pages 207–217, Abu Dhabi, UAE. Association for Computational Linguistics.

Thomas Wolf, Lysandre Debut, Victor Sanh, Julien Chaumond, Clement Delangue, Anthony Moi, Pierric Cistac, Tim Rault, Remi Louf, Morgan Funtowicz, Joe Davison, Sam Shleifer, Patrick von Platen, Clara Ma, Yacine Jernite, Julien Plu, Canwen Xu, Teven Le Scao, Sylvain Gugger, Mariama Drame, Quentin Lhoest, and Alexander Rush. 2020. Transformers: State-of-the-art natural language processing. In *Proceedings of the 2020 Conference on Empirical Methods in Natural Language Processing: System Demonstrations*, pages 38–45, Online. Association for Computational Linguistics.

Jieyu Zhao, Subhabrata Mukherjee, Saghar Hosseini, Kai-Wei Chang, and Ahmed Hassan Awadallah. 2020. Gender bias in multilingual embeddings and cross-lingual transfer. In *Proceedings of the 58th Annual Meeting of the Association for Computational Linguistics*, pages 2896–2907, Online. Association for Computational Linguistics.

Pei Zhou, Weijia Shi, Jieyu Zhao, Kuan-Hao Huang, Muhao Chen, Ryan Cotterell, and Kai-Wei Chang. 2019. Examining gender bias in languages with grammatical gender. In *Proceedings of the 2019 Conference on Empirical Methods in Natural Language*

Processing and the 9th International Joint Conference on Natural Language Processing (EMNLP-IJCNLP), pages 5276–5284, Hong Kong, China. Association for Computational Linguistics.

A Templates for Sentence Generation

In this section, we describe the details of the templates used for generating sentences in Section 3. The templates are curated based on the part-of-speech (POS) tagging of the seed words. The curated seed words contain noun and adjective tags. Based on those tags, we utilize the two templates in Table 2. The subject words for the templates are chosen carefully to ensure that the generated sentences do not contain information about specific social groups. For instance, the pronouns "he" and "she" indicate a person's gender. We chose to avoid using these pronouns as subjects because our objective is to develop a dataset focused on learning the dimensions of warmth and competence. The subject words used for the templates are: ["나 I", "너 You", "우리 We", "그 사람 A person", "저 사람 That person", "이 사람 This person"]. With the curated templates, a total of 1,710 sentences are generated. Here are sample sentences generated using the templates: "나는 능력이 있다. I have competence.", "그 사람은 친절한 사람이다. A person is a friendly person.".

LLM-C3MOD: A Human-LLM Collaborative System for Cross-Cultural Hate Speech Moderation

Junyeong Park[◇,*], **Seogyeong Jeong**[◇,*], **Seyoung Song**[◇,*], **Yohan Lee**[◇,†], **Alice Oh**[◇]

[◇]KAIST, [†]ETRI

{jjjunyeong9986, sg.jeong28, seyoung.song}@kaist.ac.kr, carep@etri.re.kr, alice.oh@kaist.edu

Abstract

Warning: *This paper contains content that may be offensive or upsetting*

Content moderation is a global challenge, yet major tech platforms prioritize high-resource languages, leaving low-resource languages with scarce native moderators. Since effective moderation depends on understanding contextual cues, this imbalance increases the risk of improper moderation due to non-native moderators' limited cultural understanding. Through a user study, we identify that non-native moderators struggle with interpreting *culturally-specific knowledge*, *sentiment*, and *internet culture* in the hate speech moderation. To assist them, we present **LLM-C3MOD**, a human-LLM collaborative pipeline with three steps: (1) RAG-enhanced cultural context annotations; (2) initial LLM-based moderation; and (3) targeted human moderation for cases lacking LLM consensus. Evaluated on a Korean hate speech dataset with Indonesian and German participants, our system achieves 78% accuracy (surpassing GPT-4o's 71% baseline), while reducing human workload by 83.6%. Notably, human moderators excel at nuanced contents where LLMs struggle. Our findings suggest that non-native moderators, when properly supported by LLMs, can effectively contribute to cross-cultural hate speech moderation.

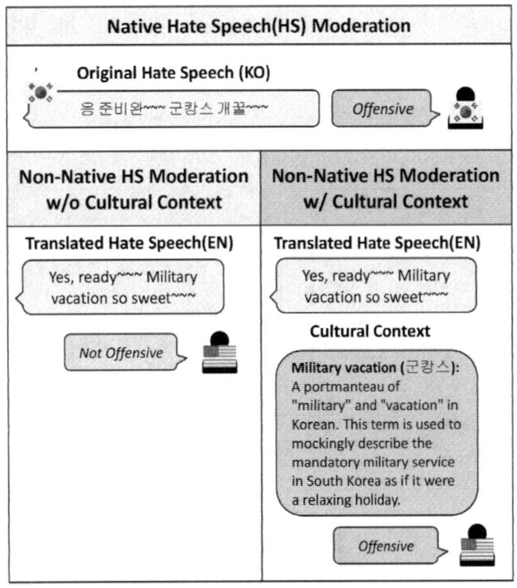

Figure 1: An example of a non-native hate speech moderator performing hate speech detection with and without cultural context.

1 Introduction

Content moderation has evolved into a global challenge, yet major tech platforms concentrate their resources primarily on high-resource languages (Witness, 2023). Meta allocates 87% of its misinformation budget to English content despite only 9% of users being English speakers, exemplifying a systemic bias in content moderation (Milmo, 2021). This imbalance has led to increased hate speech and misinformation in non-English contexts, alongside risks of improper content moderation due to insufficient cultural understanding (Nigatu and Raji, 2024; Elswah, 2024).

Given the scarcity of native moderators for many languages, we argue that exploring methods for non-native hate speech moderation is crucial. As exemplified in Figure 1, non-native moderators cannot simply rely on machine translation, as hate speech moderation task requires deeper cultural and political context to make an informed decision (Chan et al., 2024; Lee et al., 2024). Recent research has explored using Large Language Models (LLMs) for content moderation (Kolla et al., 2024a; Jha et al., 2024) and hate speech detection (Roy et al., 2023; Zhang et al., 2024), but primarily focuses on single-language scenarios, leaving cross-cultural challenges largely unexplored (Pawar et al., 2024; Hee et al., 2024).

[*]Equal contribution.

Proceedings of the 3rd Workshop on Cross-Cultural Considerations in NLP (C3NLP 2025), pages 71–88
May 4, 2025

We present **LLM-C3MOD**, a system that leverages retrieval-augmented generation (RAG)-enhanced LLMs (Lewis et al., 2020) to assist non-native moderators through three key components: (1) cultural context annotation, (2) initial LLM-based moderation, and (3) targeted human moderation. Our system leverages web search results to generate reliable cultural annotations, helping non-native moderators better understand culturally specific expressions and nuances. Also, through LLM-based initial screening, we maintain efficient workload distribution between automated and human moderation.

We evaluate **LLM-C3MOD** on KOLD (Jeong et al., 2022), a Korean hate speech dataset, with non-native participants from Indonesia and Germany. Our system achieves 78% accuracy (surpassing the 71% GPT-4o baseline) while reducing human workload by 83.6%. Notably, providing cultural context annotations improves non-native moderator accuracy from 22% to 61%. We found that human moderators particularly excel at nuanced tasks where LLMs struggle, such as interpreting internet culture, including memes and their cultural references.

Our main contributions are as follows:

- We empirically identify key challenges faced by non-native moderators in cross-cultural hate speech moderation through user study.
- We develop a RAG-enhanced cultural annotation system that demonstrably improves hate speech moderation accuracy for both humans and LLMs.
- We propose **LLM-C3MOD**, an effective human-LLM collaboration pipeline that strategically integrates machine efficiency with human judgment.

Our findings demonstrate that non-native moderators, when properly supported by LLMs, can contribute effectively to cross-cultural hate speech moderation, addressing critical needs in global online safety.

2 Related Work

2.1 Hate Speech Moderation: Cultural Considerations

Hate speech moderation is a type of content moderation that involves various tasks, including detecting (Park and Fung, 2017; Vidgen et al., 2021), explaining (Sap et al., 2020; ElSherief et al., 2021; Mathew et al., 2021), and countering (Masud et al., 2022; Chung et al., 2019) hate speech on online platforms. One of the challenges in this domain lies in understanding diverse cultural and contextual cues that differ across countries and regions (Hee et al., 2024).

To address this challenge, recent works have introduced hate speech datasets that incorporate various linguistic and cultural factors (Lee et al., 2023; Jeong et al., 2022; Jin et al., 2024; Lee et al., 2024; Arango Monnar et al., 2022; Deng et al., 2022; Demus et al., 2022; Maronikolakis et al., 2022; Ye et al., 2024; Muhammad et al., 2025). Another recent works have proposed culturally-specific hate speech moderation methods (Li et al., 2024; Ye et al., 2024). Furthermore, Masud et al. (2024) explore the potential of utilizing LLMs as hate speech annotators representing specific cultural or geographical groups. However, these approaches largely focus on moderation within specific monocultural contexts. This leaves a gap in addressing the complexities of cross-cultural hate speech moderation where human moderators are required to handle content from unfamiliar cultural or linguistic contexts. In this work, we examine the difficulties of non-native annotators and their potential in cross-cultural hate speech moderation.

2.2 Hate Speech Moderation: Human-LLM Collaboration

Recent works have investigated LLM-assisted content moderation (Kolla et al., 2024b; Kumar et al., 2024) and hate speech moderation (Vishwamitra et al., 2024; Kang and Qian, 2024; Wang et al., 2023; Yang et al., 2023; Podolak et al., 2024). However, for tasks that are heavily context-dependent, such as content moderation, human moderators are known to outperform automated systems by making more nuanced decisions that consider contextual subtleties (Alkhatib and Bernstein, 2019; Gorwa et al., 2020).

Thus, to utilize both human intelligence and machine moderator's scalability and efficiency, there is growing exploration of human-machine collaboration for hate speech moderation (Jhaver et al., 2019; Thomas et al., 2024; Ding et al., 2024; Breazu et al., 2024). Yet, it remains unclear how LLMs can be effectively leveraged in cross-cultural hate speech moderation scenarios. In this work, we utilize LLMs as cultural context annotators and hate speech moderator agents, proposing a human-

LLM collaboration cross-cultural hate speech moderation pipeline.

3 User Study: Understanding Non-Native Moderators' Challenges

In this section, we explore the challenges non-native moderators face when relying solely on basic machine translation for hate speech detection. A user study was conducted with non-Korean moderators on KOLD (Jeong et al., 2022), a Korean hate speech detection dataset.

3.1 Method

Dataset KOLD (Jeong et al., 2022) consists of comments and titles from Naver News and YouTube, annotated by native Korean speakers for offensiveness. From this dataset, we manually curated 100 culturally specific samples and categorized them into 8 themes including political, religious, historical topic. For each theme, one offensive and one non-offensive sample were selected, resulting in 16 samples for the user study. The samples were translated into English using GPT-4o (OpenAI et al., 2024), creating 16 English comment-title pairs for evaluation.

Experimental Design In this user study, two non-Korean graduate students participated as annotators. One student is from Indonesia and the other student is from Germany. Neither had prior exposure to the KOLD dataset.

The participants' task was to annotate the offensiveness of the provided comments following adapted guidelines based on the KOLD dataset annotation framework. These guidelines, as in the original KOLD guideline, included identifying and marking specific spans of text considered offensive within the comments. Aside from the usual "Offensive" and "Non-offensive" options, we introduced an additional "I don't know" option. Specifically, when the participant is uncertain about a comment's offensiveness, they were instructed to select "I don't know" and indicate what additional information would help them make a decision. Also, the participants were permitted to use an English dictionary for clarifying word meanings but were strictly prohibited from using search engines or LLMs during the annotation process.

3.2 Results

The participants struggled with the task, answering incorrectly or selecting "I don't know" for nearly half of the samples, achieving an overall accuracy of 56.25%. Participant 1 answered correctly for 9 samples, incorrectly for 2, and chose "I don't know" for 5 samples. Similarly, participant 2 answered correctly for 9 samples, incorrectly for 4, and chose "I don't know" for 3 samples.

3.3 Findings

The user study revealed three key challenges faced by non-native moderators: difficulties in understanding *culturally-specific knowledge*, *sentiment* and *internet culture*.

Cultural Knowledge Participants struggled with unfamiliar Korean-specific named entities such as "Northwest Youth League (서북청년단),". For instance, in the comment "If it were our country, it would be like the Northwest Youth League ruling the nation (우리나라로 치면 서북청년단이 나라를 지배하는 꼴)", both participants selected "I don't know" and indicated that they need more information about the named entity "Northwest Youth League".

Cultural Sentiment Another challenge arose from the cultural sentiment disparities. For example, participants marked the comment "root out pro-Japanese collaborators (친일파를 뿌리 뽑다)" as "offensive" due to the phrase "root out". However, in the Korean cultural context, "pro-Japanese collaborators" refers to individuals who cooperated with Japanese imperial policies during the colonial era, a group widely criticized and condemned in Korea. Thus, the comment is considered non-offensive within its cultural context. However, these participants marked it as offensive because they did not share the sentiments and cultural sensitivity of Koreans.

Internet Culture The participants also encountered difficulties with understanding Korean internet memes, slang, and humor such as the comment "The reason why Gag Concert has no choice but to fail...(개콘이 망할 수 밖에 없는 이유...)". Gag Concert, a popular Korean comedy show, is often referenced in internet memes to describe absurd real-life situations, especially in serious contexts like politics or religion. The meme suggests that these real events are so ironic and comedic that they outshine scripted humor, causing the comedy show to seem less relevant. Both participants marked "I don't know" due to a lack of context to understand the reference.

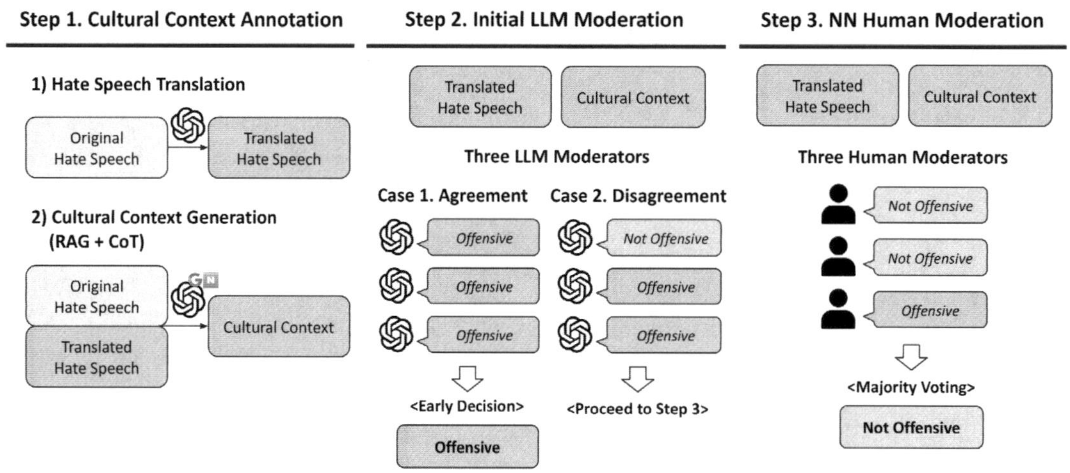

Figure 2: Overview of **LLM-C3Mod**. The pipeline consists of three steps: 1) generating cultural context annotations, 2) initial moderation using LLM moderators, and 3) final moderation by non-native human moderators. Further details are provided in Section 4.

These findings emphasize the need to provide cultural context for non-native moderators in hate speech detection tasks, especially to assist them in understanding *culturally-specific knowledge*, *sentiment*, and *internet culture*. Hate speech examples for each category are provided in Appendix A.

4 LLM-C3Mod: A Human-LLM Collaborative Hate Speech Moderation Pipeline

In this section, we suggest how LLMs can assist non-native moderators in understanding and moderating cross-cultural hate speech.

Based on our findings in Section 3, we propose **LLM-C3Mod**, a human-LLM collaborative hate speech moderation pipeine that includes 1) automatically generating cultural context 2) initial moderation with LLM moderators and 3) moderation with non-native human moderators. The process is described in Figure 2.

Step 1: Automatic Cultural Context Generation To assist hate speech moderation, we automatically generate cultural context of each title-comment pairs with GPT-4o (OpenAI et al., 2024). Notably, reliable cultural context annotations should not contain misinformation and should be able to handle up-to-date information, considering the real-time nature of content moderation. However, LLMs have limitations as they cannot process data beyond their training time and exhibit inherent hallucination (Xu et al., 2024).

To mitigate these problems, we employ RAG (Lewis et al., 2020) and CoT (Wei et al., 2022) frameworks. Specifically, we use following steps to generate cultural context annotation: (1) detect text span in the titles and comments related to following three aspects—*culturally-specific knowledge*, *sentiment*, and *internet culture*; (2) search for related articles or documents in the internet(RAG); (3) annotate objective cultural context based on the retrieved information. The samples of generated cultural context are shown in Appendix A. Furthermore, the prompts used in this process and their corresponding responses are detailed in Appendix D.1 and E, respectively.

Since our goal is to provide additional information that can assist non-native moderators in making accurate decision, we strictly limit our annotation to 'objective contexts'. In this stage, we do not task LLMs with determining whether a comment is offensive.

Step 2: Initial LLM Moderation To ensure scalability of the pipeline, we employ LLM agents for initial hate speech detection. Using the cultural context annotations generated in Step 1, three LLM moderators classify each comment as either offensive or non-offensive. The outcomes fall into one of two scenarios: (1) all three LLM moderators agree, or (2) one LLM moderator disagrees with the other two. In the first case, the pipeline concludes with the unanimous decision of the LLM moderators. In the second case, the pipeline moves to the next step for further review. In this study, we utilized three GPT-4o (OpenAI et al., 2024) agents

		Number of Samples	Baseline (GPT-4o)	Our Pipeline (GPT-4o & Human)
Total	**All Samples**	171	0.71	**0.78**
	Decision at Step 2: LLM Moderators	143	0.72	**0.78**
	Decision at Step 3: Human Moderators	28	0.67	**0.75**
Cultural Knowledge	**All Samples**	61	**0.78**	0.75
	Decision at Step 2: LLM Moderators	54	**0.76**	**0.76**
	Decision at Step 3: Human Moderators	7	**0.91**	0.71
Cultural Sentiment	**All Samples**	51	0.69	**0.78**
	Decision at Step 2: LLM Moderators	41	0.76	**0.78**
	Decision at Step 3: Human Moderators	10	0.43	**0.80**
Internet Culture	**All Samples**	59	0.67	**0.80**
	Decision at Step 2: LLM Moderators	48	0.65	**0.81**
	Decision at Step 3: Human Moderators	11	**0.73**	**0.73**

Table 1: Comparison of **LLM-C3MOD** (GPT-4o & Non-native Human) and a GPT-4o baseline(avg. of three runs) on 171 KOLD dataset samples. The samples are categorized based on the required type of cultural understanding: 1) cultural knowledge (N= 61), 2) cultural sentiment(N = 51), and 3) internet culture(N = 59). Using **LLM-C3MOD**, samples are divided into two groups: those resolved in Step 2 with agreement among LLM moderators and those requiring further review by human moderation in Step 3. **LLM-C3MOD** significantly improves performance in Step 3, increasing overall accuracy from 0.71 to 0.78. KOLD samples for each category, along with cultural context annotations, are provided in Appendix A.

as LLM moderators.

Step 3: Non-native Human Moderation Samples flagged due to LLM disagreement are passed to non-native human moderators, as such samples are implicitly more challenging. Human moderators are provided with the same cultural context annotations, titles and comments. The final decision is determined by majority voting among three non-native human moderators.

5 Experiments

5.1 Cultural Context Annotation

We conduct an A/B test to evaluate the effentiveness of cultural context annotations using a small set of 12 manually selected samples from the KOLD dataset. The samples include seven offensive and five non-offensive comments, four from each category—*culturally-specific knowledge*, *sentiment*, and *internet culture*. For human moderators, we recruited three non-Korean participants. Initially, they performed hate speech detection without the cultural context annotations, following the procedure described in Section 3.1. Then, they repeated the task on the same set of samples with the cultural context annotations provided. We conducted the same task using three GPT-4o moderators.

Table 2 shows that the generated cultural context annotations help improve the performance of both humans and LLMs in hate speech detection task. In particular, LLMs demonstrate high accuracy when the annotations are provided, showing promises.

	Cultural Context Annotation ✗	Cultural Context Annotation ✓
Human Moderators	0.22	**0.61**
GPT-4o Moderators	0.67	**0.92**

Table 2: Performance of humans and LLMs in hate speech detection with and without cultural context annotations on 12 KOLD samples. The performance is measured as the average of three non-native human moderators and three GPT-4o moderators.

5.2 LLM Moderators

We compare moderation capabilities of various LLMs to determine the most suitable LLM to serve as the moderator in our pipeline. For this section and the evaluation of pipeline, we manually select 171 samples from the KOLD dataset. Specifically, 50 samples were categorized as *cultural knowledge*, 62 as *cultural sentiment*, and 60 as *internet culture*.

Aligned with our proposed pipeline, we evaluate three LLMs as a group and compare their agreement ratios and accuracy on unanimously agreed answers. The comparison includes a GPT-4o group, a Claude-3-haiku group, a Gemini-1.5 group, and a

	Avg. Acc.	Agree. Ratio	Agree. Acc.
GPT-4o	**0.74**	**0.84**	**0.75**
Claude-3-haiku	0.71	**0.84**	0.73
Gemini-1.5	0.73	0.82	0.74
Mixed	0.72	0.78	0.72

Table 3: Comparison of LLM Moderator Groups – Each group consists of three GPT-4o, Claude-3-Haiku, Gemini-1.5, or a mix of these models. Avg. Acc. represents the average hate speech detection accuracy. Agree. Ratio indicates the proportion of samples with unanimous agreement among all models in a group. Agree. Acc. measures accuracy on those unanimously agreed samples.

mixed group consisting of one GPT-4o, one Claude-3-haiku, and one Gemini-1.5.

In Table 3, the results show that GPT-4o group achieves the highest average accuracy. While Claude-3-haiku group demonstrates the highest agreement ratio, it falls short in accuracy, making it the least suitable option for our pipeline. GPT-4o achieves the best accuracy on samples where unanimous agreement is reached. Although GPT-4o group reaches unanimous agreement on fewer samples, the accuracy of its agreed-upon samples is high, the high accuracy of these agreed-upon samples makes it a reliable choice for our pipeline. Based on these findings, we use three GPT-4o agents as the LLM moderators in our pipeline.

5.3 LLM-C3MOD Pipeline

The goal of this pipeline is to accurately and effectively conduct hate speech moderation. Based on prior findings, GPT-4o is employed as both the cultural annotation generator and the LLM moderator. For non-native human moderators, we recruited three graduate students: two from Indonesia and one from Germany. We use the same 171 KOLD samples from the LLM moderator evaluation experiment.

Table 1 compares the performance of our pipeline with a GPT-4o baseline (avg. of three runs). Our pipeline achieved 78% accuracy, exceeding the GPT-4o baseline accuracy of 71%. Furthermore, only 28 out of 171 samples failed to achieve unanimous agreement among the LLM moderators, reducing the workload for human moderators by 83.6

In Step 2, of the 143 samples that reached unanimous agreement, the LLM moderators made correct decisions on 112 samples, achieving 78% accuracy. In Step 3, majority voting among non-native human moderators achieved 75% accuracy, significantly surpassing the baseline GPT-4o's accuracy of 43%. These results demonstrate that our pipeline effectively improves the overall performance of hate speech moderation by identifying more challenging samples and delegating them to human moderators for review.

The performance of our pipeline showed no significant differences across the three categories (Table 1). However, there were several interesting features when our pipeline (human-LLM collaboration) is compared to the baselines. First, in the *cultural knowledge* category, where extracting factual data is more critical than understanding nuances, the performance decreased after applying our pipeline. However, in the *cultural sentiment* category and *internet culture* category, where understanding nuances takes precedence, the performance significantly improve through our pipeline. The accuracy comparison within the actual pipeline, specifically between the three LLM moderators and the non-native human moderator in step 3 (majority voting) can be seen in Table 4. For *cultural knowledge*, the Non-native human moderator accuracy shows significant fluctuation, sometimes higher and sometimes lower. However, for other categories, the accuracy generally tends to improve. In the case of *internet culture* category, while the final LLM moderator accuracy is slightly higher than the human moderator accuracy, this difference is only by one sample among 11 samples. When considering the overall performance across the three LLM moderators, the NN-human moderator case generally shows an upward trend in *internet culture* category.

These observations suggest that in content moderation tasks, there are aspects where humans still outperform LLMs by a substantial margin especially when understanding context and nuance is critical.

6 Discussion

6.1 Native vs. Non-native Moderator Performance

In this discussion section, we aim to compare the performance of non-native moderators to native moderators. We conduct a statistical analysis of Korean (native) annotators in the KOLD dataset and non-native participants in our experiment.

The hate speech detection accuracy of each in-

	LLM Moderator (GPT-4o)			NN Human Moderator
	1	2	3	
Total	0.43	0.57	0.61	0.75
Cultural Knowledge	0.86	0.71	0.43	0.71
Cultural Sentiment	0.30	0.80	0.50	0.80
Internet Culture	0.27	0.27	0.82	0.72

Table 4: Accuracy comparison in the Step3 in our pipeline: 3 LLM moderators(GPT-4o)' accuracy and Majority voting accuracy between 3 non-native human moderators. The comparision was done on 28 samples, and on each category; named entity (N=7), cultural sensitivity (N=10), and local memes (N=11). Cases where the LLM Moderator accuracy is lower than the NN-Human Moderator's Majority Voting accuracy are highlighted in blue, while cases where it is higher are highlighted in red.

	Non-Native Moderators			Avg.	
	1	2	3	Non-Natives	Natives
Acc.	0.68	0.82	0.68	0.73	0.89

Table 5: Comparison of hate speech detection accuracy between individual non-native moderators and native moderators. For non-native moderators, accuracy is calculated based on 28 samples from the pipeline validation experiment (Step 3). For native moderators, the average accuracy is calculated across 1,749 annotators who annotated more than 9 samples, using the entire KOLD dataset.

dividual annotator in the KOLD dataset was measured as follows. Each sample in the KOLD dataset includes the judgment results of three Korean annotators, along with their respective annotator IDs. Using this information, we identified all annotator IDs who annotated more than 9 samples from the KOLD dataset annotations. Then, we calculated the accuracy of each annotator by measuring how often their annotations matched the golden answers. The results are visualized in Figure 3.

As a result, we found that a total of 3,124 annotators contributed to annotating 40,429 samples in the KOLD dataset. on average, each annotator annotated 38.8 samples, with a median of 12 samples per annotator. Among them, 1,749 annotators annotated more than 9 samples. Within these filtered annotators, the mean accuracy was 0.89 (standard deviation: 0.074), and the median accuracy was 0.91. Note that the average accuracy cannot fall below 0.66, as the golden answers in the KOLD dataset are determined by the majority vote of the three Korean annotators.

We also calculated the hate speech detection accuracy of each non-native participants who took part in the final pipeline validation experiment. The results are presented in Table 5. Every participant showed lower performance compared to the average accuracy of the Korean annotators. This implies the persistent gap between non-native moderators and native moderators. However, it is difficult to attribute the performance difference solely to the limitations of the non-native moderators.

The average accuracy of the Korean annotators was calculated across all samples in the KOLD dataset. In contrast, the accuracy of the pipeline validation experiment participants was measured on a filtered set of samples requiring cultural knowledge and understanding for proper moderation. This suggests that non-native moderators might perform better on the full dataset, as it includes samples that do not require cultural knowledge for moderation. Meanwhile, we did not assess the accuracy of native moderators using the same set of 28 samples as the non-native moderators. This isbecause 27 KOLD annotators participated in annotating those 28 samples, with all but one (who annotated two samples) working on only one sample. Calculating accuracy with 28 samples would result in each KOLD annotator having either 0% or 100% accuracy, making the averaged accuracy meaningless.

Thus, our results indicate that non-native moderators still fall short compared to native moderators. However, these findings should be interpreted with caution due to inherent limitations in the statistical comparison.

6.2 Limitations of Early Decision-Making and Error Analysis

While our pipeline effectively reduces human workload by leaveraging LLM moderators in step 2, it has certain limitations. In our pipeline, an early decision is made in Step 2 when all three LLM moderators reach a consensus. However, if they unanimously agree on an incorrect judgment at this stage, the pipeline lacks a mechanism to correct this error. In our pipeline validation experiment, 31 out of 143 early decision samples (18% of all samples) resulted in incorrect unanimous agreements. In this discussion, we analyze the difficulty of these misclassified samples, as presented in Table 6.

We implicitly define the difficulty of a hate speech sample based on the agreement among native moderators. In the KOLD dataset, golden answers are determined by the majority vote of three

	LLM Moderators	
KOLD Annotators	Correct	Incorrect
Agree	91 (0.63)	14 (0.10)
Disagree	21 (0.15)	17 (0.12)

$$\chi^2 = 16.2064$$

$$p = 0.000057\,(< 0.05)$$

Table 6: Analysis of 143 samples that reached unanimous agreement in Step2 of our pipeline during the pipeline validation experiment. The samples were first categorized based on whether the LLM moderators' unanimous decision was correct. Then, the samples were divided according to the level of agreement among the three Korean annotators of the KOLD dataset. A Chi-square test was conducted, showing that the LLMs' decisions are significantly correlated with the agreement among the Korean annotators, reflecting the inherent difficulty of the samples.

annotators. If all three annotators agree, the sample is likely to be straightforward and reliable. Conversely, if the annotators disagree, the sample may be more ambiguous or challenging. To investigate the relationship between LLM agreement accuracy (143 samples) and the agreement level of KOLD human annotators, we conducted a Chi-square test to test the null hypothesis H_0: the accuracy of LLM-agree samples is independent of human agreement. The results showed a Chi-square value of 16.2064 and a p-value of 0.000057 (< 0.05), leading to the rejection of the null hypothesis. This indicates that the incorrect unanimous agreements in Step 2 are more likely to be inherently difficult even for native moderators. Thus, solving these samples may require a more advanced pipeline or the assistance of native moderators. The full sample analysis is in Appendix B.

7 Conclusion

We presented **LLM-C3MOD**, a system that assists non-native moderators in cross-cultural hate speech detection through RAG-enhanced cultural context annotations and strategic human-LLM collaboration. By addressing three key challenges identified from our user study—*understanding culturally-specific knowledge*, *navigating cultural sentiment differences*, and *interpreting internet culture*—our system achieves 78% accuracy while reducing human workload by 83.6% in Korean hate speech moderation with Indonesian and German participants. This demonstrates that non-native moderators, when supported with appropriate cultural context, can effectively contribute to content moderation across linguistic and cultural boundaries. In future work, we aim to explore extending **LLM-C3MOD** to examine its effectiveness across different cultural and linguistic combinations, beyond the Korean-English pairing examined in our study. We hope our findings contribute to advancing research in cross-cultural content moderation, addressing critical challenges in global online safety.

Limitations

Language Proxy Considerations The participants in our user study and pipeline evaluation experiment are from Indonesia and Germany, and English is not their first language. Thus, they relied on a proxy language (English) to understand the Korean content. This likely made it more challenging for them to fully grasp the nuances of the language when assessing the offensiveness of the content. To address this limitation, future work will involve translating the content into each participant's native language.

Early Decision-Making in the Pipeline Our pipeline makes an early decision without additional offensiveness verification when the three LLM moderators reach an unanimous agreement. As a result, our pipeline cannot correct unanimous incorrect decisions made during the early decision stage. To minimize this risk, we selected 3 GPT-4o models since it is the combination which showed highest agree accuracy(Table 3). Furthermore, errors that were not filtered out underwent quantitative analysis through Chi-square testing in Section 6.2, showing that the errors missed during early decisions in Step 2 in our pipeline were likely to involve more difficult cases or be inaccurate. However, since there remain cases where the LLMs make errors, future work should focus on addressing this limitation. Additionally, efforts to improve performance on challenging cases should also be prioritized. For example, increasing the number of LLM Moderators beyond the current three may enhance the reliability of the LLM uncertainty. Additionally, incorporating LLM consistency-checking methods alongside the use of LLM Moderators could further improve the robustness and accuracy of the system.

Ethical Considerations

Data Our study is conducted in a course project. Each participant was paid 10,000 KRW, minimum wage.

Annotator Demographics All annotators were not native speakers of both the language (English) and culture (Korean) that they were annotating. Other annotator demographics were not collected for this study, except for native language and nationality.

Compute/AI Resources All our experiments were conducted on local computers using API service. The API calls to the GPT models were done through the Azure OpenAI service. The Gemini model was accessed via the Google Gemini API service. The Claude model was accessed by Anthropic API service. Finally, we also acknowledge the usage of ChatGPT and GitHub Copilot for building our codebase.

Acknowledgements

This research project has benefitted from the Microsoft Accelerate Foundation Models Research (AFMR) grant program through which leading foundation models hosted by Microsoft Azure along with access to Azure credits were provided to conduct the research. This work was supported by Institute of Information & communications Technology Planning & Evaluation (IITP) grant funded by the Korea government(MSIT) (No.RS-2022-II220184, Development and Study of AI Technologies to Inexpensively Conform to Evolving Policy on Ethics)

References

Ali Alkhatib and Michael Bernstein. 2019. Street-level algorithms: A theory at the gaps between policy and decisions. In *Proceedings of the 2019 CHI Conference on Human Factors in Computing Systems*, CHI '19, page 1–13, New York, NY, USA. Association for Computing Machinery.

Ayme Arango Monnar, Jorge Perez, Barbara Poblete, Magdalena Saldaña, and Valentina Proust. 2022. Resources for multilingual hate speech detection. In *Proceedings of the Sixth Workshop on Online Abuse and Harms (WOAH)*, pages 122–130, Seattle, Washington (Hybrid). Association for Computational Linguistics.

Petre Breazu, Miriam Schirmer, Songbo Hu, and Napoleon Katsos. 2024. Large language models and thematic analysis: Human-ai synergy in researching hate speech on social media. *Preprint*, arXiv:2408.05126.

Fai Leui Chan, Duke Nguyen, and Aditya Joshi. 2024. "is hate lost in translation?": Evaluation of multilingual lgbtqia+ hate speech detection. *arXiv preprint arXiv:2410.11230*.

Yi-Ling Chung, Elizaveta Kuzmenko, Serra Sinem Tekiroglu, and Marco Guerini. 2019. CONAN - COunter NArratives through nichesourcing: a multilingual dataset of responses to fight online hate speech. In *Proceedings of the 57th Annual Meeting of the Association for Computational Linguistics*, pages 2819–2829, Florence, Italy. Association for Computational Linguistics.

Christoph Demus, Jonas Pitz, Mina Schütz, Nadine Probol, Melanie Siegel, and Dirk Labudde. 2022. Detox: A comprehensive dataset for German offensive language and conversation analysis. In *Proceedings of the Sixth Workshop on Online Abuse and Harms (WOAH)*, pages 143–153, Seattle, Washington (Hybrid). Association for Computational Linguistics.

Jiawen Deng, Jingyan Zhou, Hao Sun, Chujie Zheng, Fei Mi, Helen Meng, and Minlie Huang. 2022. COLD: A benchmark for Chinese offensive language detection. In *Proceedings of the 2022 Conference on Empirical Methods in Natural Language Processing*, pages 11580–11599, Abu Dhabi, United Arab Emirates. Association for Computational Linguistics.

Xiaohan Ding, Kaike Ping, Uma Sushmitha Gunturi, Buse Carik, Sophia Stil, Lance T Wilhelm, Taufiq Daryanto, James Hawdon, Sang Won Lee, and Eugenia H Rho. 2024. Counterquill: Investigating the potential of human-ai collaboration in online counterspeech writing. *Preprint*, arXiv:2410.03032.

Mai ElSherief, Caleb Ziems, David Muchlinski, Vaishnavi Anupindi, Jordyn Seybolt, Munmun De Choudhury, and Diyi Yang. 2021. Latent hatred: A benchmark for understanding implicit hate speech. In *Proceedings of the 2021 Conference on Empirical Methods in Natural Language Processing*, pages 345–363, Online and Punta Cana, Dominican Republic. Association for Computational Linguistics.

Mona Elswah. 2024. Investigating content moderation systems in the global south. *Center for Democracy and Technology*.

Robert Gorwa, Reuben Binns, and Christian Katzenbach. 2020. Algorithmic content moderation: Technical and political challenges in the automation of platform governance. *Big Data & Society*, 7(1):2053951719897945.

Ming Shan Hee, Shivam Sharma, Rui Cao, Palash Nandi, Preslav Nakov, Tanmoy Chakraborty, and Roy Ka-Wei Lee. 2024. Recent advances in online hate speech moderation: Multimodality and the role of large models. In *Findings of the Association for Computational Linguistics: EMNLP 2024*, pages

4407–4419, Miami, Florida, USA. Association for Computational Linguistics.

Younghoon Jeong, Juhyun Oh, Jongwon Lee, Jaimeen Ahn, Jihyung Moon, Sungjoon Park, and Alice Oh. 2022. KOLD: Korean offensive language dataset. In *Proceedings of the 2022 Conference on Empirical Methods in Natural Language Processing*, pages 10818–10833, Abu Dhabi, United Arab Emirates. Association for Computational Linguistics.

Prince Jha, Raghav Jain, Konika Mandal, Aman Chadha, Sriparna Saha, and Pushpak Bhattacharyya. 2024. MemeGuard: An LLM and VLM-based framework for advancing content moderation via meme intervention. In *Proceedings of the 62nd Annual Meeting of the Association for Computational Linguistics (Volume 1: Long Papers)*, pages 8084–8104, Bangkok, Thailand. Association for Computational Linguistics.

Shagun Jhaver, Iris Birman, Eric Gilbert, and Amy Bruckman. 2019. Human-machine collaboration for content regulation: The case of reddit automoderator. *ACM Trans. Comput.-Hum. Interact.*, 26(5).

Jiho Jin, Jiseon Kim, Nayeon Lee, Haneul Yoo, Alice Oh, and Hwaran Lee. 2024. KoBBQ: Korean bias benchmark for question answering. *Transactions of the Association for Computational Linguistics*, 12:507–524.

Hankun Kang and Tieyun Qian. 2024. Implanting LLM's knowledge via reading comprehension tree for toxicity detection. In *Findings of the Association for Computational Linguistics: ACL 2024*, pages 947–962, Bangkok, Thailand. Association for Computational Linguistics.

Mahi Kolla, Siddharth Salunkhe, Eshwar Chandrasekharan, and Koustuv Saha. 2024a. Llm-mod: Can large language models assist content moderation? In *Extended Abstracts of the CHI Conference on Human Factors in Computing Systems*, CHI EA '24, New York, NY, USA. Association for Computing Machinery.

Mahi Kolla, Siddharth Salunkhe, Eshwar Chandrasekharan, and Koustuv Saha. 2024b. Llm-mod: Can large language models assist content moderation? In *Extended Abstracts of the CHI Conference on Human Factors in Computing Systems*, CHI EA '24, New York, NY, USA. Association for Computing Machinery.

Deepak Kumar, Yousef Anees AbuHashem, and Zakir Durumeric. 2024. Watch your language: Investigating content moderation with large language models. *Proceedings of the International AAAI Conference on Web and Social Media*, 18(1):865–878.

Nayeon Lee, Chani Jung, Junho Myung, Jiho Jin, Jose Camacho-Collados, Juho Kim, and Alice Oh. 2024. Exploring cross-cultural differences in English hate speech annotations: From dataset construction to analysis. In *Proceedings of the 2024 Conference of the North American Chapter of the Association for Computational Linguistics: Human Language Technologies (Volume 1: Long Papers)*, pages 4205–4224, Mexico City, Mexico. Association for Computational Linguistics.

Nayeon Lee, Chani Jung, and Alice Oh. 2023. Hate speech classifiers are culturally insensitive. In *Proceedings of the First Workshop on Cross-Cultural Considerations in NLP (C3NLP)*, pages 35–46, Dubrovnik, Croatia. Association for Computational Linguistics.

Patrick Lewis, Ethan Perez, Aleksandra Piktus, Fabio Petroni, Vladimir Karpukhin, Naman Goyal, Heinrich Küttler, Mike Lewis, Wen-tau Yih, Tim Rocktäschel, Sebastian Riedel, and Douwe Kiela. 2020. Retrieval-augmented generation for knowledge-intensive nlp tasks. In *Proceedings of the 34th International Conference on Neural Information Processing Systems*, NIPS '20, Red Hook, NY, USA. Curran Associates Inc.

Cheng Li, Damien Teney, Linyi Yang, Qingsong Wen, Xing Xie, and Jindong Wang. 2024. Culturepark: Boosting cross-cultural understanding in large language models. *Preprint*, arXiv:2405.15145.

Antonis Maronikolakis, Axel Wisiorek, Leah Nann, Haris Jabbar, Sahana Udupa, and Hinrich Schuetze. 2022. Listening to affected communities to define extreme speech: Dataset and experiments. In *Findings of the Association for Computational Linguistics: ACL 2022*, pages 1089–1104, Dublin, Ireland. Association for Computational Linguistics.

Sarah Masud, Manjot Bedi, Mohammad Aflah Khan, Md Shad Akhtar, and Tanmoy Chakraborty. 2022. Proactively reducing the hate intensity of online posts via hate speech normalization. In *Proceedings of the 28th ACM SIGKDD Conference on Knowledge Discovery and Data Mining*, KDD '22, page 3524–3534, New York, NY, USA. Association for Computing Machinery.

Sarah Masud, Sahajpreet Singh, Viktor Hangya, Alexander Fraser, and Tanmoy Chakraborty. 2024. Hate personified: Investigating the role of LLMs in content moderation. In *Proceedings of the 2024 Conference on Empirical Methods in Natural Language Processing*, pages 15847–15863, Miami, Florida, USA. Association for Computational Linguistics.

Binny Mathew, Punyajoy Saha, Seid Muhie Yimam, Chris Biemann, Pawan Goyal, and Animesh Mukherjee. 2021. Hatexplain: A benchmark dataset for explainable hate speech detection. *Proceedings of the AAAI Conference on Artificial Intelligence*, 35(17):14867–14875.

Dan Milmo. 2021. Facebook revelations: what is in cache of internal documents? *The Guardian*.

Shamsuddeen Hassan Muhammad, Idris Abdulmumin, Abinew Ali Ayele, David Ifeoluwa Adelani, Ibrahim Said Ahmad, Saminu Mohammad Aliyu,

Nelson Odhiambo Onyango, Lilian D. A. Wanzare, Samuel Rutunda, Lukman Jibril Aliyu, Esubalew Alemneh, Oumaima Hourrane, Hagos Tesfahun Gebremichael, Elyas Abdi Ismail, Meriem Beloucif, Ebrahim Chekol Jibril, Andiswa Bukula, Rooweither Mabuya, Salomey Osei, Abigail Oppong, Tadesse Destaw Belay, Tadesse Kebede Guge, Tesfa Tegegne Asfaw, Chiamaka Ijeoma Chukwuneke, Paul Röttger, Seid Muhie Yimam, and Nedjma Ousidhoum. 2025. Afrihate: A multilingual collection of hate speech and abusive language datasets for african languages. *Preprint*, arXiv:2501.08284.

Hellina Hailu Nigatu and Inioluwa Deborah Raji. 2024. "i searched for a religious song in amharic and got sexual content instead": Investigating online harm in low-resourced languages on youtube. In *Proceedings of the 2024 ACM Conference on Fairness, Accountability, and Transparency*, FAccT '24, page 141–160, New York, NY, USA. Association for Computing Machinery.

OpenAI, :, Aaron Hurst, Adam Lerer, Adam P. Goucher, Adam Perelman, Aditya Ramesh, Aidan Clark, AJ Ostrow, Akila Welihinda, Alan Hayes, Alec Radford, Aleksander Mądry, Alex Baker-Whitcomb, Alex Beutel, Alex Borzunov, Alex Carney, Alex Chow, Alex Kirillov, Alex Nichol, Alex Paino, Alex Renzin, Alex Tachard Passos, Alexander Kirillov, Alexi Christakis, Alexis Conneau, Ali Kamali, Allan Jabri, Allison Moyer, Allison Tam, Amadou Crookes, Amin Tootoochian, Amin Tootoonchian, Ananya Kumar, Andrea Vallone, Andrej Karpathy, Andrew Braunstein, Andrew Cann, Andrew Codispoti, Andrew Galu, Andrew Kondrich, Andrew Tulloch, Andrey Mishchenko, Angela Baek, Angela Jiang, Antoine Pelisse, Antonia Woodford, Anuj Gosalia, Arka Dhar, Ashley Pantuliano, Avi Nayak, Avital Oliver, Barret Zoph, Behrooz Ghorbani, Ben Leimberger, Ben Rossen, Ben Sokolowsky, Ben Wang, Benjamin Zweig, Beth Hoover, Blake Samic, Bob McGrew, Bobby Spero, Bogo Giertler, Bowen Cheng, Brad Lightcap, Brandon Walkin, Brendan Quinn, Brian Guarraci, Brian Hsu, Bright Kellogg, Brydon Eastman, Camillo Lugaresi, Carroll Wainwright, Cary Bassin, Cary Hudson, Casey Chu, Chad Nelson, Chak Li, Chan Jun Shern, Channing Conger, Charlotte Barette, Chelsea Voss, Chen Ding, Cheng Lu, Chong Zhang, Chris Beaumont, Chris Hallacy, Chris Koch, Christian Gibson, Christina Kim, Christine Choi, Christine McLeavey, Christopher Hesse, Claudia Fischer, Clemens Winter, Coley Czarnecki, Colin Jarvis, Colin Wei, Constantin Koumouzelis, Dane Sherburn, Daniel Kappler, Daniel Levin, Daniel Levy, David Carr, David Farhi, David Mely, David Robinson, David Sasaki, Denny Jin, Dev Valladares, Dimitris Tsipras, Doug Li, Duc Phong Nguyen, Duncan Findlay, Edede Oiwoh, Edmund Wong, Ehsan Asdar, Elizabeth Proehl, Elizabeth Yang, Eric Antonow, Eric Kramer, Eric Peterson, Eric Sigler, Eric Wallace, Eugene Brevdo, Evan Mays, Farzad Khorasani, Felipe Petroski Such, Filippo Raso, Francis Zhang, Fred von Lohmann, Freddie Sulit, Gabriel Goh, Gene Oden, Geoff Salmon, Giulio Starace, Greg Brockman, Hadi Salman, Haiming Bao, Haitang Hu, Hannah Wong, Haoyu Wang, Heather Schmidt, Heather Whitney, Heewoo Jun, Hendrik Kirchner, Henrique Ponde de Oliveira Pinto, Hongyu Ren, Huiwen Chang, Hyung Won Chung, Ian Kivlichan, Ian O'Connell, Ian O'Connell, Ian Osband, Ian Silber, Ian Sohl, Ibrahim Okuyucu, Ikai Lan, Ilya Kostrikov, Ilya Sutskever, Ingmar Kanitscheider, Ishaan Gulrajani, Jacob Coxon, Jacob Menick, Jakub Pachocki, James Aung, James Betker, James Crooks, James Lennon, Jamie Kiros, Jan Leike, Jane Park, Jason Kwon, Jason Phang, Jason Teplitz, Jason Wei, Jason Wolfe, Jay Chen, Jeff Harris, Jenia Varavva, Jessica Gan Lee, Jessica Shieh, Ji Lin, Jiahui Yu, Jiayi Weng, Jie Tang, Jieqi Yu, Joanne Jang, Joaquin Quinonero Candela, Joe Beutler, Joe Landers, Joel Parish, Johannes Heidecke, John Schulman, Jonathan Lachman, Jonathan McKay, Jonathan Uesato, Jonathan Ward, Jong Wook Kim, Joost Huizinga, Jordan Sitkin, Jos Kraaijeveld, Josh Gross, Josh Kaplan, Josh Snyder, Joshua Achiam, Joy Jiao, Joyce Lee, Juntang Zhuang, Justyn Harriman, Kai Fricke, Kai Hayashi, Karan Singhal, Katy Shi, Kavin Karthik, Kayla Wood, Kendra Rimbach, Kenny Hsu, Kenny Nguyen, Keren Gu-Lemberg, Kevin Button, Kevin Liu, Kiel Howe, Krithika Muthukumar, Kyle Luther, Lama Ahmad, Larry Kai, Lauren Itow, Lauren Workman, Leher Pathak, Leo Chen, Li Jing, Lia Guy, Liam Fedus, Liang Zhou, Lien Mamitsuka, Lilian Weng, Lindsay McCallum, Lindsey Held, Long Ouyang, Louis Feuvrier, Lu Zhang, Lukas Kondraciuk, Lukasz Kaiser, Luke Hewitt, Luke Metz, Lyric Doshi, Mada Aflak, Maddie Simens, Madelaine Boyd, Madeleine Thompson, Marat Dukhan, Mark Chen, Mark Gray, Mark Hudnall, Marvin Zhang, Marwan Aljubeh, Mateusz Litwin, Matthew Zeng, Max Johnson, Maya Shetty, Mayank Gupta, Meghan Shah, Mehmet Yatbaz, Meng Jia Yang, Mengchao Zhong, Mia Glaese, Mianna Chen, Michael Janner, Michael Lampe, Michael Petrov, Michael Wu, Michele Wang, Michelle Fradin, Michelle Pokrass, Miguel Castro, Miguel Oom Temudo de Castro, Mikhail Pavlov, Miles Brundage, Miles Wang, Minal Khan, Mira Murati, Mo Bavarian, Molly Lin, Murat Yesildal, Nacho Soto, Natalia Gimelshein, Natalie Cone, Natalie Staudacher, Natalie Summers, Natan LaFontaine, Neil Chowdhury, Nick Ryder, Nick Stathas, Nick Turley, Nik Tezak, Niko Felix, Nithanth Kudige, Nitish Keskar, Noah Deutsch, Noel Bundick, Nora Puckett, Ofir Nachum, Ola Okelola, Oleg Boiko, Oleg Murk, Oliver Jaffe, Olivia Watkins, Olivier Godement, Owen Campbell-Moore, Patrick Chao, Paul McMillan, Pavel Belov, Peng Su, Peter Bak, Peter Bakkum, Peter Deng, Peter Dolan, Peter Hoeschele, Peter Welinder, Phil Tillet, Philip Pronin, Philippe Tillet, Prafulla Dhariwal, Qiming Yuan, Rachel Dias, Rachel Lim, Rahul Arora, Rajan Troll, Randall Lin, Rapha Gontijo Lopes, Raul Puri, Reah Miyara, Reimar Leike, Renaud Gaubert, Reza Zamani, Ricky Wang, Rob Donnelly, Rob Honsby, Rocky Smith, Rohan Sahai, Rohit Ramchandani, Romain Huet, Rory Carmichael, Rowan Zellers, Roy Chen, Ruby Chen, Ruslan Nigmatullin, Ryan Cheu, Saachi Jain, Sam Altman, Sam Schoenholz,

Sam Toizer, Samuel Miserendino, Sandhini Agarwal, Sara Culver, Scott Ethersmith, Scott Gray, Sean Grove, Sean Metzger, Shamez Hermani, Shantanu Jain, Shengjia Zhao, Sherwin Wu, Shino Jomoto, Shirong Wu, Shuaiqi, Xia, Sonia Phene, Spencer Papay, Srinivas Narayanan, Steve Coffey, Steve Lee, Stewart Hall, Suchir Balaji, Tal Broda, Tal Stramer, Tao Xu, Tarun Gogineni, Taya Christianson, Ted Sanders, Tejal Patwardhan, Thomas Cunninghman, Thomas Degry, Thomas Dimson, Thomas Raoux, Thomas Shadwell, Tianhao Zheng, Todd Underwood, Todor Markov, Toki Sherbakov, Tom Rubin, Tom Stasi, Tomer Kaftan, Tristan Heywood, Troy Peterson, Tyce Walters, Tyna Eloundou, Valerie Qi, Veit Moeller, Vinnie Monaco, Vishal Kuo, Vlad Fomenko, Wayne Chang, Weiyi Zheng, Wenda Zhou, Wesam Manassra, Will Sheu, Wojciech Zaremba, Yash Patil, Yilei Qian, Yongjik Kim, Youlong Cheng, Yu Zhang, Yuchen He, Yuchen Zhang, Yujia Jin, Yunxing Dai, and Yury Malkov. 2024. Gpt-4o system card.

Ji Ho Park and Pascale Fung. 2017. One-step and two-step classification for abusive language detection on Twitter. In *Proceedings of the First Workshop on Abusive Language Online*, pages 41–45, Vancouver, BC, Canada. Association for Computational Linguistics.

Siddhesh Pawar, Junyeong Park, Jiho Jin, Arnav Arora, Junho Myung, Srishti Yadav, Faiz Ghifari Haznitrama, Inhwa Song, Alice Oh, and Isabelle Augenstein. 2024. Survey of cultural awareness in language models: Text and beyond. *arXiv preprint arXiv:2411.00860*.

Jakub Podolak, Szymon Łukasik, Paweł Balawender, Jan Ossowski, Jan Piotrowski, Katarzyna Bakowicz, and Piotr Sankowski. 2024. LLM generated responses to mitigate the impact of hate speech. In *Findings of the Association for Computational Linguistics: EMNLP 2024*, pages 15860–15876, Miami, Florida, USA. Association for Computational Linguistics.

Sarthak Roy, Ashish Harshvardhan, Animesh Mukherjee, and Punyajoy Saha. 2023. Probing LLMs for hate speech detection: strengths and vulnerabilities. In *Findings of the Association for Computational Linguistics: EMNLP 2023*, pages 6116–6128, Singapore. Association for Computational Linguistics.

Maarten Sap, Saadia Gabriel, Lianhui Qin, Dan Jurafsky, Noah A. Smith, and Yejin Choi. 2020. Social bias frames: Reasoning about social and power implications of language. In *Proceedings of the 58th Annual Meeting of the Association for Computational Linguistics*, pages 5477–5490, Online. Association for Computational Linguistics.

Kurt Thomas, Patrick Gage Kelley, David Tao, Sarah Meiklejohn, Owen Vallis, Shunwen Tan, Blaž Bratanič, Felipe Tiengo Ferreira, Vijay Kumar Eranti, and Elie Bursztein. 2024. Supporting human raters with the detection of harmful content using large language models. *Preprint*, arXiv:2406.12800.

Bertie Vidgen, Tristan Thrush, Zeerak Waseem, and Douwe Kiela. 2021. Learning from the worst: Dynamically generated datasets to improve online hate detection. In *Proceedings of the 59th Annual Meeting of the Association for Computational Linguistics and the 11th International Joint Conference on Natural Language Processing (Volume 1: Long Papers)*, pages 1667–1682, Online. Association for Computational Linguistics.

Nishant Vishwamitra, Keyan Guo, Farhan Tajwar Romit, Isabelle Ondracek, Long Cheng, Ziming Zhao, and Hongxin Hu. 2024. Moderating new waves of online hate with chain-of-thought reasoning in large language models. In *2024 IEEE Symposium on Security and Privacy (SP)*, pages 788–806.

Han Wang, Ming Shan Hee, Md Rabiul Awal, Kenny Tsu Wei Choo, and Roy Ka-Wei Lee. 2023. Evaluating gpt-3 generated explanations for hateful content moderation. In *Proceedings of the Thirty-Second International Joint Conference on Artificial Intelligence*, IJCAI '23.

Jason Wei, Xuezhi Wang, Dale Schuurmans, Maarten Bosma, brian ichter, Fei Xia, Ed Chi, Quoc V Le, and Denny Zhou. 2022. Chain-of-thought prompting elicits reasoning in large language models. In *Advances in Neural Information Processing Systems*, volume 35, pages 24824–24837. Curran Associates, Inc.

Global Witness. 2023. How Big Tech platforms are neglecting their non-English language users. *Global Witness Org*. Investigative report analyzing social media platforms' content moderation resources across different languages in the EU, based on Digital Service Act transparency reports.

Ziwei Xu, Sanjay Jain, and Mohan Kankanhalli. 2024. Hallucination is inevitable: An innate limitation of large language models. *arXiv preprint arXiv:2401.11817*.

Yongjin Yang, Joonkee Kim, Yujin Kim, Namgyu Ho, James Thorne, and Se-Young Yun. 2023. HARE: Explainable hate speech detection with step-by-step reasoning. In *Findings of the Association for Computational Linguistics: EMNLP 2023*, pages 5490–5505, Singapore. Association for Computational Linguistics.

Haotian Ye, Axel Wisiorek, Antonis Maronikolakis, Özge Alaçam, and Hinrich Schütze. 2024. A federated approach to few-shot hate speech detection for marginalized communities. *Preprint*, arXiv:2412.04942.

Min Zhang, Jianfeng He, Taoran Ji, and Chang-Tien Lu. 2024. Don't go to extremes: Revealing the excessive sensitivity and calibration limitations of LLMs in implicit hate speech detection. In *Proceedings of the 62nd Annual Meeting of the Association for Computational Linguistics (Volume 1: Long Papers)*, pages 12073–12086, Bangkok, Thailand. Association for Computational Linguistics.

Appendix

A Cultural Context Example

Table 7 shows the samples of cultural context annotations on KOLD dataset.

Category	Label	Context(title)	Comment	Cultural Context Anntoation
Cultural Knowledge	OFF	GS25, 브레이브걸스 포스터 또 젠더 이슈 논란 GS25, Brave Girls poster, another gender issue controversy	브레이브걸스=페미아이돌 Brave Girls =feminist idol	**GS25**: A major convenience store chain in South Korea. They faced controversy over a promotional poster featuring a hand reaching for a sausage, which some critics saw as referencing a feminist symbol associated with Megalia. **Brave Girls**: Known for their viral hit Rollin'. Linked to feminist discourse in South Korea due to perceived support for gender equality.
	NOT	'N번방' 밝힌 '추적단불꽃', 與선대위 합류... 젠더 공약 돕는다 The 'Tracking Team Fire' that exposed the 'Nth Room' joins the ruling party's election committee... Helping with gender pledges	N번방을 추적해 공론화시킨 추적단불꽃을 응원합니다. I support the tracking team Flame that tracked and publicized the Nth Room.	**Nth Room**: A major digital sex crime scandal in South Korea involving the production and distribution of explicit videos, including those of minors, through Telegram chatrooms, sparking nationwide outrage. **Tracking Team Flame**: A duo of university student activists, played a crucial role in exposing the case, leading to law enforcement action and policy changes on digital sexual crimes.
Cultural Sentiment	OFF	'모든 국가와 우호적 관계'... 내부는 '공포정치' 'Friendly relations with all countries" ... internally 'politics of fear'	정은이가 친구 해 줄 거다. Jeongeun will be your friend.	**'Jeongeun'** refers to North Korean leader Kim Jong-un. He is known for ruling North Korea through a regime of fear and political repression.
	NOT	박용진이 던진 '여성 군사훈련'... 젠더 넘은 찬반 양론 불붙나 Yong-jin Park's proposal for 'women's military training' ignites debate... Will the controversy further intensify beyond gender?	남자도 무조건 애낳으면 2년 육아 전담의무화 Men should also be required to take full responsibility for childcare for two years unconditionally if they have a child.	In South Korea's **gender debate**, men's two-year mandatory military service is often compared to women's role in childbirth and the societal expectation of primary childcare responsibility.
Internet Culture	OFF	[세상읽기] 여성+가족부 해체 [Reading the World] Dissolution of the Ministry of Women and Family	웅 준비완~~~군캉스 개꿀~~~ Yes, ready~~~ Military vacation so sweet ~~~	**'Military vacation'**: a sarcastic term combining 'military' and 'vacation,' used to criticize perceptions that South Korea's mandatory military service is easier than it actually is. **'So sweet'**: a slang term where '개' (dog) intensifies '꿀' (sweet), meaning something is very easy or satisfying, often used humorously or exaggeratedly.
	NOT	(재) 흑인 농부에게 쇠사슬에 묶여 교육 당하는 중독자; (Re) An addict being chained and forced to receive education by a Black farmer.	두번째 댓글 Second comment	**'Second comment'**: a common internet trend in South Korea where users rush to comment early on articles or posts, often just to claim a spot. It is typically meaningless and unrelated to the original post.

Table 7: Example of category labeling and cultural context annotations on KOLD. Label, Context(title), and Comment is from KOLD. (OFF: offensive, NOT: not offensive, blue : culturally dependent content)

B Pipeline Sample analysis

Full Analysis on the samples used in pipeline in the following table. Chi-square analysis was done to prove / disprove the null hypothesis(H_0): the accuracy of LLM-agree samples is independent of human agreement on both LLMs-Agree case and LLMs-Disagree case. The discussion on LLMs Agree sample was done in Section 6.2. For LLMs Agree samples(143 samples), the Chi-square value was 16.2064, and the p-value was 0.000057(<0.05). Therefore, for the samples that were resolved in step 2(LLMs Agree samples), the incorrectness is dependent with the difficulty of sample. For LLMs Disagree samples(28 samples), the Chi-square value was 0.0499, with the p-value 0.823218 (>0.05). Therefore, for samples that reached step 3, the null hypothesis(H_0) failed to be rejected.

	LLMs Agree		LLMs Disagree	
Correct	✓	✗	✓	✗
Human - Agree	91	14	10	6
Human - Disagree	21	17	7	5

Table 8: Analysis of 171 samples from the pipeline experiment. Samples were categorized based on whether the three LLMs in the second stage of the pipeline reached unanimous agreement. Each category was further divided by the Human majority voting outcome, assessing whether it aligned with the golden answers in the KOLD dataset. Finally, samples were analyzed based on agreement among the three Korean annotators of the KOLD dataset.

C KOLD Annotators analysis

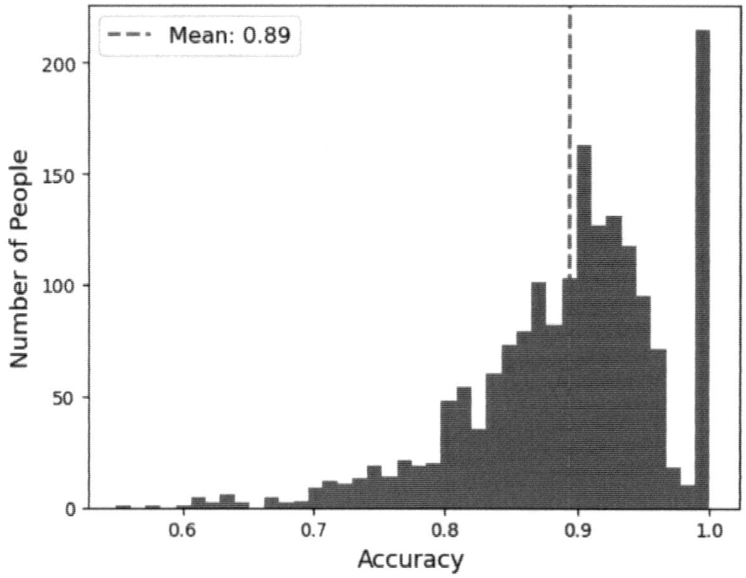

Figure 3: Histogram showing the accuracy distribution of 1,749 Korean annotators(out of 3,124 Korean annotators, who annotated more than 9 samples) in the KOLD dataset.

D Prompt

Appendix D.1 describes the prompts utilized to generated annotation. Appendix D.2 is the prompt used for LLM to classify the offensiveness of the text.

D.1 Prompt for Annotation

This is the prompt selected for annotation generation. It consists of two steps: the RAG step and the annotation generation step. Together, this entire process represents a Chain-of-Thought (CoT) approach.

D.1.1 RAG-step Prompt

Below is the original prompt used in **RAG step**, and prompt translated in English. The original prompt contains both English and Korean. The parts that were originally written in English and hasn't been additionally translated are written in blue font.

Original Prompt

> 다음 기사의 제목과 댓글에서 한국 문화나 한국의 인물, 또는 한국 인터넷 밈이 포함되어 있는지 확인하고, 그 부분을 인터넷 검색 (web search) 후 관련된 한국 문화나 인물, 인터넷 밈에 대해서 인터넷 출처와 함께 알려줘.
>
> Title: **{Article text title in Korean}**
> Comment: **{Article text comment in Korean}**

Translated Prompt

> Check whether the following article's title and comments include any references to Korean culture, Korean figures, or Korean internet memes. Then, perform an internet search (web search) on those parts and provide information about the related Korean culture, figures, or internet memes along with internet sources.
>
> Title: **{Article text title in Korean}**
> Comment: **{Article text comment in Korean}**

D.1.2 Annotation Generation-step Prompt

Below is the original prompt used in **annotation generation step**, and prompt translated in English. The original prompt contains both English and Korean. The parts that were originally written in English and hasn't been additionally translated are written in blue font. The LLM must know the response of the previous prompt(**RAG step** prompt) before given the following prompt.

Original Prompt

> 외국인이 이해할 수 있도록 예시처럼 영어로 간결하게 설명해줘.
> 예시)
> Title: ""Suicide bombing at a mosque in northwest Pakistan... 'Over 40 dead'""
> Comment: If Dori Dori gets elected, you'll end up like that.
> - ""Dori Dori"": is a nickname used in South Korea to refer to President Yoon Suk-yeol. This nickname originated from his habit of moving his head side to side during speeches or public appearances. The term became an internet meme, often used in a political context to mock or criticize him.
> 설명은 객관적이어야만 해. 아래의 번역된 기사 제목과 댓글을 참고하도록 해.
> Title: **{Article text title in translated in English}**
> Comment: **{Article text comment translated in English}**

Translated Prompt

Explain it concisely in English so that foreigners can understand, like in the example below.
Example)
Title: ""Suicide bombing at a mosque in northwest Pakistan... 'Over 40 dead'""
Comment: If Dori Dori gets elected, you'll end up like that.
- ""Dori Dori"": is a nickname used in South Korea to refer to President Yoon Suk-yeol. This nickname originated from his habit of moving his head side to side during speeches or public appearances. The term became an internet meme, often used in a political context to mock or criticize him.
The explanation must remain objective. Refer to the translated article title and comments below.
Title: **{Article text title translated in English}**
Comment: **{Article text comment translated in English}**

D.2 Offensiveness Classification Prompt

This prompt is used to guide an LLM in evaluating the offensiveness of a given text by utilizing external information (annotations generated by the prompt in Appendix D.1). This is also the prompt used in the second stage of the pipeline.

Consider the following definitions.
1. offensive: the text which contains one of the following type:
(a) Word Modification: Instances where offensive language is altered to evade censorship but remains clearly recognizable as an insult.
(b) Reverse Discrimination Statements: Remarks expressing dissatisfaction with privileges or benefits attributed to a particular group, while portraying the speaker's group as a victim of discrimination.
(c) Incitement of Violence: Statements that incite or support violence or hate groups.
(d) Derogatory Remarks: Statements that imply or state that a particular group or individual is inferior to others. This includes dehumanizing language, such as comparing people to animals, insects, objects, etc.
(e) Satire: Statements that use sarcasm, humor, or satire to attack a particular group or individual.
(f) Stereotyping / Fact Distortion: Statements associating a specific group with negative attributes, like murder or terrorism, or delivering unsubstantiated and negatively distorted information about a specific group.
2. normal: the text which is not offensive and adheres to social norms.
Classify the post delimited by two backticks as offensive and normal. It is a Korean-written corpus translated in English. Refer to the annotation in your decision.
If it is offensive, span the parts(sentence, phrase or word) which you think it is offensive.
Example output for offensive :
Offensiveness : True
Span : [span]
Example output for normal :
Offensiveness : False
'Title: {**Article text title translated in English**}
Comment: {**Article text comment translated in English**} '
Annotation:
{**Annotation generated by the prompt in Appendix D.1**}

E Annotation Generation Example

The following is an example of the generated annotation. The given title and comments are as follows:

> **Title (KOR)**: [SNS세상] ""노래할 땐 사투리 안 쓰냐고?... 지방말투 차별 마세요""
> **Comment (KOR)**: 무까끼하이
> **Title (ENG)**: [SNS World] ""Don't you speak dialect when you sing?... Don't discriminate against regional accents""
> **Comment (ENG)**: Mukakki high

E.1 Response of RAG-step prompt

This is the response of the LLM after the **RAG-step** Prompt in Appendix D.1.1. Since the original prompt is written mostly in Korean, and the given input title and comment is in Korean, the output response of the LLM is also in Korean. Therefore, the translated response is also given below. The parts that were originally written in English and hasn't been additionally translated are written in blue font.

Original Response

> 제목과 댓글에서 한국 문화와 관련된 요소를 확인한 결과, 댓글에 '무까끼하이'라는 표현이 등장합니다. '무까끼하이'는 경상도 사투리로 '무식하게'라는 의미를 지니며, 힙합 듀오 메타와 렉스(Meta & Wreckx)의 곡 제목이기도 합니다. 이 곡은 음악 산업에서 돈만을 추구하는 이들을 비판하는 내용을 담고 있으며, 전체 가사가 경상도 사투리로 구성되어 있습니다. (출처: 마니아DB)
> 또한, 이 곡은 2012년 한국대중음악상에서 최우수 랩&힙합 노래 부문을 수상하며 그 가치를 인정받았습니다. (출처: KOREAN MUSIC AWARDS)
> 이처럼 '무까끼하이'는 한국 힙합 문화에서 사투리의 독특한 표현을 활용한 사례로, 음악 산업에 대한 비판적 시각을 담고 있어 한국 대중음악사에서 의미 있는 작품으로 평가받고 있습니다.

Translated Response

> As a result of checking the title and comments for elements related to Korean culture, the comment includes the phrase 'Mukakki High.' 'Mukakki High' is a phrase from the Gyeongsang-do dialect meaning 'recklessly' or 'ignorantly.' It is also the title of a song by the hip-hop duo Meta and Wreckx(Meta & Wreckx). The song criticizes those in the music industry who pursue money above all else, and its entire lyrics are written in the Gyeongsang-do dialect. (Source: ManiaDB)
> Furthermore, this song was recognized for its value by winning the Best Rap & Hip-Hop Song award at the 2012 Korean Music Awards. (Source: Korean Music Awards)
> In this way, 'Mukakki High' is an example of utilizing unique expressions from regional dialects in Korean hip-hop culture. It conveys a critical perspective on the music industry and is regarded as a significant work in the history of Korean popular music.

E.2 Response of annotation generation-step prompt

This is the response of the LLM after **the annotation generation step** prompt in Appendix D.1.2. This prompt asks to generate annotation in English, therefore the original response is in English.

> Title: [SNS World] "Don't you speak dialect when you sing?... Don't discriminate against regional accents"
> Comment: Mukakki high
> **"Mukakki high"**: This phrase originates from a regional dialect in South Korea, specifically the Gyeongsang Province dialect, meaning "recklessly" or "brashly." It gained popularity through

a song by the South Korean hip-hop duo Meta & Wreckx titled "Mukakki High," which uses Gyeongsang dialect throughout its lyrics. The song criticizes the greed-driven nature of the music industry and became a cultural reference in Korean hip-hop.

F LLM Offensiveness Classification Example

The following is an example of the classification response. The given title, comments, generated annotations, and the golden answer are as follows:

Title (KOR): [자막뉴스] '노마스크' 백인 남성에 "마트에서 나가라" 본때 보여준 한인들 / JTBC News
Comment (KOR): 하다하다 이런걸로 국뽕질이네
Title (ENG): [Subtitled News] Koreans Teach a Lesson to "No Mask" White Man with "Get Out of the Store" / JTBC News
Comment (ENG): Doing this kind of thing out of **extreme national pride**, seriously.
Annotation (ENG):

> **"Extreme national pride (국뽕)"**: This term is a Korean internet slang combining "nation" and "methamphetamine," used to mock or criticize excessive patriotism or over-the-top national pride. It implies being overly proud of one's country to the point of irrationality or exaggeration. The term is popular in online discussions in South Korea, often appearing in contexts where people feel certain actions or statements are driven by undue nationalistic sentiment.

Offensive? : TRUE

This is the response provided by the LLM when tasked with classifying the offensiveness of a post. The classification was conducted using external information (generated annotations), as outlined in the prompt included in Appendix D.2.

Offensiveness : True
Span : ["Doing this kind of thing out of extreme national pride"]

One world, one opinion? The superstar effect in LLM responses

Sofie Goethals
University of Antwerp, Belgium
sofie.goethals@uantwerpen.be

Lauren Rhue
Robert H. Smith School of Business,
University of Maryland, USA

Abstract

As large language models (LLMs) are shaping the way information is shared and accessed online, their opinions have the potential to influence a wide audience. This study examines who is predicted by the studied LLMs as the most prominent figures across various fields, while using prompts in ten different languages to explore the influence of linguistic diversity. Our findings reveal low diversity in responses, with a small number of figures dominating recognition across languages (also known as the "*superstar effect*"). These results highlight the risk of narrowing global knowledge representation when LLMs retrieve subjective information.

1 Introduction

Large Language Models (LLMs) are becoming increasingly integrated into various aspects of society. With applications such as educational tools, writing assistance, and content generation, they have considerable potential to shape people's opinions and decisions (Vida et al., 2024; Buyl et al., 2024; Qadri et al., 2025). A report from the World Bank estimates that since the launch of ChatGPT, LLMs and other generative AI (GenAI) have already become embedded in the daily routines of approximately half a billion people worldwide (Liu and Wang, 2024), illustrating their widespread potential influence.

Although many LLMs originate in the United States, these LLMs are increasingly able to converse in multiple languages. These models can be used for tasks such as synthesizing information (Evans et al., 2024), replacing human input in surveys (Bisbee et al., 2023), or performing general information retrieval (Zhu et al., 2023). LLMs are thus transforming the way information is accessed and transmitted online (Burton et al., 2024; Qadri et al., 2025).

The use of LLMs for these tasks may have unintended consequences. In this paper, we explore one such consequence – whether LLMs narrow the variety of perspectives (Shumailov et al., 2024; Padmakumar and He, 2024; Pedreschi et al., 2024). Cultural opinions, such as those about celebrities and other prominent figures, naturally vary by culture and language. Differences in linguistic and cultural diffusion should, in principle, lead LLMs to generate responses that reflect local perspectives. However, because LLMs share common embeddings and similar training data, their responses may be more uniform than expected, potentially narrowing cultural diversity and elevating global figures over nationally or culturally significant ones.

This paper specifically focuses on how LLMs answer opinion-based prompts about celebrated figures. These questions, such as "*Who is the greatest artist?*", reveal aspirational figures for society and for specific professional fields. We explore whether varying the language of the opinion-based prompt leads LLMs to provide different responses. Since opinion-based prompts do not have objectively correct answers and rely heavily on societal and cultural knowledge, we might expect models to adjust their responses based on the language of the prompt.

Furthermore, we investigate whether these LLM responses exhibit the "superstar effect".[1] We examine the superstar effect by assessing the frequency and novelty of names in the LLM-generated responses. Do the LLM responses reflect a language-specific spectrum of celebrated individuals from different cultures, or do the responses suggest a tendency to focus on a narrow subset of globally well-known individuals? In case of the latter, this

[1]This effect, observed in various domains, suggest that recognition and admiration is concentrated among a small number of figures. There is a long-tail of figures sharing the remaining recognition. This superstar effect emerges as an artifact of technology mediation (Elberse and Oberholzer-Gee, 2006).

Proceedings of the 3rd Workshop on Cross-Cultural Considerations in NLP (C3NLP 2025), pages 89–107
May 4, 2025 ©2025 Association for Computational Linguistics

could sideline regionally important individuals, ultimately narrowing global knowledge over time. This effect of cultural homogenization is also discussed in other research (Bommasani et al., 2022; Durmus et al., 2023; AlKhamissi et al., 2024).

Lastly, we analyze how individuals' professions shape the LLM results. Some professional fields are more international than others due to their inherent characteristics. Science, for example, is characterized by contributions that transcend cultural, linguistic, and national boundaries. This transcendence occurs due to the universality of scientific methods and principles, as well as international collaborations in modern scientific research, so that scientific contributions are less tied to specific local contexts and more universally recognized (Leydesdorff and Wagner, 2008). Landmark contributions, such as Einstein's theory of relativity or Newton's laws of motion, have global relevance, irrespective of cultural or linguistic boundaries. In contrast, contributions in arts and politics are often deeply embedded in local culture, history, and societal values (Benedict, 2019). Artistic works, such as literature, music, or visual art, frequently draw upon the specific traditions, languages, and experiences of their creators. Politics is inherently a contested and subjective domain, shaped by diverse perspectives, ideologies, and cultural contexts. What may be celebrated as visionary leadership in one context can be condemned as authoritarianism in another. As a result, we anticipate stronger consensus in scientific fields and more diversity in areas like the arts or politics.

Surprisingly, our findings reveal a substantial degree of consensus in LLM responses across languages, with many of the same individuals appearing regardless of the language used. For example, in every language, the most returned person for prompts about the most celebrated '*mathematician*' is Isaac Newton. In contrast, for prompts about the most celebrated '*political figure*' the responses are more diverse, but Gandhi is the most returned person for almost every language except for Russian and Chinese (Mao Zedong) and for Urdu and Bengali (Nelson Mandela). We consistently find this concentration of names, which we refer to as the "superstar effect". For every profession, there is a single individual (or a small group of individuals) who appear in over two-thirds of the responses across languages, LLMs and prompt variations (see Table 10). This result illustrates the strong convergence in LLM outputs regardless of linguistic or model-specific differences. However, we did find some variation depending on the field of the profession, where professions related to science lead to more consensus and professions related to art and politics to less. Our findings also indicate that languages with greater lexical similarity yield more aligned responses, suggesting a form of cultural consensus in the long tail of responses. We discuss potential causes and implications for this in Section 5.

The paper is structured as follows. We discuss related work in Section 2, and give more details about the materials, methods and metrics we use in Section 3. Our results are presented in Section 4. We discuss the implications and potential future research directions in Section 5, and end with listing the limitations of our study in Section 6.

2 Background

There have been many studies that focus on LLMs for multilingual input, primarily focused on their accuracy (Watts et al., 2024). As much of the initial training data on LLMs is written in English, LLMs tend to perform worse for non-English languages, particularly in under-resourced languages (Ahuja et al., 2023a,b). Rajaratnam (2024) makes the analogy with a library predominantly filled with English books: a reader looking for resources in another language may struggle to find what they need—and LLMs face similar challenges. This study also investigate how LLM outputs vary across multilingual inputs, but this paper focuses on alignment in opinions across languages rather than performance across languages, as there is no ground truth for these opinion-based tasks.

Another related area of research focuses on the cultural undertones in LLMs. One research stream evaluates language models' retention of culture-related commonsense by testing their responses to geographically diverse facts (Nguyen et al., 2023; Yin et al., 2022; Keleg and Magdy, 2023). Several studies investigate the cultural values that LLMs exhibit and find that these are more closely aligned with Western, Rich and Industrialized ideologies (Cao et al., 2023; Tao et al., 2024; Buyl et al., 2024; Rao et al., 2023). Vida et al. (2024) highlight that the language of the prompt significantly influences LLM response behaviors, while AlKhamissi et al. (2024) demonstrate stronger cultural alignment when LLMs are prompted in the dominant language of a given culture. Furthermore,

Durmus et al. (2023) compare LLM output with opinions of different countries on global issues. These studies study alignment in cultural values (often based on the World Values Survey (Haerpfer et al., 2020)) . More in line with our research is Naous et al. (2023) who find that when operating in Arabic, LLM's exhibit a bias towards Western entities, failing in appropriate cultural adaptation.

This study explores the responses of LLMs about high achievers in different aspects of society because celebrities reflect the values of society (Gorin and Dubied, 2011; Allison and Goethals, 2016) and, under certain circumstances, can influence social norms (Cohen et al., 2024). These notable figures, heroes with elevated social stature, are a means to represent cultural values in a way that is easy to communicate to all members of society and reflect the behaviors that should be modeled (Sun et al., 2024). The identification of specific figures as the pinnacle of their field indicate the attributes that are valued in that field, and provide a lens to understand how others in this field are judged. Several studies in other fields observe the emergence of the "superstar effect" in the technology-mediated sales (Weeds, 2012; Brynjolfsson et al., 2010), where there is a concentration of demand among a few items and a very long tail among the others. This study will assess whether generative AI reveals similar trends when responding to opinion-based questions regarding notable figures.

3 Materials and Methods

3.1 Experimental set-up

Our goal is to explore the variation across LLMs and across languages in response to a series of opinion-based prompts about celebrated individuals. To that end, this study consists of an experimental design with four dimensions: LLMs, languages, professional field, and prompt adjective. First, this study uses three of the most well-known large language models, namely GPT-4 from OpenAI (Achiam et al., 2023), Claude-3-Opus from Anthropic (Anthropic, 2024), and Llama-3.1-70B-Instruct from Meta (Dubey et al., 2024). We use the default parameters for every LLM to reflect the way most users would use them. Second, we vary the prompt language. To avoid any selection bias, we choose the ten most-used languages (Central Intelligence Agency, 2025) .

This aspect of methodological set-up is presented in Figure 1.

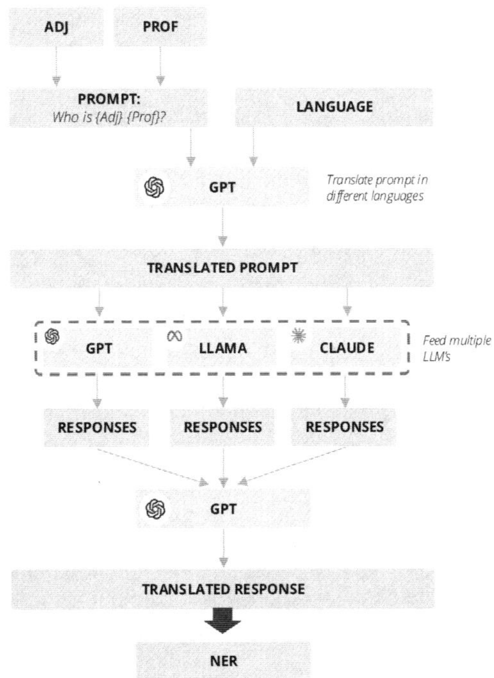

Figure 1: Overview of experimental set-up for the multilingual prompt analysis

Next, we systematically vary the adjective and the professional field in the opinion-based prompt. Translated into English, each prompt is a variation of the following format: "*Who is the {adjective} {profession}?*". The prompts cover fifteen professions with five descriptive adjectives. Profession is broadly defined and encompasses specific occupations such as writer or poet as well as vague terms such as person or leader. The used adjectives, professions and languages are shown in Table 1.

Languages	Adjectives	Professions
English	Greatest	Leader
Spanish	Most Influential	Military Leader
Russian	Most Important	Poet
Chinese	Most Famous	Philosopher
Hindi	Most Impactful	Artist
Arabic		Political Figure
French		Composer
Bengali		Writer
Portuguese		Physicist
Urdu		Chemist
		Economist
		Medical Researcher
		Mathematician
		Computer Scientist
		Person

Table 1: Languages, Adjectives, and Professions

Each adjective and profession are combined into a prompt. For each prompt, we use GPT-4o to translate the initial prompt to the selected language. The translated prompt is submitted to each of the three LLMs and the LLMs' response is captured. Then, we use GPT-4o to translate the answer back to English.[2] Based on the translated responses, we use Named Entity Recognition (NER) to identify the persons in the responses. We execute every combination of LLM, adjective, profession, and language five times (as LLMs behave stochastically and can return different results each run), resulting in a total of 11,250 iterations.[3]

Entity recognition To identify individuals mentioned in the responses, we apply Named Entity Recognition (NER) using the spaCy library ("*en_core_web_trf*" model).[4] We process each translated response to extract named entities classified as 'PERSON' labels. We perform manual verification of all extracted names to ensure consistency and to merge different writing styles.

3.2 Consensus between the language pairs

We use **cosine similarity** to assess the consensus between LLM responses to prompts in two different languages. We convert the responses of each language in a frequency vector. Cosine similarity measures the angle between the two vectors, where a smaller angle indicates greater similarity.

As a proxy for the cultural similarity of a language pair, we use the Similarity Database of modern lexicons of Bella et al. (2021). When languages have higher lexical similarity, it means they share a larger number of words with similar forms and meanings. This similarity often arises because the languages have a common linguistic ancestry (e.g., Latin for Romance languages), have historically interacted closely, or have borrowed words from each other over time (Hock and Joseph, 2009).

We use the **Spearman correlation** coefficient (Spearman, 1961) to measure the alignment between the lexical similarity and the average consensus between one language pair. This metric measures the strength and direction of a monotonic relationship between two variables by comparing their rank orders. [5]

3.3 Metrics

We measure the **novelty** of a set of responses R as is done in the recommender literature (Zhou et al., 2010; Kaminskas and Bridge, 2016):

$$\text{Novelty}(R) = \frac{\sum_{i \in R} -\log_2 p(i)}{|R|} \quad (1)$$

where $p(i)$ is the fraction of responses in the overall distribution that mention person i. For each name i in the response set R, we will evaluate its novelty relative to the overall response distribution and subsequently compute the average novelty of the entire response set R.[6]

We use the **Gini coefficient** (Dorfman, 1979) to measure the inequality in the distribution of name occurrences for each profession. This metric quantifies how unequal the distribution is by comparing the cumulative proportions of the population (which are all the unique persons that are returned for one profession) and the recognition they hold:

$$G = \frac{\sum_{i=1}^{n} \sum_{j=1}^{n} |x_i - x_j|}{2n^2\mu} \quad (2)$$

where:

- n is the number of observations,
- x_i and x_j are the number of occurrences for individuals i and j,
- μ is the mean of the distribution.

A Gini coefficient of 0 reflects complete diversity in responses whereas values closer to 1 represent concentration (one person gets most of the recognition).

4 Results

In this section, we present our aggregate results. We discuss the analysis for LLMs, prompt language and profession here, but the analysis for adjectives can be found in Section A.1. The results for each LLM separately can also be found in the Appendix in Table 7 (LLM -Adjective), 8 (LLM - Language) and 9 (LLM - Profession). The top ten names for every profession can be found in Table 10. On average, each response contained 5.80 names, and in total, 2412 unique names were returned.

[2]Jiao et al. (2023) show that the performance of GPT-4 is comparable to commercial translation products, even for distant languages.

[3]Calculated as: 3 LLMs * 10 languages * 15 professions * 5 adjectives * 5 runs = 11, 250 iterations

[4]`https://spacy.io/api/entityrecognizer`

[5]We use the implementation in `https://docs.scipy.org/doc/scipy/reference/generated/scipy.stats.spearmanr.html`.

[6]In our experiments, we will measure this for every profession separately, and then take the average over the different professions.

4.1 LLM

The choice of LLM has a large impact on the results, as shown in Table 2. LLMs differ in the scope and novelty of their responses. On average, using Claude returns more than double the number of persons than using Llama, the LLM with the lowest average number of names, suggesting that Claude provides more expansive responses in each iteration. However, despite returning the least persons on average for each run, Llama by far returns the most unique names across the different runs, adjectives and languages suggesting that Llama has more diversity in its responses. This is reflected in the higher novelty score of Llama as well.

LLM	Avg. # of names	Unique names	Novelty
GPT	5.01	1158	1.99
Claude	8.60	1023	2.14
Llama	3.80	1386	2.61

Table 2: General results by LLM.
Avg. # of names represent the average number of persons returned in one response, Unique names represents how many unique names are returned over all the responses and the novelty score represents how novel the results of one LLM are compared to the overall response distribution of all LLMs (average over the professions).

Figure 2 demonstrates the overlap in unique names between the LLMs. Llama generates more names that are not present in the results of the other LLMs, again highlighting the variation in knowledge across LLMs.

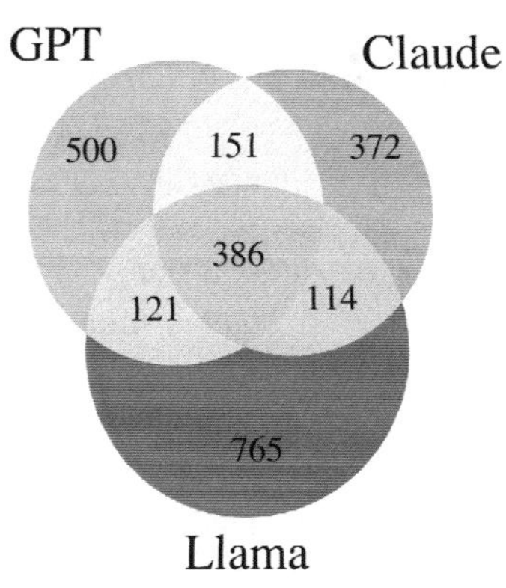

Figure 2: Overlap in names between the LLMs

4.2 Prompt Language

Second, we report the variation in responses across languages. Table 3 reports the general statistics for each language (aggregated across all LLMs). On average, we see that prompts in English return the most names and prompts in Arabic return the least (this pattern also holds for each LLM separately, see Table 8 in the Appendix). Urdu returns more unique names compared to the other languages, a pattern that we also see for every LLM separately but that is most striking for Llama (Table 8). This finding is reflected in the novelty scores as well. We can see that prompts in Urdu or Chinese tend to return more novel names than prompts in French or Spanish.

Language	Avg. # of names	Unique names	Novelty
English	7.90	520	2.11
Spanish	6.66	477	1.95
Russian	5.45	490	1.91
Chinese	5.93	647	2.43
Hindi	5.24	618	2.29
Arabic	4.08	591	2.28
French	6.43	468	1.93
Bengali	5.37	642	2.26
Portuguese	6.13	551	2.03
Urdu	4.86	918	2.91

Table 3: General results by language

To understand which languages yield similar responses, we quantify the consensus between two languages by measuring the cosine similarity between the frequency distributions of their responses. We use MDS to visualize the similarity of the responses in a 2D-plot for every LLM in Figure 3.[7] Languages with similar cultures and history produce results that are closer together. For example, for each of the LLMs, the responses from languages from European origin appear in one centroid, while theresponses from Asian languages appear more distant.

To verify this pattern statistically, we compare these results with the Similarity Database of Modern Lexicons (Bella et al., 2021). We verify for each LLM separately whether there is a pairwise correlation between the average consensus of each language pair and the lexical similarity of that language pair. We see a significant correlation for every LLM in Table 4. This means that languages with higher lexicon similarity tend to have more consensus on which persons should be venerated.

[7]MDS is a dimensionality reduction technique that projects high-dimensional data into a lower-dimensional space, preserving the pairwise distances between points as closely as possible (Cox and Cox, 2000).

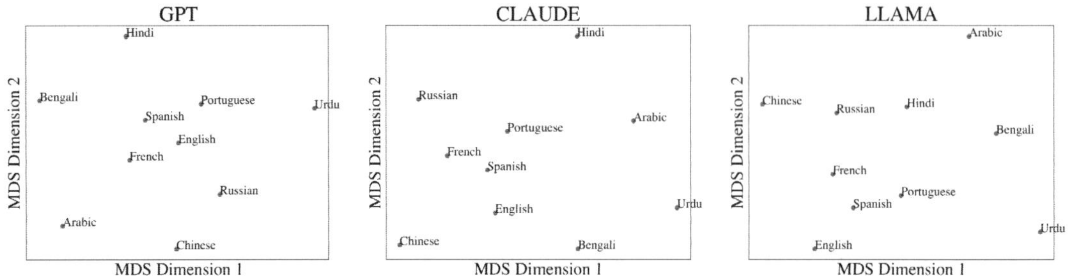

(a) GPT (b) Claude (c) Llama

Figure 3: Similarity of the responses between languages (by LLM)

LLM	GPT	Claude	Llama
Correlation	0.450	0.532	0.401
p-value	0.002**	0.002**	0.006**

Table 4: Spearman correlation between the similarity in modern lexicons and the consensus between languages

4.3 Profession

The general results for each profession can be found in Table 5. If we divide the professions according to their overarching categories (Science, Politics, Art and General), we can see differences in the average response rate. We see that general, vague 'professions' such as 'person' lead to the most names per response, while science-related professions such as physicist or chemist consistently generate fewer names in the returned responses.

Profession	Avg. # of names	Unique names	Novelty
Artist	5.64	227	2.19
Computer Scientist	4.65	119	1.88
Chemist	3.99	174	2.34
Composer	5.38	208	2.01
Poet	6.30	384	3.00
Leader	7.08	260	2.38
Physicist	4.28	97	1.74
Medical Researcher	4.85	203	2.33
Philosopher	6.79	152	1.67
Person	8.21	266	2.36
Political Figure	7.33	333	2.38
Economist	4.74	85	1.32
Writer	6.39	365	2.89
Military Leader	5.77	286	2.42
Mathematician	5.66	237	2.25

Table 5: General results by profession

Table 5 suggests that scientific professions also tend to yield fewer unique names compared to professions such as politics or art. For each profession, we also calculate the average novelty score across the languages. [8]

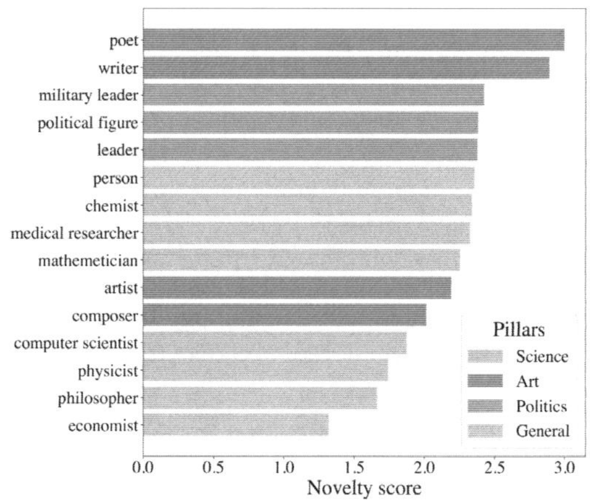

Figure 4: Novelty by field and category

Figure 4 shows that fields such as 'poet' and 'writer' that heavily depend on the language, and more subjective fields such as 'military leader' and 'political figure' lead to the most novel names. This means that prompting in a different language generally leads to more novel names. This aligns with our expectation that science represents a field with more globally recognized contributors whose influence transcends national boundaries, whereas politics and art are fields that often reflect more localized and culturally specific perspectives.

4.4 The superstar effect

The superstar effect is quantified in multiple ways. First, we analyze the frequency distribution of names returned for each profession. The superstar effect is characterized by the power-law distribution – a distribution with a heavy concentration on

[8] To calculate the novelty of a profession, we do not compare the responses of the different professions with each other. Instead, we calculate the novelty score per profession by calculating the the novelty score of every language for that profession, and taking the average.

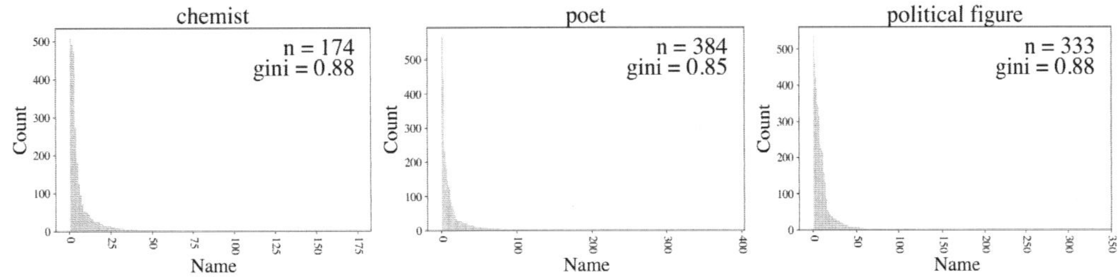

Figure 5: Frequency distribution for three professions (across LLMs). The number of unique names and Gini coefficient are depicted in the right corner (n). The other frequency distributions are available in the Appendix.

some and a long tail for others. The inequality in the distribution is captured by the Gini coefficient.

The superstar effect for three professions across LLMs in shown in Figure 5. The other professions show similar patterns and can be found in the Appendix in Figure 9, as well as the Figures for every LLM separately (Figures 10 - 12). For every profession, a total of 750 responses are generated.[9] All the distributions share a sharp peak and a long tail, where the sharp peak indicates a few people who are consistently included in the answers across all parameters. All professions exhibit a long tail of names that are returned only a few times or even just once. To quantify the concentration in the responses, we calculate the Gini coefficient for each profession and consistently find values higher than 0.70, which indicates very unequal distributions. [10]

For instance, Alan Turing is present in 96.4% (n = 723) of the responses for computer scientist (so across different adjectives, runs, languages and LLMs), and Adam Smith is present in 96.3% (n = 722) of the responses for economist. For every profession, there is a person that is present in more than 2/3 of the responses ($n > 500$). We display the results for computer scientists in Table 6. For the detailed view of the results by individual names across all professions, see Table 10 in the Appendix.

Table 6: Results for computer scientist. Count (n) is the number of responses with the name. Percentage (%) is the fraction of responses with the name ($n/750$).

Name	n	%
Alan Turing	723	96.4
John Neumann	364	48.5
Tim Berners	314	41.9
Lee	313	41.7
Hopper	257	34.3
Ada Lovelace	230	30.7
Dennis Ritchie	193	25.7
Claude Shannon	166	22.1
Charles Babbage	146	19.5
Donald Knuth	134	17.9

5 Discussion

In this study, we systematically vary the prompt, the prompt language, and the used language model to explore the relationship between language and opinions returned by LLMs. This study identifies two important factors when using LLMs to generate opinions about prominent figures: the influence of culture, measured by lexical similarity, and the impact of the professional field. We also find that LLM responses exhibit the superstar effect, common in other technologically mediated contexts.

Our findings indicate that the opinions vary with cultural elements. The names in the LLM responses display higher consensus in languages with greater lexical similarities. This outcome aligns with expectations, as linguistic overlap often reflects cultural interconnectedness. LLMs are expected to vary their responses to align with the norms of the culture associated with the prompt language.

Next, we observe the influence of the professional field on the LLM responses. Internationally influential professions such as computer science and physics often yield consensus on globally renowned figures, such as Alan Turing or Albert Einstein, who dominate the LLM responses. There is less consensus on professional fields with more regional influence or fields that are more tied to cultural norms, such as military leaders and writers. However, even in more locally appreciated profes-

[9] 3 LLMs * 10 languages * 5 adjectives * 5 runs = 750 responses

[10] The Gini values are displayed in Figure 5 and Figures 9 - 12.

sions such as the arts, LLMs exhibit a preference towards dominant figures, often from the Western hemisphere. For example, William Shakespeare consistently emerges as the most celebrated writer in every language, and this result could indicate that the LLMs are overshadowing culturally specific authors. Future research could investigate this phenomenon further.

This pattern highlights a broader trend: LLMs prioritize popular opinions, often at the expense of cultural diversity. Such behavior is consistent with the narrowing of knowledge discussed in prior literature. Shumailov et al. (2024) illustrate the risk of homogeneity in AI-generated content, as when AI predicts what to generate, the path of least resistance is an averaging of the content in its source material. Similarly, Doshi and Hauser (2024) argue that while using AI can boost individual creativity, it comes at the expense of less varied content overall. Pedreschi et al. (2024) warn that human-AI coevolution might lead to a loss of diversity in generated content, while Burton et al. (2024) discuss how the use of large language models can reshape collective intelligence by reducing functional diversity among individuals. Lastly, Qadri et al. (2025) study how the use of large language models can lead to cultural erasure. This type of knowledge homogeneity could stem from the training data and processes underlying these models (Prabhakaran et al., 2022). Training datasets may overrepresent globally influential figures or sources from a few dominant cultures. Moreover, the architecture of LLMs promotes shared embeddings and parameters across languages, resulting in consistent output. Cross-linguistic transfer learning (Lai et al., 2024) amplifies this effect by encoding general, cross-linguistic knowledge rather than language-specific nuances.

While this paper does not aim to prescribe whether LLMs should prioritize producing more consensus or embracing greater diversity in their opinions, it is crucial to consider some of its implications. For example, teenagers writing a school paper about "a great writer" might no longer consult their parents or teachers but instead ask an LLM for inspiration. If the models consistently suggest a narrow set of globally renowned authors like Shakespeare or Tolstoy, it could limit exposure to regionally significant writers, leading to a narrowing of global knowledge over time. Alternatively, if news agencies or content creators use LLMs for research or writing assistance, they may unintentionally amplify the prominence of already well-known figures, leading to reduced media diversity and limited recognition for less-known local figures.

Different levels of consensus or diversity might be appropriate depending on the context. For example, in fields like physics or mathematics, a higher degree of consensus might be desirable due to its universal nature, while in literature or politics, diversity and cultural specificity might be more suited. The discussed phenomenon is not necessarily good or bad, but its appropriateness is context-dependent. The goal is this paper is to observe the existence of the superstar effect in LLM opinions and contribute to the discussion about its implications.

Several avenues for future research emerge from this work. Our main direction of future research is to compare the LLM responses with human responses. It would be interesting to compare the diversity in human opinions to that of LLMs. Do people who speak these languages agree with the assessment of LLMs on who should be celebrated for their achievements in these fields? Do they produce more or less diverse opinions? Another avenue of future research is experimenting with prompts that stress that the response should be relative to the culture or language in question. Although this does not necessarily reflect a typical user, this type of prompt could encourage culturally-specific responses and reduce the narrowing of knowledge. Lastly, the global figures appear to be historical figures (such as Shakespeare). Future research could evaluate the temporal relationship between the superstar effect and the LLM responses, and whether time moderates the tension between global and cultural responses.

With LLMs rapidly changing the way information is accessed and shared online, it is vital to proactively anticipate some of its unintended consequences. This study explores the tension between global consensus and cultural specificity in AI-generated content and encourages users to be aware of this behavior when relying on LLMs to retrieve information that can involve subjective perspectives.

6 Limitations

As can be seen in our methodological set-up, all responses are translated back to English before the consequent analysis. The manner of translation could have some influence on the results. However, as we do not use the actual responses (except for the sentiment analysis in the Appendix) but only the named entities present in the response, the translation manner will have less impact. We also manually verify some of the responses to ensure that the LLM does not alter the returned persons. The fact that we only investigate the persons present in the response can also be seen as a limitation, as we do not analyse the remainder of the response or the ordering in which the persons occur. Naous et al. (2023) also found that NER works better for Western persons than for Arabic persons, which could influence the returned persons from other cultures.

The choice of languages and models is also a limiting factor. To avoid any selection bias, we opted for the ten most spoken languages, and three of the most popular LLMs. However, we could extend the analysis to some less popular languages as well. The lower language support may lead to an increase in the superstar effect, as there may be less local cultural awareness. Similarly, an interesting follow-up experiment could be using LLMs developed in different countries and see how this would affect these results. Additionally, we use language as a proxy for culture, while there are obviously important differences between the two (Hershcovich et al., 2022).

Besides this, we use the current version of the LLMs for our experiments, which presents challenges for reproducibility as they can be updated at anytime, potentially altering the results. Lastly, we used the default parameters for every LLM but varying some of the parameters (such as temperature) could also influence the diversity of the response. We opted for the default parameters to reflect the way that most users would interact with the LLMs.

Acknowledgments

This research was funded by Flemish Research Foundation (grant number 1247125N).

References

Josh Achiam, Steven Adler, Sandhini Agarwal, Lama Ahmad, Ilge Akkaya, Florencia Leoni Aleman, Diogo Almeida, Janko Altenschmidt, Sam Altman, Shyamal Anadkat, et al. 2023. Gpt-4 technical report. *arXiv preprint arXiv:2303.08774*.

Kabir Ahuja, Harshita Diddee, Rishav Hada, Millicent Ochieng, Krithika Ramesh, Prachi Jain, Akshay Nambi, Tanuja Ganu, Sameer Segal, Maxamed Axmed, et al. 2023a. Mega: Multilingual evaluation of generative ai. *arXiv preprint arXiv:2303.12528*.

Sanchit Ahuja, Divyanshu Aggarwal, Varun Gumma, Ishaan Watts, Ashutosh Sathe, Millicent Ochieng, Rishav Hada, Prachi Jain, Maxamed Axmed, Kalika Bali, et al. 2023b. Megaverse: Benchmarking large language models across languages, modalities, models and tasks. *arXiv preprint arXiv:2311.07463*.

Badr AlKhamissi, Muhammad ElNokrashy, Mai AlKhamissi, and Mona Diab. 2024. Investigating cultural alignment of large language models. *arXiv preprint arXiv:2402.13231*.

Scott T Allison and George R Goethals. 2016. Hero worship: The elevation of the human spirit. *Journal for the Theory of Social Behaviour*, 46(2):187–210.

AI Anthropic. 2024. The claude 3 model family: Opus, sonnet, haiku. *Claude-3 Model Card*, 1.

Gábor Bella, Khuyagbaatar Batsuren, and Fausto Giunchiglia. 2021. A database and visualization of the similarity of contemporary lexicons. In *International Conference on Text, Speech, and Dialogue*, pages 95–104. Springer.

Ruth Benedict. 2019. *Patterns of culture*. Routledge.

James Bisbee, Joshua D Clinton, Cassy Dorff, Brenton Kenkel, and Jennifer M Larson. 2023. Synthetic replacements for human survey data? the perils of large language models. *Political Analysis*, pages 1–16.

Rishi Bommasani, Kathleen A Creel, Ananya Kumar, Dan Jurafsky, and Percy S Liang. 2022. Picking on the same person: Does algorithmic monoculture lead to outcome homogenization? *Advances in Neural Information Processing Systems*, 35:3663–3678.

Erik Brynjolfsson, Yu Hu, and Michael D Smith. 2010. Research commentary—long tails vs. superstars: The effect of information technology on product variety and sales concentration patterns. *Information Systems Research*, 21(4):736–747.

Jason W Burton, Ezequiel Lopez-Lopez, Shahar Hechtlinger, Zoe Rahwan, Samuel Aeschbach, Michiel A Bakker, Joshua A Becker, Aleks Berditchevskaia, Julian Berger, Levin Brinkmann, et al. 2024. How large language models can reshape collective intelligence. *Nature Human Behaviour*, pages 1–13.

Maarten Buyl, Alexander Rogiers, Sander Noels, Iris Dominguez-Catena, Edith Heiter, Raphael Romero, Iman Johary, Alexandru-Cristian Mara, Jefrey Lijffijt, and Tijl De Bie. 2024. Large language models reflect the ideology of their creators. *arXiv preprint arXiv:2410.18417*.

Yong Cao, Li Zhou, Seolhwa Lee, Laura Cabello, Min Chen, and Daniel Hershcovich. 2023. Assessing cross-cultural alignment between chatgpt and human societies: An empirical study. *arXiv preprint arXiv:2303.17466*.

Central Intelligence Agency. 2025. The world factbook: World - people and society. Accessed: 2025-03-03.

Elizabeth L Cohen, Mckay West, Koji Yoshimura, Molly E Farrell, and Ashleigh Swain. 2024. Normative influence of the stars: The relative indirect effects of celebrity exemplars on vaping norm perceptions through liking, parasocial relationship strength, and wishful identification. *Health Communication*, 39(9):1877–1887.

Trevor F Cox and Michael AA Cox. 2000. *Multidimensional scaling*. CRC press.

Robert Dorfman. 1979. A formula for the gini coefficient. *The review of economics and statistics*, pages 146–149.

Anil R Doshi and Oliver P Hauser. 2024. Generative ai enhances individual creativity but reduces the collective diversity of novel content. *Science Advances*, 10(28):eadn5290.

Abhimanyu Dubey, Abhinav Jauhri, Abhinav Pandey, Abhishek Kadian, Ahmad Al-Dahle, Aiesha Letman, Akhil Mathur, Alan Schelten, Amy Yang, Angela Fan, et al. 2024. The llama 3 herd of models. *arXiv preprint arXiv:2407.21783*.

Esin Durmus, Karina Nyugen, Thomas I Liao, Nicholas Schiefer, Amanda Askell, Anton Bakhtin, Carol Chen, Zac Hatfield-Dodds, Danny Hernandez, Nicholas Joseph, et al. 2023. Towards measuring the representation of subjective global opinions in language models. *arXiv preprint arXiv:2306.16388*.

Anita Elberse and Felix Oberholzer-Gee. 2006. *Superstars and underdogs: An examination of the long tail phenomenon in video sales*, volume 7. Citeseer.

Julia Evans, Jennifer D'Souza, and Sören Auer. 2024. Large language models as evaluators for scientific synthesis. *Preprint*, arXiv:2407.02977.

Valerie Gorin and Annik Dubied. 2011. Desirable people: Identifying social values through celebrity news. *Media, Culture & Society*, 33:599–618.

Christian Haerpfer, Ronald Inglehart, Alejandro Moreno, Christian Welzel, Kseniya Kizilova, Jaime Diez-Medrano, Marta Lagos, Pippa Norris, Eduard Ponarin, and Bi Puranen. 2020. World values survey wave 7 (2017-2020) cross-national data-set. *(No Title)*.

Daniel Hershcovich, Stella Frank, Heather Lent, Miryam de Lhoneux, Mostafa Abdou, Stephanie Brandl, Emanuele Bugliarello, Laura Cabello Piqueras, Ilias Chalkidis, Ruixiang Cui, et al. 2022. Challenges and strategies in cross-cultural nlp. *arXiv preprint arXiv:2203.10020*.

Hans Henrich Hock and Brian D Joseph. 2009. *Language history, language change, and language relationship: An introduction to historical and comparative linguistics*. Mouton de Gruyter.

Wenxiang Jiao, Wenxuan Wang, Jen-tse Huang, Xing Wang, Shuming Shi, and Zhaopeng Tu. 2023. Is chatgpt a good translator? yes with gpt-4 as the engine. *arXiv preprint arXiv:2301.08745*.

Marius Kaminskas and Derek Bridge. 2016. Diversity, serendipity, novelty, and coverage: a survey and empirical analysis of beyond-accuracy objectives in recommender systems. *ACM Transactions on Interactive Intelligent Systems (TiiS)*, 7(1):1–42.

Amr Keleg and Walid Magdy. 2023. Dlama: A framework for curating culturally diverse facts for probing the knowledge of pretrained language models. *arXiv preprint arXiv:2306.05076*.

Wen Lai, Mohsen Mesgar, and Alexander Fraser. 2024. Llms beyond english: Scaling the multilingual capability of llms with cross-lingual feedback. *Preprint*, arXiv:2406.01771.

Loet Leydesdorff and Caroline S Wagner. 2008. International collaboration in science and the formation of a core group. *Journal of informetrics*, 2(4):317–325.

Yan Liu and He Wang. 2024. Who on earth is using generative ai? *Washington, DC: World Bank*.

Steven Loria et al. 2018. textblob documentation. *Release 0.15*, 2(8):269.

Tarek Naous, Michael J Ryan, Alan Ritter, and Wei Xu. 2023. Having beer after prayer? measuring cultural bias in large language models. *arXiv preprint arXiv:2305.14456*.

Tuan-Phong Nguyen, Simon Razniewski, Aparna Varde, and Gerhard Weikum. 2023. Extracting cultural commonsense knowledge at scale. In *Proceedings of the ACM Web Conference 2023*, pages 1907–1917.

Vishakh Padmakumar and He He. 2024. Does writing with language models reduce content diversity? *Preprint*, arXiv:2309.05196.

Dino Pedreschi, Luca Pappalardo, Emanuele Ferragina, Ricardo Baeza-Yates, Albert-László Barabási, Frank Dignum, Virginia Dignum, Tina Eliassi-Rad, Fosca Giannotti, János Kertész, et al. 2024. Human-ai coevolution. *Artificial Intelligence*, page 104244.

Vinodkumar Prabhakaran, Rida Qadri, and Ben Hutchinson. 2022. Cultural incongruencies in artificial intelligence. *arXiv preprint arXiv:2211.13069*.

Rida Qadri, Aida M Davani, Kevin Robinson, and Vinodkumar Prabhakaran. 2025. Risks of cultural erasure in large language models. *arXiv preprint arXiv:2501.01056*.

Vaikunthan Rajaratnam. 2024. Why i'm committed to breaking the bias in large language models. *Nature*.

Abhinav Rao, Aditi Khandelwal, Kumar Tanmay, Utkarsh Agarwal, and Monojit Choudhury. 2023. Ethical reasoning over moral alignment: A case and framework for in-context ethical policies in llms. *arXiv preprint arXiv:2310.07251*.

Ilia Shumailov, Zakhar Shumaylov, Yiren Zhao, Nicolas Papernot, Ross Anderson, and Yarin Gal. 2024. Ai models collapse when trained on recursively generated data. *Nature*, 631(8022):755–759.

Charles Spearman. 1961. The proof and measurement of association between two things.

Yuning Sun, Elaine L. Kinsella, and Eric R. Igou. 2024. On cultural differences of heroes: Evidence from individualistic and collectivistic cultures. *Personality and Social Psychology Bulletin*, 50(6):841–856. PMID: 36727610.

Yan Tao, Olga Viberg, Ryan S Baker, and René F Kizilcec. 2024. Cultural bias and cultural alignment of large language models. *PNAS nexus*, 3(9):pgae346.

Karina Vida, Fabian Damken, and Anne Lauscher. 2024. Decoding multilingual moral preferences: Unveiling llm's biases through the moral machine experiment. In *Proceedings of the AAAI/ACM Conference on AI, Ethics, and Society*, volume 7, pages 1490–1501.

Ishaan Watts, Varun Gumma, Aditya Yadavalli, Vivek Seshadri, Manohar Swaminathan, and Sunayana Sitaram. 2024. Pariksha: A large-scale investigation of human-llm evaluator agreement on multilingual and multi-cultural data. *arXiv preprint arXiv:2406.15053*.

Helen Weeds. 2012. Superstars and the long tail: The impact of technology on market structure in media industries. *Information Economics and Policy*, 24(1):60–68.

Da Yin, Hritik Bansal, Masoud Monajatipoor, Liunian Harold Li, and Kai-Wei Chang. 2022. Geomlama: Geo-diverse commonsense probing on multilingual pre-trained language models. *arXiv preprint arXiv:2205.12247*.

Tao Zhou, Zoltán Kuscsik, Jian-Guo Liu, Matúš Medo, Joseph Rushton Wakeling, and Yi-Cheng Zhang. 2010. Solving the apparent diversity-accuracy dilemma of recommender systems. *Proceedings of the National Academy of Sciences*, 107(10):4511–4515.

Yutao Zhu, Huaying Yuan, Shuting Wang, Jiongnan Liu, Wenhan Liu, Chenlong Deng, Haonan Chen, Zheng Liu, Zhicheng Dou, and Ji-Rong Wen. 2023. Large language models for information retrieval: A survey. *arXiv preprint arXiv:2308.07107*.

A Appendix

A.1 Adjectives

As explained in Section 3, we test different versions of the prompt by varying the adjective and running each version 5 times. We see in Figure 6 that the adjective 'Greatest' leads to the most returned names on average, and that this is consistent across the LLMs (see Table 7 in the Appendix).

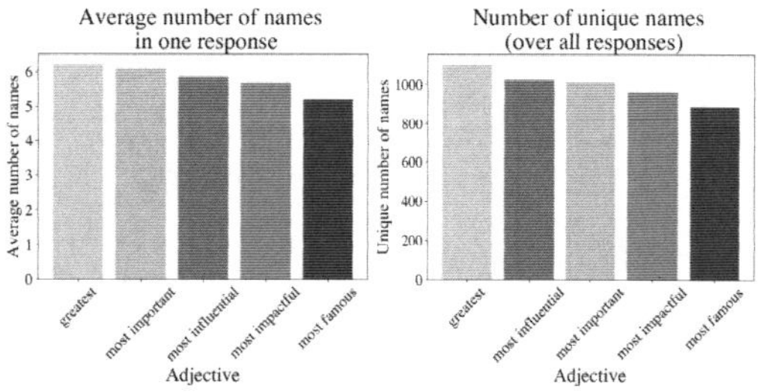

Figure 6: General analysis by adjective

The adjective 'Most Famous' consistently returns the least names. Similarly 'Greatest' leads to the most unique names, and 'Most Famous' to the least. We hypothesize that there may be more universal agreement on the criteria for fame whereas the criteria for adjectives like 'Greatest' may be harder to define. We see in Figure 7 that the adjective 'Greatest' also leads to the most novel names across the professions, although there is only a slight difference. We also conduct a sentiment analysis to assess how the adjectives impact the polarity and subjectivity of the responses and present the results in Section A.2.

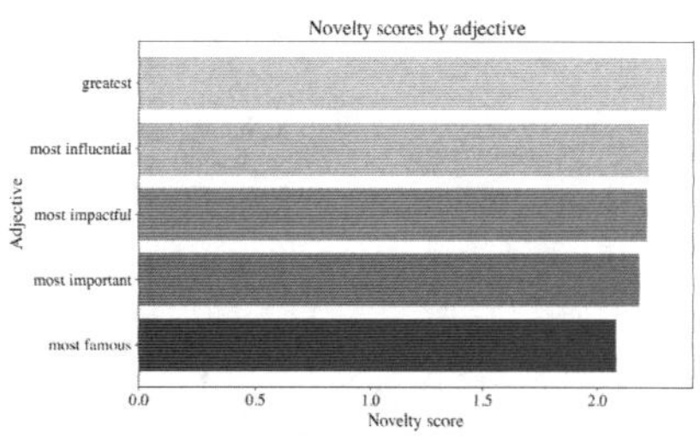

Figure 7: Novelty of responses by adjective

A.2 Sentiment analysis

We use TextBlob to analyze the sentiment of the text responses, measuring polarity (the positivity or negativity) and subjectivity (the degree of opinion versus fact) for each response (Loria et al., 2018). The sentiment of the responses is analyzed after the LLMs' responses are translated back into English. In this case, we use the complete text responses and not only the returned names.

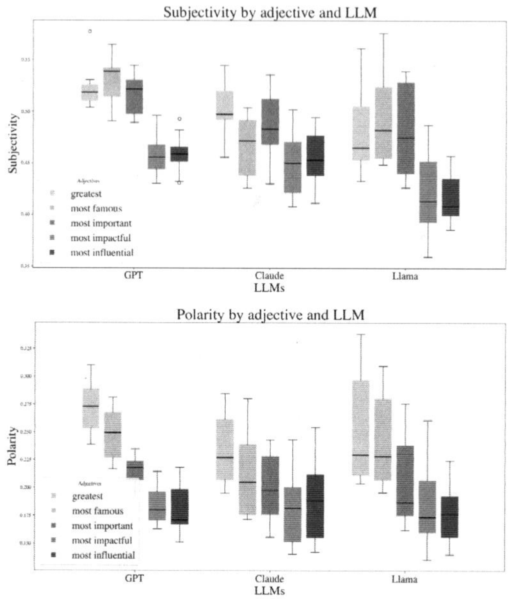

Figure 8: Sentiment analysis

We see in Figure 8 that the average polarity and subjectivity of the text response can vary a lot depending on the used adjective.

A.3 Additional results

In this Section, we present some of the additional results. We display the full results by LLM and adjective in Table 7, by LLM and language in Table 8 and by LLM and profession in Table 9. Table 7 reveals that Claude generates the highest number of unique names within a single adjective. However, it produces the fewest unique names when considering results across different adjectives. This suggests that Claude's outputs are the least affected by variations in prompt phrasing (adjective choice). Table 8 illustrates that Claude produces the most unique names within one language, but the least unique names when we look at the results of all the languages combined. This suggests that the output of Claude is the least affected by the language of the prompt as well. We visualise the frequency distributions across LLMs for every profession in Figure 9, and for each LLM separately in Figure 10 (GPT), Figure 11 (Claude) and Figure 12 (Llama).

Lastly, we visualise the top 10 results for every profession across the different languages, adjectives, LLMs and runs in Table 10.

	Average #names/response				Unique names				
Model	GPT	Claude	Llama	all LLMs		GPT	Claude	Llama	all LLMs
greatest	5.24	8.72	4.63	6.20		509	566	613	1098
most famous	4.25	8.26	3.10	5.20		444	492	435	886
most impactful	5.11	8.48	3.45	5.68		454	536	505	962
most important	5.34	8.81	4.13	6.09		478	549	503	1011
most influential	5.14	8.75	3.67	5.85		426	539	586	1023
All adjectives	5.01	8.60	3.80	5.80	Avg. (per adj.)	462.2	536.4	528.4	998.4
					Total (across adj.)	1158	1023	1386	2409

Table 7: General results by LLM and adjective. We present the average number of names/response and the number of unique names per LLM and adjective.

	Average #names/response				Unique names				
Language	GPT	Claude	Llama	all LLMs		GPT	Claude	Llama	all LLMs
Hindi	5.53	7.64	2.56	5.24		369	360	236	618
Spanish	5.12	9.88	4.97	6.66		193	293	326	477
Urdu	5.11	6.33	3.16	4.86		419	301	558	918
Russian	4.85	8.47	3.04	5.45		204	318	272	490
English	4.57	9.78	9.35	7.90		165	281	401	520
French	5.09	9.63	4.56	6.43		188	309	297	468
Chinese	5.75	9.75	2.30	5.93		360	415	224	647
Portuguese	4.22	9.71	4.45	6.13		160	297	410	551
Bengali	5.58	8.38	2.15	5.37		371	354	244	642
Arabic	4.32	6.49	1.42	4.08		333	289	227	591
All languages	5.02	8.60	3.80	5.80	Avg. (per lang.)	276.2	321.7	319.5	592.2
					Total (across lang.)	1158	1023	1386	2409

Table 8: General results by LLM and language

	Average #names/response				Unique names				
Profession	GPT	Claude	Llama	all LLMs		GPT	Claude	Llama	all LLMs
Artist	4.56	8.44	3.94	5.64		86	96	157	227
Computer Scientist	3.50	8.06	2.39	4.65		74	36	68	119
Chemist	3.38	6.22	2.37	3.99		83	62	94	174
Composer	4.56	8.11	3.47	5.38		123	62	98	208
Poet	5.36	9.35	4.20	6.30		162	225	147	384
Leader	7.41	8.53	5.32	7.08		120	116	158	260
Physicist	2.86	7.66	2.31	4.28		27	53	52	97
Medical Researcher	4.42	7.29	2.85	4.85		106	59	118	203
Philosopher	5.97	10.50	3.90	6.79		84	74	75	152
Person	7.13	11.52	5.99	8.21		123	126	161	266
Political Figure	7.72	8.34	5.92	7.33		155	91	216	333
Economist	3.26	7.80	3.16	4.74		39	31	52	85
Writer	5.20	9.66	4.30	6.39		190	134	206	365
Military Leader	5.08	8.77	3.47	5.77		109	162	126	286
Mathematician	4.82	8.82	3.34	5.66		90	70	158	237
All professions	5.02	8.60	3.80	5.80	Avg. (per prof.)	104.7	93.1	125.7	226.4
					Total (across lang.)	1158	1023	1386	2409

Table 9: General results by LLM and profession

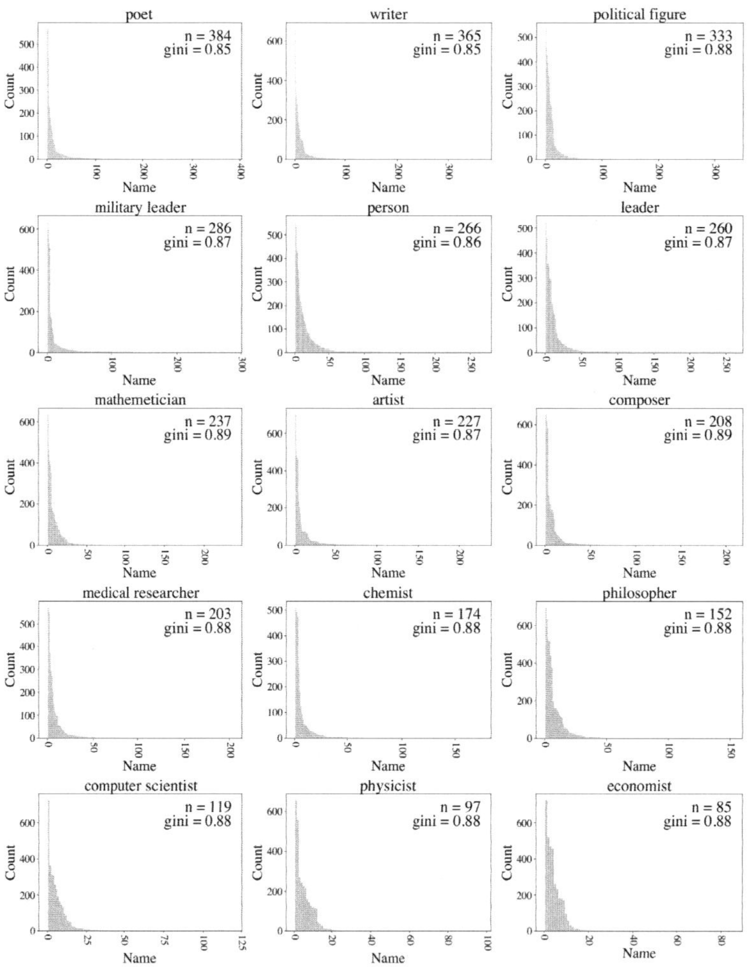

Figure 9: Frequency distribution for every profession (across LLMs). The number of unique names is depicted in the right corner (n).

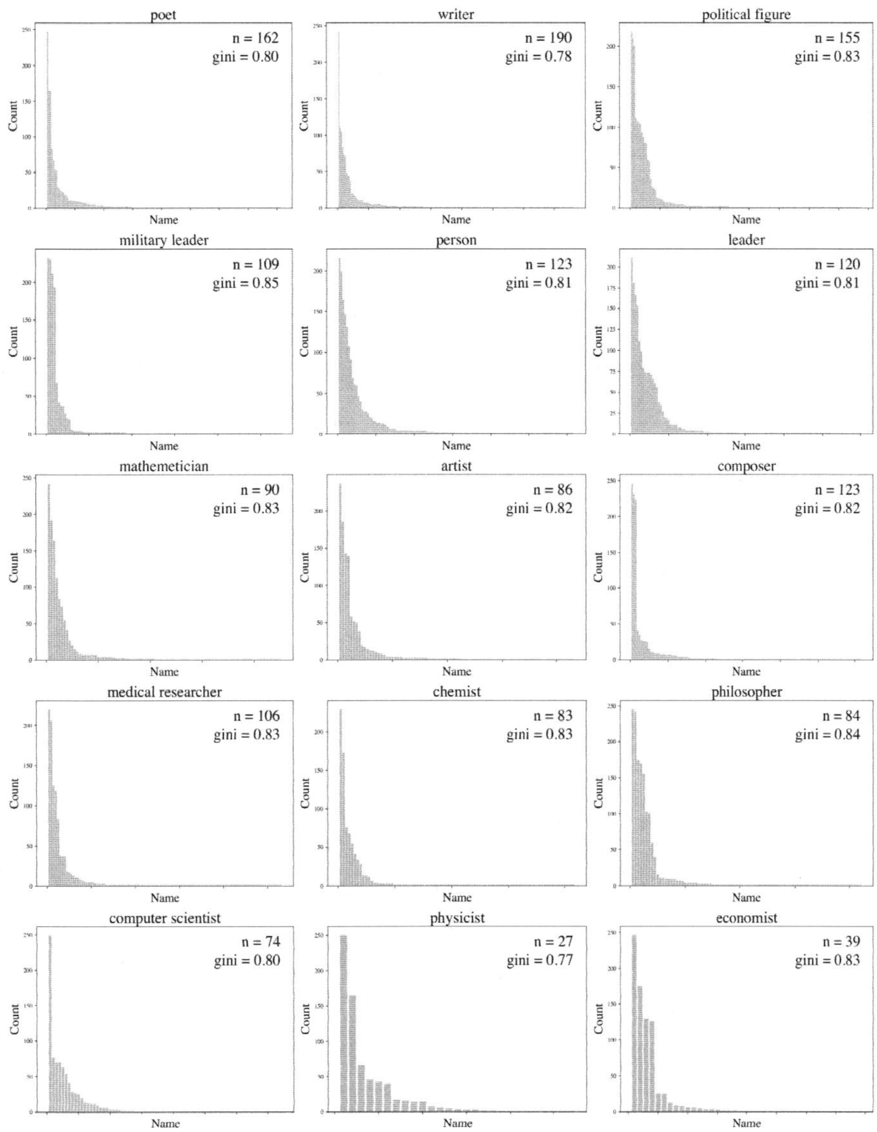

Figure 10: Frequency distribution for every profession (GPT)

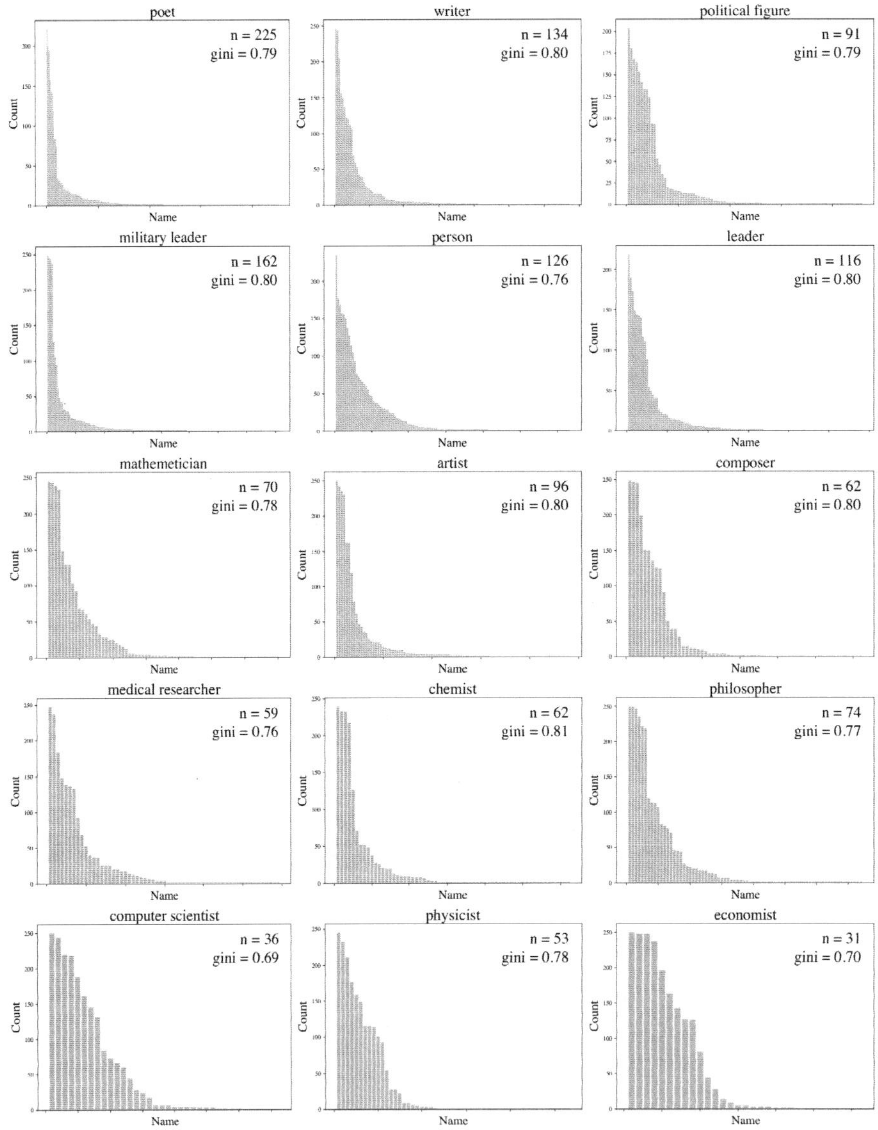

Figure 11: Frequency distribution for every profession (Claude)

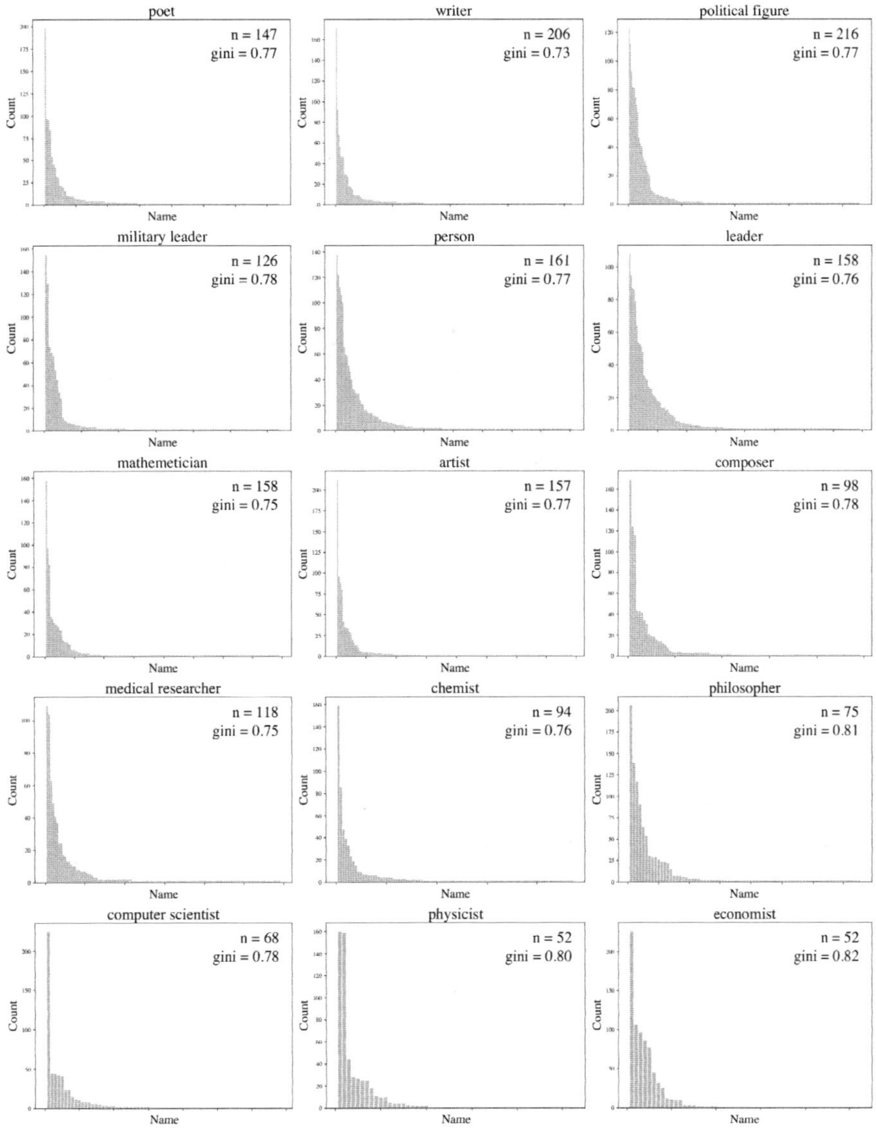

Figure 12: Frequency distribution for every profession (Llama)

Table 10: Results for each profession. We display the count (n) which is the number of responses in which they occur and the percentage (%) which is the percentage of responses in which they occur ($n/750$).

(a) Artist

Name	n	%
Leonardo Da Vinci	699	93.2
Pablo Picasso	508	67.7
Michelangelo	470	62.7
Vincent Van Gogh	464	61.9
Rembrandt	232	30.9
Charles David	204	27.2
Claude Monet	171	22.8
Salvador Dali	112	14.9
William Shakespeare	77	10.3
Ludwig Beethoven	76	10.1

(b) Computer Scientist

Name	n	%
Alan Turing	723	96.4
John Neumann	364	48.5
Tim Berners	314	41.9
Lee	313	41.7
Hopper	257	34.3
Ada Lovelace	230	30.7
Dennis Ritchie	193	25.7
Claude Shannon	166	22.1
Charles Babbage	146	19.5
Donald Knuth	134	17.9

(c) Chemist

Name	n	%
Marie Curie	509	67.9
Dmitri Mendeleev	492	65.6
Lavoisier	474	63.2
Linus Pauling	274	36.5
Dalton	180	24.0
Alfred Nobel	126	16.8
Robert Boyle	96	12.8
Louis Pasteur	72	9.6
Frederick Sanger	54	7.2
Rosalind Franklin	53	7.1

(d) Composer

Name	n	%
Mozart	649	86.5
Beethoven	617	82.3
Bach	584	77.9
Wagner	249	33.2
Chopin	218	29.1
Tchaikovsky	204	27.2
Schubert	179	23.9
Stravinsky	176	23.5
Debussy	164	21.9
Brahms	130	17.3

(e) Poet

Name	n	%
Shakespeare	565	75.3
Homer	565	75.3
Dante	443	59.1
Neruda	236	31.5
Tagore	230	30.7
Rumi	197	26.3
Goethe	181	24.1
Li Bai	144	19.2
Virgil	136	18.1
Whitman	128	17.1

(f) Leader

Name	n	%
Gandhi	525	70.0
Mandela	458	61.1
Churchill	360	48.0
Lincoln	355	47.3
Alexander the Great	347	46.3
Napoleon	296	39.5
MLK Jr.	295	39.3
Julius Caesar	293	39.1
Mao Zedong	198	26.4
Genghis Khan	193	25.7

(g) Physicist

Name	n	%
Einstein	655	87.3
Newton	557	74.3
Galileo	272	36.3
Niels Bohr	243	32.4
Maxwell	227	30.3
Feynman	217	28.9
Hawking	160	21.3
Marie Curie	145	19.3
Max Planck	127	16.9
Faraday	121	16.1

(h) Medical Researcher

Name	n	%
Louis Pasteur	571	76.1
Alexander Fleming	552	73.6
Edward Jenner	373	49.7
Hippocrates	295	39.3
Jonas Salk	270	36.0
Robert Koch	202	26.9
Leon Harvey	152	20.3
Marie Curie	117	15.6
Albert Sabin	108	14.4
Francis Crick	99	13.2

(i) Philosopher

Name	n	%
Plato	695	92.7
Aristotle	634	84.5
Socrates	522	69.6
Kant	516	68.8
Nietzsche	440	58.7
Descartes	373	49.7
Confucius	196	26.1
Sartre	159	21.2
Karl Marx	158	21.1
Hegel	153	20.4

(j) Person

Name	n	%
Einstein	556	74.1
Jesus Christ	531	70.8
Newton	432	57.6
Muhammad	422	56.3
Buddha	353	47.1
Gandhi	317	42.3
Alexander the Great	242	32.3
Mandela	218	29.1
Confucius	213	28.4
Darwin	195	26.0

(k) Political Figure

Name	n	%
Gandhi	534	71.2
Mandela	464	61.9
Churchill	425	56.7
Lincoln	392	52.3
Mao Zedong	347	46.3
Julius Caesar	341	45.5
Napoleon	316	42.1
Alexander the Great	235	31.3
Hitler	227	30.3
Lenin	220	29.3

(l) Economist

Name	n	%
Adam Smith	722	96.3
Keynes	519	69.2
Karl Marx	469	62.5
Friedman	455	60.7
Ricardo	262	34.9
Samuelson	233	31.1
Marshall	181	24.1
Hayek	179	23.9
Schumpeter	171	22.8
Amartya Sen	96	12.8

Table 10: Results for each profession (continued)

(m) Writer

Name	n	%
Shakespeare	659	87.9
Tolstoy	417	55.6
Homer	324	43.2
Cervantes	278	37.1
Dante	275	36.7
Dickens	242	32.3
Dostoevsky	192	25.6
Goethe	175	23.3
Marquez	157	20.9
Victor Hugo	147	19.6

(n) Military Leader

Name	n	%
Alexander the Great	636	84.8
Napoleon	596	79.5
Genghis Khan	531	70.8
Julius Caesar	506	67.5
Hannibal	192	25.6
Erwin Rommel	173	23.1
Sun Tzu	163	21.7
George Patton	117	15.6
Saladin	98	13.1
George Washington	83	11.1

(o) Mathematician

Name	n	%
Newton	634	84.5
Gauss	464	61.9
Archimedes	409	54.5
Euclid	395	52.7
Euler	350	46.7
Leibniz	180	24.0
Einstein	165	22.0
Hilbert	159	21.2
Riemann	146	19.5
Ramanujan	118	15.7

Towards Region-aware Bias Evaluation Metrics

Angana Borah[1] **Aparna Garimella**[2] **Rada Mihalcea**[1]
[1]University of Michigan, Ann Arbor, USA, [2]Adobe Research, India

anganab@umich.edu garimell@adobe.com mihalcea@umich.edu

Abstract

When exposed to human-generated data, language models are known to learn and amplify societal biases. While previous works introduced metrics that can be used to assess the bias in these models, they rely on assumptions that may not be universally true. For instance, a gender bias dimension commonly used by these metrics is that of *family–career*, but this may not be the only common bias in certain regions of the world. In this paper, we identify topical differences in gender bias across different regions and propose a region-aware bottom-up approach for bias assessment. Several of our proposed region-aware gender bias dimensions are found to be aligned with the human perception of gender biases in these regions.

1 Introduction

Human bias refers to the tendency of prejudice or preference towards a certain group or an individual and can reflect social stereotypes concerning gender, age, race, religion, and so on. Biases can be especially problematic when prior information is derived from *harmful precedents* like prejudices and social stereotypes. Early work in detecting biases includes the Word Embedding Association Test (WEAT) (Caliskan et al., 2017) and the Sentence Encoder Association Test (SEAT) (May et al., 2019). WEAT is inspired by the Implicit Association Test (IAT) (Greenwald et al., 1998) in psychology, which gauges people's propensity to unconsciously link particular characteristics—like *family* versus *career*—with specific target groups—like female (F) versus male (M). WEAT measures the distances between target and attribute word sets in word embeddings using dimensions[1] similar to those used in IAT.

Biases toward or against a group can vary across different regions due to the influence of an individual's culture and demographics (Grimm and Church, 1999; Kiritchenko and Mohammad, 2018a; Garimella et al., 2022; Jha et al., 2023). Psychological studies that demonstrate human stereotypes vary by continental regions (Damann et al., 2023; Blog, 2017) and even larger concepts like the western and eastern worlds (Markus and Kitayama, 2003; Jiang et al., 2019) serve as an inspiration for the use of continental regions to determine biases across cultures. However, existing bias evaluation metrics like WEAT and SEAT follow a "one-size-fits-all" approach to detect biases across different regions[2]. As biases can be diverse depending on the demographic lens, a fixed or a small set of dimensions (such as family–career, math–arts) may not be able to cover all the possible biases in society. In this paper, we address two main research questions about gender bias: (1) Is it possible to use current NLP techniques to automatically identify gender bias characteristics (such as family, career) specific to various regions? (2) How do these gender dimensions compare to the current generic dimensions included in WEAT/SEAT?

Our paper makes four main contributions:

1. An automatic method to uncover gender bias topic pairs in various regions that uses (a) topic modeling to identify dominant topics aligning with the F/M (Female/Male) groups for different regions, and (b) an embedding-based approach to identify F-M topic pairs for different regions that can be viewed as gender bias dimensions in those regions.

2. An IAT-style test to assess our predicted gender bias topic pairs with human annotators. To the best of our knowledge, this is the first study to use a data-driven, bottom-up method to evaluate bias across regional boundaries.

3. A WEAT-based evaluation setup using region-aware topic pairs to evaluate gender biases in different data domains (Reddit and UN General Debates) across regions.

[1]'Topic pairs' and 'topic dimensions' are used equivalently.

[2]In our study, a region refers to a continental region

Proceedings of the 3rd Workshop on Cross-Cultural Considerations in NLP (C3NLP 2025), pages 108–131
May 4, 2025 ©2025 Association for Computational Linguistics

4. An analysis of how well our predicted bias dimensions align with those of custom LLMs, including open-source models like `Llama-3-8b` and `Mistral-7b-Instruct`; as well as closed-source models such as `GPT-4`, `Gemini-Pro` and `Claude-3-Sonnet`.

2 Data

For our study, we require a geographical corpus that covers several regions of the world. Tthe selection of regions is based on data availability and representation in existing geographical datasets, and aligns with established frameworks for regional analysis [3]. We use GeoWAC (Dunn and Adams, 2020a), a geographically balanced corpus consisting of web pages from Common Crawl, spanning 150 countries. Language samples are geo-located using country-specific domains, such as an *.in* domain suggesting Indian origin (Dunn and Adams, 2020b). We draw inspiration from Garimella et al. (2022) to select the top three countries with the highest number of English examples from each region: Asia, Africa, Europe, North America, South America, and Oceania. For each region, we randomly sample 282,000 English examples, allocating 94,000 examples to each selected country within the region. Dataset details are included in Appendix A.

3 Variations in Gender Bias Tests Across Regions

We start by investigating the differences in existing gender bias tests like WEAT across different regions. WEAT takes in *target words* such as male names and female names, to indicate a specific group, and *attribute words* that can be associated with the target words, such as *math* and *art*. Bias is computed using the cosine distance between the embeddings of the target and attribute words. We use word2vec embeddings (Mikolov et al., 2013) trained on six regions separately to compute bias. Table 1 shows the region-wise bias scores for the three gender-specific tests in WEAT.

Although we observe a positive bias for most topic pairs, scores vary across regions. For example, the highest scoring regions vary for the target words-attribute words groups. For *family–career*, North America exhibits the highest bias, whereas Africa demonstrates the highest bias for the *math–arts* and *science–arts*. Interestingly, Europe and South America have negative scores on *science–arts* and *career–family* respectively (indicating stronger F-science, F-career and M-arts, M-family associations). These results provide preliminary support to our hypothesis that bias dimensions vary across regions, thus propelling a need for further bias dimensions to better capture gender biases in these regions in addition to the existing generic ones in WEAT.

[3] `https://unstats.un.org/unsd/methodology/m49/`

TARGET WORDS - ATTRIBUTE WORDS	REGION	WEAT
career vs family - Male names vs Female names	Africa	1.798
	Asia	1.508
	North America	1.885
	South America	-0.574
	Europe	1.610
	Oceania	1.727
Math vs Arts - Male terms vs Female terms	Africa	1.429
	Asia	1.187
	North America	0.703
	South America	0.532
	Europe	0.334
	Oceania	1.158
Science vs Arts - Male terms vs Female terms	Africa	1.247
	Asia	0.330
	North America	0.036
	South America	0.912
	Europe	-0.655
	Oceania	0.725

Table 1: Region-wise WEAT scores using word2vec.

4 A Method to Automatically Detect Bias Dimensions Across Regions

Building upon our WEAT findings, we propose a two-stage approach to automatically detect region-aware bias dimensions that likely capture the biases in specific regions in a bottom-up manner. In the first stage, we utilize topic modeling to identify prominent topics in each region. In the second stage, we use an embedding-based approach to find female-male topic pairs among those identified in the first stage that are likely to represent prominent gender bias dimensions in each region. Fig 1 shows the pipeline of our methodology.

4.1 Identifying Region-wise Bias Topics

We use topic modeling to identify dominant topics in the male and female examples in each region.

We first build F(emale)- and M(ale)-aligned datasets using the examples from GeoWAC for each region. Leveraging 52 pairs of gender-defining, non-stereotypical words (e.g., wife, brother) from Bolukbasi et al. (2016) (see Appendix G), we identify examples containing these words. An example is assigned to the F- or M-aligned dataset if it contains a higher frequency of female or male words, respectively, and the difference in frequency between F and M words exceeds a threshold of three. These datasets are then used to

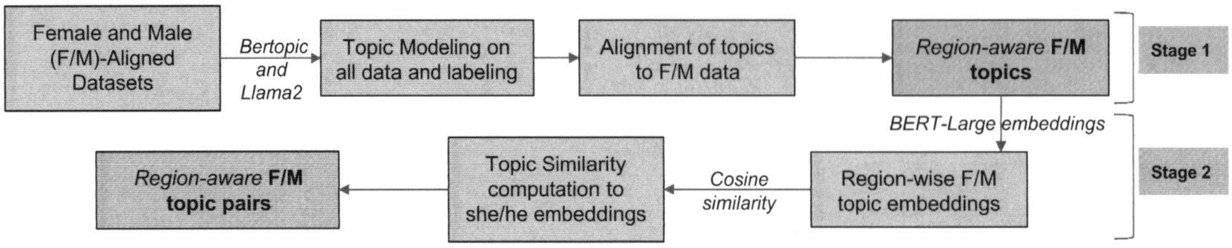

Figure 1: Methodology Pipeline: Stage 1 refers to the extraction of region-aware gender topics using topic modeling, Stage 2 refers to extraction of region-aware gender topic pairs using an embedding based approach

detect gender-aligned topics from GeoWAC. The dataset statistics are specified in Table 6 in Appendix B.

For topic modeling, we use `Bertopic` (Grootendorst, 2022), which identifies an optimal number of topics n for a given dataset (see Appendix L.1 for implementation details). We further refine the resulting topics using `Llama2` (Touvron et al., 2023) to label and better understand the topic clusters identified by `Bertopic`. The prompting mechanism for `Llama2` is provided in Appendix H.

We then compute the topic alignment to either of the F/M groups. To achieve this, we first calculate the topic distribution of a data point, which gives the probability p_{it} of an example i belonging to each topic t. For a topic t, we take n examples that dominantly belong to that topic: $i_1, i_2, ..., i_n$. If m out of n data points belong to the F group in the F-M dataset, and the other (n - m) belongs to the M group, we compute the average of topic probabilities for both groups separately: $p_{Ft} = \frac{(p_{i_1 t} + p_{i_2 t} + ... + p_{i_m t})}{m}$ and $p_{Mt} = \frac{(p_{i_{m+1} t} + p_{i_{m+2} t} + ... + p_{i_n t})}{(n-m)}$, where p_{Ft} and p_{Mt} refer to the average probability by which a topic belongs to the F and M groups respectively. If $p_{Ft} > p_{Mt}$, we say the topic is a *bias topic* that aligns with the F group and vice-versa.

4.2 Finding Topic Pairs as Region-wise Bias Dimension Indicators

We use an embedding-based approach to generate F-M topic pairs from the pool of topics identified in the previous stage. These topic pairs would be comparable to IAT/WEAT pairs.

We use BERT-large (`stsb-bert-large`) from SpaCy's (Honnibal and Montani, 2017) `sentencebert` library to extract contextual embeddings for topic words extracted in Stage 1. For a topic t consisting of topic words $w_1, ..w_n$, the topic embedding is given by the average of embeddings of the top ten topic words in that topic.

Next, we identify topic pairs from the embeddings inspired by Bolukbasi et al. (2016): let the embeddings of the words she and he be E_{she} and E_{he} respectively. The embedding of a topic t_i be E_{t_i}. A female topic F_{t_i} and a male topic M_{t_j} are a topic pair if: $cos(E_{F_{t_i}}, E_{she}) \sim cos(E_{M_{t_j}}, E_{he})$ and/or $cos(E_{F_{t_i}}, E_{he}) \sim cos(E_{M_{t_j}}, E_{she})$, where $cos(i,j)$ refers to the cosine similarity between embeddings i and j, given by $cos(i,j) = \frac{i.j}{||i||||j||}$. For two topics to be in a pair, the threshold considered for the difference between the cosine similarities is 0.01, i.e., two topics $(t1, t2)$ are considered a pair if the difference of cosine similarities cos($t1$, she)/cos($t1$, he) and cos($t2$, he)/cos($t2$, she) respectively is < 0.01. We manually choose 0.01 since differences close to 0.01 are almost $= 0$.

4.3 Human Validation Setup

We validate our topic pairs using an IAT-style test with six volunteer annotators per region (three female and three male). Alongside our region-aware topic pairs, we evaluate existing WEAT dimensions related to gender (*family–career, math–arts, science–arts*).

As done in IAT, we show the topic names and female/male faces to our annotators along with a set of guidelines. [4] As shown in Fig 2, each topic pair test form contains two tasks. First, the annotators have to press one key for a female face f and a female topic T_f and another key for a male face m and a male topic T_m, timing responses as r_1 and r_2. In the reverse task, they pair T_m with f and T_f with m, timing these as r_3 and r_4. We average r_1 and r_2 for the 'un-reversed' case and r_3 and r_4 for the 'reversed' case. The annotators' implicit association of a gender to a topic may influence their response time. A lower response time suggests easier recollection of the guidelines and potential implicit gender-topic associations, and thus lower bias with respect to these topics. We also varied the test order for different annotators to avoid initial pairing bias. We conduct the survey with six

[4]Note that faces are used exclusively in the Human Validation Set-up for IAT testing, consistent with the original IAT methodology, and are not employed in other experiments.

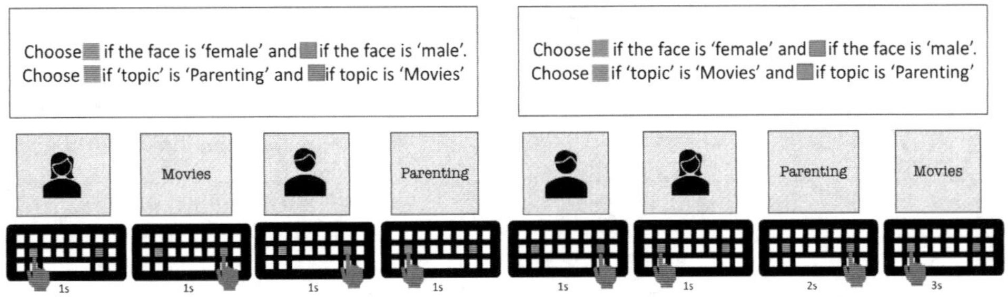

Figure 2: IAT-style test with region-aware topic pairs for human validation. The above example shows the user implicitly associates female to *parenting* and male to *movies*: When guidelines are reversed, they take longer time, indicating the presence of bias. Note that we randomize the order of tests for participants to ensure initial pairing bias is accounted for. We also have several pages showing faces and topics for each guideline.

annotators each from Africa, Asia, Europe, North America, and South America and randomize the reversed and un-reversed tests to prevent primacy bias. We provide screenshots of our annotation framework in Appendix N.

4.4 Results: Bias Dimensions across Regions

4.4.1 Region-wise Bias Topics

Table 2 displays the top topics based on u_{mass} coherence (Mimno et al., 2011), that is based on word co-occurrence within a given corpus for each region. Several topics that are exclusive to certain regions are identified. Additionally, some topics like *family* and *parenting*; *cooking*; *pets* and *animal care* are common across several regions for F. Similarly *movies*; *politics* and *government*; and *sports* are common topics for M. Finally, there are differences between regions in terms of *education*, *reading*, and *research* (F-Europe, NA, and M-Africa); *fashion* and *lifestyle* (F-Europe, NA, and M-Africa) and *music and culture* (F-SA and M-NA and Oceania). Some other popular topics across regions are *religion and spirituality*, *Christian theology* in M; *obituaries and genealogy*, *online dating*, *travel*, and *sailing* in F (see Appendix D for a comprehensive list of topics). We also provide an example of a topic cluster (Africa region) in Appendix J.

4.4.2 Region-wise Bias Dimensions

Table 3[5] shows the top five topic pairs per region, chosen based on the u_{mass} score from the top 10 topics each for F and M from the topic modeling scheme. As expected, topic pairs differ by region, and new topic pairs emerge that do not appear in previous tests like WEAT. Among the top pairs, there are recurring topics in F such as *dating and marriage*, *family and relationships*, *luxury sailing*, and *education*, whereas in M, there are *politics*, *religion*, *sports*, and *movies*. These region-specific pairs may supplement generic tests like WEAT/SEAT in NLP to detect regional biases. Thus, several topics are shared across regions, while others differ, potentially revealing diverse perceptions of biases. To explore this further, we compute and analyze the top unigrams and bigrams for topic pairs that are common across regions, as detailed in Appendix E.

4.4.3 Human Validation Results

Fig 3 shows response times for the top five topic pairs in each region for both un-reversed and reversed scenarios. Larger time differences indicate more bias, suggesting that the pair could be a potential gender bias dimension for that region. If un-reversed time is lower, it suggests a stronger association of T_f with the F group and T_m with the M group, showing the existence of biases. Please refer to Table 3 for topic pairs corresponding to (P1...P5). The *family–career* pair shows the highest bias across all three general IAT topic pairs except South America. There are smaller differences among *math–arts* and *science–arts*. Certain pairs—such as P5 for Africa, P1 for Asia, P1, P4, and P5 for Europe, P1 and P2 for North America, and P3 and P5 for South America show greater differences than one(or more) generic WEAT dimensions in their respective regions. This suggests that participants associated stronger biases with region-specific topic pairs than with the existing WEAT dimensions. These findings support our hypothesis and bring preliminary evidence that the region-aware bias dimensions we uncover are in line with the human perception of bias in those

[5] Note that the topics that appear in the top topic pairs here may not necessarily be among the top five topics for each region as shown in Table 2 because we use a different approach to compute pairs. However, they are among the top ten topics for each region.

REGION	FEMALE	MALE
Africa	Credit cards and finances, Royalty and Media, Trading strategies and market analysis, Dating and relationships guides, Parenting and family relationships	Fashion and Lifestyle, Male enhancement and sexual health, Nollywood actresses and movies, Nigerian politics and government, Essay writing and research
Asia	Hobbies and Interests, Healthy eating habits for children, Social media platforms, Royal wedding plans, Online Dating and Chatting	DC comic characters, Mobile Application, Phillippine Politics and Government, Sports and Soccer, Career
Europe	Pets and animal care, Fashion and Style, Education, Obituaries and Genealogy, Luxury sailing	Political developments in Northern Ireland, Christian Theology and Practice, Crime and murder investigation, EU Referendum and Ministerial Positions, Criminal Justice System
North America	Pets, Cooking: culinary delights and chef recipes, Fashion and style, Family dynamics and relationships, Reading and fiction	Civil War and history, Middle East conflict and political tensions, Movies and filmmaking, Political leadership and party dynamics in Bermuda, Rock Music and songwriting
South America	Luxury and Cruise, Regional Development in South America, Cultural events, Food and recipes, Gender and Social inequality	Colonial Wine Industry, Chilean politics and violence, Gaming, Football and Sports, Startup and Entrepreneurship
Oceania	Cooking and culinary delights, Romance, Weight loss and nutrition for women, Water travel experience, Woodworking plans and projects	Harry Potter adventures, Art and Photography, Superheroes and their Universes, Music recording and Artists, Football in Vanuatu

Table 2: Top five topics for F and M for each region, extracted using Bertopic and Llama2.

REGION	F-M TOPIC PAIR
Africa	Parenting and family relationships-Nollywood Actress and Movies (P1) Marriage and relationships - Sports and Football (P2) Womens' lives and successes - Fashion and Lifestyle (P3) Music - Social Media (P4) Dating and relationships advice - Religious and Spiritual growth (P5)
Asia	Hotel royalty - Political leadership in India (P1) Healthy eating habits for children - Sports and Soccer (P2) Royal wedding plans - Social Media platforms for video sharing (P3) Royal wedding plans - Religious devotion and spirituality (P4) Marriage - Bollywood actors and films (P5)
Europe	Education - Music (P1) Comfortable hotels - Political decision and impact on society (P2) Luxury sailing - UK Government Taxation policies (P3) Obituaries and Genealogy - Christian Theology and Practice (P4) Fashion and style - Christian theology and practice (P5)
North America	Online Dating for Singles - Religion and Spirituality (P1) Fashion and Style - Reproductive Health (P2) Education and achievements - Reinsurance and capital markets (P3) Family dynamics and relationships - Nike shoes and fashion (P4) Reading and fiction - Cape Cod news (P5)
South America	Food and Recipes - Professional Wrestling and MMA Events (P1) Health issues among schoolchildren - Insect Biology (P2) Chilean Olympic team and successes - Chilean Politics and Violence (P3) Gender and Social Inequality - Colonial Wine Industry (P4) Movies and Filmmakers - Football and Sports (P5)
Oceania	Family relationships - Religious beliefs and figures (P1) Woodworking plans and projects - Music record and Artists (P2) Weight loss and nutrition for women - Building and designing boats (P3) Exercises for hormone development - Superheroes and their Universes (P4) Kids' furniture and decor - Building and designing boats (P5)

Table 3: Top five region-aware topic pairs for F and M for each region using an embedding-based approach.

regions [6]. We find that all regions exhibit biases aligned with our topic pairs' gender associations, except for P3: *education–reinsurance and capital markets* in North America. Additionally, South America shows a negative bias for *family–career*, consistent with our findings in Table 1. These results highlight the importance of considering topic pair differences when identifying and evaluating biases.

5 WEAT-based Evaluation Using Region-aware Topic Pairs

To measure biases across data domains and regions, we use region-specific topics extracted from the GeoWAC dataset and set up a WEAT-style evaluation, demonstrating how region-aware bias dimensions integrate with existing bias evaluation frameworks.

Data. We consider two datasets: (i) Reddit data and (ii) UN General Debates (Baturo et al., 2017). The Reddit data consists of data from subreddits corresponding to specific regions: `r/asia`, `r/africa`, `r/europe`, `r/northamerica`, and `r/oceania`. We use the official Reddit API to extract data, consisting of 500 top posts[7] from each subreddit. The posts are pre-processed to remove URLs and signs, and each post contains at least 30 words. The UN General Debate Corpus (UNGDC) includes texts of General Debate statements from 1970 to 2016. These statements are delivered by leaders and senior officials to present their government's perspective on global issues. We filter the countries for each region and extract 500 data points per region, maintaining equal representation across region. [8] These datasets demonstrate how topic pairs can be integrated into WEAT, without controlling for the speaker or author. While

[6] It is not always evident whether gender associations in these pairs stem from direct stereotypes or reverse associations (e.g., females linked to T because males are strongly linked to P and not because females are strongly linked to T). Future work should investigate this distinction.

[7] The Official Reddit API has rate limits, therefore 500 top posts ensures an equal number of examples for each region.

[8] Oceania has limited available countries in UNGDC, hence we adhere to 500 data points for each region.

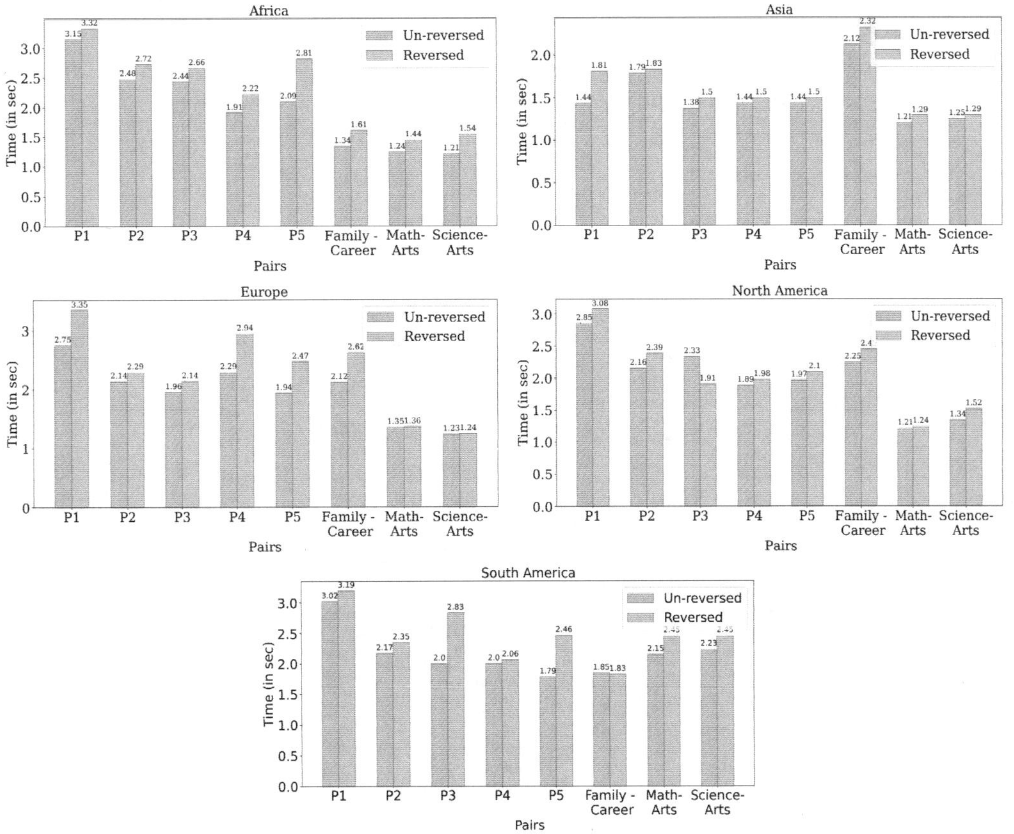

Figure 3: Human validation results across regions. 'Unreversed' refers to bias dimensions with the same gender associations as our topic pairs, 'Reversed' refers to bias dimensions with the opposite gender associations.

speaker/author bias may also play a role, exploring this influence is beyond the scope of these experiments and presents a direction for future research.

Method. WEAT tests consist of keywords corresponding to each attribute (like family-career) and target sets (like male-female terms). For attribute sets, we use KeyBERT (Grootendorst, 2020) to gather top topic representative words corresponding to each topic extracted from GeoWAC. For target sets, i.e., male/female terms, we use the same representative words from WEAT. To further make it specific to a particular region, we employ GPT-4 (OpenAI et al., 2024) to generate 10 commonly used male/female names in each region, validate them with the help of region-specific annotators (100% agreement) and add them to the list. We provide the list of words in Table 12 of Appendix F. We use fastText (Bojanowski et al., 2017)[9] to generate embeddings of the lists and compute the region-aware WEAT scores.

Results. Table 4 displays the results of WEAT scores across region-aware topic pairs for the two datasets. We intentionally exclude generic WEAT dimensions such as *family–career*, as their effectiveness has been extensively evaluated in prior studies. Instead, our focus is to demonstrate how our region-specific bias pairs can be integrated into an already established test framework. A high number of positive scores means a presence of biases with the same gender association as our topic pairs. For example, if *'music-social media'* is an F-M topic pair in Africa, a positive score on the Reddit dataset means that bias is associated with the same genders. The few negative scores indicate that some topic pairs do not conform to the same gender bias associations. Additionally, scores with magnitudes greater than 0.5 indicate a strong presence of bias (positive or negative). We also observe that high-bias topics vary across regions and datasets. For example, *'music-social media'* has the highest bias in Africa for both datasets, however for Asia, we find that *'marriage - Bollywood actors and films'* and *'Hotel royalty - Political leadership in India'* exhibit the highest biases in Reddit and UN General Debates respectively, suggesting that biased topic pairs may be domain-dependent.

[9]We choose fastText because it allows us to compute embeddings of words that are not present in the target text (as our topics are derived from a different dataset GeoWAC).

REGION	F-M TOPIC PAIR	REDDIT	UN GENERAL DEBATES
Africa	Parenting and family relationships-Nollywood Actress and Movies	0.500	0.979
	Marriage and relationships - Sports and Football	-0.051	0.224
	Womens' lives and successes - Fashion and Lifestyle	0.480	0.493
	Music - Social Media	1.894	1.721
	Dating and relationships advice - Religious and Spiritual growth	1.475	1.061
Asia	Hotel royalty - Political leadership in India	1.365	1.768
	Healthy eating habits for children - Sports and Soccer	0.006	-0.068
	Royal wedding plans - Social Media platforms for video sharing	1.05	1.393
	Royal wedding plans - Religious devotion and spirituality	1.183	1.335
	Marriage - Bollywood actors and films	1.543	0.918
Europe	Education - Music	1.261	1.920
	Comfortable hotels - Political decision and impact on society	0.324	0.485
	Luxury sailing - UK Government Taxation policies	1.232	1.558
	Obituaries and Genealogy - Christian Theology and Practice	0.001	-0.405
	Fashion and style - Christian theology and practice	1.730	1.028
North America	Online Dating for Singles - Religion and Spirituality	1.728	1.830
	Fashion and Style - Reproductive Health	1.723	1.095
	Education and achievements - Reinsurance and capital markets	-0.148	-0.364
	Family dynamics and relationships - Nike shoes and fashion	0.109	0.691
	Reading and fiction - Cape Cod news	0.251	0.506
South America	Food and Recipes - Professional Wrestling and MMA Events	1.462	0.880
	Health issues among schoolchildren - Insect Biology	1.551	1.763
	Chilean Olympic team and successes - Chilean Politics and Violence	-0.062	0.795
	Gender and Social Inequality - Colonial Wine Industry	0.315	0.587
	Movies and Filmmakers - Football and Sports	0.179	1.399
Oceania	Family relationships - Religious beliefs and figures	0.305	0.267
	Woodworking plans and projects - Music record and Artists	0.056	-0.258
	Weight loss and nutrition for women - Building and designing boats	0.336	0.582
	Exercises for hormone development - Superheroes and their Universes	-0.05	-0.07
	Kids' furniture and decor - Building and designing boats	0.612	0.524

Table 4: Region-aware WEAT-based evaluation on Reddit and UNGDC. Highest scores are highlighted for each dataset across regions.

Using our topic pairs in a WEAT-style evaluation setup illustrates how our automatically curated region-aware bias dimensions can be used in designing a region-aware bias evaluation test. It also shows the effectiveness of our region-aware bias topic pairs in capturing the dimensions that are likely to contain gender biases across regions.[10]

6 Alignment of Region-Aware Bias Dimensions with LLM generations

To determine if LLMs generate biases similar to our region-aware bias topic pairs, we design a persona generation task for the models. We prompt the LLM to output personas interested in different 'topics' from the topic pairs extracted using GeoWAC. Fig 7 in Appendix M shows an example of the prompt provided to an LLM to generate personas. We experiment with different LLMs: `GPT-3.5` (Brown et al., 2020), `GPT-4`, `Mistral-7b-Instruct` (Jiang et al., 2023), `Claude-3 Sonnet`,[11] and `Gemini-Pro` (Team et al., 2024). Many studies have utilized LLM-generated personas for multi-agent interactions across different societal contexts (Park et al., 2023; Zhou et al., 2024). However, if LLMs generate biased personas—such as always associating a female persona with childcare responsibilities and a male persona with strength and handling emergencies—this can reinforce and perpetuate biases in subsequent downstream tasks and interactions. Given this concern, we employ persona generation as a tool to assess whether any biases are present in the personas created by LLMs. To measure these biases, we compare the gender associations of the LLM-generated personas to the gender associations of our region-aware topic pairs. To ensure robustness, we average the results over seven runs.

Results. We plot the results of persona gender mismatch between LLMs and topic pairs in Fig 4. A

[10]Note that while our topic pairs are extracted from GeoWAC and may generalize to datasets like Reddit and UNGDC, we do not claim they are the optimal pairs, as topic pairs are data-dependent. However, our methodology can be used to identify bias-related topic pairs in specific datasets.

[11]https://claude.ai/

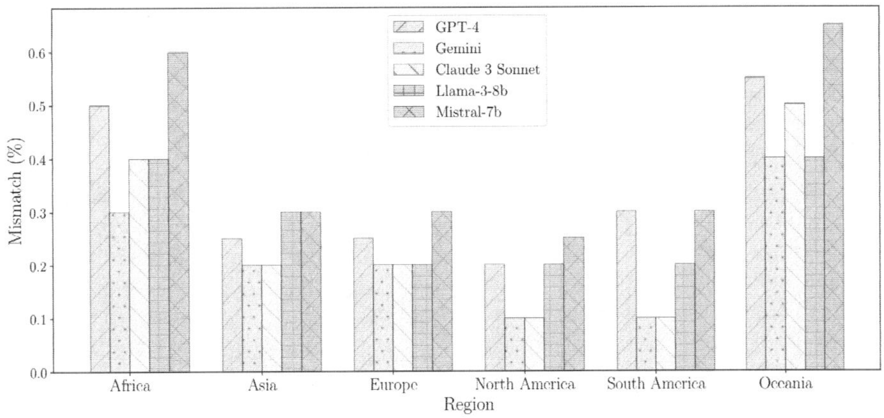

Figure 4: Bias Evaluation of LLM outputs using region-aware bias topic pairs through 'persona generation'.

mismatch occurs when an LLM generates a persona with a 'female' gender for a topic like Politics in Asia, which, according to our findings, is typically associated with a 'male' gender. Fewer mismatches mean the existence of region-aware biases. Regions with relatively higher representation: North America, South America, Europe, and Asia have fewer mismatches, with North America having the lowest mismatch. Conversely, regions like Africa and Oceania show higher mismatch rates. Among models, `Mistral-7b` (7B) has the highest mismatch rate while `Gemini-Pro` (50T) has the least, which may stem from varying model sizes. Overall, all the models exhibit similar mismatch trends for both highly-represented and other regions. Fewer mismatches in highly-represented regions show the importance of evaluation using region-specific topic pairs. Higher mismatches in regions like Africa and Oceania suggest LLMs do not mimic these regions' biases, which can be beneficial. However, due to growing research on LLM cultural alignment, a more precise, region-specific bias evaluation metric becomes essential.

7 Related Work

IAT (Greenwald et al., 1998) is one of the earliest method for measuring implicit social biases in humans. Inspired by the IAT, WEAT (Caliskan et al., 2017) and SEAT (May et al., 2019) use word and sentence embeddings respectively to measure biases in text. Additionally, various bias detection measures in NLP focus on post-training model predictions, such as gender swapping (Stanovsky et al., 2019). Moreover, there are specific gender bias evaluation test sets in tasks like coreference resolution (Rudinger et al., 2018; Zhao et al., 2018; Webster et al., 2018) and sentiment analysis (Kiritchenko and Mohammad, 2018b). Several studies have emphasized the significance of considering cultural awareness in the study of social phenomena. The demographics of individuals can shape their worldviews and thoughts (Garimella et al., 2016), potentially influencing their language preferences and biases in daily life. Notably, some studies have observed a bias towards Western nations in current LLMs (Dwivedi et al., 2023). Recent research has focused on cross-cultural aspects of LLMs, including aligning them with human values from different cultures (Glaese et al., 2022; Sun et al., 2023) and exploring them as personas representing diverse cultures (Gupta et al., 2024). To our knowledge, no prior work has proposed a data-driven approach to extract region-aware bias topics. Given the biases in LLMs, region-specific metrics can enable more accurate bias evaluations and enhance downstream tasks involving demographic-aware social simulations. This research is crucial for addressing cross-cultural biases effectively.

8 Conclusion

In this paper, we propose a bottom-up data-dependent approach to identify region-aware topic pairs that capture gender biases across different regions. Our human evaluation results demonstrate the validity of our proposed topic pairs.

We employ a region-aware WEAT-based evaluation setup to assess biases in two additional datasets: Reddit and UNGDC. The presence of region-specific biases in these datasets underscores the importance of a region-aware bias evaluation metric. Additionally, when examining LLM outputs against the gender associations in our region-aware topic pairs, we find that biases align closely for relatively highly represented regions such as North America, South America, Europe, and Asia. This emphasizes the value of region-aware topic pairs in LLM bias evaluation. Future work includes incorporating testing different model/dataset combinations and topic-pair dependency on data. We also intend to carry out a large-scale human validation experiment to further strengthen the validation of our approach. Finally, we aim to study biases in multiple languages and explore region-aware bias mitigation techniques. Our code and data are available at `https://github.com/MichiganNLP/DemographicAwareBiasEval`.

Limitations

Dataset limitations. We utilized the GeoWAC corpus as our sole data source for extracting topic pairs from various regions. However, we acknowledge the importance of incorporating additional datasets in our future work. It is important to note that the countries selected to represent each continent are based solely on data availability in GeoWAC. We do not claim that these three countries can fully encapsulate the diversity or complexity of an entire continent. This limitation should be considered when interpreting the results. Additionally, our WEAT-based evaluation was conducted on relatively smaller datasets. So, we intend to conduct further analysis on larger datasets to ensure a comprehensive evaluation based on WEAT.

Multilingualism and fine-grained bias evaluation. Our study did not account for different languages due to the diverse linguistic landscape of the regions (continents) included in our study. However, the significance of conducting a more detailed and multi-lingual analysis to examine variations among different countries would be interesting. Furthermore, we recognize that dividing the world by continent is an oversimplified approach, as it obscures nuanced regional differences. For example, Africa, with its large population and geographic diversity, is often condensed into a single category, while regions such as Oceania are treated similarly despite their smaller scale. This imbalance highlights the need for more granular or fine-grained frameworks for bias evaluation in future research.

Limited participants for human validation. In our study, we unfortunately encountered difficulties in finding participants from Oceania for human validation. Moving forward, we plan to include insights and findings from Oceania and also incorporate a larger population to ensure a more comprehensive human validation of our region-aware bias methodology.

Intersectional biases and gender diversity. We do not address intersectional biases, the overlapping systems of discrimination based on race, class, gender, ability, and so on, which are critical for understanding inequality (Lalor et al., 2022). Addressing these biases represents a valuable direction for future research. Additionally, our analysis is limited to a binary gender framework (female and male), excluding non-binary and gender nonconforming individuals. Future research directions can adopt diverse gender identities to ensure more inclusive and representative findings.

Ethical Considerations

When developing our region-aware topic pairs, it is essential to consider the ethical implications:

Broad cultural categorization: Since we utilize a much broader aspect of culture, i.e. continents to distinguish among cultures, the region-aware topic pairs we extract may not translate to cultures of communities that are not well-represented in models. Hence, it is important that we utilize topic pairs carefully.

Biases. AI models have been shown to frequently produce responses that align with Western, educated, industrialized, rich, and democratic (WEIRD) perspectives (Henrich et al., 2010; Mihalcea et al., 2025). Our findings also reveal that LLMs exhibit the strongest alignment with Western-centric biases. Therefore, it is essential to approach LLM-generated results with caution. Furthermore, it is important to note that in our persona experiment, we employ names generated by LLMs for various continents. Although these names were manually reviewed, they may still carry inherent LLM biases, therefore it is important to remain mindful of these biases when interpreting findings, and carefully consider their implications in future research. Such awareness is critical to ensuring more equitable and representative outcomes.

Offensive content. The Reddit data used for our region-aware evaluation metric may include offensive or inappropriate content, as it is sourced from a public platform with diverse user contributions. To mitigate privacy concerns, we have anonymized the data by removing usernames and any personally identifiable information. While this step helps protect user privacy, it does not eliminate the potential presence of offensive material. We emphasize the need for careful handling and interpretation of such data in research contexts.

Acknowledgments

We thank the anonymous reviewers for their constructive feedback. We are also grateful to the members of the Language and Information Technologies lab at the University of Michigan for the insightful discussions during the early stage of the project. This project was partially funded by a National Science Foundation award (#2306372), an award from the Robert Wood Johnson Foundation (#80345), a grant from OpenAI, and a Microsoft Foundational Model grant. Any opinions, findings, and conclusions or recommendations expressed in this material are those of the authors and do not necessarily reflect the views of the National Science Foundation, the Robert Wood Johnson Foundation, OpenAI, or Microsoft.

References

Alexander Baturo, Niheer Dasandi, and Slava J. Mikhaylov. 2017. Understanding state preferences with text as data: Introducing the un general debate corpus. *Research & Politics*, 4(2):2053168017712821.

National Geographic Education Blog. 2017. What continent do you think they are from? drawing humans to reveal internalized bias.

Piotr Bojanowski, Edouard Grave, Armand Joulin, and Tomas Mikolov. 2017. Enriching word vectors with subword information. *Transactions of the Association for Computational Linguistics*, 5:135–146.

Tolga Bolukbasi, Kai-Wei Chang, James Y Zou, Venkatesh Saligrama, and Adam T Kalai. 2016. Man is to computer programmer as woman is to homemaker? debiasing word embeddings. *Advances in neural information processing systems*, 29.

Tom B. Brown, Benjamin Mann, Nick Ryder, Melanie Subbiah, Jared Kaplan, Prafulla Dhariwal, Arvind Neelakantan, Pranav Shyam, Girish Sastry, Amanda Askell, Sandhini Agarwal, Ariel Herbert-Voss, Gretchen Krueger, Tom Henighan, Rewon Child, Aditya Ramesh, Daniel M. Ziegler, Jeffrey Wu, Clemens Winter, Christopher Hesse, Mark Chen, Eric Sigler, Mateusz Litwin, Scott Gray, Benjamin Chess, Jack Clark, Christopher Berner, Sam McCandlish, Alec Radford, Ilya Sutskever, and Dario Amodei. 2020. Language models are few-shot learners. *CoRR*, abs/2005.14165.

Aylin Caliskan, Joanna J Bryson, and Arvind Narayanan. 2017. Semantics derived automatically from language corpora contain human-like biases. *Science*, 356(6334):183–186.

Taylor J Damann, Jeremy Siow, and Margit Tavits. 2023. Persistence of gender biases in europe. *Proceedings of the National Academy of Sciences*, 120(12):e2213266120.

Jacob Devlin, Ming-Wei Chang, Kenton Lee, and Kristina Toutanova. 2019. BERT: Pre-training of deep bidirectional transformers for language understanding. In *Proceedings of the 2019 Conference of the North American Chapter of the Association for Computational Linguistics: Human Language Technologies, Volume 1 (Long and Short Papers)*, pages 4171–4186, Minneapolis, Minnesota. Association for Computational Linguistics.

Jonathan Dunn and Ben Adams. 2020a. Geographically-balanced gigaword corpora for 50 language varieties. In *Proceedings of the Twelfth Language Resources and Evaluation Conference*, pages 2528–2536.

Jonathan Dunn and Ben Adams. 2020b. Mapping languages and demographics with georeferenced corpora. *arXiv preprint arXiv:2004.00809*.

Ashutosh Dwivedi, Pradhyumna Lavania, and Ashutosh Modi. 2023. EtiCor: Corpus for analyzing LLMs for etiquettes. In *Proceedings of the 2023 Conference on Empirical Methods in Natural Language Processing*, pages 6921–6931, Singapore. Association for Computational Linguistics.

Aparna Garimella, Rada Mihalcea, and Akhash Amarnath. 2022. Demographic-aware language model fine-tuning as a bias mitigation technique. In *Proceedings of the 2nd Conference of the Asia-Pacific Chapter of the Association for Computational Linguistics and the 12th International Joint Conference on Natural Language Processing (Volume 2: Short Papers)*, pages 311–319, Online only. Association for Computational Linguistics.

Aparna Garimella, Rada Mihalcea, and James Pennebaker. 2016. Identifying cross-cultural differences in word usage. In *Proceedings of COLING 2016, the 26th International Conference on Computational Linguistics: Technical Papers*, pages 674–683, Osaka, Japan. The COLING 2016 Organizing Committee.

Amelia Glaese, Nat McAleese, Maja Trębacz, John Aslanides, Vlad Firoiu, Timo Ewalds, Maribeth Rauh, Laura Weidinger, Martin Chadwick, Phoebe Thacker, Lucy Campbell-Gillingham, Jonathan Uesato, Po-Sen Huang, Ramona Comanescu, Fan Yang, Abigail See, Sumanth Dathathri, Rory Greig, Charlie Chen, Doug Fritz, Jaume Sanchez Elias, Richard Green, Soňa Mokrá, Nicholas Fernando, Boxi Wu, Rachel Foley, Susannah Young, Iason Gabriel, William Isaac, John Mellor, Demis Hassabis, Koray Kavukcuoglu, Lisa Anne Hendricks, and Geoffrey Irving. 2022. Improving alignment of dialogue agents via targeted human judgements.

Anthony G Greenwald, Debbie E McGhee, and Jordan LK Schwartz. 1998. Measuring individual differences in implicit cognition: the implicit association test. *Journal of personality and social psychology*, 74(6):1464.

Stephanie D Grimm and A Timothy Church. 1999. A cross-cultural study of response biases in personality measures. *Journal of Research in Personality*, 33(4):415–441.

Maarten Grootendorst. 2020. Keybert: Minimal keyword extraction with bert.

Maarten Grootendorst. 2022. Bertopic: Neural topic modeling with a class-based tf-idf procedure.

Akshat Gupta, Xiaoyang Song, and Gopala Anumanchipalli. 2024. Self-assessment tests are unreliable measures of llm personality.

Joseph Henrich, Steven J Heine, and Ara Norenzayan. 2010. The weirdest people in the world? *Behavioral and brain sciences*, 33(2-3):61–83.

Matthew Honnibal and Ines Montani. 2017. spaCy 2: Natural language understanding with Bloom embeddings, convolutional neural networks and incremental parsing. To appear.

Akshita Jha, Aida Davani, Chandan K Reddy, Shachi Dave, Vinodkumar Prabhakaran, and Sunipa Dev. 2023. Seegull: A stereotype benchmark with broad geo-cultural coverage leveraging generative models. *arXiv preprint arXiv:2305.11840*.

Albert Q. Jiang, Alexandre Sablayrolles, Arthur Mensch, Chris Bamford, Devendra Singh Chaplot, Diego de las Casas, Florian Bressand, Gianna Lengyel, Guillaume Lample, Lucile Saulnier, Lélio Renard Lavaud, Marie-Anne Lachaux, Pierre Stock, Teven Le Scao, Thibaut Lavril, Thomas Wang, Timothée Lacroix, and William El Sayed. 2023. Mistral 7b.

Mengyin Jiang, Shirley KM Wong, Harry KS Chung, Yang Sun, Janet H Hsiao, Jie Sui, and Glyn W Humphreys. 2019. Cultural orientation of self-bias in perceptual matching. *Frontiers in Psychology*, 10:1469.

Svetlana Kiritchenko and Saif Mohammad. 2018a. Examining gender and race bias in two hundred sentiment analysis systems. In *Proceedings of the Seventh Joint Conference on Lexical and Computational Semantics*, pages 43–53, New Orleans, Louisiana. Association for Computational Linguistics.

Svetlana Kiritchenko and Saif Mohammad. 2018b. Examining gender and race bias in two hundred sentiment analysis systems. In *Proceedings of the Seventh Joint Conference on Lexical and Computational Semantics*, pages 43–53, New Orleans, Louisiana. Association for Computational Linguistics.

John P Lalor, Yi Yang, Kendall Smith, Nicole Forsgren, and Ahmed Abbasi. 2022. Benchmarking intersectional biases in nlp. In *Proceedings of the 2022 conference of the North American chapter of the association for computational linguistics: Human language technologies*, pages 3598–3609.

Claudia Malzer and Marcus Baum. 2020. A hybrid approach to hierarchical density-based cluster selection. In *2020 IEEE International Conference on Multisensor Fusion and Integration for Intelligent Systems (MFI)*. IEEE.

Hazel Rose Markus and Shinobu Kitayama. 2003. Models of agency: sociocultural diversity in the construction of action.

Chandler May, Alex Wang, Shikha Bordia, Samuel R. Bowman, and Rachel Rudinger. 2019. On measuring social biases in sentence encoders. In *Proceedings of the 2019 Conference of the North American Chapter of the Association for Computational Linguistics: Human Language Technologies, Volume 1 (Long and Short Papers)*, pages 622–628, Minneapolis, Minnesota. Association for Computational Linguistics.

Leland McInnes, John Healy, Nathaniel Saul, and Lukas Großberger. 2018. Umap: Uniform manifold approximation and projection. *Journal of Open Source Software*, 3(29):861.

Rada Mihalcea, Oana Ignat, Longju Bai, Angana Borah, Luis Chiruzzo, Zhijing Jin, Claude Kwizera, Joan Nwatu, Soujanya Poria, and Thamar Solorio. 2025. Why ai is weird and should not be this way: Towards ai for everyone, with everyone, by everyone. In *Association for the Advances of Artificial Intelligence*.

Tomas Mikolov, Kai Chen, Greg Corrado, and Jeffrey Dean. 2013. Efficient estimation of word representations in vector space.

David Mimno, Hanna Wallach, Edmund Talley, Miriam Leenders, and Andrew McCallum. 2011. Optimizing semantic coherence in topic models. In *Proceedings of the 2011 Conference on Empirical Methods in Natural Language Processing*, pages 262–272, Edinburgh, Scotland, UK. Association for Computational Linguistics.

Dugan Nichols. 2011. Men and must-have shoes. *Retrieved from*.

OpenAI, Josh Achiam, Steven Adler, Sandhini Agarwal, Lama Ahmad, Ilge Akkaya, Florencia Leoni Aleman, Diogo Almeida, Janko Altenschmidt, Sam Altman, Shyamal Anadkat, Red Avila, Igor Babuschkin, Suchir Balaji, Valerie Balcom, Paul Baltescu, Haiming Bao, Mohammad Bavarian, Jeff Belgum, Irwan Bello, Jake Berdine, Gabriel Bernadett-Shapiro, Christopher Berner, Lenny Bogdonoff, Oleg Boiko, Madelaine Boyd, Anna-Luisa Brakman, Greg Brockman, Tim Brooks, Miles Brundage, Kevin Button, Trevor Cai, Rosie Campbell, Andrew Cann, Brittany Carey, Chelsea Carlson, Rory Carmichael, Brooke Chan, Che Chang, Fotis Chantzis, Derek Chen, Sully Chen, Ruby Chen, Jason Chen, Mark Chen, Ben Chess, Chester Cho, Casey Chu, Hyung Won Chung, Dave Cummings, Jeremiah Currier, Yunxing Dai, Cory Decareaux, Thomas Degry, Noah Deutsch, Damien Deville, Arka Dhar, David Dohan, Steve Dowling, Sheila Dunning, Adrien Ecoffet, Atty Eleti, Tyna Eloundou, David Farhi, Liam Fedus, Niko Felix, Simón Posada Fishman, Juston Forte, Isabella Fulford, Leo Gao, Elie Georges, Christian Gibson, Vik Goel, Tarun Gogineni, Gabriel Goh, Rapha Gontijo-Lopes, Jonathan Gordon, Morgan Grafstein, Scott Gray, Ryan Greene, Joshua Gross, Shixiang Shane

Gu, Yufei Guo, Chris Hallacy, Jesse Han, Jeff Harris, Yuchen He, Mike Heaton, Johannes Heidecke, Chris Hesse, Alan Hickey, Wade Hickey, Peter Hoeschele, Brandon Houghton, Kenny Hsu, Shengli Hu, Xin Hu, Joost Huizinga, Shantanu Jain, Shawn Jain, Joanne Jang, Angela Jiang, Roger Jiang, Haozhun Jin, Denny Jin, Shino Jomoto, Billie Jonn, Heewoo Jun, Tomer Kaftan, Łukasz Kaiser, Ali Kamali, Ingmar Kanitscheider, Nitish Shirish Keskar, Tabarak Khan, Logan Kilpatrick, Jong Wook Kim, Christina Kim, Yongjik Kim, Jan Hendrik Kirchner, Jamie Kiros, Matt Knight, Daniel Kokotajlo, Łukasz Kondraciuk, Andrew Kondrich, Aris Konstantinidis, Kyle Kosic, Gretchen Krueger, Vishal Kuo, Michael Lampe, Ikai Lan, Teddy Lee, Jan Leike, Jade Leung, Daniel Levy, Chak Ming Li, Rachel Lim, Molly Lin, Stephanie Lin, Mateusz Litwin, Theresa Lopez, Ryan Lowe, Patricia Lue, Anna Makanju, Kim Malfacini, Sam Manning, Todor Markov, Yaniv Markovski, Bianca Martin, Katie Mayer, Andrew Mayne, Bob McGrew, Scott Mayer McKinney, Christine McLeavey, Paul McMillan, Jake McNeil, David Medina, Aalok Mehta, Jacob Menick, Luke Metz, Andrey Mishchenko, Pamela Mishkin, Vinnie Monaco, Evan Morikawa, Daniel Mossing, Tong Mu, Mira Murati, Oleg Murk, David Mély, Ashvin Nair, Reiichiro Nakano, Rajeev Nayak, Arvind Neelakantan, Richard Ngo, Hyeonwoo Noh, Long Ouyang, Cullen O'Keefe, Jakub Pachocki, Alex Paino, Joe Palermo, Ashley Pantuliano, Giambattista Parascandolo, Joel Parish, Emy Parparita, Alex Passos, Mikhail Pavlov, Andrew Peng, Adam Perelman, Filipe de Avila Belbute Peres, Michael Petrov, Henrique Ponde de Oliveira Pinto, Michael, Pokorny, Michelle Pokrass, Vitchyr H. Pong, Tolly Powell, Alethea Power, Boris Power, Elizabeth Proehl, Raul Puri, Alec Radford, Jack Rae, Aditya Ramesh, Cameron Raymond, Francis Real, Kendra Rimbach, Carl Ross, Bob Rotsted, Henri Roussez, Nick Ryder, Mario Saltarelli, Ted Sanders, Shibani Santurkar, Girish Sastry, Heather Schmidt, David Schnurr, John Schulman, Daniel Selsam, Kyla Sheppard, Toki Sherbakov, Jessica Shieh, Sarah Shoker, Pranav Shyam, Szymon Sidor, Eric Sigler, Maddie Simens, Jordan Sitkin, Katarina Slama, Ian Sohl, Benjamin Sokolowsky, Yang Song, Natalie Staudacher, Felipe Petroski Such, Natalie Summers, Ilya Sutskever, Jie Tang, Nikolas Tezak, Madeleine B. Thompson, Phil Tillet, Amin Tootoonchian, Elizabeth Tseng, Preston Tuggle, Nick Turley, Jerry Tworek, Juan Felipe Cerón Uribe, Andrea Vallone, Arun Vijayvergiya, Chelsea Voss, Carroll Wainwright, Justin Jay Wang, Alvin Wang, Ben Wang, Jonathan Ward, Jason Wei, CJ Weinmann, Akila Welihinda, Peter Welinder, Jiayi Weng, Lilian Weng, Matt Wiethoff, Dave Willner, Clemens Winter, Samuel Wolrich, Hannah Wong, Lauren Workman, Sherwin Wu, Jeff Wu, Michael Wu, Kai Xiao, Tao Xu, Sarah Yoo, Kevin Yu, Qiming Yuan, Wojciech Zaremba, Rowan Zellers, Chong Zhang, Marvin Zhang, Shengjia Zhao, Tianhao Zheng, Juntang Zhuang, William Zhuk, and Barret Zoph. 2024. Gpt-4 technical report.

Joon Sung Park, Joseph C. O'Brien, Carrie J. Cai, Meredith Ringel Morris, Percy Liang, and Michael S. Bernstein. 2023. Generative agents: Interactive simulacra of human behavior. In *In the 36th Annual ACM Symposium on User Interface Software and Technology (UIST '23)*, UIST '23, New York, NY, USA. Association for Computing Machinery.

Nils Reimers and Iryna Gurevych. 2019. Sentence-BERT: Sentence embeddings using Siamese BERT-networks. In *Proceedings of the 2019 Conference on Empirical Methods in Natural Language Processing and the 9th International Joint Conference on Natural Language Processing (EMNLP-IJCNLP)*, pages 3982–3992, Hong Kong, China. Association for Computational Linguistics.

Rachel Rudinger, Jason Naradowsky, Brian Leonard, and Benjamin Van Durme. 2018. Gender bias in coreference resolution. In *Proceedings of the 2018 Conference of the North American Chapter of the Association for Computational Linguistics: Human Language Technologies, Volume 2 (Short Papers)*, pages 8–14, New Orleans, Louisiana. Association for Computational Linguistics.

Rebecca Ross Russell. 2010. *Gender and jewelry: A feminist analysis*. Rebecca Ross Russell.

Gabriel Stanovsky, Noah A. Smith, and Luke Zettlemoyer. 2019. Evaluating gender bias in machine translation. In *Proceedings of the 57th Annual Meeting of the Association for Computational Linguistics*, pages 1679–1684, Florence, Italy. Association for Computational Linguistics.

Zhiqing Sun, Yikang Shen, Qinhong Zhou, Hongxin Zhang, Zhenfang Chen, David Cox, Yiming Yang, and Chuang Gan. 2023. Principle-driven self-alignment of language models from scratch with minimal human supervision. In *Thirty-seventh Conference on Neural Information Processing Systems*.

Gemini Team, Machel Reid, Nikolay Savinov, Denis Teplyashin, Dmitry, Lepikhin, Timothy Lillicrap, Jean baptiste Alayrac, Radu Soricut, Angeliki Lazaridou, Orhan Firat, Julian Schrittwieser, Ioannis Antonoglou, Rohan Anil, Sebastian Borgeaud, Andrew Dai, Katie Millican, Ethan Dyer, Mia Glaese, Thibault Sottiaux, Benjamin Lee, Fabio Viola, Malcolm Reynolds, Yuanzhong Xu, James Molloy, Jilin Chen, Michael Isard, Paul Barham, Tom Hennigan, Ross McIlroy, Melvin Johnson, Johan Schalkwyk, Eli Collins, Eliza Rutherford, Erica Moreira, Kareem Ayoub, Megha Goel, Clemens Meyer, Gregory Thornton, Zhen Yang, Henryk Michalewski, Zaheer Abbas, Nathan Schucher, Ankesh Anand, Richard Ives, James Keeling, Karel Lenc, Salem Haykal, Siamak Shakeri, Pranav Shyam, Aakanksha Chowdhery, Roman Ring, Stephen Spencer, Eren Sezener, Luke Vilnis, Oscar Chang, Nobuyuki Morioka, George Tucker, Ce Zheng, Oliver Woodman, Nithya Attaluri, Tomas Kocisky, Evgenii Eltyshev, Xi Chen, Timothy Chung, Vittorio Selo, Siddhartha Brahma, Petko Georgiev, Ambrose Slone, Zhenkai Zhu, James Lottes, Siyuan Qiao, Ben Caine, Sebastian Riedel,

Alex Tomala, Martin Chadwick, Juliette Love, Peter Choy, Sid Mittal, Neil Houlsby, Yunhao Tang, Matthew Lamm, Libin Bai, Qiao Zhang, Luheng He, Yong Cheng, Peter Humphreys, Yujia Li, Sergey Brin, Albin Cassirer, Yingjie Miao, Lukas Zilka, Taylor Tobin, Kelvin Xu, Lev Proleev, Daniel Sohn, Alberto Magni, Lisa Anne Hendricks, Isabel Gao, Santiago Ontanon, Oskar Bunyan, Nathan Byrd, Abhanshu Sharma, Biao Zhang, Mario Pinto, Rishika Sinha, Harsh Mehta, Dawei Jia, Sergi Caelles, Albert Webson, Alex Morris, Becca Roelofs, Yifan Ding, Robin Strudel, Xuehan Xiong, Marvin Ritter, Mostafa Dehghani, Rahma Chaabouni, Abhijit Karmarkar, Guangda Lai, Fabian Mentzer, Bibo Xu, YaGuang Li, Yujing Zhang, Tom Le Paine, Alex Goldin, Behnam Neyshabur, Kate Baumli, Anselm Levskaya, Michael Laskin, Wenhao Jia, Jack W. Rae, Kefan Xiao, Antoine He, Skye Giordano, Lakshman Yagati, Jean-Baptiste Lespiau, Paul Natsev, Sanjay Ganapathy, Fangyu Liu, Danilo Martins, Nanxin Chen, Yunhan Xu, Megan Barnes, Rhys May, Arpi Vezer, Junhyuk Oh, Ken Franko, Sophie Bridgers, Ruizhe Zhao, Boxi Wu, Basil Mustafa, Sean Sechrist, Emilio Parisotto, Thanumalayan Sankaranarayana Pillai, Chris Larkin, Chenjie Gu, Christina Sorokin, Maxim Krikun, Alexey Guseynov, Jessica Landon, Romina Datta, Alexander Pritzel, Phoebe Thacker, Fan Yang, Kevin Hui, Anja Hauth, Chih-Kuan Yeh, David Barker, Justin Mao-Jones, Sophia Austin, Hannah Sheahan, Parker Schuh, James Svensson, Rohan Jain, Vinay Ramasesh, Anton Briukhov, Da-Woon Chung, Tamara von Glehn, Christina Butterfield, Priya Jhakra, Matthew Wiethoff, Justin Frye, Jordan Grimstad, Beer Changpinyo, Charline Le Lan, Anna Bortsova, Yonghui Wu, Paul Voigtlaender, Tara Sainath, Shane Gu, Charlotte Smith, Will Hawkins, Kris Cao, James Besley, Srivatsan Srinivasan, Mark Omernick, Colin Gaffney, Gabriela Surita, Ryan Burnell, Bogdan Damoc, Junwhan Ahn, Andrew Brock, Mantas Pajarskas, Anastasia Petrushkina, Seb Noury, Lorenzo Blanco, Kevin Swersky, Arun Ahuja, Thi Avrahami, Vedant Misra, Raoul de Liedekerke, Mariko Iinuma, Alex Polozov, Sarah York, George van den Driessche, Paul Michel, Justin Chiu, Rory Blevins, Zach Gleicher, Adrià Recasens, Alban Rrustemi, Elena Gribovskaya, Aurko Roy, Wiktor Gworek, Sébastien M. R. Arnold, Lisa Lee, James Lee-Thorp, Marcello Maggioni, Enrique Piqueras, Kartikeya Badola, Sharad Vikram, Lucas Gonzalez, Anirudh Baddepudi, Evan Senter, Jacob Devlin, James Qin, Michael Azzam, Maja Trebacz, Martin Polacek, Kashyap Krishnakumar, Shuo yiin Chang, Matthew Tung, Ivo Penchev, Rishabh Joshi, Kate Olszewska, Carrie Muir, Mateo Wirth, Ale Jakse Hartman, Josh Newlan, Sheleem Kashem, Vijay Bolina, Elahe Dabir, Joost van Amersfoort, Zafarali Ahmed, James Cobon-Kerr, Aishwarya Kamath, Arnar Mar Hrafnkelsson, Le Hou, Ian Mackinnon, Alexandre Frechette, Eric Noland, Xiance Si, Emanuel Taropa, Dong Li, Phil Crone, Anmol Gulati, Sébastien Cevey, Jonas Adler, Ada Ma, David Silver, Simon Tokumine, Richard Powell, Stephan Lee, Kiran Vodrahalli, Samer Hassan, Diana Mincu, Antoine Yang, Nir Levine, Jenny Brennan, Mingqiu Wang, Sarah Hodkinson, Jeffrey Zhao, Josh Lipschultz, Aedan Pope, Michael B. Chang, Cheng Li, Laurent El Shafey, Michela Paganini, Sholto Douglas, Bernd Bohnet, Fabio Pardo, Seth Odoom, Mihaela Rosca, Cicero Nogueira dos Santos, Kedar Soparkar, Arthur Guez, Tom Hudson, Steven Hansen, Chulayuth Asawaroengchai, Ravi Addanki, Tianhe Yu, Wojciech Stokowiec, Mina Khan, Justin Gilmer, Jaehoon Lee, Carrie Grimes Bostock, Keran Rong, Jonathan Caton, Pedram Pejman, Filip Pavetic, Geoff Brown, Vivek Sharma, Mario Lučić, Rajkumar Samuel, Josip Djolonga, Amol Mandhane, Lars Lowe Sjösund, Elena Buchatskaya, Elspeth White, Natalie Clay, Jiepu Jiang, Hyeontaek Lim, Ross Hemsley, Zeyncep Cankara, Jane Labanowski, Nicola De Cao, David Steiner, Sayed Hadi Hashemi, Jacob Austin, Anita Gergely, Tim Blyth, Joe Stanton, Kaushik Shivakumar, Aditya Siddhant, Anders Andreassen, Carlos Araya, Nikhil Sethi, Rakesh Shivanna, Steven Hand, Ankur Bapna, Ali Khodaei, Antoine Miech, Garrett Tanzer, Andy Swing, Shantanu Thakoor, Lora Aroyo, Zhufeng Pan, Zachary Nado, Jakub Sygnowski, Stephanie Winkler, Dian Yu, Mohammad Saleh, Loren Maggiore, Yamini Bansal, Xavier Garcia, Mehran Kazemi, Piyush Patil, Ishita Dasgupta, Iain Barr, Minh Giang, Thais Kagohara, Ivo Danihelka, Amit Marathe, Vladimir Feinberg, Mohamed Elhawaty, Nimesh Ghelani, Dan Horgan, Helen Miller, Lexi Walker, Richard Tanburn, Mukarram Tariq, Disha Shrivastava, Fei Xia, Qingze Wang, Chung-Cheng Chiu, Zoe Ashwood, Khuslen Baatarsukh, Sina Samangooei, Raphaël Lopez Kaufman, Fred Alcober, Axel Stjerngren, Paul Komarek, Katerina Tsihlas, Anudhyan Boral, Ramona Comanescu, Jeremy Chen, Ruibo Liu, Chris Welty, Dawn Bloxwich, Charlie Chen, Yanhua Sun, Fangxiaoyu Feng, Matthew Mauger, Xerxes Dotiwalla, Vincent Hellendoorn, Michael Sharman, Ivy Zheng, Krishna Haridasan, Gabe Barth-Maron, Craig Swanson, Dominika Rogozińska, Alek Andreev, Paul Kishan Rubenstein, Ruoxin Sang, Dan Hurt, Gamaleldin Elsayed, Renshen Wang, Dave Lacey, Anastasija Ilić, Yao Zhao, Adam Iwanicki, Alejandro Lince, Alexander Chen, Christina Lyu, Carl Lebsack, Jordan Griffith, Meenu Gaba, Paramjit Sandhu, Phil Chen, Anna Koop, Ravi Rajwar, Soheil Hassas Yeganeh, Solomon Chang, Rui Zhu, Soroush Radpour, Elnaz Davoodi, Ving Ian Lei, Yang Xu, Daniel Toyama, Constant Segal, Martin Wicke, Hanzhao Lin, Anna Bulanova, Adrià Puigdomènech Badia, Nemanja Rakićević, Pablo Sprechmann, Angelos Filos, Shaobo Hou, Víctor Campos, Nora Kassner, Devendra Sachan, Meire Fortunato, Chimezie Iwuanyanwu, Vitaly Nikolaev, Balaji Lakshminarayanan, Sadegh Jazayeri, Mani Varadarajan, Chetan Tekur, Doug Fritz, Misha Khalman, David Reitter, Kingshuk Dasgupta, Shourya Sarcar, Tina Ornduff, Javier Snaider, Fantine Huot, Johnson Jia, Rupert Kemp, Nejc Trdin, Anitha Vijayakumar, Lucy Kim, Christof Angermueller, Li Lao, Tianqi Liu, Haibin Zhang, David Engel, Somer Greene, Anaïs White, Jessica Austin, Lilly Taylor, Shereen Ashraf, Dangyi Liu, Maria Georgaki, Irene Cai, Yana Kulizhskaya, Sonam Goenka, Brennan Saeta, Ying Xu, Christian Frank, Dario de Cesare, Brona Robenek,

Harry Richardson, Mahmoud Alnahlawi, Christopher Yew, Priya Ponnapalli, Marco Tagliasacchi, Alex Korchemniy, Yelin Kim, Dinghua Li, Bill Rosgen, Kyle Levin, Jeremy Wiesner, Praseem Banzal, Praveen Srinivasan, Hongkun Yu, Çağlar Ünlü, David Reid, Zora Tung, Daniel Finchelstein, Ravin Kumar, Andre Elisseeff, Jin Huang, Ming Zhang, Ricardo Aguilar, Mai Giménez, Jiawei Xia, Olivier Dousse, Willi Gierke, Damion Yates, Komal Jalan, Lu Li, Eri Latorre-Chimoto, Duc Dung Nguyen, Ken Durden, Praveen Kallakuri, Yaxin Liu, Matthew Johnson, Tomy Tsai, Alice Talbert, Jasmine Liu, Alexander Neitz, Chen Elkind, Marco Selvi, Mimi Jasarevic, Livio Baldini Soares, Albert Cui, Pidong Wang, Alek Wenjiao Wang, Xinyu Ye, Krystal Kallarackal, Lucia Loher, Hoi Lam, Josef Broder, Dan Holtmann-Rice, Nina Martin, Bramandia Ramadhana, Mrinal Shukla, Sujoy Basu, Abhi Mohan, Nick Fernando, Noah Fiedel, Kim Paterson, Hui Li, Ankush Garg, Jane Park, DongHyun Choi, Diane Wu, Sankalp Singh, Zhishuai Zhang, Amir Globerson, Lily Yu, John Carpenter, Félix de Chaumont Quitry, Carey Radebaugh, Chu-Cheng Lin, Alex Tudor, Prakash Shroff, Drew Garmon, Dayou Du, Neera Vats, Han Lu, Shariq Iqbal, Alex Yakubovich, Nilesh Tripuraneni, James Manyika, Haroon Qureshi, Nan Hua, Christel Ngani, Maria Abi Raad, Hannah Forbes, Jeff Stanway, Mukund Sundararajan, Victor Ungureanu, Colton Bishop, Yunjie Li, Balaji Venkatraman, Bo Li, Chloe Thornton, Salvatore Scellato, Nishesh Gupta, Yicheng Wang, Ian Tenney, Xihui Wu, Ashish Shenoy, Gabriel Carvajal, Diana Gage Wright, Ben Bariach, Zhuyun Xiao, Peter Hawkins, Sid Dalmia, Clement Farabet, Pedro Valenzuela, Quan Yuan, Ananth Agarwal, Mia Chen, Wooyeol Kim, Brice Hulse, Nandita Dukkipati, Adam Paszke, Andrew Bolt, Kiam Choo, Jennifer Beattie, Jennifer Prendki, Harsha Vashisht, Rebeca Santamaria-Fernandez, Luis C. Cobo, Jarek Wilkiewicz, David Madras, Ali Elqursh, Grant Uy, Kevin Ramirez, Matt Harvey, Tyler Liechty, Heiga Zen, Jeff Seibert, Clara Huiyi Hu, Andrey Khorlin, Maigo Le, Asaf Aharoni, Megan Li, Lily Wang, Sandeep Kumar, Norman Casagrande, Jay Hoover, Dalia El Badawy, David Soergel, Denis Vnukov, Matt Miecnikowski, Jiri Simsa, Praveen Kumar, Thibault Sellam, Daniel Vlasic, Samira Daruki, Nir Shabat, John Zhang, Guolong Su, Jiageng Zhang, Jeremiah Liu, Yi Sun, Evan Palmer, Alireza Ghaffarkhah, Xi Xiong, Victor Cotruta, Michael Fink, Lucas Dixon, Ashwin Sreevatsa, Adrian Goedeckemeyer, Alek Dimitriev, Mohsen Jafari, Remi Crocker, Nicholas FitzGerald, Aviral Kumar, Sanjay Ghemawat, Ivan Philips, Frederick Liu, Yannie Liang, Rachel Sterneck, Alena Repina, Marcus Wu, Laura Knight, Marin Georgiev, Hyo Lee, Harry Askham, Abhishek Chakladar, Annie Louis, Carl Crous, Hardie Cate, Dessie Petrova, Michael Quinn, Denese Owusu-Afriyie, Achintya Singhal, Nan Wei, Solomon Kim, Damien Vincent, Milad Nasr, Christopher A. Choquette-Choo, Reiko Tojo, Shawn Lu, Diego de Las Casas, Yuchung Cheng, Tolga Bolukbasi, Katherine Lee, Saaber Fatehi, Rajagopal Ananthanarayanan, Miteyan Patel, Charbel Kaed, Jing Li, Shreyas Rammohan Belle, Zhe Chen, Jaclyn Konzelmann, Siim Põder, Roopal Garg, Vinod Koverkathu, Adam Brown, Chris Dyer, Rosanne Liu, Azade Nova, Jun Xu, Alanna Walton, Alicia Parrish, Mark Epstein, Sara McCarthy, Slav Petrov, Demis Hassabis, Koray Kavukcuoglu, Jeffrey Dean, and Oriol Vinyals. 2024. Gemini 1.5: Unlocking multimodal understanding across millions of tokens of context.

Hugo Touvron, Louis Martin, Kevin Stone, Peter Albert, Amjad Almahairi, Yasmine Babaei, Nikolay Bashlykov, Soumya Batra, Prajjwal Bhargava, Shruti Bhosale, Dan Bikel, Lukas Blecher, Cristian Canton Ferrer, Moya Chen, Guillem Cucurull, David Esiobu, Jude Fernandes, Jeremy Fu, Wenyin Fu, Brian Fuller, Cynthia Gao, Vedanuj Goswami, Naman Goyal, Anthony Hartshorn, Saghar Hosseini, Rui Hou, Hakan Inan, Marcin Kardas, Viktor Kerkez, Madian Khabsa, Isabel Kloumann, Artem Korenev, Punit Singh Koura, Marie-Anne Lachaux, Thibaut Lavril, Jenya Lee, Diana Liskovich, Yinghai Lu, Yuning Mao, Xavier Martinet, Todor Mihaylov, Pushkar Mishra, Igor Molybog, Yixin Nie, Andrew Poulton, Jeremy Reizenstein, Rashi Rungta, Kalyan Saladi, Alan Schelten, Ruan Silva, Eric Michael Smith, Ranjan Subramanian, Xiaoqing Ellen Tan, Binh Tang, Ross Taylor, Adina Williams, Jian Xiang Kuan, Puxin Xu, Zheng Yan, Iliyan Zarov, Yuchen Zhang, Angela Fan, Melanie Kambadur, Sharan Narang, Aurelien Rodriguez, Robert Stojnic, Sergey Edunov, and Thomas Scialom. 2023. Llama 2: Open foundation and fine-tuned chat models.

Kellie Webster, Marta Recasens, Vera Axelrod, and Jason Baldridge. 2018. Mind the GAP: A balanced corpus of gendered ambiguous pronouns. *Transactions of the Association for Computational Linguistics*, 6:605–617.

Thomas Wolf, Lysandre Debut, Victor Sanh, Julien Chaumond, Clement Delangue, Anthony Moi, Pierric Cistac, Tim Rault, Rémi Louf, Morgan Funtowicz, and Jamie Brew. 2019. Huggingface's transformers: State-of-the-art natural language processing. *CoRR*, abs/1910.03771.

Jieyu Zhao, Tianlu Wang, Mark Yatskar, Vicente Ordonez, and Kai-Wei Chang. 2018. Gender bias in coreference resolution: Evaluation and debiasing methods. In *Proceedings of the 2018 Conference of the North American Chapter of the Association for Computational Linguistics: Human Language Technologies, Volume 2 (Short Papers)*, pages 15–20, New Orleans, Louisiana. Association for Computational Linguistics.

Xuhui Zhou, Hao Zhu, Leena Mathur, Ruohong Zhang, Haofei Yu, Zhengyang Qi, Louis-Philippe Morency, Yonatan Bisk, Daniel Fried, Graham Neubig, and Maarten Sap. 2024. SOTOPIA: Interactive evaluation for social intelligence in language agents. In *The Twelfth International Conference on Learning Representations*.

REGION	COUNTRY	#EXAMPLES
Africa	Nigeria Mali Gabon	3,153,761 660,916 645,769
Asia	India Singapore Philippines	12,327,494 6,130,047 3,166,971
Europe	Ireland United Kingdom Spain	8,689,752 7,044,434 465,780
North America	Canada United States Bermuda	7.965,736 8,521,094 244,500
South America	Chile Colombia Brazil	84,452,354 3,553,216 237,134
Oceania	New Zealand Palau Vanuatu	94,476 486,437 165,355

Table 5: Region-specific details in GeoWAC

A GeoWAC dataset details

Table 5 contain the total number of examples per country in a region. We consider the top three countries with the highest number of examples per region.

B F-M Dataset statistics

Table 6 displays the total number of examples from female and male groups per region for the region-specific F-M dataset.

REGION	TOTAL	#FEMALE	#MALE
Africa	57895	20153	37742
Asia	56877	21400	35477
Europe	59121	21049	38072
North America	70665	27627	43038
Oceania	62101	25951	36150

Table 6: F-M dataset statistics for regions (Total refers to the total number of examples in each region, therefore, total = #female + #male)

C Cultural differences in biases using WEAT

Table 7 shows the WEAT scores for all WEAT dimensions defined in (Caliskan et al., 2017). We find that scores and p-values differ across regions for different dimensions. High bias dimensions differ across regions, hence it is important to consider region-specific topic pairs.

D Region-wise topic lists in GeoWAC

Table 8 displays a comprehensive list of topics for female and male groups across all regions.

E Unigram/Bigram Analysis

Table 10 shows the unigrams and bigrams of common topics with different gender associations. We find that 'fashion' is highly associated with shoes when it is a male topic in Africa, whereas in Europe and North America, it is mostly associated with accessories like sunglasses, rings, etc. This shows the typical association of women with jewelry and men with shoes (Russell, 2010; Nichols, 2011). In the case of 'Music', we see that unigrams and bigrams pertaining to Africa contain words related to hip-hop music and artists. For Europe, we find location references and metal music. And finally, Oceania shows references of jazz and rock. We do not find any obvious gender associations in the analysis of the music topic. Table 11 provides a unigram/bigram analysis of topics that are commonly associated with a specific gender across regions. For *parenting and family relationships*, Africa has mentions of children, while Asia and Oceania contain mentions of family events, etc. In North America, we mostly find text about maintaining health in families. For *religion and spirituality*, the unigrams/bigrams are mostly about Jesus and Christianity across regions. For *politics*, we find mentions of specific regions, as expected. *Education* topic is more about being successful in Europe, where it is about degrees in North America. Finally, 'social media' trends are mostly similar. Overall for topics with same gender associations across regions, do not have stark differences.

F WEAT-based evaluation setup details

For male/female terms, we use the same representative words from WEAT: *brother, father, uncle, grandfather, son, he, his, him, man, boy, male* for male and *sister, mother, aunt, grandmother, daughter, she, hers, her, woman, girl, female for female*. We also utilize GPT-4 to output the ten most common male/female names specific to each region. We provide the lists of word belonging to each topic in Table 12.

G Paired-list for F-M datasets

Here is the list of the 52 pairs used to create the F-M datasets per region inspired from the foundational work on bias detection and mitigation in NLP using word embedding techniques (Bolukbasi et al., 2016):

TARGET WORDS - ATTRIBUTE WORDS	REGION	REGION-SPECIFIC P-VALUE	REGION-SPECIFIC WEAT SCORE	ORIGINAL WEAT SCORE, P-VALUE
Male names vs Female names - career vs family	Africa	0.016	1.798	1.81, 0.001
	Asia	0.007	1.508	
	North America	0.04	1.885	
	South America	0.082	-0.574	
	Europe	$6 \cdot 10^{-4}$	1.610	
	Oceania	0.03	1.727	
Math vs Arts - Male vs Female terms	Africa	0.003	1.429	1.06, 0.018
	Asia	0.045	1.187	
	North America	0.007	0.703	
	South America	0.0006	0.532	
	Europe	0.005	0.334	
	Oceania	0.03	1.158	
Science vs Arts - Male vs Female terms	Africa	0.048	1.247	1.24, 0.01
	Asia	0.004	0.330	
	North America	$1 \cdot 10^{-5}$	0.036	
	South America	0.004	0.912	
	Europe	$1 \cdot 10^{-7}$	-0.655	
	Oceania	$2 \cdot 10^{-4}$	0.725	
Young people names vs old people names - pleasant vs unpleasant	Africa	$3 \cdot 10^{-5}$	0.855	1.21, 0.01
	Asia	$4 \cdot 10^{-4}$	0.917	
	North America	0.032	1.325	
	South America	0.0021	1.223	
	Europe	0.009	0.917	
	Oceania	0.014	0.947	
European American names vs African American names - pleasant vs unpleasant	Africa	$1 \cdot 10^{-5}$	0.008	1.28, 0.001
	Asia	$1 \cdot 10^{-6}$	-0.453	
	North America	0.009	1.29	
	South America	0.02	1.127	
	Europe	0.001	0.617	
	Oceania	$1 \cdot 10^{-4}$	0.492	
Instruments vs Weapons - pleasant vs unpleasant	Africa	0.03	1.443	1.53, $< 10^{-7}$
	Asia	0.009	1.001	
	North America	0.01	1.202	
	South America	0.045	0.672	
	Europe	0.02	1.21	
	Oceania	0.001	0.951	
Flowers vs Insects - pleasant vs unpleasant	Africa	0.002	0.312	1.5, $< 10^{-7}$
	Asia	0.009	0.869	
	North America	0.003	0.382	
	South America	0.009	0.412	
	Europe	0.001	0.332	
	Oceania	0.009	0.660	
Mental disease vs Physical disease - temporary vs permanent	Africa	0.008	0.835	1.38, 0.01
	Asia	0.02	1.201	
	North America	0.008	0.692	
	South America	0.01	1.123	
	Europe	0.04	1.382	
	Oceania	0.009	1.620	

Table 7: Region-wise WEAT scores and p-values across all dimensions specific in WEAT using word2vec. Negative scores are highlighted. We compare our region specific scores and p-values with the scores and p-values of the Original paper by (Caliskan et al., 2017)

REGION	FEMALE	MALE
Africa	Credit cards and finances, Royalty and Media, Trading strategies and market analysis, Dating and relationships guides, Parenting and family relationships, Fashionable Ankara Styles, women's lives and successes, online dating	Fashion and Lifestyle, Male enhancement and sexual health, Nollywood actresses and movies, Nigerian politics and government, Essay writing and research, Medical care for children and adults, Journalism and Media Conference, Music industry news and releases, Football league standing and player performances, Academic success and secondary school education, Religious inspiration and spiritual growth, Economic diversification and Socio-economic development
Asia	Hobbies and Interests, Healthy eating habits for children, Social media platforms, Royal wedding plans, Online Dating and Chatting, Adult Services, Gift ideas for Valentine's Day	DC comic characters, Mobile Application, Philippine Politics and Government, Sports and Soccer, Career, Bike enthusiasts, Artists and their work, Youth Soccer Teams, Career in film industry, Political leadership in India, Bollywood actors and films, Religious devotion and spirituality, Phone accessories
Europe	Pets and animal care, Fashion and Style, Education, Obituaries and Genealogy, Luxury sailing, Traveling, Energy and climate change, Family and relationships, Pension and costs, Tech and business operations, Dating, Comfortable hotels, Government transportation policies	Political developments in Northern Ireland, Christian Theology and Practice, Crime and murder investigation, EU Referendum and Ministerial Positions, Criminal Justice System, Israeli politics and International relations, Cancer and medications, UK Government Taxation policies, Art Exhibitions, Political decision and impact on society, Music Gendres and artists, Medical specialties and university training, Political discourse and parliamentary debates
North America	Pets, Cooking: culinary delights and chef recipes, Fashion and style, Family dynamics and relationships, Reading and fiction, Scheduling and dates, Life and legacy of Adolf Hitler, Gender roles and inequality, Education and achievements, Online dating for singles, Luxury handbags, Footwear and Apparel brands, Essay writing and literature	Civil War and history, Middle East conflict and political tensions, Movies and filmmaking, Political leadership and party dynamics in Bermuda, Rock Music and songwriting, Wartime aviation adventures, Religion and Spirituality, Reproductive health, Reinsurance and Capital markets, Nike shoes and fashion, Cape Cod news, NHL players
South America	Luxury and Cruise, Regional Development in South America, Cultural events, Food and recipes, Gender and Social inequality, Immigrants lifestyles, Travel and Beauty essentials, yoga and fitness for women, family and school life, motherhood and family characteristics	Colonial Wine Industry, Chilean politics and violence, Gaming, Football and Sports, Startup and Entrepreneurship, movies and actors, men's health and sexual wellness, startup and entrepreneurship, Chilean business leaders and Innovation, Religious texts and figures, Superhero movies and TV shows
Oceania	Cooking and culinary delights, Romance, Weight loss and nutrition for women, Water travel experience, Woodworking plans and projects, Time management and productivity, Inspiring stories and books for alleges, Sexual violence and abuse, Car insurance, Exercises for hormone development, kid's furniture and decor	Harry Potter adventures, Art and Photography, Superheroes and their Universes, Music recording and Artists, Football in Vanuatu, Pet care and veterinary services, Building and designing boats, Religious beliefs and figures, Fashion, Classic movie stars, Men's hairstyle and fashion, Male sexual health and supplements

Table 8: Region-wise topics for female and male.

[monastery, convent], [spokesman, spokeswoman], [Catholic priest, nun], [Dad, Mom], [Men, Women], [councilman, councilwoman], [grandpa, grandma], [grandsons, granddaughters], [prostate cancer, ovarian cancer], [testosterone, estrogen], [uncle, aunt], [wives, husbands], [Father, Mother], [Grandpa, Grandma], [He, She], [boy, girl], [boys, girls], [brother, sister], [brothers, sisters], [businessman, businesswoman], [chairman, chairwoman], [colt, filly], [congressman, congresswoman], [dad, mom], [dads, moms], [dudes, gals], [ex girlfriend, ex boyfriend], [father, mother], [fatherhood, motherhood], [fathers, mothers], [fella, granny], [fraternity, sorority], [gelding, mare], [gentleman, lady], [gentlemen, ladies], [grandfather, grandmother], [grandson, granddaughter], [he, she], [himself, herself], [his, her], [king, queen], [kings, queens], [male, female], [males, females], [man, woman], [men, women], [nephew, niece], [prince, princess], [schoolboy, schoolgirl], [son, daughter], [sons, daughters], [twin brother, twin sister].
Each pair in the above is denoted as a [male, female] pair.

H Llama 2 prompt for topic modeling

The prompt scheme for `Llama2` consists of three prompts: (1) System Prompt: a general prompt that describes information given to all conversations, (2) Example Prompt: an example that demonstrates the output we are looking for, and (3) Main Prompt: describes the structure of the main question, that is with a given set of documents and keywords, we ask the model to create a short label for the topic. Fig 5 displays the three prompts as used in the code.

I Topic Cluster Labels using other LLMs

We use `Llama2` to fine-tune our topics to label them for better coherence in our paper. However, we also experiment with `GPT-4` and arrive at similar topics in Table 9. (see Table 2 for comparison with `Llama2` topic labels).

J Topic Word Clusters Example - Africa

Here, we provide an example of how topics look in our data. In Fig 6, we provide word clusters of topics from Africa. The word clusters contain the top 10 words from each topic in Africa. We find that topic labels by `Llama2` are coherent in terms of top topic words.

K Region specific BERTs to identify top words in F/M direction

To motivate our case to investigate differences in biases across regions, we use BERT to compute

```
[ ] # System prompt describes information given to all conversations
    system_prompt = """
    <s>[INST] <<SYS>>
    You are a helpful, respectful and honest assistant for labeling topics.
    <</SYS>>
    """

[ ] # Example prompt demonstrating the output we are looking for
    example_prompt = """
    I have a topic that contains the following documents:
    - Traditional diets in most cultures were primarily plant-based with a little meat on top, but with the rise of industrial style meat
    production and factory farming, meat has become a staple food.
    - Meat, but especially beef, is the word food in terms of emissions.
    - Eating meat doesn't make you a bad person, not eating meat doesn't make you a good one.

    The topic is described by the following keywords: 'meat, beef, eat, eating, emissions, steak, food, health, processed, chicken'.

    Based on the information about the topic above, please create a short label of this topic. Make sure you to only return the label and nothing more.

    [/INST] Environmental impacts of eating meat
    """

[ ] # Our main prompt with documents ([DOCUMENTS]) and keywords ([KEYWORDS]) tags
    main_prompt = """
    [INST]
    I have a topic that contains the following documents:
    [DOCUMENTS]

    The topic is described by the following keywords: '[KEYWORDS]'.

    Based on the information about the topic above, please create a short label of this topic. Make sure you to only return the label and nothing more.
    [/INST]
    """
```

Figure 5: Llama2 prompt

Figure 6: Topic Word Clusters - Africa

REGION	FEMALE TOPICS	MALE TOPICS
Africa	Credit card-based financial services	Fashion - footwear and celebrities
	Royalty and femininity	Male enhancement and sexual health
	Financial trading	Nollywood
	Dating guides	Nigerian politics
	Motherhood and parenting	Academic writing
Asia	Hobbies	Superhero comic books
	Food and nutrition	Mobile applications
	Social media platforms and content creation	Philippines politics and people
	Royal weddings	Sports
	Online social interaction and dating	Career
Europe	Pets	Irish politics
	Fashion	Christianity
	Education	Law enforcement and crime
	Deaths and funerals	EU and Brexit
	Luxury yachting and sailing	Criminal justice system
North America	Pets	Civil War Military
	Cooking and Food	Middle Eastern politics and conflicts
	Fashion	Movies and direction
	Family and relationships	Bermuda politics
	Reading novels	Rock music
Oceania	Food and eating habits	Harry Potter
	Romance and emotions	Artistic expressions
	Weight loss and nutrition	Superheroes of Marvel and DC
	Boat and sailing experience	Albums, songs and artists
	Woodworking and carpentry	Vanuatu Football

Table 9: Topic labels by `gpt-4`, see Table 2 for comparison with `Llama2` topic labels

the top words corresponding to the *she-he* axis in the embedding space. BERT is a pre-trained transformer-based language model that consists of a set of encoders. As a motivation experiment to identify differences in the contextual embedding space for different regions, we fine-tune BERT with the masked language modeling task (no labels) for each region separately. For a given word, we compute its embeddings by averaging out all sentence embeddings where it occurs across the dataset.Similarly, we compute embeddings for all words in the dataset. The tokenized input goes through the BERT model and we take the hidden states at the end of the last encoder layer (in our case, BERT-base, i.e. 12 encoder layers) as sentence embeddings. We identify the top words with the highest projection across the *she-he* axis in the region-specific datasets. If we find differences in the top words across regions, it is possible that dominating bias topics vary by region as well. Fig 8 shows the top words closest to 'she' and 'he' contextual embeddings in our data for each region. We

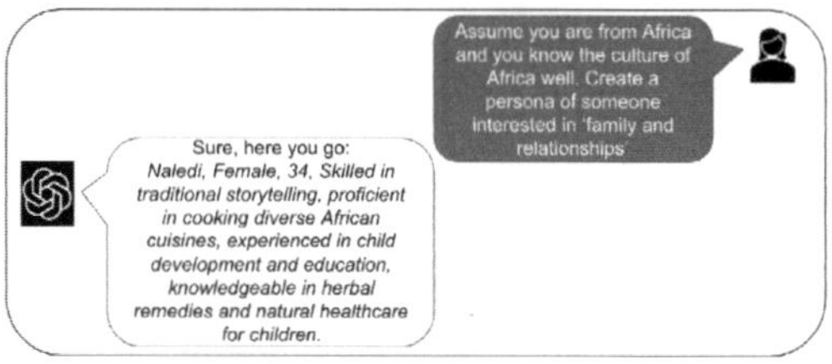

Figure 7: Example Prompt for Persona Generation

find that top words differ quite a bit across different regions. We find many differences in the top F (close to she) and M (close to he) words across regions. Some top F words are soprano, archaeological (Africa); graduate, secretary (Asia); innovative, graphics (Europe); poets, sentiments (NA); and arts, sleep (Oceania). Some top M words are history, leading (Africa); astronomer, commissioners (Asia); honorary, songwriters (Europe); owner, hospital (NA); and wrestlemania, orbits (Oceania). Gender-neutral words such as poets, secretaries, astronomers, commissioners, songwriters, owners, and so on are closer to either the she or he axes. Although comparable to the findings of (Bolukbasi et al., 2016), the variances among regions inspire us to look deeper into the data to arrive at culture-specific bias themes.

L Implementations details

For training our `Bertopic` model, we use `Google Colab's` Tesla T4 GPU, and it takes 15 min to run topic modeling for a region-specific F-M dataset. Region-specific BERTs are run on NVIDIA RTX2080 GPUs. Each BERT training experiment takes 1 GPU hour. For our LLM experiment, we used NVIDIA-A40 for `Mistral-7b-Instruct` and `Llama-3-8b` for an hour. We do not use any GPUs for `GPT-4`, `Claude-3-Sonnet` and `Gemini-Pro`.

L.1 Bertopic

We use Bertopic's default models: `SBERT` (Reimers and Gurevych, 2019) to contextually embed the dataset, `UMAP` (McInnes et al., 2018) to perform dimensionality reduction, `HDBSCAN` (Malzer and Baum, 2020) for clustering to perform topic modeling. We choose the embedding model `BAAI/bge-small-en` from *Huggingface* (Wolf et al., 2019). We set `top_n_words` to 10 and `verbose` as True and set the `min_topic_size` to 100 for the `Bertopic` model. Finally, we use Bertopic's official library to implement the model.

TOPIC	REGION	UNIGRAMS	BIGRAMS
Fashion and lifestyle	Africa (male)	march, outlet, air, max, tods, man, said, pas, cher, people	air max, pas cher, princess j, roshe run, nike air, tods outlet, j march, roger vivier, posts email, notify new
	Europe (female)	one, women, fashion, like, new, look, make, hair, girl, dress	oakley sunglasses, louis vuitton, red carpet, new york, fashion model, engagement rings, per cent, year old, christian louboutin, diamond ring
	North America (female)	one, love, like, little, new, made, time, get, make, women	s cooper, cooper main, t shirt, new york, little girl, men women, look good, main store, years ago, check out
Music	Africa (female)	music, song, album, new, video, single, one, singer, also, songs	music industry, hip hop, record label, single titled, new single, chris brown, tiwa savage, ice prince, kanye west, niegrian music
	Europe (male)	man, single, stage, years, world, many, metal, guitar, solo, irish	year shelfmark, black metal, time exercise, musical content, dundee repertory, singer songwriter, edinburgh year, zumba days, male vocalists, millions men
	Oceania (male)	music, album, new, songs, band, first, time, jazz, released, rock	new york, elizabth ii, debut album, years later, big band, rock roll, first time, studio album, los angeles, solo artist

Table 10: Common topics with different gender associations across regions

L.2 Llama2

We use `Llama2` to finetune the topics to give shorter labels for each topic. We set the `temperature` to 0.1, `max_new_tokens` to 500 and `repetition_penalty` to 1.1. We utilize Bertopic's built-in representation models to use `Llama2` in our topic model.

L.3 LLM experiment

For `GPT-4`, and `Mistral-7b-Instruct` and `Llama-3-8b`, we utilize the Microsoft Azure API[12], huggingface[13], and huggingface[14] for inference respectively. We use a temperature 0.8 for all models. For `Gemini-Pro` and `Claude-3-Sonnet`, we use the available chat interface.

L.4 Region-specific BERT

We use the uncased version BERT (Devlin et al., 2019) for our region-specific BERT model trained for the MLM objective. We use a batch size of 8, a learning rate of $1 \cdot 10^{-4}$, and an AdamW optimizer to train our BERT models for 3 epochs.

M Persona Generation Task

Figure 7 shows an example of the persona generation procedure for bias detection in LLMs.

N Human Validation

Students and staff from a college campus were recruited as annotators, who volunteered for the study. We have 6 annotators per region (3 male and 3 female) not necessarily from the same countries but belonging to the regions. Screenshots of the form are displayed in Fig 9.

O Reproducibility

We open-source our codes, which are uploaded to the submission system. We include commands with hyperparameters in our codes. This would help future work to reproduce our results.

[12]`https://learn.microsoft.com/en-us/rest/api/azure/`

[13]`https://huggingface.co/mistralai/Mistral-7B-Instruct-v0.1`

[14]`https://huggingface.co/meta-llama/Meta-Llama-3-8B`

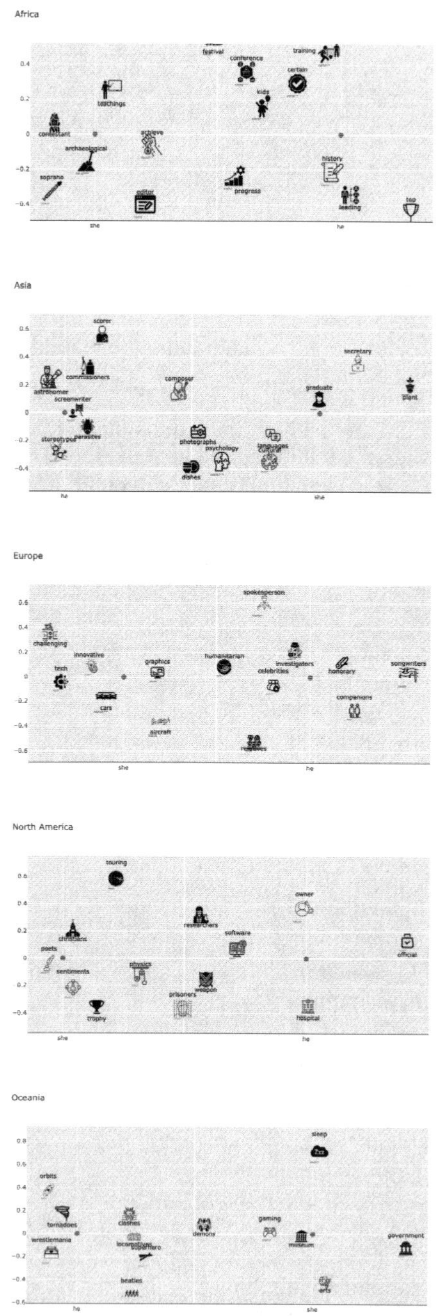

Figure 8: Top words for each region(Africa, Asia, Europe, North America and Oceania) using region-specific BERTs

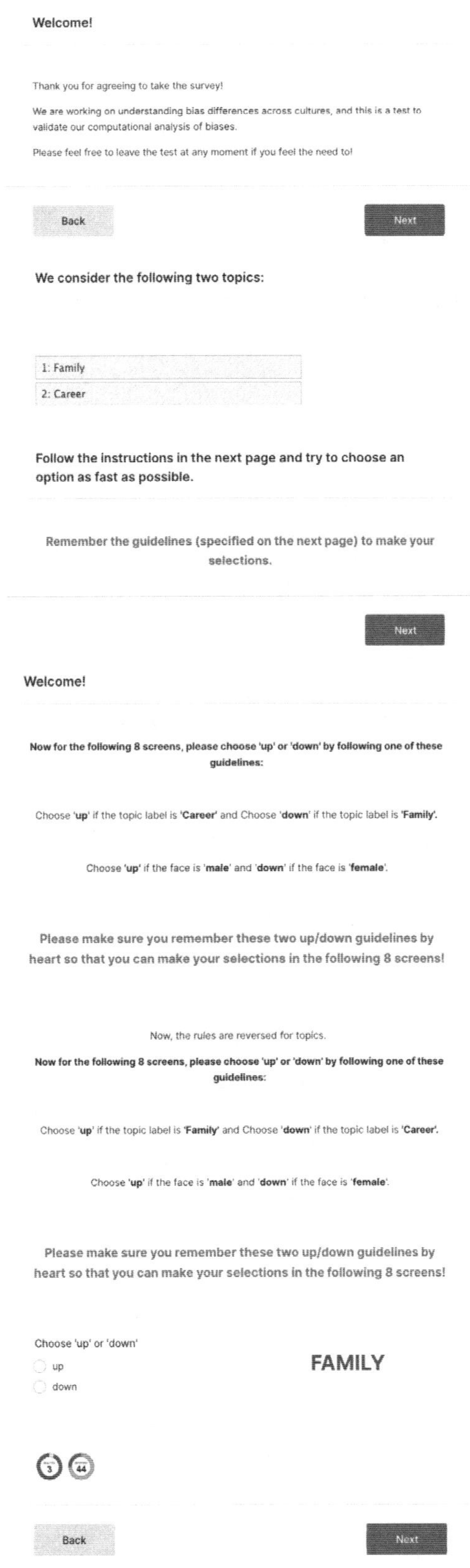
Welcome!

Thank you for agreeing to take the survey!

We are working on understanding bias differences across cultures, and this is a test to validate our computational analysis of biases.

Please feel free to leave the test at any moment if you feel the need to!

Back

Next

We consider the following two topics:

1: Family

2: Career

Follow the instructions in the next page and try to choose an option as fast as possible.

Remember the guidelines (specified on the next page) to make your selections.

Next

Welcome!

Now for the following 8 screens, please choose 'up' or 'down' by following one of these guidelines:

Choose **'up'** if the topic label is **'Career'** and Choose **'down'** if the topic label is **'Family'**.

Choose **'up'** if the face is **'male'** and **'down'** if the face is **'female'**.

Please make sure you remember these two up/down guidelines by heart so that you can make your selections in the following 8 screens!

Now, the rules are reversed for topics.

Now for the following 8 screens, please choose 'up' or 'down' by following one of these guidelines:

Choose **'up'** if the topic label is **'Family'** and Choose **'down'** if the topic label is **'Career'**.

Choose **'up'** if the face is **'male'** and **'down'** if the face is **'female'**.

Please make sure you remember these two up/down guidelines by heart so that you can make your selections in the following 8 screens!

Choose 'up' or 'down'

up

down

FAMILY

3 44

Back

Next

Figure 9: Annotation Form Screenshots (We do not include screenshots with faces to protect privacy)

TOPIC	REGION	UNIGRAMS	BIGRAMS
Parenting and family relationships	Africa (female)	child, registration, form, information, sent, women, foster, best, catholic, women	registration form, form information, child assigned, surgery doctors, new catholic, catholic women, contemporary challenge, best everything, foster short, doctors clinic
	Asia (female)	year, old, weekly, fortnightly, clicking, create, alert, state, 1, terms	year old, weekly fortnightly, create alert, stated agree, conditions acknowledge, finals appearances, together playing, dial guarded, came work, outlet jackets
	North America (female)	women, healthday, loss, three, worked, closely, together, she, elegant, dignified	three women, women worked, closely together, elegant dignified, very pleasant, soft spoken, women men, healthday reporter, tuesday march, participate more
	Oceania (female)	laurel, school, moved, one, day, royal, wedding, house, sister, hopefully	moved one, royal wedding, laurel school, 1 california, weeks dad, high school, one hopefully, nobody knew, sister means, fu school
Religion and Spirituality	Africa (male)	god, man, church, one, life, people, jesus, us, lord, christ,	short description, jesus christ, man god, holy spirit, god said, thank god, bible says, catholic church, today god, every man
	Asia (male)	life, jesus, us, church, one, man ,lord, said, father, christ	holu spirit, jesus christ, pope francis, brothers sisters, son god, men women, holy father, opus dei, eternal life, paul ii
	Europe (male)	god, one, jesus, church, life, people, father, man , said, christ	jesus christ, son man, catholic church, holy spirit, men women, said him, holy father, john paul, jesus said, word god
	North America (male)	god, jesus, one, man, us, life, would, christ, lord, people	recognizable cheering, section league, jesus christ, exact synonyms, past years, god said, years before, thanks mostly, mostly steph, father dell
	Oceania (male)	also, said, best, love, new, come, good, like, men, made	god said, jesus christ, holy spirit, lord krishna, temple god, father devil, eternal life, son god, son man, god father
Politics	Asia (male)	said, one, India, time, people, minister, government, years, state, police, court	indian congress, government plans, modi ministry, human rights, foreign politics, armed forces, international warfare, foreign ministry, middle east, united nations
	Europe (male)	government, said, minister, people, international, country, one, foreign, president, state	make statement, prime minister, human rights, armed forces, secretary state, middle east, united nations, hon friend, foreign secretary, united states
Education	Europe (female)	school, primary, teacher, founder, CEO, judgment, group, named, ranking, prestigious	as founder, founder CEO, judgment group, named fortune, ranking prestigious, world scientist, scientist women, students comprehend, program support, support students
	North America (female)	bachelor, years, student, leader, degree, animal, veterinary, music, taught, communication	bachelors degree, animal veterinary, bachelor music, alison taught, privately years, students ranging, development programmes, including leader, art communication, recent years
Social Media	Africa (male)	onigbinder, aura, pictures, first, gained, popularity, match, beaut, designed, music	aura pictures, gained popularity, match beaut, designed wonder, attending music, music festival, schomburg library, Instagram account, sugar coating, schedule tomorrow
	Asia (male)	time, later, latest, tracks, speedy, Zulfiqar, nasty, children, tweeted, guys	gets later, latest tracks, speedy zulfiqar, children pti, pti tweeted, taking long, long time, hosted pageant, time vincent, love fleeting

Table 11: Common topics with same-gender associations across regions

Region	Topics: Word lists
AFRICA	**Nollywood Actress and Movies**: nollywood, actress, actors, drama, celebrity, movie, acting, movies, producer, tv **Parenting and family relationships**: mother, mom, mothers, mum, moms, parent, her, child, momodu, parents **Sports and Football**: players, sports, fifa, team, player, football, mourinho, scored, league, champions **Marriage and relationships**: wives, marriage, husbands, marriages, married, wife, relationships, husband, marry, relationship **Fashion and lifestyle**: cher, nike, max, air, looked, face, love, tods, soldes, scarpe **Womens lives and successes**: women, ladies, woman, female, girls, men, gender, ones, employees, male **Social Media**: instagram, facebook, social, twitter, tweet, snapchat, tweets, tweeted, hashtag, followers **Music**: song, songs, album, hits, music, released, rap, singer, tracks, rapper **Religious and Spiritual Growth**: god, almighty, bible, christ, faith, believers, christian, jesus, prayer, religion **Dating and relationships advice**: dating, women, relationships, ladies, sites, singles, online, single, escorts, websites **Male terms**: male, man, boy, brother, he, him, his, son, Kwame, Mandela, Moyo, Jelani, Tariq, Keita, Obi, Simba, Ayo, Kofi, Jabari, Tunde, Mekonnen, Anwar, Chukwuemeka **Female terms**: sister, mother, aunt, grandmother, daughter, she, hers, her, Aisha, Zahara, Nia, Sade, Amara, Chinelo, Layla, Ayana, Nala, Zuri, Imani, Lola, Kamaria, Nyala, Kaya
ASIA	**Political Leardership in India**: modi, political, said, bjp, told, says, leader, congress, minister, public **Hotel Royalty**: visited, places, stayed, hotels, adventure, pictures, favourite, guest, hiking, hemingway **Sports and Soccer**: sports, team, basketball, players, nba, league, championship, coach, rebounds, finals **Healthy eating habits for children**: food, foods, eating, meals, nutrition, cuisine, diet, dishes, cooking, eat **Social Media platforms for video sharing**: instagram, video, videos, twitter, tweet, facebook, gifs, vlog, youtube, followers **Royal wedding plans**: meghan, duchess, engagement, england, royal, royalty, prince, kate, london, married **Religious devotion and spirituality**: god, bible, holy, faith, prayer, believe, christian, blessed, christ, spiritual **Royal wedding plans**: meghan, duchess, engagement, england, royal, royalty, prince, kate, london, married **Bollywood actors and films**: bollywood, bachchan, kapoor, actors, acting, kareena, actor, film, shahrukh, hindi **Marriage**: married, marriage, marriages, couple, couples, wife, marry, wedding, husband, divorced **Male terms**: male, man, boy, brother, he, him, his, son, Hiroshi, Ravi, Kazuki, Jin, Satoshi, Rohan, Haruki, Dai, Akira, Yuan **Female terms**: sister, mother, aunt, grandmother, daughter, she, hers, her, Sakura, Mei, Aiko, Yuna, Lina, Ji-hye, Mika, Nami, Anika, Rina
EUROPE	**Music**: music, songs, vocalists, album, albums, singing, vocals, singles, rock, song **Education**: school, schools, classroom, students, education, educational, pupils, boys, academy, college **Political decisions and impact on society**: government, public, minister, said, hon, people, first, the, column, committee **Comfortable hotels**: guests, staying, rooms, friendly, welcoming, stayed, hotel, beds, stay, comfortable **UK Government Taxation Policies**: corbyn, taxation, fiscal, tax, taxes, exchequer, labour, governments, government, deficit **Luxury Sailing**: yachts, yacht, boat, sailing, sails, cruising, sail, berths, cruiser, cabin **Christian Theology and Practice**: god, bible, christ, jesus, faith, christian, religious, religion, holy, gave **Obituaries and Genealogy**: died, edward, relatives, anne, lived, elizabeth, funeral, irish, mrs, galway **Christian Theology and Practice**: god, bible, christ, jesus, faith, christian, religious, religion, holy, gave **Fashion and style**: fashion, shoes, style, clothes, clothing, shoe, wear, nike, dress, stylish **Male terms**: male, man, boy, brother, he, him, his, son, Lukas, Matteo, Sebastian, Alexander, Gabriel, Nikolai, Maximilian, Leonardo, Daniel, Adrian **Female terms**: sister, mother, aunt, grandmother, daughter, she, hers, her, Emma, Sophia, Olivia, Isabella, Ava, Mia, Charlotte, Amelia, Lily, Emily
NORTH AMERICA	**Religion and Spirituality**: god, christ, jesus, bible, christian, holy, christians, scripture, faith, heaven **Online Dating for Singles**: dating, singles, hookup, single, relationships, dates, flirting, personals, date, mingle **Reproductive Health**: download, available, pdf, online, edition, manual, free, reprint, kindle, file **Fashion and style**: fashion, dresses, dress, wardrobe, clothes, clothing, style, outfit, vintage, wear **Reinsurance and capital markets**: reinsurance, reinsurers, insurers, insurance, securities, investors, investment, finance, trading, pension **Education and achievements**: school, schools, graduated, college, students, undergraduate, graduation, graduate, attended, education **Nike shoes and fashion**: nike, shoes, sneakers, jordans, jeans, tops, black, boys, men, casual **Family dynamics and relationships**: family, families, children, kids, grandchildren, relatives, grandparents, parents, child, parent **Cape Cod news**: lifeguard, drowned, drowns, newstweet, hospitalized, snorkeling, cape, reported, reuterstweet, pulled **Reading and fiction**: books, book, reading, novels, series, enjoyed, novel, romance, katniss, readers **Male terms**: male, man, boy, brother, he, him, his, son, Liam, Noah, Ethan, Jacob, William, Michael, James, Alexander, Benjamin, Matthew **Female terms**: sister, mother, aunt, grandmother, daughter, she, hers, her, Emma, Olivia, Ava, Sophia, Isabella, Mia, Charlotte, Amelia, Harper, Evelyn
OCEANIA	**Religious beliefs and figures**: god, gods, bible, mankind, faith, christ, spiritual, christian, religion, jesus **Family relationships**: mum, mother, mom, mums, parent, family, parents, baby, dad, father **Music record and Artists**: music, album, albums, jazz, songs, hits, musicians, artists, recordings, blues **Woordworking plans and projects**: plans, furniture, woodwork, wood, woodcraft, woodworking, plywood, carpentry, cabinets, wooden **Building and designing boats**: boatbuilder, boatbuilding, boats, plans, boat, sauceboat, sailboat, build, catamaran, kits **Weight loss and nutrition for women**: diet, workout, exercise, foods, weight, food, eating, healthy, pounds, fat **Superheroes and their Universes**: superhero, superheroes, avengers, marvel, comics, superman, aquaman, heroes, comic, hero **Exercises for hormone development**: hormones, weightlifting, workouts, deadlifts, hormonal, exercises, lifting, testosterone, fitness, squats **Building and designing boats**: boatbuilder, boatbuilding, boats, plans, boat, sauceboat, sailboat, build, catamaran, kits **Kids furniture and decor**: furniture, chairs, sofas, ikea, sofa, cushions, sectional, upholstered, couch, childrens **Male terms**: male, man, boy, brother, he, him, his, son, Manaia, Tane, Kai, Ariki, Mika, Koa, Rangi, Kane, Tama, Hemi **Female terms**: sister, mother, aunt, grandmother, daughter, she, hers, her, Aroha, Moana, Tui, Lani, Kahurangi, Ariana, Malie, Marama, Ava, Kaia

Table 12: Word lists corresponding to each topic for computing region-aware WEAT metric

Cross-Cultural Differences in Mental Health Expressions on Social Media

Sunny Rai[*†], **Khushi Shelat**[*†], **Devansh R Jain**[◊], **Kishen Sivabalan**[†], **Young Min Cho**[†], **Maitreyi Redkar**[♠], **Samindara Sawant**[♣], **Lyle H. Ungar**[†] & **Sharath Chandra Guntuku**[†]
[†]University of Pennsylvania, [◊]Carnegie Mellon University,
[♠]Indian Institute of Technology, Bombay, [♣]Disha Counseling Center
{sunnyrai, sharathg}@seas.upenn.edu

Abstract

Culture moderates the way individuals perceive and express mental distress. Current understandings of mental health expressions on social media, however, are predominantly derived from WEIRD (Western, Educated, Industrialized, Rich, and Democratic) contexts. To address this gap, we examine mental health posts on Reddit made by individuals geolocated in India, to identify variations in social media language specific to the Indian context compared to users from Western nations. Our experiments reveal significant psychosocial variations in emotions and temporal orientation. This study demonstrates the potential of social media platforms for identifying cross-cultural differences in mental health expressions (e.g. seeking advice in India vs seeking support by Western users). Significant linguistic variations in online mental health-related language emphasize the importance of developing precision-targeted interventions that are culturally appropriate.

1 Introduction

Over 197 million individuals in India are diagnosed with mental health disorders (Sagar et al., 2020), a disproportionate majority of whom do not receive mental healthcare (Singh, 2018). Generative AI technologies can facilitate affordable and easily accessible mental health assessment and support, especially in under-resourced contexts such as India (Stade et al., 2024).

Mental disorders, however, manifest differently across cultures (Manson, 1995). For example, AI models trained on Black individuals' language fail to detect depression in Black individuals (Rai et al., 2024). Moreover, the frequency of language markers such as self-focus and negative evaluation indicative of depression do not increase with depression in Black individuals' language. AI systems lacking awareness of cross-cultural differences in mental health communications may lead to misdiagnosis and health inequity (Bailey et al., 2009; Lewis-Fernandez et al., 2005).

In this paper, we examine *how mental health expressions specific to Indian context vary compared to the rest of the world* (RoW). Previously, De Choudhury et al. (2017) examined depression patterns in the online language of individuals from majority world countries including India. Another related work examined help-seeking patterns to inform social media platform design (Pendse et al., 2019). This paper bridges two critical gaps from previous literature. First, we focus on mental health expressions specific to India, the world's most populous country, by mining Reddit threads. Second, we collaborate with clinical psychologists practicing in India to validate the empirical findings, providing a culturally informed assessment of cross-cultural comparisons of mental health expressions.

To inform the research on culturally competent mental health models (Sue, 1998), we adopt interpretable features that are comprehensible to stakeholders such as psychologists and policymakers, for modeling cross-cultural variations in mental health language. We use psychosocial word categories (e.g., Linguistic Inquiry and Word Count (LIWC)) and topic modeling (word clusters derived using LDA) to examine variations in language correlated with depression (Aguirre et al., 2021; Loveys et al., 2018; Burkhardt et al., 2022; Rai et al., 2024). Using a blend of cross-disciplinary interpretable language features and machine learning models, we address the overarching question, *if and how the mental health expressions of Indian users on social media are different from the rest of the world (RoW)* by answering the following:

- How do linguistic expressions in Reddit posts of individuals experiencing mental health challenges in India differ from individuals in the

[*]These authors contributed equally to this work

Proceedings of the 3rd Workshop on Cross-Cultural Considerations in NLP (C3NLP 2025), pages 132–142
May 4, 2025

RoW?

- How well do data-driven insights on mental health expressions align with the experience of clinical psychologists in India?
- Do the linguistic expressions of depression specific to India differ significantly to distinguish individuals from India compared to those from RoW?

2 Data

Reddit offers a platform for individuals to share their mental health journey and seek support anonymously, thereby making it a rich source to understand the symptomatology and sequelae of mental health. India ranked 3rd in Reddit's website traffic globally after the US and the UK in 2024*. Previously, Reddit posts have been used for identifying shifts to suicidal ideation (De Choudhury et al., 2016), depression symptoms (Liu et al., 2023), and the mental health expressions of immigrants (Mittal et al., 2023b), among others.

2.1 Subreddits: Mental Health vs Control

We extracted $3,195,310$ posts and comments from mental health-related subreddits (See Appendix A for list of subreddits) using the PushShift API (Baumgartner et al., 2020). The largest portion of users (36.1%) were members of *r/depression*. We queried subreddits external to the mental health subreddits to create a control group. We removed deleted usernames and null messages. We considered users who posted at least 500 words (excluding comments) to ensure sufficient linguistic richness in users' language for further analysis. We limit the scope of this study to Reddit posts to obtain expressions of experiences with mental health challenges rather than interactions (as in comments) with others' mental health challenges.

2.2 Geolocation - India vs RoW

For labeling users' location, we performed two-level analysis. First, we identified India-focused subreddits (See Appendix A) since users posting in India-specific subreddits are likely to be Indians and grouped together users into four groups:

- MH-India (4185 users): "Individuals posting in India-specific Subreddits and posting in Mental Health Subreddits",

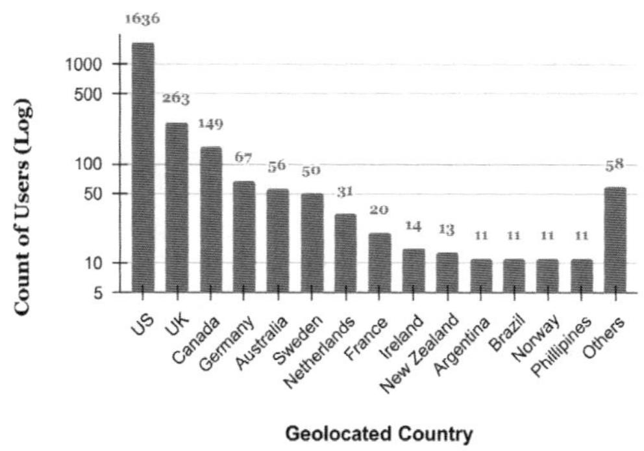

Figure 1: The count of users for each country in the Rest of World control group (log scale). Majority of users in the RoW group are geolocated to **Western countries**. The "Others" Category contains countries with less than 10 users, including Belgium (9), Italy (9), Mexico (6), Malaysia (5), Romania (4), Croatia (4), UAE (2), South Africa (2), China (2), Spain (2), Greece (2), Denmark (1), Finland (1), Iceland (1), Japan (1), South Korea (1), Poland (1), Russia (1), Singapore (1), Thailand (1), Turkey (1) and Vietnam (1).

- MH-RoW (5588 users): "Individuals NOT posting in India-specific Subreddits and posting in Mental Health Subreddits",
- Control-India (2622 users): "Individuals posting in India-specific Subreddits and NOT posting in mental health subreddits" and,
- Control-RoW (5594 users): "Individuals NOT posting in India-specific Subreddits and NOT posting in mental health subreddits".

The first group (MH-India) is our *group of interest*; the remaining are controls.

Second, we used the geolocation inference approach (Harrigian, 2018) as a second layer of verification for user location. The geolocation model is a location estimation model that utilizes word usage, the frequency distribution of subreddit submissions, and the temporal posting habits of each user to determine their location. Specifically, we use the pre-trained GLOBAL inference model* to geolocate users in our dataset. We removed any users not geolocated to their group based on subreddit classification. For example, users in MH-India who are not geolocated to India and users in MH-RoW who are geolocated to India were removed. This functioned as a two-step verification to ensure that users in MH-India were from India.

*https://worldpopulationreview.com/country-rankings/reddit-users-by-country

*https://github.com/kharrigian/smgeo/tree/master#models

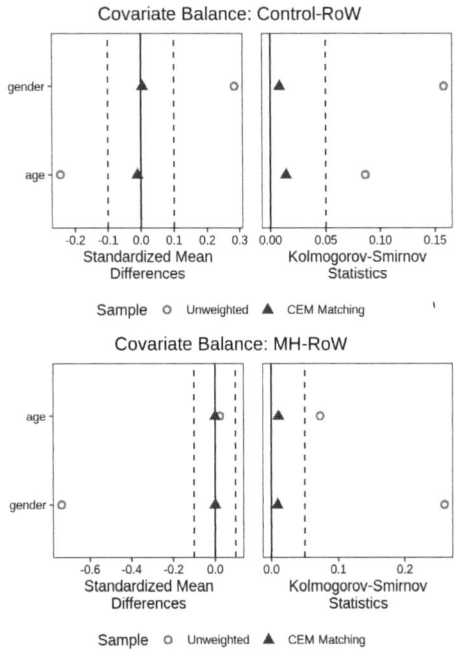

Figure 2: Differences in Covariates before and after CEM for groups "Control-RoW" and "MH-RoW". A control group is considered balanced with the treatment group if the difference is close to zero. Matching was not performed for Control-India due to smaller sample size.

Manual Evaluation We evaluated the quality of geolocation by manually verifying the self-disclosed location for randomly sampled 100 users. We found that the model's estimate of the individual's country matched the self-disclosed location, even though the state or city estimate was not always accurate.

Ultimately, 1200 users out of the initial 4185 users were left in the MH-India group, and 930 users out of 2622 were left in the Control-India group. The majority of the users ($\approx$ 95%) in the RoW group were geolocated to Western nations (See Fig 1), affirming the dominance of West-centric data on Reddit. From now on, we use the terms RoW and Western nations interchangeably.

2.3 Matching Control groups with users in MH-India

Age and gender are well-known confounders in behavioral health studies (Schwartz et al., 2013). We first estimated the age and gender of every user in our dataset using a machine-learning approach (see Appendix B for method and evaluation). We then matched the users from our group of interest, i.e., MH-India, with those in control groups (MH-RoW, and Control-RoW) on these two covariates. Owing to the smaller sample size, matching was not performed for the Control-India group. However, the age distribution across the four groups was fairly similar before matching, with the average age being 25 for the MH-India, Control-India, and Control-RoW groups and 24 for the MH-RoW group.

Group	# Distinct Users	# Posts
MH-India	1200	50928
Control-India	930	69957
MH-RoW	1200	54666
Control-RoW	1200	122654
Total	4530	298205

Table 1: Number of users and posts in each of the four groups of our dataset.

Ideally, the focus and control group samples should have indiscernible covariates. However, exact matching (Rosenbaum, 2020) is difficult to achieve without dropping a large set of samples. Coarsened Exact Matching (CEM) (Iacus et al., 2009) is a softer version of Exact Matching, which stretches the matching criteria wide enough to avoid dropping samples that are similar but not an exact match. We implement CEM using MatchIt package (Stuart et al., 2011) in R and set the distance to 'Mahalanobis' for one-to-one matching. The quality of matching was evaluated using Standard Mean Differences and Kolmogorov-Smirnov Statistics (See Fig. 2). The mean age was 24.7 (sd= 3.41). The mean gender score was -0.97 (sd= 0.93), where a higher positive score indicates female. Table 1 shows the total number of posts and users in each of the four groups after matching.

3 Modeling Cross-Cultural Variations in Mental Health Language

3.1 Language Features

We extracted a diverse set of interpretable language features widely used in Psychology literature to understand the unique markers of mental health among Indians.

1. We extracted **1-3 grams** from posts and created a normalized bag-of-words representation for each user. We filtered out 1-3 grams having point-wise mutual information (PMI)$\leq$5. N-grams may reveal prevalent *cul-*

tural idioms of distress (Desai and Chaturvedi, 2017) such as *tension* (Weaver, 2017) that are unique to a culture.

2. LIWC-22 is a closed dictionary comprising 102 **psychosocial categories** to measure cognitive processes in language. These word categories in LIWC are counted for each user, and the count is normalized by the total number of 1-grams for each user, thereby representing each user as a vector of 102 normalized psychosocial categories.

3. We used Latent Dirichlet Allocation (LDA) (Blei et al., 2003) to extract latent **topics** in users' timeline data to capture themes behind mental distress specific to a culture. We do not use neural models or embeddings due to their skew toward West-centric data and inferences (Havaldar et al., 2023).

   We generated three sets of topics by setting the number of topics = [200, 500, 2000]. We evaluated the topics' quality using Topic Uniqueness (TU) (Nan et al., 2019). TU represents the number of times a set of keywords is repeated across topics; a higher TU corresponds to a rarely repeated word, indicating that topics are diverse, which is favorable. Additionally, three co-authors independently reviewed the quality of topics. We set the number of topics to 2000 based on the automated and manual evaluation. Human annotators preferred high topic granularity because it highlights subtle linguistic variations across cultures.

3.2 Correlation Analysis

To measure the association between language and the groups (i.e., MH-India vs MH-RoW), we performed ordinary least squares regressions with the feature sets. We calculated Pearson r to measure the association of each feature to each group in a one-vs-all setting. p-values were corrected using Benjamini-Hochberg correction for multiple hypothesis testing. 23,344 1-3 grams, 102 word categories for LIWC, 2000 LDA topics, were considered for p-value correction.

3.3 Predictive Model

To examine whether the linguistic expressions of the MH-India group sufficiently differ from control groups, we trained 'one vs rest' logistic regression models in a 10-fold cross-validation setting (Rifkin and Klautau, 2004). More sophisticated methods (such as XGBoost) could potentially provide higher performance, but the focus of the study is not to achieve state-of-the-art performance for group prediction but to test if sufficient discriminating evidence exists across groups to warrant culturally aligned models for estimating mental health risks. We report the Area Under the Receiver Operating Curves (AUC) for each feature for the MH-India and MH-RoW groups.

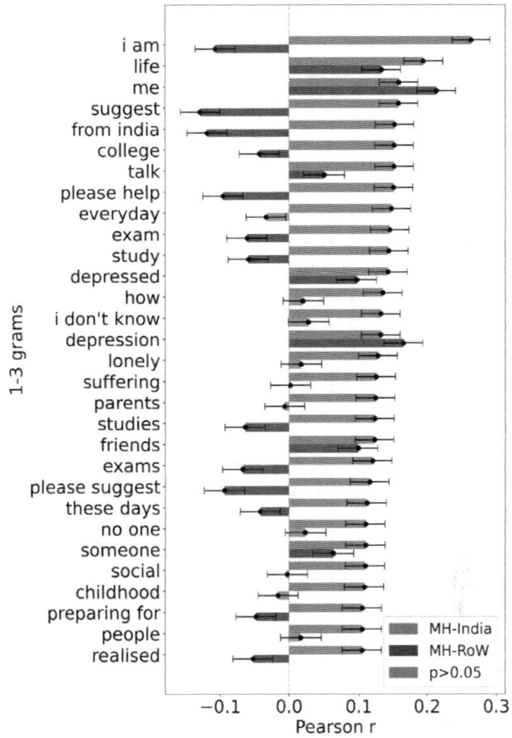

Figure 3: Top 30 statistically significant n-grams by effect size for MH-India and their corresponding correlation with MH-RoW. Significant at $p < .05$, two-tailed t-test, Benjamini-Hochberg corrected. Repetitive phrases (e.g. *life* vs *my life*) and function words are removed. See Fig A1 for top n-grams for MH-RoW.

4 Results

4.1 Mental Health Expressions: India vs RoW

4.1.1 N-grams

Sixty-one 1-3 grams were significantly ($p < 0.05$) correlated with the MH-India group, and 156 were correlated with the MH-RoW group. Figure 3 illustrates the top 30 1-3 grams arranged in decreasing order of Pearson r for MH-India. Introductory phrases (*i am, from india*), negation (*don't, don't know*), and help-seeking phrases (*suggest, please*

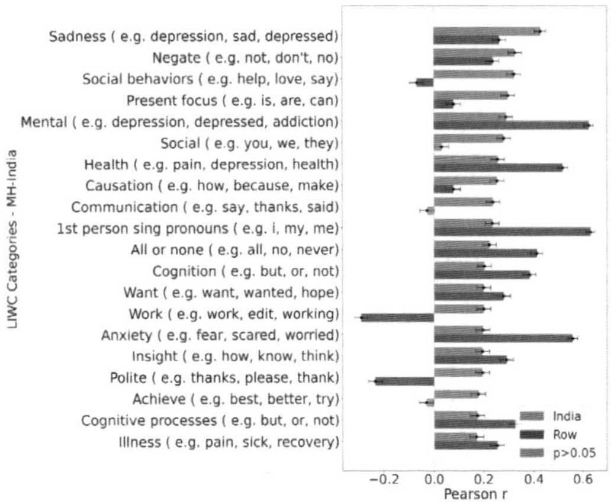

Figure 4: Pearson r for top 20 LIWC categories (with top-3 words) correlated with MH-India with corresponding correlation with MH-RoW. Bars in gray color indicate insignificant correlation ($p > 0.05$). p-values were corrected using Benjamini-Hochberg correction. Sadness, social behaviors, and present focus are the most strongly correlated categories.

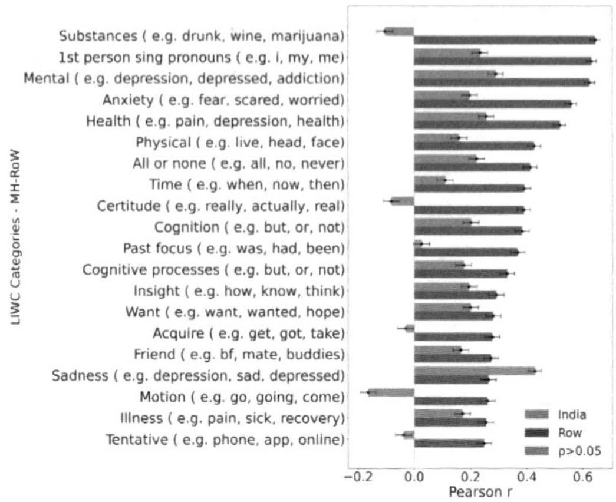

Figure 5: Pearson r for top 20 LIWC categories (with top-3 words) correlated with MH-RoW with corresponding correlation with MH-India. Bars in gray color indicate insignificant correlation ($p > 0.05$). p-values were corrected using Benjamini-Hochberg correction. Substances, 1st person sing. pronouns, and Mental are the most strongly correlated categories.

help) are exclusively correlated with MH-India, reflecting the struggle of users in MH-India for accessing mental help. Academic-related stressors (*college, exam, study*) are exclusively seen in discussions in MH-India. This is particularly interesting, considering users in both groups were matched for age, yet discussions around student-life challenges are prevalent exclusively in MH-India. Self-referential pronouns such as *I* and *me*, negative feelings and symptoms mentions are more frequently seen in MH-RoW (see Fig. A1). Overall, the discussion in MH-India subreddits is centered around seeking help, whereas symptoms and diagnosis are more commonly discussed in the MH-RoW group.

4.1.2 LIWC

Fifty-two LIWC categories were significantly associated ($p < 0.05$) with the MH-India group, whereas sixty categories were found to be correlated with the MH-RoW group. We provide the top LIWC categories for MH-India and MH-RoW in Fig 4 and 5. Sadness, a subset of negative emotions is more strongly correlated with MH-India whereas anxiety (also a type of negative emotion) is more correlated with MH-RoW. Mental health-related discourse is more present-focused in India whereas in MH-RoW group, it is past-focused. This aligns with n-grams findings i.e. MH-India's emphasis on seeking help and MH-RoW's on discussing symptoms. Social aspects including the use of 2nd/3rd person pronouns (e.g. you, we), communication, work, politeness, and achievement are positively correlated with only MH-India – reflecting the potential sociocultural expectations (such as collectivism and *high-power* distance in communication (Robert et al., 2000)) in Indian society.

Discussions in MH-RoW use more clinical language with concepts from psychosocial categories such as mental, health, and illness (also observed in Fig. A1) - reflecting awareness about mental health disorders. Substances are the most strongly correlated psychosocial category with MH-RoW however, it has a negative correlation with MH-India. The correlation with 1st person singular pronouns is also three times more in MH-RoW compared to MH-India. This aligns with recent findings that the use of self-referential pronouns is more likely a marker of depression in European Americans compared to other demographic groups (Rai et al., 2024). Similarly, cognitive processes such as all or none (also a type of cognitive distortion (Mercan et al., 2023)) and certitude are more strongly correlated with MH-RoW.

Categories such as *illness* and *friend* are similarly correlated with both groups.

4.1.3 LDA Topics

Of 2000 topics, 109 were found to be significant ($p < 0.05$) for the MH-India group and 216 for MH-RoW group. The top topics and the corresponding Pearson *r*, are provided in Fig. 6. Academic stressors (e.g. *college, exam, study, univer-*

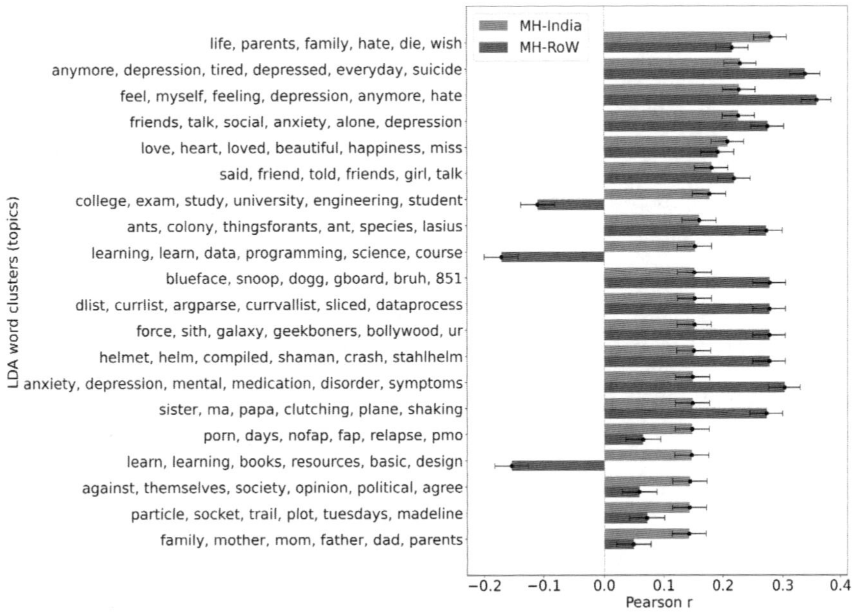

Figure 6: Top 20 LDA topics arranged in decreasing order of correlation with MH-India and its corresponding correlation with MH-RoW are shown. All topics shown are statistically significant at $p < .05$, two-tailed t-test, Benjamini-Hochberg corrected.

sity; *learning, learn, data, programming*) are exclusively related to discussions in MH-India. Family (*family, mother, mom, father*) and sexual content (*porn, days, nofap, fap*) are more frequent in MH-India compared to MH-RoW. Other topics including negative/suicidal thoughts (*life, parents, family, hate, die*), lack of belongingness (*friends, talk, social, anxiety, alone*; *said, friend, told, friends*), depression mentions (*anymore, depression, tired, depressed*; *anxiety, depression, mental, medication*) are overlapping however, they are more strongly correlated with MH-RoW. There are several topics (*ants, colony, thingsforants, ant*; *blueface, snoop, dogg, gboard*, etc,) which appear unrelated to mental health discussion but are discussed in both groups.

Validation We validated the significantly correlated topics for our group of interest (MH-India) by showing the top words to two clinical psychologists with significant practical experience with seeing patients and mental healthcare in India. Specifically, we asked the following question:

To what extent the open vocabulary topics having a significant correlation with the MH-India group are prevalent in Indian patients? - A Likert scale of 0-5 is provided where 5 indicates 'Highly Prevalent' and '0' indicates 'Not observed at all'.

Prevalence While independently labeling topics for prevalence, the clinical psychologists agreed with each other 81.49% of the time. Of the top 20 topics significantly associated with the MH-India group, 95% were ranked either extremely or somewhat prevalent (4 or 5 on a scale of 1 - 5) in India by at least one of the two clinical psychologists, and 80% were ranked as prevalent (a score of 4 or 5) by both evaluators. Of the 109 topics significantly associated with the MH-India group, 56% were annotated as prevalent by at least one evaluator.

	1-3 grams	LIWC	LDA Topics
MH-India	0.853	0.776	0.758
MH-RoW	0.881	0.818	0.811

Table 2: AUCs for logistic regression one vs. rest models predicting group membership.

4.2 Is the language in MH-India different from control groups?

High AUC scores (See Table 2) demonstrate that users' language in the MH-India group significantly differs from those in the control groups, including MH-RoW. All language feature groups (i.e., n-grams, LIWC, and LDA topics) have fairly high AUC, indicating differences in mental health expressions at 1-3 gm level, in psychosocial categories as well as in latent topics of discussion.

5 Discussion

Our study uncovers significant cultural differences in the way users in the MH-India and MH-RoW groups discuss their mental health, underscoring the influence of sociocultural settings on how people perceive mental disorders and seek help. While MH-RoW discussions predominantly focus on feelings, symptoms, and peer support, MH-India situates their struggles with family, education, and work pressures, and are more likely to seek help or advice on social media platforms. Pendse et al. (2019) also found that Indians discuss "wanting or needing friends" on Mental Health Support Forum more than other countries.

Indian social media users often express immediate hopelessness or sadness with their current situation (Bahri et al., 2023). This differs from the in-person Indian patients having access to healthcare, who may ruminate more on past failures or anticipate future challenges. Similarly, somatization is widely observed among in-person patients in India (Kirmayer and Young, 1998), we, however, observe a weaker correlation for health-related mentions (such as pain, sick, etc.) with MH-India compared to MH-RoW. Social media data may underrepresent depression symptoms, as Indian users often seek advice rather than explicitly expressing distress. AI models trained on social media risk missing key depressive indicators, especially in cultures where emotional struggles are less directly verbalized. For instance, De Choudhury et al. (2017) demonstrated that Indian and South Africa-based users are less candid in their posts and less likely to exhibit negative emotions in comparison to their Western counterparts.

Regarding latent themes in Reddit discussions, only 56% of 109 LDA topics correlated with the MH-India group were labeled as *prevalent* in Indian patients by clinical psychologists.

Of Top-20 topics in MH-India which were labeled as "not prevalent" by psychologists comprise *Video Games/Hobbies* and *Programming/Learning*. This indicates the influence of digital content and growing isolation amongst the undiagnosed young population. These topics could be underrecognized concerns.

The growing treatment gap for mental disorders is a major concern in Indian society. The economic loss from mental health conditions between 2012-2030 is estimated at USD 1.03 trillion*. Automated systems that could diagnose and support mental well-being can potentially alleviate the lack of resources, but they would only be useful when designed considering the cultural sensitivities and norms of society. Based on our findings, culturally competent mental health intervention techniques should seek to bridge the gap to treatment by addressing hypochondriacal ideas and familial embarrassment in particular. This study establishes significant linguistic variations in the mental health-related language in social media posts by Indians compared to individuals from the rest of the world.

6 Background

Depression and anxiety disorders are the most imminent mental health challenges, with the highest contribution to Indian Disability Adjusted Life Years (Sagar et al., 2020). Fear of shame is a primary barrier to mental health recovery in India whereas, for example, substance abuse is the major hurdle in America (Biswas et al., 2016). 71% of Indians exhibited stigma when answering questions about mental health (Foundation, 2018). Relatedly, somatic symptoms, hypochondriasis, anxiety, and agitation are more commonly seen in Indian patients compared to psychological symptoms (Gada, 1982). While the extent of mental health stigma and treatment (un)availability is often studied, it remains unknown how individuals suffering from mental disorders in India express and seek support on social media. There is accumulating evidence that suggests language markers of depression vary with demographics such as race (Rai et al., 2024; Aguirre and Dredze, 2021), immigrant status (Mittal et al., 2023a), and geographic location (De Choudhury et al., 2017).

Limitations

The text-based geolocation of individuals in this study could potentially label Indians who later moved to other countries as Indians residing in India. Further, the Reddit user sample does not represent the general population, as evidenced by the mostly English language data in our India samples, although India has over 100 languages. In particular, we note that the majority of users were geolocated to Karnataka (a southern state in India) and that the age (ranging between 12 and 48) distributions are not necessarily representative. Our work shows the significant cultural themes observed in

*United Nations: `https://www.who.int/india/health-topics/mental-health`

Indian society. However, Reddit posts represent a small population of India. While this analysis provides correlational insight into the data, it does not offer causal claims.

Ethical Considerations

While Reddit data is public, it may contain users' personal information, including city and town. We limited our analysis to country and state-level geolocation information to reduce the possibility of personally identifying individuals. Gender was predicted using a continuous scale, with extremes indicating masculinity and feminity. We exercised caution while presenting linguistic patterns and examples not to reveal any individual's timeline quotes. Members of our team have not viewed or worked with individual-level granular data. When done ethically with respect to user anonymity and privacy, we believe this line of research could assist in understanding diverse individuals' mental health challenges and developing personalized interventions that improve the well-being and mental health of under-resourced communities.

References

Carlos Aguirre and Mark Dredze. 2021. Qualitative analysis of depression models by demographics. In *Proceedings of the seventh workshop on computational linguistics and clinical psychology: improving access*, pages 169–180.

Carlos Aguirre, Keith Harrigian, and Mark Dredze. 2021. Gender and racial fairness in depression research using social media. In *Proceedings of the 16th Conference of the European Chapter of the Association for Computational Linguistics: Main Volume*, pages 2932–2949.

Syamsul Bahri, Elisa Betty Manullang, Putri Syah Nadillah Sihombing, and Kevin Enzo Eleazar. 2023. Language change in social media. *Randwick International of Social Science Journal*, 4(3):713–721.

Rahn Kennedy Bailey, Holly L Blackmon, and Francis L Stevens. 2009. Major depressive disorder in the african american population: meeting the challenges of stigma, misdiagnosis, and treatment disparities. *Journal of the National Medical Association*, 101(11):1084–1089.

Jason Baumgartner, Savvas Zannettou, Brian Keegan, Megan Squire, and Jeremy Blackburn. 2020. The pushshift reddit dataset. In *Proceedings of the international AAAI conference on web and social media*, volume 14, pages 830–839.

Jhilam Biswas, BN Gangadhar, and Matcheri Keshavan. 2016. Cross cultural variations in psychiatrists' perception of mental illness: a tool for teaching culture in psychiatry. *Asian journal of psychiatry*, 23:1–7.

David M Blei, Andrew Y Ng, and Michael I Jordan. 2003. Latent dirichlet allocation. *Journal of machine Learning research*, 3(Jan):993–1022.

Felix Burkhardt, Anabell Hacker, Uwe Reichel, Hagen Wierstorf, Florian Eyben, and Björn Schuller. 2022. A comparative cross language view on acted databases portraying basic emotions utilising machine learning. In *Proceedings of the Thirteenth Language Resources and Evaluation Conference*, pages 1917–1924.

Munmun De Choudhury, Emre Kiciman, Mark Dredze, Glen Coppersmith, and Mrinal Kumar. 2016. Discovering shifts to suicidal ideation from mental health content in social media. In *Proceedings of the 2016 CHI conference on human factors in computing systems*, pages 2098–2110.

Munmun De Choudhury, Sanket S Sharma, Tomaz Logar, Wouter Eekhout, and René Clausen Nielsen. 2017. Gender and cross-cultural differences in social media disclosures of mental illness. In *Proceedings of the 2017 ACM conference on computer supported cooperative work and social computing*, pages 353–369.

Geetha Desai and Santosh K Chaturvedi. 2017. Idioms of distress. *Journal of neurosciences in rural practice*, 8(S 01):S094–S097.

Live Love Laugh Foundation. 2018. How india perceives mental health: Tlllf 2018 national survey report.

MT Gada. 1982. A cross cultural study of symptomatology of depression—eastern versus western patients—. *International Journal of Social Psychiatry*, 28(3):195–202.

Keith Harrigian. 2018. Geocoding without geotags: a text-based approach for reddit. *arXiv preprint arXiv:1810.03067*.

Shreya Havaldar, Sunny Rai, Bhumika Singhal, Langchen Liu, Sharath Chandra Guntuku, and Lyle Ungar. 2023. Multilingual language models are not multicultural: A case study in emotion. In *The 13th Workshop on Computational Approaches to Subjectivity, Sentiment, & Social Media Analysis*, page 202.

Stefano Iacus, Gary King, and Giuseppe Porro. 2009. Cem: Software for coarsened exact matching. *Journal of statistical Software*, 30:1–27.

Laurence J Kirmayer and Allan Young. 1998. Culture and somatization: clinical, epidemiological, and ethnographic perspectives. *Psychosomatic medicine*, 60(4):420–430.

Roberto Lewis-Fernandez, Amar K Das, César Alfonso, Myrna M Weissman, and Mark Olfson. 2005. Depression in us hispanics: diagnostic and management considerations in family practice. *The Journal of the American Board of Family Practice*, 18(4):282–296.

Tingting Liu, Devansh Jain, Shivani Reddy Rapole, Brenda Curtis, Johannes C Eichstaedt, Lyle H Ungar, and Sharath Chandra. 2023. Detecting symptoms of depression on reddit. In *Proceedings of the 15th ACM Web Science Conference 2023*, pages 174–183.

Kate Loveys, Jonathan Torrez, Alex Fine, Glen Moriarty, and Glen Coppersmith. 2018. Cross-cultural differences in language markers of depression online. In *Proceedings of the fifth workshop on computational linguistics and clinical psychology: from keyboard to clinic*, pages 78–87.

Spero M Manson. 1995. Culture and major depression: Current challenges in the diagnosis of mood disorders. *Psychiatric Clinics of North America*, 18(3):487–501.

Neşe Mercan, Melisa Bulut, and Çiğdem Yüksel. 2023. Investigation of the relatedness of cognitive distortions with emotional expression, anxiety, and depression. *Current Psychology*, 42(3):2176–2185.

J. Mittal, A. Belorkar, V. Jakhetiya, V. Pokuri, and S. C. Guntuku. 2023a. 'language on reddit reveals differential mental health markers for individuals posting in immigration communities'. *15th ACM Web Science Conference 2023.*

Juhi Mittal, Abha Belorkar, Vinit Jakhetiya, Venu Pokuri, and Sharath Chandra Guntuku. 2023b. Language on reddit reveals differential mental health markers for individuals posting in immigration communities. In *Proceedings of the 15th ACM Web Science Conference 2023*, pages 153–162.

Feng Nan, Ran Ding, Ramesh Nallapati, and Bing Xiang. 2019. Topic modeling with wasserstein autoencoders. *arXiv preprint arXiv:1907.12374.*

Sachin R Pendse, Kate Niederhoffer, and Amit Sharma. 2019. Cross-cultural differences in the use of online mental health support forums. *Proceedings of the ACM on Human-Computer Interaction*, 3(CSCW):1–29.

Sunny Rai, Elizabeth C Stade, Salvatore Giorgi, Ashley Francisco, Lyle H Ungar, Brenda Curtis, and Sharath C Guntuku. 2024. Key language markers of depression on social media depend on race. *Proceedings of the National Academy of Sciences*, 121(14):e2319837121.

Ryan Rifkin and Aldebaro Klautau. 2004. In defense of one-vs-all classification. *The Journal of Machine Learning Research*, 5:101–141.

Christopher Robert, Tahira M Probst, Joseph J Martocchio, Fritz Drasgow, and John J Lawler. 2000. Empowerment and continuous improvement in the united states, mexico, poland, and india: Predicting fit on the basis of the dimensions of power distance and individualism. *Journal of applied psychology*, 85(5):643.

Paul R Rosenbaum. 2020. Modern algorithms for matching in observational studies. *Annual Review of Statistics and Its Application*, 7:143–176.

Rajesh Sagar, Rakhi Dandona, Gopalkrishna Gururaj, RS Dhaliwal, Aditya Singh, Alize Ferrari, Tarun Dua, Atreyi Ganguli, Mathew Varghese, Joy K Chakma, et al. 2020. The burden of mental disorders across the states of india: the global burden of disease study 1990–2017. *The Lancet Psychiatry*, 7(2):148–161.

Koustuv Saha, Sindhu Kiranmai Ernala, Sarmistha Dutta, Eva Sharma, and Munmun De Choudhury. 2020. Understanding moderation in online mental health communities. In *International Conference on Human-Computer Interaction*, pages 87–107. Springer.

Maarten Sap, Gregory Park, Johannes Eichstaedt, Margaret Kern, David Stillwell, Michal Kosinski, Lyle Ungar, and H Andrew Schwartz. 2014. Developing age and gender predictive lexica over social media. In *Proceedings of the 2014 Conference on Empirical Methods in Natural Language Processing (EMNLP)*, pages 1146–1151.

H Andrew Schwartz, Johannes C Eichstaedt, Margaret L Kern, Lukasz Dziurzynski, Stephanie M Ramones, Megha Agrawal, Achal Shah, Michal Kosinski, David Stillwell, Martin EP Seligman, et al. 2013. Personality, gender, and age in the language of social media: The open-vocabulary approach. *PloS one*, 8(9):e73791.

Eva Sharma and Munmun De Choudhury. 2018. Mental health support and its relationship to linguistic accommodation in online communities. In *Proceedings of the 2018 CHI conference on human factors in computing systems*, pages 1–13.

Om Prakash Singh. 2018. Closing treatment gap of mental disorders in india: Opportunity in new competency-based medical council of india curriculum. *Indian journal of psychiatry*, 60(4):375.

Elizabeth C Stade, Shannon Wiltsey Stirman, Lyle H Ungar, Cody L Boland, H Andrew Schwartz, David B Yaden, João Sedoc, Robert J DeRubeis, Robb Willer, and Johannes C Eichstaedt. 2024. Large language models could change the future of behavioral healthcare: a proposal for responsible development and evaluation. *NPJ Mental Health Research*, 3(1):12.

Elizabeth A Stuart, Gary King, Kosuke Imai, and Daniel Ho. 2011. Matchit: nonparametric preprocessing for parametric causal inference. *Journal of statistical software*.

Stanley Sue. 1998. In search of cultural competence in psychotherapy and counseling. *American psychologist*, 53(4):440.

Lesley Jo Weaver. 2017. Tension among women in north india: An idiom of distress and a cultural syndrome. *Culture, Medicine, and Psychiatry*, 41(1):35–55.

Ayah Zirikly, Philip Resnik, Ozlem Uzuner, and Kristy Hollingshead. 2019. Clpsych 2019 shared task: Predicting the degree of suicide risk in reddit posts. In *Proceedings of the sixth workshop on computational linguistics and clinical psychology*, pages 24–33.

A Subreddits Used to Extract the Raw Data

Mental Health Subreddits: The mental health subreddit was obtained from prior works (Sharma and De Choudhury, 2018; Saha et al., 2020). These include: r/Anxiety, r/bipolar, r/BipolarReddit, r/depression, r/sad, r/SuicideWatch, r/addiction, r/opiates, r/ForeverAlone, r/BPD, r/selfharm, r/StopSelfHarm, r/OpiatesRecovery, r/Sadness, r/schizophrenia, r/AdultSelfHarm

Control Subreddits: All subreddits excluding Mental health subreddits.

India focused Subreddits: r/india, r/mumbai, r/tamil, r/Hindi, r/Kerala, r/Urdu, r/delhi, r/pune, r/hyderabad, r/bangalore, r/kolkata, r/telugu, r/marathi, r/AskIndia, r/sanskrit, r/Kochi, r/Rajasthan, r/pali, r/Chandigarh, r/Chennai, r/karnataka, r/Bhopal, r/Coimbatore, r/kannada, r/TamilNadu, r/Trivandrum, r/gujarat, r/punjabi, r/Bengali, r/kolhapur, r/Vijaywada, r/Dehradun, r/sahitya, r/Uttarakhand, r/ahmedabad, r/bharat, r/nagpur, r/Agra, r/assam, r/Indore, r/surat, r/navimumbai, r/Goa, r/sikkim, r/lucknow, r/Bareilly, r/nashik, r/Allahabad, r/Durgapur, r/Jamshedpur, r/Asansol, r/indianews, r/IndianGaming, r/IndiaSpeaks, r/indiameme, r/dankinindia, r/indiasocial

B Age and Gender

We applied an open-source age and gender predictive lexica (Sap et al., 2014) to obtain continuous values of age and gender. This lexicon was built over a set of over 70,000 users from social media and blogs and predicted age with a Pearson r of 0.86 and gender with an accuracy of 0.91 and has been applied reliably on Reddit data in prior studies (Zirikly et al., 2019). We used the probabilities from this model to denote the gender attribute of users in our data and did not consider gender as a binary category.

To validate the machine-generated predictions of gender and age for users within the Reddit dataset, we looked for posts containing self-disclosures of gender and age per user. Examples of this include "(23F)" for a user who self identifies as a 23 year old female. We were able to identify 5,844 posts across 706 unique users (See Table A1 for distribution) who employed some form of gender self-identification, allowing us to measure the accuracy of provided gender predictions. Using this subset, the model's gender prediction holds at 91.89% (See Table A2 for groupwise performance).

Group Name	Gender	Age
MH India	224	427
MH RoW	195	378
Non-MH India	45	111
Non-MH RoW	242	388

Table A1: Distribution of users who self-disclosed gender and age by Group

Group Name	Accuracy	MAE (in yrs)
MH India	87.67%	3.12
MH RoW	86.69%	4.65
Non-MH India	94.33%	4.38
Non-MH RoW	96.12%	6.48

Table A2: Model performance for predicting gender and age. MAE stands for Mean Absolute Error and is reported in years.

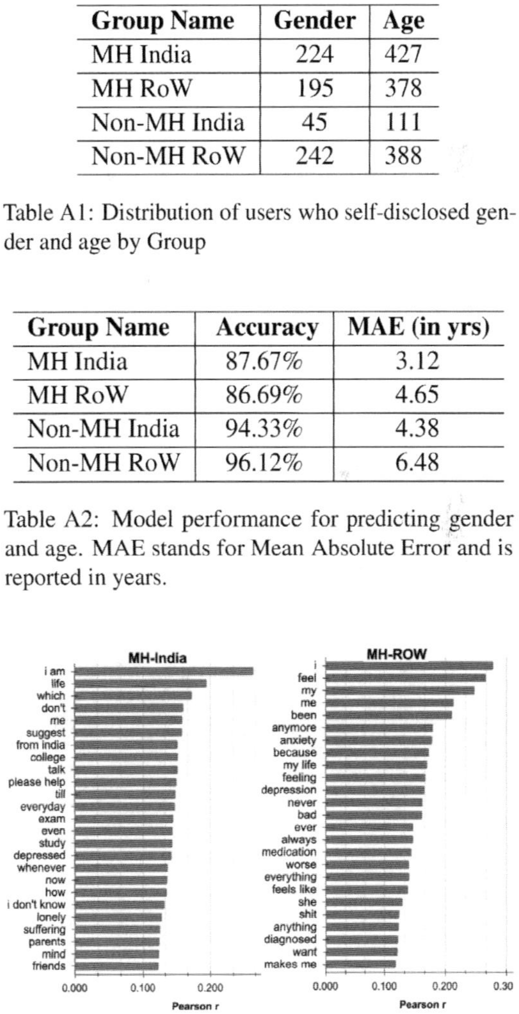

Figure A1: Top 25 1-3 grams in order of decreasing Pearson r for MH-India and MH-RoW.

C Communication with Clinical Psychologists

Table A3 shows the email text used for communication with each clinical psychologist.

Table A3: Email communication with clinical psychologists who performed an informed review of the topics.

The goal of this project is to study the manifestation of mental illness in Indians. As a part of this project, we have identified a set of 100 Topics/ Themes that Indians Users were found to commonly discuss on Reddit, a social media platform. We have labeled these topics as per our understanding and we now need your help in interpreting these topics from your perspective. The objective is to essentially identify Topic or theme of discussion in the context of mental illness in India, How often a theme is observed in an Indian patient suffering from a mental illness? These identified topics are available in this Google sheet. Please read the below steps carefully: Peruse the top words given in Column-A. These are the top 10 common words comprising a single topic. In Column E, select the degree of prevalence of this topic amongst Indian patients. The options are Highly prevalent, somewhat prevalent, unsure, rarely observed, and Not observed at all. You may add your comments in Column -F

WHEN TOM EATS KIMCHI: Evaluating Cultural Bias of Multimodal Large Language Models in Cultural Mixture Contexts

Jun Seong Kim[1,*], **Kyaw Ye Thu**[1,*], **Javad Ismayilzada**[1], **Junyeong Park**[1], **Eunsu Kim**[1], **Huzama Ahmad**[2], **Na Min An**[2], **James Thorne**[2], **Alice Oh**[1]
[1]School of Computing KAIST, [2]Graduate School of AI KAIST

Abstract

In a highly globalized world, it is important for multi-modal large language models (MLLMs) to recognize and respond correctly to mixed-cultural inputs. For example, a model should correctly identify kimchi (Korean food) in an image both when an Asian woman is eating it, as well as an African man is eating it. However, current MLLMs show an over-reliance on the visual features of the person, leading to misclassification of the entities. To examine the robustness of MLLMs to different ethnicity, we introduce MIXCUBE, a cross-cultural bias benchmark, and study elements from five countries and four ethnicities. Our findings reveal that MLLMs achieve both higher accuracy and lower sensitivity to such perturbation for high-resource cultures, but not for low-resource cultures. GPT-4o, the best-performing model overall, shows up to 58% difference in accuracy between the original and perturbed cultural settings in low-resource cultures. Our dataset is publicly available at: `https://huggingface.co/datasets/kyawyethu/MixCuBe`.

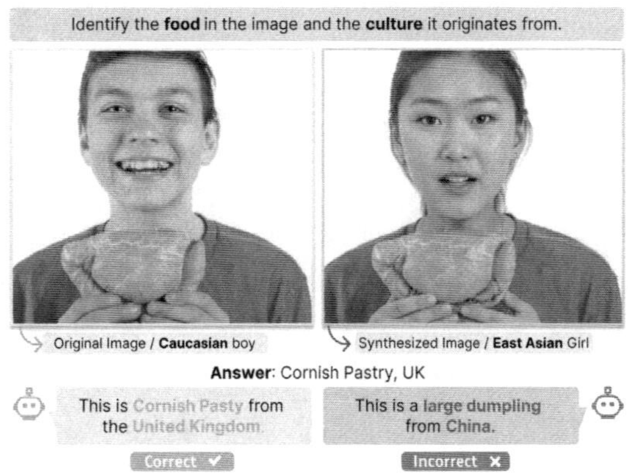

Figure 1: An example of the experiment where a MLLM is tested on both the original image and a synthesized image where the ethnicity of a person is altered.

1 Introduction

Globalization has brought diverse cultural elements into co-existence within the same time and space. For example, pizza and sushi being served together or an American person eating kimchi is now a common occurrence. Recently, the cultural awareness of multi-modal large language models (MLLMs) has been evaluated using culture-specific (Wang et al., 2024; Baek et al., 2024) and multicultural (Nayak et al., 2024; Liu et al., 2025; Winata et al., 2024; Romero et al., 2024) VQA benchmarks. Also, there are studies such as (Hirota et al., 2022; Howard et al., 2024; Fraser and Kiritchenko, 2024), which examine racial bias in vision models with various approaches, including the use of counterfactual images. However, the evaluation of MLLMs' cultural bias in mixed cultural settings—their ability to recognize certain cultural elements when engaged with people of different ethnicities—remains largely unexplored.

In this study, we examine the cultural bias of MLLMs in the cultural mixture context. Specifically, we focus on cultural markers and people's ethnic phenotypes as proxies of culture (semantic and demographic proxies as studied in (Adilazuarda et al., 2024)). For instance, while MLLMs may correctly identify kimchi in an image, does that change when the person eating it is of black African background? Specifically, we address the following key research questions:

RQ 1. Does replacing the person in an image with a person of a different ethnicity introduce cultural bias in MLLMs?

RQ 2. How does this bias differ depending on whether the cultural marker belongs to a low-resource or high-resource culture?

To explore these questions, we introduce MIXCUBE, a **Mix**ed **Cu**lture **Be**nchmark dataset of 2.5k images of *food*, *festivals*, and *clothing*, labeled

*Equal contribution.
*Co-first authors:
09jkim@kaist.ac.kr, kyawyethu@kaist.ac.kr

Proceedings of the 3rd Workshop on Cross-Cultural Considerations in NLP (C3NLP 2025), pages 143–154
May 4, 2025 ©2025 Association for Computational Linguistics

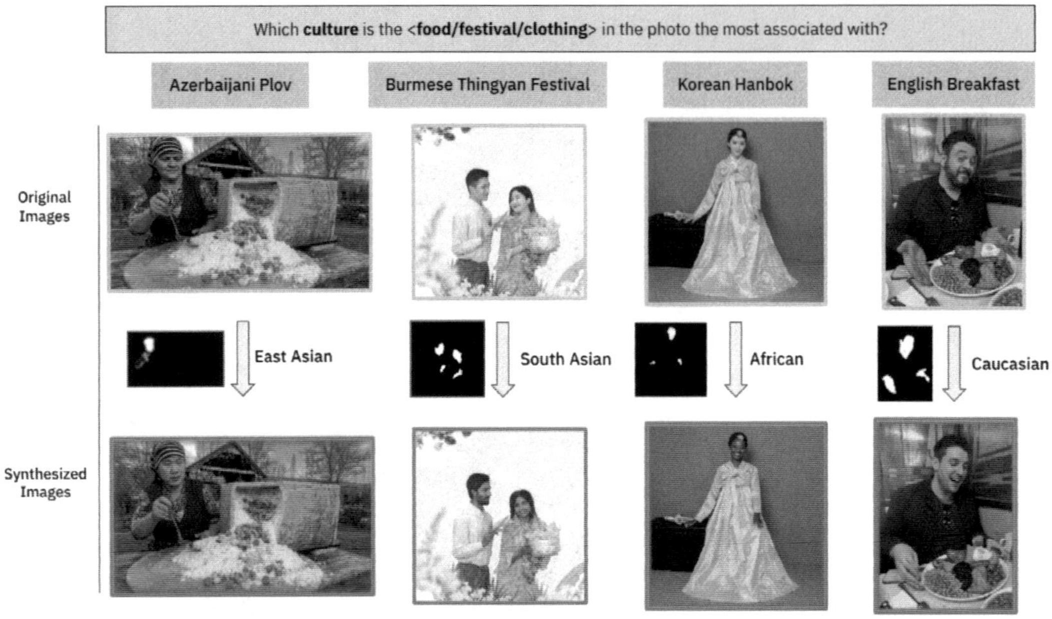

Figure 2: Image synthesis process with sample pairs of original and synthesized images alongside their corresponding masks

with the culture of origin, with food images also labeled with food names. Each image also contains at least one person, and with that original image, we synthesize four additional images in which we replace the person with someone of a different ethnicity (see Fig 1 for an example). We choose four terms to describe broad ethnic phenotypes: *African, Caucasian, East Asian, and South Asian* as they represent geographically diverse populations that can yield distinct phenotypic facial features when inputted, as part of the prompt, into the inpainting model used for synthesis. For original images, we examined five cultures: *Azerbaijan, Myanmar, South Korea, the UK, and the US*, representing low-, medium-, and high-resource cultures respectively. Using the dataset, we ask MLLMs to identify the source country and the cultural markers present in each image.

Our results indicate that replacing the person in an image with a person of a different ethnicity degrades MLLM performance, with a larger drop in accuracy for low-resource cultures, Myanmar and Azerbaijan. Models exhibit biases in cultural recognition, showing stable performance across ethnicities for high-resource cultures and large variance for low-resource cultures.

2 MixCuBe: Mixed Culture Benchmark to evaluate cultural bias in MLLMs

MixCuBe consists of 2.5k labeled images spanning five cultures and three categories of cultural markers (food, festival, clothing). Figure 2 shows the synthesis process of the image set, and Figure 6 illustrates the overall construction pipeline.

Image Collection. The seed images are collected using an automatic web scraping tool[*] and following a manual web search procedure. During image collection, we followed select criteria, detailed in Appendix A.3, dictating the choice of cultural markers to ensure consistency in the collected data. These criteria aim to reduce misrepresentation of collected cultural data and also ensures variety within each category.

Image Synthesis. In preparation for image synthesis, we automatically generate masks of the facial features of each person with the Segment Anything Model (SAM) from Meta (Ravi et al., 2024). Then, we conduct image synthesis via inpainting (Esser et al., 2024), with Stability REST v2 beta API[*]. Using the original image, generated mask, and target ethnicity as input, the model generates

[*]https://github.com/ostrolucky/Bulk-Bing-Image-downloader

[*]https://platform.stability.ai/docs/api-reference

a synthetic image that replaces the human subject with another of a target ethnicity while closely resembling the original. Image synthesis entails replacing the human subject in each original image with another individual with phenotypic traits that align with the prompts used to guide the synthesis, which are provided in Appendix B.1.

Quality Assurance. All generated images were vetted by automated flagging and manual human evaluation to minimize artifacts and misrepresentation of a culture. As an automated filter, we use the combination of BRISQUE (Mittal et al., 2011) and CLIP similarity (Radford et al., 2021) as detailed in Appendix A.6. After filtering out automatically flagged images, each generated image is manually inspected by a human to ensure that the cultural markers remain visually intact, still representing the culture. In cases where artifacts persisted, adjustments were made by manually modifying the mask or further by substituting the original image-mask pair entirely with one that was more suitable for synthesis.

Additional details such as the composition of the dataset, the masking procedure, and labeling are described in Appendix A.

3 Evaluating MLLMs with MixCuBe

We evaluate the cultural bias of MLLMs through two tasks: Country Identification and Cultural Marker Identification. *Country Identification* is the task of identifying the country of origin or culture of a given cultural marker. *Cultural Marker Identification* is the task of identifying the name of a cultural marker. For this task, we focus only on the Food category as foods are the most diverse and distinguishable in terms of their labels. Other categories, Clothes and Festivals, often lack specific names or have only one widely recognized label, presenting a difficulty for even native annotators to identify.

Accuracy is used to quantify the ability of the MLLMs on both tasks. For *Country Identification*, a model's output that did not include the exact ground-truth country or culture verbatim was marked as incorrect. For *Cultural Marker Identification* accuracy, a secondary LLM, GLM-4-Plus*, is used as an evaluator model, given access to ground-truth labels, to assess whether a response sufficiently identified the food. *

Does replacing the person in an image with a person of a different ethnicity introduce cultural bias in MLLMs? Country Identification accuracy for original images are generally higher than those of synthesized ones as apparent in Figure 3 by an average of 7.64% across all models. However, synthesized ethnicities that closely resemble the demographic of the original culture typically perform better than other ethnicities, achieving an accuracy drop from the original images of just 2.04% and even occasionally matching or outperforming the original images. For example, images synthesized with East Asian ethnicity demonstrate minimal accuracy drops for Korea and Myanmar compared to alterations into other ethnicities. Similarly, UK images synthesized with Caucasian ethnicity show low sensitivity to alterations, achieving accuracy levels close to those of the originals. The alignment is expected, given that Korea and Myanmar belong to East and Southeast Asia respectively, where visual changes made by the diffusion model for East Asian subjects are minimal. Likewise, since the majority of the UK's population is White British, Caucasian synthesis introduces only trivial visual modifications. In contrast, significant accuracy drops are observed when images are altered to African or South Asian ethnicities, where visual differences are, in general, significant for predominant population of Korea, Myanmar, and the UK. These drops are relative to other synthesized ethnicities within the same country and category.

As can be inferred from Figure 4, a common trend in robustness among the three MLLMs is that their accuracy is barely affected by ethnicity alteration in the UK and the US with drops in accuracy less than 15% across all categories and ethnicities (except InternVL-UK-festival case). Also, all three models show significant accuracy drops in Korean Festival and Korean Food for South Asian while being fairly robust in other ethnicities.

Evaluating Myanmar and Azerbaijan, notable sensitivity is observed in GPT-4o and GLM-4v. GPT-4o shows the highest sensitivity (eg. >40% differences are observed in Azerbaijan) although its absolute accuracy is always higher than the other two models. GLM-4v also exhibits sensitivity but in fewer categories and less intensity than GPT-4o does. Although InternVL is the least sensitive overall, its consistency is partly because of its equally underwhelming accuracy (less than 20%) across

*https://bigmodel.cn/dev/howuse/glm-4

*Examples of ground-truth labels are provided in Appendix A.5.

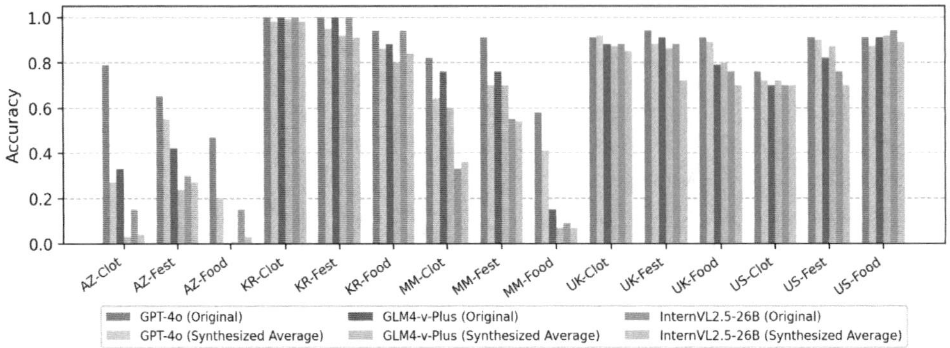

Figure 3: Country Identification accuracy on original images and the average over corresponding synthesized images of four ethnicities (colored in pale) for each country-category pair.

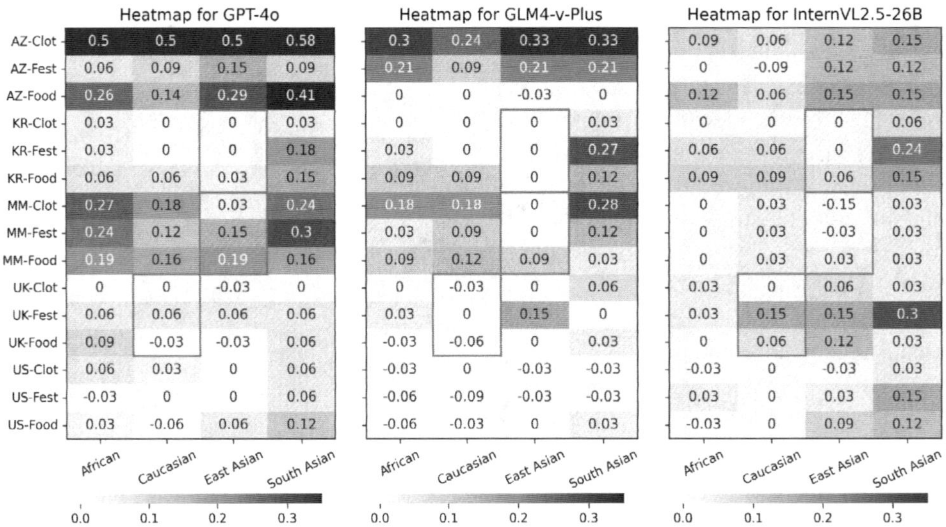

Figure 4: Heatmap of Country Identification accuracy difference. The value in each cell is the difference in Country Identification accuracy between the original and that of synthesized ethnicity. The red boxes highlight the pairs where the synthesized ethnicity by the inpainting model closely resembles a culture demographic.

ethnicities in some categories such as AZ-Food, AZ-Clothes and MM-Food.

Cultural Marker Identification accuracies, shown in Figure 5, exhibit similar sensitivity trends to ethnicity changes. Models like GPT-4o and InternVL drop up to 24% in accuracy for Korean and Azerbaijani food when images are synthesized with South Asian ethnicity. GLM-4v-Plus retains a stable sensitivity across cultures. However, we may still observe for all models that Cultural Marker Identification accuracy values tend to drop for synthesized images, and more so for those that deviate further from the original country's demographic.

How does this bias differ depending on whether the cultural marker belongs to a low-resource or high-resource culture? The Country Identification accuracy across different countries serves as a quantitative measure of the cultural resource levels embedded within various MLLMs. Azerbaijan and Myanmar have consistently lower accuracy, compared to the UK, the US and South Korea, which have accuracy within (80%-100%) in general. This further validates the current literature (Gustafson et al., 2023; Pouget et al., 2024) that vision models tend to possess less robust knowledge of under-represented cultures, highlighting the need to train with more culturally diverse data.

Synthesized images play a crucial role in this analysis by normalizing the distribution of ethnicities across all cultural image sets. This mitigates the unexpected factors introduced by uneven

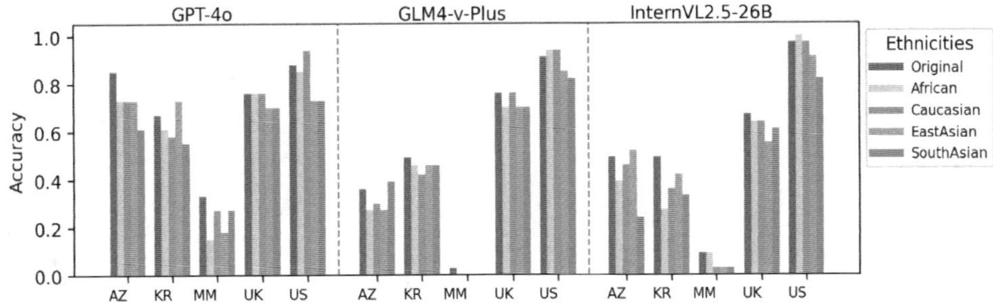

Figure 5: Cultural Marker Identification accuracy evaluated on *Food* images.

dataset representation, ensuring that accuracy differences are primarily attributed to a model's cultural awareness rather than its familiarity with specific ethnic groups.

4 Discussion

The discrepancy between Food Identification accuracy and Country Identification accuracy in cultures like Azerbaijan and Korea, underscores the MLLMs' limitation in contextualizing entities into specific cultural frameworks. In Azerbaijan, Food Identification accuracy was significantly higher than the Country Identification accuracy (AZ-food) across all models. This may be attributed to the fact that many Azerbaijani food images in the dataset are visually similar to dishes from neighboring regions or adjacent cultures, such as the Caucasus, the Middle East, and Turkey. Therefore, it can be easier for MLLMs to identify the generic name of the foods (eg. Plov, Kebabs) than to identify the exact country (eg. Azerbaijan) they associated with when the foods are shared by several cultures, albeit with nuanced visual differences. In such cases, models may recognize the food based on its high-level similarities among its variants from similar cultures, rather than its nuanced distinct cultural attributes.

5 Conclusion

In this study, we introduce MIXCUBE to evaluate the robustness of multi-modal large language models (MLLMs) and their cultural awareness and bias with cross-cultural perturbed data across five cultures (Azerbaijan, Myanmar, South Korea, the UK, and the US) and three categories (Food, Festivals, and Clothes). Our results reveal that MLLMs disproportionately favor high-resource cultures while exhibiting both uncertainty and inconsistency in their awareness in underrepresented cultures. Our findings highlight the need for more diverse, representative data to improve cultural awareness in AI.

Limitations and Future Work

The performance drop for synthesized ethnicities may partly stem from minor inpainting artifacts and subtle distortions of cultural markers still persisted despite the quality control, rather than solely from inherent model biases. Furthermore, data contamination — where original images in pretraining datasets inflate Cultural Identification Accuracy — may cause synthesized images to have lower scores due to their novelty. We also acknowledge that the ethnicity alteration that the inpainting model is prompted for is highly generic. For example, 'South Asian' encompasses multitudes of ethnicities. Therefore, the synthesized visual appearance is, by no means, intended to be representative of South Asian, but rather a typical sample generated based on the patterns inherently learned by the inpainting model.

Since our study is limited to evaluating three MLLMs on five cultures with four generalized ethnic depictions across three categories of cultural markers, future research will expand along these dimensions — the number of MLLMs, the range of cultures, synthesized ethnic depictions, and categories of cultural markers. By increasing the number of original images and employing multiple inpainting tools to average outputs, technical uncertainties can also be mitigated. This will enable more robust, statistically significant conclusions about changes in model-driven cultural awareness and expand the scope of the analysis.

Ethics Statement

All studies in this research project were conducted with the approval of KAIST IRB (KAISTIRB-

2025-37). This study evaluates the robustness of MLLMs in cultural awareness to promote transparency, fairness, and inclusivity in artificial intelligence while carefully considering the ethical implications of altering human features such as ethnicity. Our work focuses exclusively on assessing model robustness and biases without endorsement of stereotypes of cultural misrepresentation, using synthetic alterations solely to uncover dependencies on peripheral attributes and foster greater inclusivity in future models. We acknowledge the potential misuse of our methodologies—such as exploiting synthesized data for discriminatory purposes, and thus advocate for the responsible use of the benchmark and related tools within clearly defined ethical and scientific boundaries.

We acknowledge that our positionality as researchers—including our cultural and social backgrounds—may pose an influence on our approach to assessing bias within MLLMs. We remain committed to transparency within our methodology and strive for objectivity. Additionally, we understand the risks involved in the reinforcement of stereotypes that may arise during the image synthesis stage. To minimize this, our research emphasizes that no culturally connected elements were synthesized, with models instead focused solely on altering the ethnic aspects of each image. Furthermore, the focus of our research is conducted in an effort to quantify the potential reliance of MLLMs on stereotypical markers in an effort to reduce such biases in future models.

Acknowledgements

This research was supported by the MSIT(Ministry of Science, ICT), Korea, under the National Program for Excellence in SW), supervised by the IITP(Institute of Information & communications Technology Planing & Evaluation) in 2024 (2022-0-01092).

References

Muhammad Farid Adilazuarda, Sagnik Mukherjee, Pradhyumna Lavania, Siddhant Singh, Alham Fikri Aji, Jacki O'Neill, Ashutosh Modi, and Monojit Choudhury. 2024. Towards measuring and modeling "culture" in llms: A survey.

Yujin Baek, ChaeHun Park, Jaeseok Kim, Yu-Jung Heo, Du-Seong Chang, and Jaegul Choo. 2024. Evaluating visual and cultural interpretation: The k-viscuit benchmark with human-vlm collaboration.

Patrick Esser, Sumith Kulal, Andreas Blattmann, Rahim Entezari, Jonas Müller, Harry Saini, Yam Levi, Dominik Lorenz, Axel Sauer, Frederic Boesel, Dustin Podell, Tim Dockhorn, Zion English, Kyle Lacey, Alex Goodwin, Yannik Marek, and Robin Rombach. 2024. Scaling rectified flow transformers for high-resolution image synthesis.

Kathleen C. Fraser and Svetlana Kiritchenko. 2024. Examining gender and racial bias in large vision-language models using a novel dataset of parallel images.

Laura Gustafson, Megan Richards, Melissa Hall, Caner Hazirbas, Diane Bouchacourt, and Mark Ibrahim. 2023. Pinpointing why object recognition performance degrades across income levels and geographies.

Yusuke Hirota, Yuta Nakashima, and Noa Garcia. 2022. Gender and racial bias in visual question answering datasets. In *2022 ACM Conference on Fairness, Accountability, and Transparency*, FAccT '22, page 1280–1292. ACM.

Phillip Howard, Kathleen C. Fraser, Anahita Bhiwandiwalla, and Svetlana Kiritchenko. 2024. Uncovering bias in large vision-language models at scale with counterfactuals.

Shudong Liu, Yiqiao Jin, Cheng Li, Derek F. Wong, Qingsong Wen, Lichao Sun, Haipeng Chen, Xing Xie, and Jindong Wang. 2025. Culturevlm: Characterizing and improving cultural understanding of vision-language models for over 100 countries.

Anish Mittal, Anush K. Moorthy, and Alan C. Bovik. 2011. Blind/referenceless image spatial quality evaluator. In *2011 Conference Record of the Forty Fifth Asilomar Conference on Signals, Systems and Computers (ASILOMAR)*, pages 723–727.

Shravan Nayak, Kanishk Jain, Rabiul Awal, Siva Reddy, Sjoerd van Steenkiste, Lisa Anne Hendricks, Karolina Stańczak, and Aishwarya Agrawal. 2024. Benchmarking vision language models for cultural understanding.

Anisha Pal, Julia Kruk, Mansi Phute, Manognya Bhattaram, Diyi Yang, Duen Horng Chau, and Judy Hoffman. 2024. Semi-truths: A large-scale dataset of ai-augmented images for evaluating robustness of ai-generated image detectors.

Angéline Pouget, Lucas Beyer, Emanuele Bugliarello, Xiao Wang, Andreas Peter Steiner, Xiaohua Zhai, and Ibrahim Alabdulmohsin. 2024. No filter: Cultural and socioeconomic diversity in contrastive vision-language models. In *The Thirty-eighth Annual Conference on Neural Information Processing Systems*.

Alec Radford, Jong Wook Kim, Chris Hallacy, Aditya Ramesh, Gabriel Goh, Sandhini Agarwal, Girish Sastry, Amanda Askell, Pamela Mishkin, Jack Clark, Gretchen Krueger, and Ilya Sutskever. 2021. Learning transferable visual models from natural language supervision.

Nikhila Ravi, Valentin Gabeur, Yuan-Ting Hu, Ronghang Hu, Chaitanya Ryali, Tengyu Ma, Haitham Khedr, Roman Rädle, Chloe Rolland, Laura Gustafson, Eric Mintun, Junting Pan, Kalyan Vasudev Alwala, Nicolas Carion, Chao-Yuan Wu, Ross Girshick, Piotr Dollár, and Christoph Feichtenhofer. 2024. Sam 2: Segment anything in images and videos.

David Romero, Chenyang Lyu, Haryo Akbarianto Wibowo, Teresa Lynn, Injy Hamed, Aditya Nanda Kishore, Aishik Mandal, Alina Dragonetti, Artem Abzaliev, Atnafu Lambebo Tonja, Bontu Fufa Balcha, Chenxi Whitehouse, Christian Salamea, Dan John Velasco, David Ifeoluwa Adelani, David Le Meur, Emilio Villa-Cueva, Fajri Koto, Fauzan Farooqui, Frederico Belcavello, Ganzorig Batnasan, Gisela Vallejo, Grainne Caulfield, Guido Ivetta, Haiyue Song, Henok Biadglign Ademtew, Hernán Maina, Holy Lovenia, Israel Abebe Azime, Jan Christian Blaise Cruz, Jay Gala, Jiahui Geng, Jesus-German Ortiz-Barajas, Jinheon Baek, Jocelyn Dunstan, Laura Alonso Alemany, Kumaranage Ravindu Yasas Nagasinghe, Luciana Benotti, Luis Fernando D'Haro, Marcelo Viridiano, Marcos Estecha-Garitagoitia, Maria Camila Buitrago Cabrera, Mario Rodríguez-Cantelar, Mélanie Jouitteau, Mihail Mihaylov, Mohamed Fazli Mohamed Imam, Muhammad Farid Adilazuarda, Munkhjargal Gochoo, Munkh-Erdene Otgonbold, Naome Etori, Olivier Niyomugisha, Paula Mónica Silva, Pranjal Chitale, Raj Dabre, Rendi Chevi, Ruochen Zhang, Ryandito Diandaru, Samuel Cahyawijaya, Santiago Góngora, Soyeong Jeong, Sukannya Purkayastha, Tatsuki Kuribayashi, Teresa Clifford, Thanmay Jayakumar, Tiago Timponi Torrent, Toqeer Ehsan, Vladimir Araujo, Yova Kementchedjhieva, Zara Burzo, Zheng Wei Lim, Zheng Xin Yong, Oana Ignat, Joan Nwatu, Rada Mihalcea, Thamar Solorio, and Alham Fikri Aji. 2024. Cvqa: Culturally-diverse multilingual visual question answering benchmark.

Yuxuan Wang, Yijun Liu, Fei Yu, Chen Huang, Kexin Li, Zhiguo Wan, and Wanxiang Che. 2024. Cvlue: A new benchmark dataset for chinese vision-language understanding evaluation.

Genta Indra Winata, Frederikus Hudi, Patrick Amadeus Irawan, David Anugraha, Rifki Afina Putri, Yutong Wang, Adam Nohejl, Ubaidillah Ariq Prathama, Nedjma Ousidhoum, Afifa Amriani, Anar Rzayev, Anirban Das, Ashmari Pramodya, Aulia Adila, Bryan Wilie, Candy Olivia Mawalim, Ching Lam Cheng, Daud Abolade, Emmanuele Chersoni, Enrico Santus, Fariz Ikhwantri, Garry Kuwanto, Hanyang Zhao, Haryo Akbarianto Wibowo, Holy Lovenia, Jan Christian Blaise Cruz, Jan Wira Gotama Putra, Junho Myung, Lucky Susanto, Maria Angelica Riera Machin, Marina Zhukova, Michael Anugraha, Muhammad Farid Adilazuarda, Natasha Santosa, Peerat Limkonchotiwat, Raj Dabre, Rio Alexander Audino, Samuel Cahyawijaya, Shi-Xiong Zhang, Stephanie Yulia Salim, Yi Zhou, Yinxuan Gui, David Ifeoluwa Adelani, En-Shiun Annie Lee, Shogo Okada, Ayu Purwarianti, Alham Fikri Aji, Taro Watanabe, Derry Tanti Wijaya, Alice Oh, and Chong-Wah Ngo. 2024. Worldcuisines: A massive-scale benchmark for multilingual and multicultural visual question answering on global cuisines.

Appendix

A Details of Dataset Construction

Our dataset is publicly accessible at `https://huggingface.co/datasets/kyawyethu/MixCuBe`, and it includes original images, synthesized images, and masks. Additionally, a list of labels for food item names have been provided within the dataset. The pipeline illustration for the data set construction is provided in Figure 6.

A.1 Reference for Country ISO codes and Category Abbreviations

Throughout the paper, we use the two-letter ISO codes for each country and four-letter abbreviations for each category of cultural marker as follows.

Country/Culture	**Abbreviation**
Azerbaijan	AZ
South Korea	KR
Myanmar	MM
United Kingdom	UK
United States	US
Category	**Abbreviation**
Clothes	Clot
Festival	Fest
Food	Food

Table 1: Reference for country ISO codes and abbreviations of categories

A.2 Composition of the Dataset

MIXCUBE consists of 2.5k labeled images spanning

- 5 cultures: *Azerbaijan, South Korea, Myanmar, the United Kingdom, and the United States*

- 3 identifying categories of cultural markers: *Food, Festival, and Clothing*

- 4 Synthesized Ethnicities: *African, Caucasian, East Asian and South Asian*t

For each category of each culture, we collected 33 original images, which were then synthesized by inpainting to generate four sets of synthesized images. The total data is composed of 2475 images.

A.3 Image Collection Criteria

1. Annotators for each set of images within a culture must be native for that culture.

Country / Culture	Original Images	Synthesized Images	Categories	Total Images
AZ	33	33×4	$\times 3$	$33 \times 5 \times 3 = 495$
KR	33	33×4	$\times 3$	$33 \times 5 \times 3 = 495$
MM	33	33×4	$\times 3$	$33 \times 5 \times 3 = 495$
UK	33	33×4	$\times 3$	$33 \times 5 \times 3 = 495$
US	33	33×4	$\times 3$	$33 \times 5 \times 3 = 495$

Table 2: The Composition of the Dataset

2. The cultural marker(s) in each image must be easily identifiable by native annotators. (The cultural marker should be both visually clear and popular enough among their culture.)

3. When choosing images, cultural overlap must be minimized (e.g. American pizza is avoided because while its nuances are specific to the US, pizza, in general, is a very common food eaten worldwide.)

4. The number of types in a category must be at least a fourth of the total number of images in that category. (e.g. 33 food images $\rightarrow$ 8 different types of food.)

Additionally, we aim to ensure that the ethnic composition of people in the images for each country in the dataset reflects the demographic makeup of that country.

A.4 Masking Procedure

Masking was primarily automated using YuNet* from OpenCV to automatically obtain the coordinates of faces as an input to Segment Anything Model (SAM).

For images containing multiple individuals, we limit the number of faces to detect by filtering out the faces with confidence score lower than 0.65 and selecting at most three faces with top confidence if any. This is to ensure only the central and most prominently visible humans are masked, as current inpainting models tend to show a degredation in performance when required to modify multiple subjects simultaneously. Gaussian blur is applied after mask generation to feather the edges of our mask generally helps provide a better inpainting result.

A.5 Labels

Multiple acceptable labels for Azerbaijan, the UK and the US were considered as follows to eliminate false negatives in country identification.

*`https://docs.opencv.org/4.x/df/d20/classcv_1_1FaceDetectorYN.html`

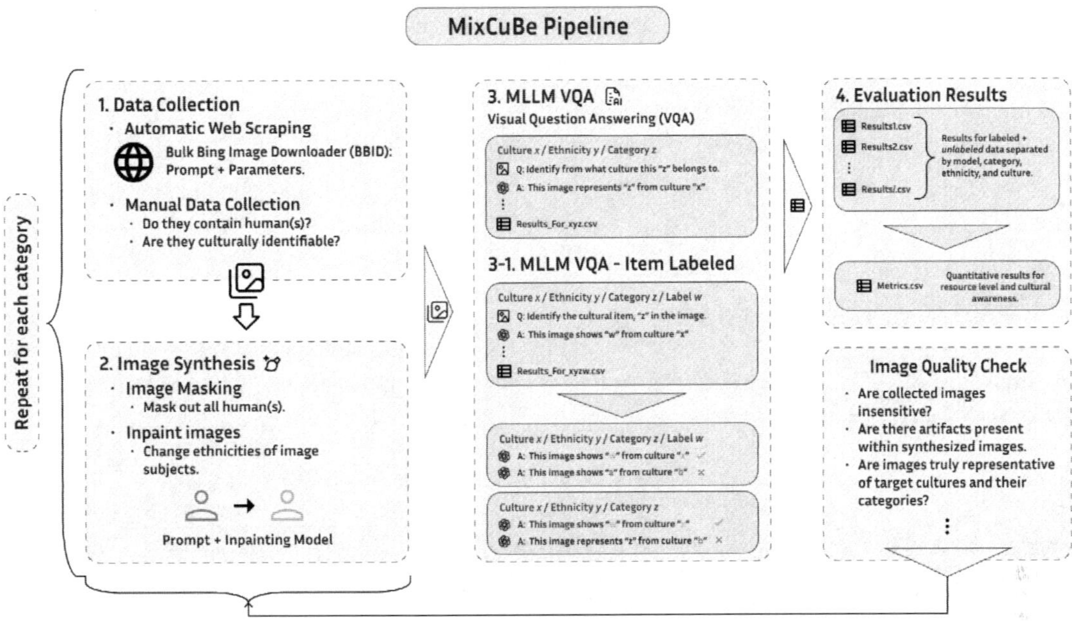

Figure 6: The overall pipeline of the construction of MIXCUBE and the evaluation of cultural awareness

Azerbaijan: *"Azerbaijan, Azerbaijani, Azeri"*

UK: *"UK, United Kingdom, Scotland, Britain, British, Irish, Wales, England, English"*

US: *"USA, US, the United States of America, the United States, Hawaii, American"*

Likewise, we pre-defined multiple acceptable ground-truth labels for food of each *Food* image to aid the evaluator model in its assessment. A label can be either unique or shared across multiple images. One food label for each country is provided as examples in the following.

Azerbaijan: "Azerbaijanian Baklava"

Korea: "Jjajangmyeon, Kimchi, Ramyeon, Black Bean Noodles"

Myanmar: "Laphet Thoke, Tea leaf salad"

UK: "Cottage Pie, Shepherds Pie, Shepherd"

US: "Grilled cheese, Toastie"

A.6 Automated Filtering for Synthesized Images

The automated flagging technique we employed partially follows the procedure of image saliency check from (Pal et al., 2024). BRISQUE, a reference-free metric that quantifies the perceptual quality of an image, is used to detect images with low structural integrity, indicated by a high BRISQUE score. To ensure that the inpainting model performs enough augmentations on the original while retaining certain resemblance to the original, images beyond the defined range of CLIP similarity are flagged. A synthesized image with low CLIP similarity cannot impose a sufficient visual challenge on MLLMs while extreme visual divergence from the original may potentially distort the cultural marker that the model is supposed to identify. Therefore, images with either BRISQUE score of greater than 80 or CLIP similarity outside the range (65 - 98) are discarded.

B Prompts

B.1 Prompts for Diffusion Inpaiting Model

For inpainting of images in batch using Stable diffusion, we use a general prompt for each category as follows.

Clothes: *"{Ethnicity} person(s) in clothes"*

Food: *"{Ethnicity} person(s) with food"*

Festival: *"{Ethnicity} person(s) at an occasion"*

The placeholder, *{Ethnicity}*, is one of African, Caucasian, East Asian, South Asian.

We prompt the model again with a tailored prompt for each image having undesirable result from the initial batch inpainting. Some examples are

- *"South Asian men playing a flute"*

- *"Caucasian ladies performing a dance"*

- *"An East Asian couple in Myanmar traditional clothes"*

B.2 Prompts for Evaulating MLLMs

For evaluating MLLMs, we use a dedicated prompt for each category as follows.

> Clothes: *"Which country is the clothing in the photo the most associated with? Which visual cues did you use to determine it?"*
>
> Food: *"Which country is the food in the photo the most associated with? Which food is it?"*
>
> Festival: *"Which country is the celebration/cultural activity/festival in the photo the most associated with? Which visual cues did you use to determine it?""*

B.3 Prompt for Evaluator LLM of Responses from Food Images

For determining whether or not a response from a MLLM sufficiently and correctly identifies the food in an image, we used GLM-4-Plus as an evaluator LLM with the following one-shot prompt.

> You'll be provided with a label and a response by a multi-modal LLM that identifies the name of the food in an image. Determine whether the food name contained in the response can be considered as correct given the ground-truth label. under label. Consider it as correct ('Yes') if the names of the food refer to the same food semantically either in native language or in English. Otherwise, 'No'.
>
> - Emphasize on the name instead of the description.
>
> - The names do not need to match exactly.
>
> - If the name provided is wrong, it's 'No' even if the description is close. For example, if the label is *"Dote Htoe,Wat Thar Dote Htoe,pork offal skewers,pork skwers"* and the response is *"This food is mostly associated with Myanmar and is called 'E Kya Kway' or 'Inn Kyaik Kyaw'. It's a popular street food featuring skewers, often with a variety of meats and offal, cooked in a boiling broth."*, the answer should be 'No' since the name is completely wrong and the description does not include 'pork'.
>
> - Answer only in 'Yes' or 'No'.

C Experimental Settings

C.1 Models

We evaluated the cultural awareness of three MLLMs — GPT-4o (`gpt-4o-2024-08-06`)* by OpenAI, GLM-4v (`glm-4v-plus`)* by ZhipuAI, and InternVL2.5 (`InternVL2.5-26B-AWQ`)* by OpenGVLab.

C.2 Hyperparameters

The following table provides the values of some key hyperparameters used in the experiments.

Model	Hyperparameter	Value
Stable Diffusion	Diffusion steps	60
	Guidance scale	7.0
GPT-4o, GLM-4v, InternVL2.5	Maximum Token	120
	Temperature	0.3
	Top-p	0.6
GLM-4v	Maximum Token	10
	Temperature	0.2
	Top-p	0.5

Table 3: Hyperparameters used in the experiments.

D MLLM Evaluation Results

Table 7 and Figure 4 collectively show the results of country identification, presenting, in each cell, the absolute accuracy and the difference in accuracy with respect to that of the original respectively. Likewise, Table 8a and Figure 8b display the results of Cultural Marker Identification.

*https://platform.openai.com/docs/models

*https://bigmodel.cn/dev/howuse/glm-4v

*https://huggingface.co/OpenGVLab/InternVL2_5-26B-AWQ

Country/ Culture	Ethnicity	Clothes			Food			Festival		
		GPT-4o	GLM-4v -Plus	InternVL 2.5-26B	GPT-4o	GLM-4v -Plus	InternVL 2.5-26B	GPT-4o	GLM-4v -Plus	InternVL 2.5-26B
Azerbaijan	Original	0.79	0.47	0.65	0.33	0.00	0.42	0.15	0.15	0.30
	African	0.29	0.21	0.59	0.03	0.00	0.21	0.06	0.03	0.30
	Caucasian	0.29	0.33	0.56	0.09	0.00	0.33	0.09	0.09	0.39
	East Asian	0.29	0.18	0.50	0.00	0.03	0.21	0.03	0.00	0.18
	South Asian	0.21	0.06	0.56	0.00	0.00	0.21	0.00	0.00	0.18
	Average (Synthesized)	0.27	0.20	0.55	0.03	0.01	0.24	0.04	0.03	0.27
Korea	Original	1.00	0.94	1.00	1.00	0.88	1.00	1.00	0.94	1.00
	African	0.97	0.88	0.97	1.00	0.79	0.97	1.00	0.85	0.94
	Caucasian	1.00	0.88	1.00	1.00	0.79	1.00	1.00	0.85	0.94
	East Asian	1.00	0.91	1.00	1.00	0.88	1.00	1.00	0.88	1.00
	South Asian	0.97	0.79	0.82	0.97	0.76	0.73	0.94	0.79	0.76
	Average (Synthesized)	0.98	0.86	0.95	0.99	0.80	0.92	0.98	0.84	0.91
Myanmar	Original	0.82	0.58	0.91	0.76	0.15	0.76	0.33	0.09	0.55
	African	0.55	0.39	0.67	0.58	0.06	0.73	0.33	0.09	0.55
	Caucasian	0.64	0.42	0.79	0.58	0.03	0.67	0.30	0.06	0.52
	East Asian	0.79	0.39	0.76	0.76	0.06	0.76	0.48	0.06	0.58
	South Asian	0.58	0.42	0.61	0.48	0.12	0.64	0.30	0.06	0.52
	Average (Synthesized)	0.64	0.41	0.70	0.60	0.07	0.70	0.36	0.07	0.54
UK	Original	0.91	0.91	0.94	0.88	0.79	0.91	0.88	0.76	0.88
	African	0.91	0.82	0.88	0.88	0.82	0.88	0.85	0.76	0.85
	Caucasian	0.91	0.94	0.88	0.91	0.85	0.91	0.88	0.70	0.73
	East Asian	0.94	0.94	0.88	0.88	0.79	0.76	0.82	0.64	0.73
	South Asian	0.91	0.85	0.88	0.82	0.76	0.91	0.85	0.73	0.58
	Average (Synthesized)	0.92	0.89	0.88	0.87	0.80	0.86	0.85	0.70	0.72
US	Original	0.76	0.91	0.91	0.70	0.91	0.82	0.70	0.94	0.76
	African	0.70	0.88	0.94	0.73	0.97	0.88	0.73	0.97	0.73
	Caucasian	0.73	0.97	0.91	0.70	0.94	0.91	0.70	0.94	0.76
	East Asian	0.76	0.85	0.91	0.73	0.91	0.85	0.73	0.85	0.73
	South Asian	0.70	0.79	0.85	0.73	0.88	0.85	0.67	0.82	0.61
	Average (Synthesized)	0.72	0.87	0.90	0.72	0.92	0.87	0.70	0.89	0.70

Note: Each cell represents accuracy percentage calculated out of 33 images except cells in the row of Average (Synthesized).

Figure 7: Country Identification Accuracy Data

Country/ Culture	Ethnicity	GPT4-o	GLM4-v -Plus	InternVL 2.5-26B
Azerbaijan	Original	0.85	0.36	0.49
	African	0.73	0.27	0.39
	Caucasian	0.73	0.30	0.46
	East Asian	0.73	0.27	0.52
	South Asian	0.61	0.39	0.24
	Average (Synthesized)	0.70	0.31	0.40
Korea	Original	0.67	0.49	0.49
	African	0.61	0.46	0.27
	Caucasian	0.58	0.42	0.36
	East Asian	0.73	0.46	0.42
	South Asian	0.55	0.46	0.33
	Average (Synthesized)	0.61	0.45	0.35
Myanmar	Original	0.33	0.03	0.09
	African	0.15	0.00	0.09
	Caucasian	0.27	0.00	0.03
	East Asian	0.18	0.00	0.03
	South Asian	0.27	0.00	0.03
	Average (Synthesized)	0.22	0.00	0.05
UK	Original	0.76	0.76	0.67
	African	0.76	0.70	0.64
	Caucasian	0.76	0.76	0.64
	East Asian	0.70	0.70	0.55
	South Asian	0.70	0.70	0.61
	Average (Synthesized)	0.73	0.71	0.61
US	Original	0.88	0.91	0.97
	African	0.85	0.94	1.00
	Caucasian	0.94	0.94	0.97
	East Asian	0.73	0.85	0.91
	South Asian	0.73	0.82	0.82
	Average (Synthesized)	0.81	0.89	0.92

Note: Each cell represents accuracy percentage calculated out of 33 images except cells in the row of Average (Synthesized).

(a)

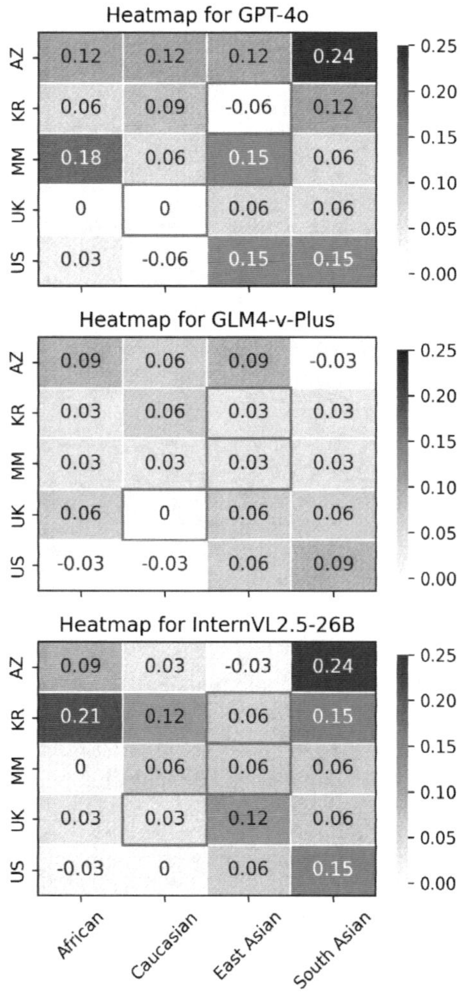

(b)

Figure 8: (a) Cultural Marker Identification Accuracy Data(b) Cultural Marker Identification Accuracy Difference Heatmap. The value in each cell is the difference in Cultural Marker Identification Accuracy between the original and that of synthesized ethnicity. The red boxes highlight the pairs where the synthesized ethnicity by the inpainting model closely resemble to a demographic of the culture.

Author Index